Iconography and the Professional Reader

MEDIEVAL CULTURES

SERIES EDITORS
Rita Copeland
Barbara A. Hanawalt
David Wallace

Sponsored by the Center for Medieval Studies at the University of Minnesota

Volumes in the series study the diversity of medieval cultural histories and practices, including such interrelated issues as gender, class, and social hierarchies; race and ethnicity; geographical relations; definitions of political space; discourses of authority and dissent; educational institutions; canonical and non-canonical literatures; and technologies of textual and visual literacies.

VOLUME 15
Kathryn Kerby-Fulton and Denise L. Despres
Iconography and the Professional Reader: The Politics of Book Production in the Douce "Piers Plowman"

VOLUME 14
Edited by Marilynn Desmond
Christine de Pizan and the Categories of Difference

VOLUME 13
Alfred Thomas
Anne's Bohemia: Czech Literature and Society, 1310–1420

VOLUME 12
Edited by F. R. P. Akehurst and Stephanie Cain Van D'Elden
The Stranger in Medieval Society

VOLUME 11
Edited by Karma Lochrie, Peggy McCracken, and James A. Schultz
Constructing Medieval Sexuality

VOLUME 10
Claire Sponsler
Drama and Resistance: Bodies, Goods, and Theatricality in Late Medieval England

VOLUME 9
Edited by Barbara A. Hanawalt and David Wallace
Bodies and Disciplines: Intersections of Literature and History in Fifteenth-Century England

VOLUME 8
Marilynn Desmond
Reading Dido: Gender, Textuality, and the Medieval "Aeneid"

For other books in the series, see p. 269

Iconography and the Professional Reader

The Politics of Book Production in the Douce *Piers Plowman*

✣

Kathryn Kerby-Fulton and Denise L. Despres

Medieval Cultures
Volume 15

University of Minnesota Press
Minneapolis
London

Copyright 1999 by the Regents of the University of Minnesota

All rights reserved. No part of this publication may be reproduced, stored in a retrieval system, or transmitted, in any form or by any means, electronic, mechanical, photocopying, recording, or otherwise, without the prior written permission of the publisher.

Published by the University of Minnesota Press
111 Third Avenue South, Suite 290
Minneapolis, MN 55401-2520
http://www.upress.umn.edu

Library of Congress Cataloging-in-Publication Data
Kerby-Fulton, Kathryn.
   Iconography and the professional reader : the politics of book production in the Douce Piers Plowman / Kathryn Kerby-Fulton and Denise L. Despres.
     p.   cm. — (Medieval cultures ; v. 15)
   Includes bibliographical references (p.   ) and index.
   ISBN 0-8166-2976-5
   1. Langland, William, 1330?-1400? Piers the Plowman—Illustrations.   2. Illumination of books and manuscripts, Medieval—Ireland.   3. Langland, William, 1330?-1400—Appreciation—Ireland. 4. Book industries and trade—Ireland—History—To 1500. 5. Christian poetry, English (Middle)—Illustrations.   6. Authors and readers—Ireland—History—To 1500.   7. Langland, William, 1330?-1400?—Manuscripts.   8. Books and reading—Ireland—History—To 1500.   9. Bodleian Library. Manuscript. Douce 104. 10. Manuscripts, English (Middle)—Ireland.   I. Despres, Denise Louis, 1958–   . II. Title. III. Series.
PR2017.I37K47   1998
821'.1—dc21   98-31505

Printed in the United States of America on acid-free paper

The University of Minnesota is an equal-opportunity educator and employer.

10 09 08 07 06 05 04 03 02 01 00 99   10 9 8 7 6 5 4 3 2 1

For Derek Pearsall and Lawrence Clopper
"Ac þe way is full wikked, but ho-so hadde a gyde"

Contents

⁙

Preface   xi

Introduction   1
Kathryn Kerby-Fulton
    The Professional Reader at Work — The Douce Manuscript in Brief —
    Medieval Reading, Scribe-Illustrators, and the "Utility-Grade"
    Manuscript

Part I: Visual Politics
Kathryn Kerby-Fulton

1. Visual Literacy and the Iconography of Reformist Polemics   17
   Clericist Iconography and the Civil Service Scribe — Retraining the
   Reader's Eye: Reform or Dissent?

2. Visual Literacy and the Iconography of Social Dissent   42
   Legal Illustration and the Origins of Douce — History, Social Realism,
   and the Giraldian Visual Tradition — Authority and Visual Dissent:
   Piers Plowman for the Anglo-Irish Reader

3. The Professional Reader as Annotator   68
   The Professional Reader and the Politics of Annotation — Ethical,
   Polemical, and Literary Responses: Types of Annotations — The
   Annotators of Douce 104 and Huntington 143: Two Professional
   Readers at Work

4. Visual Politics   92
   Informal Book Illustration and the Anglo-Irish Civil Service —
   Voicing the Text: Representing and Remembering Voices — The
   Artisans of Douce 104 and Their Division of Labor

Part II: Visual Heuristics
Denise L. Despres

5. Visualizing the Text: The Heuristics of the Page   119
   Visualizing the Text—Marginal Illustration and Meditative Reading—
   The Physical Shape of the Poem for the Medieval Reader

6. Visual Heuristics   147
   Performative Reading—The Seven Ages of Man

Conclusion: Reading *Piers Plowman* in a Manuscript Culture   169
Denise L. Despres

Appendix 1: The Hands of Douce's Main Scribe and
Corrector-Annotator   177

Appendix 2: The Marginal Annotations of Douce 104:
A Complete Transcription   181

Appendix 3: Translations   193

Notes   205

Index   253
    Index of Illustrations in Douce 104—Index of Manuscripts

Frontispiece. Dublin Court of Exchequer at Work. *The Red Book of the Exchequer* (original now destroyed); copy reproduced from John Gilbert, *Facsimiles of the National Manuscripts of Ireland,* vol. 3 (London: Longman et al., 1879), plate 37, Princeton University Library. Anglo-Irish, second quarter of fifteenth century.

Preface

⁂

A coauthored book is still relatively rare in medieval studies—although heaven knows that the interdisciplinarity of our field places demands unusual enough on individual scholars to warrant a good deal more collaboration than there is. For that reason alone, it seems appropriate to say a little about how this study developed, what the division of labor has been, and, most important, why a single person could not have managed to research and write it. We chose to work on this study together, over seven years ago now, precisely because it demanded interdisciplinary skills in a range of areas (art history, literature, codicology, paleography, and ecclesiastical, political, and cultural history)—a range that neither of us felt able to cope with single-handedly. We have never regretted the decision, although at times we have regretted the unusual problems it presented, many of which were purely practical (domestic and geographical). But we have learned a tremendous amount from each other, and we simply could not have presented so much information any other way.

This study began (while we were huddled over a little slide viewer in Kathryn Kerby-Fulton's kitchen) merely as a projected article on the extraordinary way in which the marginal figures in the Douce *Piers Plowman* related to the text on its pages. Neither of us had ever seen anything like Douce, and the more we looked at what art historians published on contemporary manuscripts, the stranger Douce seemed. The few scholarly comments about it in print emphasized its idiosyncrasy, but this seemed an inadequate explanation. So we embarked on an exercise in cultural archaeology, and, amid the detritus rejected by the art historians, we found a submerged stratum of economically illustrated manuscripts in which Douce looked perfectly at home.

Perhaps because we have worked as a team ourselves, we have been quicker than previous scholars to note the division of labor (and the workshop tensions) among the medieval artisans who produced Douce—but unlike them, we have never disagreed or diverged in our interpretations of the manuscript, and this we think is remarkable. The one difficulty we've had is in merging our two authorial voices in the writing, and this was partly because, we eventually realized, we had different jobs. Since Kathryn Kerby-Fulton had the task of writing the introduction and the chapters involving historical, polemical, and paleographical-codicological work, her chapters have laid the foundation for the study almost by the mere fact of their chronology and subject matter. Denise Despres's work on the iconography of visual meditation and mnemonics follows, exploring how the medieval reader actually approached the page. What is new about this book is its emphasis on rarely studied aspects of reception, forcing both of us to develop new methodologies for excavating medieval response; in this, our work has been mutually revelatory, supportive, and complementary. But the scope of it also lies, broadly, in two different camps: roughly, the ideological and the didactic. So the book falls very naturally into part I, "Visual Politics" (which contains Kerby-Fulton's chapters), and part II, "Visual Heuristics" (which contains Despres's).

This study began as a close iconographical and codicological analysis of a single manuscript of *Piers Plowman*, Oxford, Bodleian Library, MS Douce 104, the only medieval copy of the poem containing a cycle of illustrations. Douce is still central to the book, but we now see the study of the manuscript as an opportunity to explore and exemplify a number of broader questions about the medieval reading process; it has become a book about how manuscripts were "prepared" for readers, and about certain reading audiences: readers of *Piers Plowman*, Anglo-Irish readers, and "professional" readers, both "lay" and "clerical." (These last two terms we've come to realize are unhelpfully blunt instruments—especially in relation to the men who were "clerks" in that other sense of those who "live by the pen.") Most important, this is a book about how medieval readers actually read. We are conscious of breaking—we hope not too clumsily—new ground in some of these areas. For instance, to our knowledge, ours is the first to attempt to draw a detailed profile of what a team of "professional readers"[1] (those who edited, annotated, and illustrated books for the medieval reading public) looked for, ideologically and heuristically, when producing a vernacular literary text; ours is the first lengthy analysis (outside of work done on Matthew Paris) of a late medieval scribe-illustrator; and it is certainly the first to study the scribe-illustrator's role in the making of books for the lower socio-economic end of the illustrated book market. We also examine in detail, especially in Despres's section, the role of illustrations in a manuscript of a visionary work: we discuss how the manuscript pages were used (meditatively and mnemonically), and we have coined the term "visionary *ordinatio*" to describe the physical presentation of the poem required for such use. Moreover, because Douce is written in a Hiberno-English dialect, we have made the first sustained attempt (known to us) to trace and define an Anglo-Irish iconographical tradition of the later Middle Ages (almost all study of illustration in medieval Ireland is either of the preconquest period or of later Gaelic-Irish productions). Ours is also the first attempt to identify or examine the "vogue" for *Piers Plowman* in medieval Anglo-Ireland, especially in light of the quite neglected extant literature of the colony, which is largely reformist, satirical, and antiauthoritarian in character. In chapter 3 (and the appendixes) we present new evidence about how medieval annotators annotated—in accordance with both medieval literary theory and contemporary scribal practice—and how the ideological agenda of annotators might influence their work. Finally, we present for the first time evidence suggesting that Douce was produced by a scribe-illustrator trained in the civil service (likely in the Dublin Exchequer, which was closely modeled on Westminster's). In the Douce illustrator, then, we have just the kind of reader Langland's own Westminster preoccupations project.

Outside of Pearsall's and Scott's introductions to the facsimile of Douce 104, the manuscript has received very little sustained attention.[2] Our debt to Pearsall and Scott for their ever-useful descriptive analysis and catalog of the illustrations will be apparent throughout. On substantive points of both fact and interpretation, we rarely disagree with them. But the publication of a facsimile marks the beginning, not the end, of future scholarship on a manuscript, and in the space of a facsimile introduction Scott and Pearsall could not explore many facets of Douce or any of its most explosive ideological and iconographic implications.

Many aspects of this study are quite technical, and in the interests of reaching a wider audience than manuscript studies normally command, we have shifted much of the technical evidence and discussion to the appendixes and the notes. Our policy on transcriptions has been to follow, with few modifications, the procedures set out in Malcolm Parkes, *English Cursive Hands, 1250–1500* (see appendix 2), with the addition of braces { } to indicate words written over erasure in the text (as happens fairly frequently in the main text of Douce, which was heavily corrected). Quotations from Douce itself are followed by a folio number and the corresponding passus and line numbers in Pearsall: for example, fol. 42; VIII.15.[3] To make the study more accessible we normally quote from Pearsall's text, since the Hiberno-English dialect in Douce is less familiar to most readers; however, where the Douce version differs enough textually (as it frequently does) to warrant citing the manuscript, we offer transcriptions from it. In appendix 3 we give translations of the quotations. We should also note that we follow the practice of other scholars of medieval Ireland in using the term "Gaelic-Irish" to refer to the native Irish of Celtic descent and "Anglo-Irish" to refer to natives of Ireland of English descent; the dialect of the latter group we refer to as Middle Hiberno-English (MHE); we reserve "English" to refer to those born in England (preserving the distinction in medieval colonial records of "English by birth" and "English by blood").[4]

With regard to pictorial choices, the attempt to make this book affordable has necessitated a reduction in the number of plates we could publish, and we have not been able to publish any in color for that reason. Library fees for reproduction range from minimal to staggering, and we

Preface

have sometimes had to forgo certain pictures, to our great regret. We are grateful to the University of Minnesota Press for generously making space in the Medieval Cultures series for a many-pictured book like ours, and we hope that the affordability of the book will make up for the inherent inconveniences to readers. During the tortuous process of selecting plates, we have tried to make a priority of those not easily available elsewhere or not yet published, and to provide references to accessible studies where plates we've not been able to include may be seen.

Finally, we wish to clarify our use of a couple of vexed terms. The adjectives "progressive" and "democratizing" we have used throughout this study, although not without misgivings. Both are, of course, problematically anachronistic in relation to the Middle Ages (thus their guard of quotation marks). We use them here not with any teleological purpose in mind (we are not writing Whig history), but rather as a shorthand to indicate the radical social and political generosities exhibited in both the Douce manuscript and in certain other texts and cultural productions of Anglo-Ireland. Faced with some of the astonishing social gestures of this manuscript (like the decision to portray Contemplatif as a layman, or to make a merchant the single witness of Grace's gifts to the professions, or to use gold to dust the poorest beggars in the cycle), one needs a terminology of some sort.[5] As Steven Justice suggested to us, "The artist works hard to derive from Langland a utopian vision of governance that Langland himself gives only the most transient expression to."

By the term "illustrator" we mean the person who designed the subjects for illustration in Douce 104 and likely initially sketched in, however roughly, the pictures, or at least decided upon the placement of them all (in a large atelier the person in this role was sometimes called a *paginator*).[6] We believe that in Douce this person was also the one who carried out at least the lion's share of the finishing work (the drawing and painting) and a good deal of the rubrication. We are well aware that in a larger workshop, designing the cycle might be a wholly separate job from executing the pictures, but given the modest nature of the manuscript, the intensity of the relationship between text and image, and other production evidence, this division of labor seems unlikely here, so we have retained the word "illustrator" (in the singular) to describe these combined roles. Opinion is currently divided on whether the work of more than one artist can be distinguished in the pictures of Douce: no one can (yet) rule out the possibility that the illustrator might have had help working up some of his drawings to their final painted form or that he had help with some of the rubrication, but there are alternative explanations for certain distinctive styles apparent throughout the manuscript. What is beyond doubt is that the illustrator sometimes wielded the rubricator's inks and washes and that, when doing so, he sometimes wrote in the main scribe's hand.[7] This is, in fact, precisely what one would expect of an Exchequer-trained scribe-illustrator. As even a casual look at the fifteenth-century Dublin Court of Exchequer picture (see frontispiece) will confirm, such artists shifted easily between two levels of formality: finer, professional drawing (as in the image of the judge or baron in the lower left-hand corner) and spontaneously rough "cartoon" sketching (as in the facing images of the three suitors on the lower right).[8] These are clearly the work of a single Exchequer illustrator, yet these images are as different in "quality" as the images of Douce's knight (figure 11) and Douce's lawyer (figure 15)—who bear such striking stylistic resemblances to the Court of Exchequer judge and suitors, respectively, as to suggest artists of shared training. For these artists, the boundary between text and image was endlessly permeable (they worked mainly as scribes, after all): in the Court of Exchequer picture, not only are the words of the figures and the document incipit for each text inscribed irreverently and playfully right over the pictures themselves, but the artist has made use of all the available iconography of speaking gestures to "set off" these little texts as well: note the judge's authoritative *declamatio* gesture (curved index finger of the pointing right hand), the first suitor's "open hand speaking gesture" (with the back of the hand toward the viewer), and the second suitor's satirical "announcing" gesture (raised hand with palm turned toward the viewer).[9] We will see exactly this kind of detailed attention to the pictorial dramatization of voicing the text in Douce. Such scribe-illustrators are also innovators at the rubricator's inkpot: if our frontispiece reproduction were in color, one could see that rubrication colors were used without reserve to highlight or exaggerate facial features, just as in Douce.[10] With two detailed technical studies of the artistic work in the Douce manuscript pending,[11] it would be foolish, at this stage, for us to try to offer definitive answers to all the problems and possibilities raised by the artwork, but on the basis of evidence both in the manuscript itself and in the work of scribe-illustrators from the same milieu, we have no hesitation in pointing to a single scribe-illustrator. This man was also working, by times, as the rubricator and was at least mainly responsible for the text and pictorial program—one man wearing two hats, and sometimes three.

We would like to thank Rita Copeland for her enthusiastic interest in this book from our earliest contact with the Minnesota Medieval Cultures series editors; Rita Copeland and Barbara Hanawalt for their gracious and unflinching support during the tribulations of the reading process; and all the series editors for their willingness to take a risk on that least salable of all academic genres, a "single-manuscript study," especially at a time when even studies of single authors (like Langland) are said to be out of favor. Also at the University of Minnesota Press we are especially grateful to Robin Moir and Anne Running, both of whom labored for hours over the manuscript. Thanks are also due to Kelly Parsons, Linda Olson, and John Van Engen for their invaluable assistance during the indexing and proofreading of the book.

Preface

The following librarians and archivists went out of their way to help us: Dorothy Africa (who checked Harvard Law School, MS 12, for us during the Medieval Academy Conference in Boston when the library was closed); Adelaide Bennett, of the Index of Christian Art, Princeton University, for advice about illustrated legal manuscripts; and Josephine Matthews of the Public Record Office in London, for kindly and patiently tracking down the documentary sources of the Exchequer pictures in figure 69; Marcia Tucker and Pat Bernard, of the Institute for Advanced Study, Princeton, New Jersey, who energetically searched out ancient and elephantine Irish facsimiles and manuscript catalogs for Kathryn Kerby-Fulton. We would like to offer heartfelt thanks to the following libraries for waiving reproduction fees: the British Library, London; the Chester Beatty Library, Dublin; Harvard Law School Library, Cambridge, Massachusetts; Lincoln Cathedral Library, Lincoln, England; Merton College Library, Oxford; the Parker Library, Corpus Christi College, Cambridge; the Archives Department, Saint Bartholomew's Hospital, London; and the Pierpont Morgan Library, New York. We would also like to thank two photographers who took special pains: John Blazejewski, of the Index of Christian Art, Princeton (frontispiece), and Margaret Fincke-Keeler, of the University of Victoria (figure 69).

We owe individual debts to the following institutions: to the University of Victoria, its President's Committee on Research and Travel, and its Research Administration; to the Social Sciences and Humanities Research Council of Canada for several grants for travel to England and Ireland and for conference travel to present work in progress; and to the School of Historical Studies, Institute for Advanced Study, Princeton, for supporting Kathryn Kerby-Fulton's time in Princeton (and her moonlighting on Douce).

Denise Despres would like to thank the University of Puget Sound Enrichment Committee, Holly Jones for her gracious help in preparing the manuscript, and Gail McMurrary Gibson, Davidson College, Davidson, North Carolina, for inviting the authors to present their conclusions in her session, "Word and Image," at the 1995 Meeting of the Medieval Academy. Both the authors are very grateful to the President's Office of the University of Puget Sound, Tacoma, Washington, for providing us with a Humanities Grant, which paid a significant portion of the large reproduction fees we encountered for plates; we are also grateful to the University of Victoria work-study program for providing funds for a student research assistant and to Deborah Moore for so cheerfully agreeing to be that assistant and shouldering its myriad burdens with energy and good humor. We would also like to thank the dean of Graduate Studies at the University of Victoria, Gordana Lazarevich, for kindly providing an honorarium for the invaluable advisory work Maidie Hilmo has done for us.

A number of individuals commented on partial sections of the book and offered timely advice, including Malcolm Parkes, Jeremy Smith, De Lloyd Guth, Carter Revard, and Kathleen Scott. Kathleen provided insightful and enthusiastic commentary in her role as chair of our plenary session at the Early Book Society in Dublin in 1991 (and we are grateful to the organizers for risking so much on an unknown study in the early stages of its development). We are also grateful to Linda Olson for permission to cite her unpublished study, "A Fifteenth-Century Reading of *Piers Plowman* and the Tradition of Monastic Autobiography," and to other students in Kathryn Kerby-Fulton's graduate seminars (especially Kevin Kennedy, Carl Grindley, Corinna Gilliland, Pamela Jouris, and Tanya Schaap) for allowing us to cite their original observations on the making of Douce. We would also like to thank Mary Patricia Gibson for expert advice on technical aspects of drawing.

For attentiveness, beyond the call of common duty, to full-length draft versions of this study, we would like to offer our sincerest thanks to Michael Camille, Alan Fletcher, Steven Justice, Maidie Hilmo, and the two dedicatees of the book, Lawrence Clopper and Derek Pearsall. Michael Camille's faith in our earliest draft and his infectious enthusiasm for our unorthodox study have been sources of great comfort and cheer. Alan Fletcher gave selflessly of his wisdom and precision on matters of medieval Irish culture (as will be evident in many of our notes); he also heroically tracked down and transcribed material in the Public Record Office of Northern Ireland for us. Steven Justice was an engaged and uncompromising reader who clarified for us the ideological focus of the book, rigorously distinguishing readers' responses in Douce (which is the main business of our book) from anything we might wish to say about what Langland as an author "intended" (which is another kind of study). Without Maidie Hilmo's capacious art-historical knowledge and unflaggingly generous engagement with every step of our work, this would have been a much poorer book in every respect. We would also like to thank Maidie for permission to cite her dissertation (in progress), "Transcending Boundaries: Image and Text in the *Pearl* Manuscript, the Ellesmere Manuscript of the *Canterbury Tales*, and the Douce 104 *Piers Plowman*," and her article in *Fifteenth-Century Studies* 23 (1997): "Retributive Violence and the Reformist Agenda in the Illustrated Douce 104 MS of *Piers Plowman*."

Finally, in this list, Lawrence Clopper (who supervised Denise Despres's doctoral dissertation) and Derek Pearsall (who supervised Kathryn Kerby-Fulton's) have been, to each of us respectively, a source of endless moral support, judicious guidance, and perpetual inspiration. Their love of Langland and their love of life are exemplary, both. Derek Pearsall very kindly sent a prepublication typescript of his essay "Manuscript Illustration of Late Middle English Literary Texts, with Special Reference

Preface

to the Illustration of *Piers Plowman* in Bodleian Library MS Douce 104"[12] and an early draft of his introduction to the Douce facsimile. Lawrence Clopper kindly read the penultimate draft of the book and generously shared his own research from his forthcoming book with Denise Despres.

The two people to whom we owe the greatest personal debts are the two people to whom we would not have dared dedicate this book: Stephen Mead and Gordon Fulton have had to put up with this study for far too long, but they never failed to provide the patient and loving support that got us over the multitude of humps (never-ending) in this book's long gestation. Our deepest thanks to them both.

Note

While this book was in press, new evidence came to light suggesting that the Douce artist and the artist of the *Red Book* may in fact be the same (and not simply, as argued here, scribes of shared training). This evidence will be published in Kathryn Kerby-Fulton's "Professional and Private Readers of Langland at Home and Abroad," in the proceedings of the "New Directions in Manuscript Studies" conference, Harvard University, October 22–25, 1998, to be edited by Derek Pearsall.

Introduction

Kathryn Kerby-Fulton

The Professional Reader at Work

There was a politics as well as an art to medieval book production, and that politics had this in common with what we would today call censorship: neither process cares much for the sanctity of the authorial text. As Annabel Patterson writes in *Censorship and Interpretation*, it is not authorial intention so much as audience reception that "determines the meaning and impact of a literary work," an impact that "makes itself heard inferentially, in the *space* between what is written... and what the audience, knowing what they know, might expect to read."[1] This is a book about what occurs in the "space" between author and audience, a "space" that, in the Middle Ages, was far less notional than it is for modern children of print culture. Those who prepared manuscripts were constantly negotiating between authorial intention and reader expectation, and this is a case study of how those expectations were met (or dashed or manipulated) by those responsible for physically making books. This is not, therefore, a study of *Piers Plowman* in the usual sense, but a study of the politics of producing *Piers Plowman* for the medieval reader, and of medieval reading processes generally. Our main focus is the only extant illustrated manuscript of Langland's poem, Oxford, Bodleian Library, MS Douce 104,[2] which we set alongside a number of contemporary manuscripts, especially those similarly illustrated and annotated for low-budget book owners, in many of which, as in Douce, the scribe is also known or believed to be the artist. Despite its large number of pictures, Douce 104 is, by contemporary standards for illustrated books, a modest early-fifteenth-century manuscript. Written in 1427, it contains the C text of *Piers Plowman*, translated into a Hiberno-English dialect and economically illustrated for an unknown patron; its unframed marginal miniatures have the distinction of being the only cycle of illustrations among more than fifty extant medieval copies of Langland's poem.[3] Because of its format, it provides a uniquely revealing instance of how the makers of manuscripts intended medieval readers to *use* text-image pages and of how scribes and artists packaged a poem like *Piers* for reader consumption. Such a study seems particularly appropriate given Langland's own obsessive concern with audience reception, and it provides clues as to how he may have anticipated (or feared) that his poem might be read. By restoring audience reception to the equation with which literary critics have traditionally sought to formulate the meaning of early texts, we hope to provide a fuller understanding of the hermeneutics of medieval reading.

We are interested in both the *politics* of late medieval manuscript preparation (Kerby-Fulton, part I) and the *heuristics* of manuscript use (Despres, part II). Scribes and illuminators were the filters, so to speak, through which all texts passed before reaching medieval readers; the codicological evidence of their filtering activity on behalf of their audiences survives, but it remains an underutilized resource for the study of cultural literacies.[4] Modern scholars understand as yet so few of the assumptions and passions these "middlemen" (and a few women)[5] brought to their work, and even less about how those assumptions influenced both what writers wrote and what bookshop clientele expected.[6] But scribes and illuminators are the very medieval readers whose testimony is most accessible to us; it was the job of those artisans who labored in scriptoria and bookshops to "prepare"—an apparently neutral word with cultural ramifications far from neutral—literature for presentation to the community (whether to a religious community or a particular patron or a chance customer). Medieval illustrators or their supervisors inevitably brought their own ethical and ideological sensibilities to their work; even when developing pictorial programs to suit a specific patron, they "translated" the ideas of the text into iconography on the basis of their own interpretations, ideologies, and assumptions about audience visual literacy.[7] The Douce manuscript is intriguing precisely because it provides unusual evidence of these assumptions at work, and of the kinds of tensions between and among illustrator, annotator, and, apparently, patron that the competition for interpretive control might produce.[8] It is further intriguing precisely because modern editors have always considered it a "bad manuscript," and that is simply because its makers did their jobs so well: medieval scribes, annotators, and correctors, much to the exasperation of modern editors, were trained to render a text intelligible to their *immediate* audience—that is, to "correct" dialect, meter, doctrine, anything that might impede the understanding of simpler readers or irritate wealthy patrons or the authorities generally.[9] Douce is an instructive instance of just such "professional" editorializing and adaptation for the local reader, including linguistic adaptation to a Hiberno-English dialect.[10] It is a particularly clear instance of the "filtering"—or if one prefers a less ideologically loaded label, "social authorship"—of poetic texts on behalf of the medieval reader.[11] Such laborers in the medieval literacy industry, for the purposes of this study (and with the necessary qualifications delineated later), will be referred to as "professional readers." Professional readers are those whose job it was to make decisions about the copying, illustration, editing, correcting, and annotating of a text *on be-*

half of the medieval reader or consumer. (The term therefore does not include those whose job it was simply to carry out uncritically a supervisor's decisions.) This book is a case study of professional readers at work.

The Douce Manuscript in Brief

In an influential essay published in 1962, Rosemary Woolf wrote that it is "self-evident that *Piers Plowman* is insusceptible of illustration" because "none of the very numerous manuscript texts of the poem are illustrated."[12] Although even as an Oxford don Woolf apparently did not know about the seventy-four pictures that populate the pages of the Bodleian's Douce 104,[13] perhaps the sheer unconventionality of its program of illustrations vindicates her. In an unfavorable comparison with the brilliant backdrops of *Pearl*, she astutely complained that "the background against which [Langland's] characters meet is quite unknown,"[14] so she would hardly have been surprised to see that all of Douce's seventy-three miniatures, with the exception of the first, are placed austerely against the bare vellum of the margins, unframed, and utterly destitute of even the merest suggestion of setting: the diapered frames or suggestive foliage that give a sense of terra firma to even the most rudimentary of medieval illustrations are nonexistent in Douce 104.

There are, in fact, a striking number of absences in the manuscript. For instance, those who approach its illustrations expecting to find a visual guide to the poem's narrative events, such as is provided, for example, by the illustrations of Lydgate's *Troy Book*,[15] will be sadly disappointed: of the seventy-three illustrations, only five show an event or episode from the poem actually taking place. While it is true that the narrative structure of *Piers* is hardly obvious—what Dr. Johnson remarked of Samuel Richardson's novels, "If you were to read Richardson for the story... you would hang yourself,"[16] is equally applicable to Langland—one cannot help noticing that, even where clear narrative occurs, the illustrator is rarely tempted by it. Nor is he—perhaps for reasons of religious dissent—tempted by the poem's major biblical events, the lineaments of which were well established in model books: there is not even an illustration of the Crucifixion or of any single divine or saintly nonallegorical character mentioned in the poem. Furthermore, passus like IX and XI, with virtually no action scenes and a great deal of dialogue, are heavily illustrated, while passus XX, which contains the Tournament, the Crucifixion, and the Harrowing, is one of the most sparsely illustrated.[17] While some of these omissions might be explained by the choice of marginal format, which, as Kathleen Scott has suggested, was no doubt partly motivated by a need for economy, the illustrator is quite capable of handling or suggesting multiple figures (where he wants to) by clever use of perspective or expansion into other margins;[18] thus, lack of space cannot entirely account for his avoidance of narrative subjects. Rather, his startling neglect of setting and narrative give Douce 104, as we shall argue, the look of a manuscript designed in part to enhance the mnemonic and meditative potential of a visionary work. Mary Carruthers has already briefly pointed out the mnemonic function of some of Douce's images,[19] but no one has so far commented on the apparent meditative function of the cycle, which seems designed to trace a visionary progress through a *mental* (not physical) landscape. The empty backgrounds Woolf complained of in *Piers Plowman* were recognized by the Douce illustrator as a function of the meditator's insistent foregrounding of key images, a process that seeks to discard surrounding imagery as distracting. The bare backgrounds of Douce 104 were consequently intended for just such mental work. Moreover, they make—in tandem with the cycle's defiant avoidance of orthodox religious iconography—an austerely reformist statement.

There is another peculiarity of Douce not entirely explained even by its meditative function: that is, its heavy representation of single human figures and its dearth of nonhuman images. Some sixty-four out of the seventy-three pictures are of human figures, drawn from the ranks of the poem's many speakers or type figures. The lack of inanimate objects and animal symbols is startling: Elizabeth Salter's sensitive study, "*Piers Plowman* and the Visual Arts," would have led us to expect many of the kinds of pictures that fill the *Holkam Bible Picture Book* (London, British Library, MS Add. 47682) and spiritual encyclopedias, but there is no Tree of Charity, no Barn of Unity, no Cart of Christendom—in fact none of the diagrammatic images that fill the pages of such manuscripts, often in marginal positions.[20] Rather, forty-three of the seventy-three pictures serve to identify speakers, of whom thirty-six are actually speaking in the lines beside which their pictures are placed. The fact that the Douce illustrator is at pains both to show speakers in relation to their speech and to portray acts of discourse under way suggests a sensitive response to the large amount of intellectual struggle and debate in Langland's poem. Formal discourse is heavily represented: at least fifteen of the illustrations represent a speech-act, in the strict sense of the term, in progress; that is, utterances "viewed as performing specific actions," as *doing* something through the act of speaking. In the Douce illustrations, for instance, one sees acts of confessing (e.g., Mede and a friar, fol. 11v), preaching (Dobet, figure 21), teaching (Franciscan friar, figure 20), litigating (lawyer, figure 15), disputing (Recklessness, figure 25; Trajan, figure 27), writing (Will, figure 24)—even proclaiming a marriage charter (Liar, fol. 9).[21] This suggests an emphasis on the text's voices that may surprise modern readers, yet it is quite consistent with the visionary genre of the poem (visions are full of dialogue and debate) and also with the manuscript's mnemonic function (the illustrator is striving to associate voices with images in the mind of the reader). But it is also consistent with attention to the orality of the medieval reading process itself, something that interests this illustrator immensely.

Medieval iconography of narration was heavily influenced by orality, even after the development of silent reading sometime during the fourteenth century.[22] An emphasis on representing speakers is especially marked, as Michael Camille has shown, in a tradition of marginal illustration that began during the period M. T. Clanchy distinguishes as transitional "from memory to written record" (1066–1307) and that later developed to include, with the spread of silent reading, depictions of *readers* as well as *speakers*. Such illustrations function to "voice" the text beside which they occur. We refer to this as a *performative* tradition of illustration (because it visually dramatizes the voice in performance).[23] It was tenacious long after silent reading began; one thinks of even the Ellesmere manuscript (San Marino, Huntington Library, MS Ellesmere 26 C 9), with its emphasis on tale *narrators* in *The Canterbury Tales*, rather than tale *narratives*.[24]

The illustrator's interest in the poem's voices and its visionary structure does much to illuminate his unusual lack of interest, as Kathleen Scott has noted, in *ordinatio*.[25] Although the written text of Douce meets the basic requirements of a tradition of *ordinatio* in the poem's copying[26] (with its blue "Lombard" initials and red flourishing at passus openings, crude rubrication of Latin, and more ambitious gold-leaf initials at the three "Vita" openings),[27] the illustrator has made virtually no attempt to align pictures with divisions in the text. In fact he generally avoids passus openings, especially where they occur on a verso, because there the illustration would have to compete with the flourishing. This might be taken as an indication of his nonprofessional status, but his pictures are rarely either technically or interpretively naive.[28] What seems to have influenced picture placement more than anything is the fact that the vast majority of the pictures represent speakers, and speakers have—or raise—iconographic issues of authority. And these matter to this artist.

It is perhaps no accident, then, that the clearest discernible principle of selection in the Douce cycle is not *ordinatio*, in the usual sense, but visionary structure and reformist ideology. The illustrator's awareness of these features is acute: (1) he follows the development of the dreamer, Will, through the various stages of his spiritual progress:[29] at least six of the illustrations seem designed to portray or recall Will in some spiritual state (usually in relation to the Ages of Man iconography), while no other figure, not even Piers, is portrayed more than once; (2) he emphasizes the common visionary theme of pilgrimage (he was well aware of the iconography of the "pilgrimage of life" genre)[30] with his numerous portraits of travelers and wanderers—staves, scrips, and worn-out shoes abound on these pages, even among characters whom Langland has not explicitly designated as pilgrims; (3) he plays off the medieval reader's standard iconographic expectations by a series of provocative, perhaps dissenting, certainly reformist pictorial choices, dashing some orthodox reader expectations, surprising or manipulating others; and (4) he emphasizes the text's voices, which as any reader of *Piers* knows, is extremely helpful, more helpful than guidance to passus divisions ever could be (which are, after all, fairly useless for interpretive purposes). Knowing who is speaking in *Piers Plowman* is perhaps the biggest challenge a reader faces, especially a manuscript reader. As any editor of the poem knows, to assign modern quotation marks to the text is to make major interpretive decisions in many places, and the Douce illustrator was not afraid of making major interpretive decisions on the reader's behalf.[31] In short, the illustrator seems to have been bent on encouraging a certain kind of *reading process* as well as a certain kind of *reading* of the poem. We are only beginning to understand how radically different these were from what late-twentieth-century scholars might have expected of an illustrated *Piers* manuscript (speaking of dashed expectations). We assume that one reason the manuscript has received so little attention is that its reading of the poem is often barely recognizable as the *Piers Plowman* constructed by decades of New Critical scholarship. As such, the illustrations have much to teach us about medieval perceptions.

A less obvious but equally decisive set of interpretive decisions made on the reader's behalf lies in the Douce annotations. Immediately after Douce 104 was written, decorated, and illustrated, it was provided with 257 marginal annotations that were apparently meant to guide the reader through the main points of the allegorical narrative, to signal new topics, to highlight moral and spiritual doctrine, and to give vent to social and ecclesiastical commentary. The annotations, all (with three exceptions) in a single hand, present a remarkably consistent set of responses to the poem and can be broadly categorized, as we shall see in chapter 3, according to medieval literary theory. They are also very similar to the kinds of annotation developed originally by Robert Grosseteste for theological writing. The annotator actually highlights, with an apparent neutrality that is quite deceptive, the most controversial passages in matters of faith, ecclesiology, and socioreligious issues, passages usually ignored or glossed over by the more conservative *Piers* annotators. Paleographical evidence shows, in fact, that—contrary to the suggestion of the scruffy appearance of his page—he was a "professional reader" (that is, a *scribe* whose job it was to provide annotation for reader guidance, not a scribbling owner). Although the annotator and the illustrator of Douce can differ dramatically in their perspectives on the poem, several of the purposes for which the illustrations were created are evident in the annotations as well: notably, they highlight interests in mnemonics, in distinguishing voices in the text, in singling out images that epitomize or explain whole passages, and especially in noting challenges to faith and authority.

Authority is a provocative theme in Douce partly because of its geographical origin.[32] It illuminates what might be called "the Anglo-Irish connection" in the early dissemination of Langland's poem specifically and in the satirical poetry of social and ecclesiastical disgruntlement generally. It has not yet really been noticed that a variety of geographical and ecclesiastical factors converged to make Anglo-Ireland a center for the creation and dissemination of poetry with *both* a satirical and a reformist (sometimes even dissenting) slant.[33] The illustrator's attitude toward religious images and religious authority is unusually negative, but both the illustrator and the annotator saw authority issues as paramount and thought it their duty to sort out the hierarchy of voices in the poem on behalf of the reader—which they did somewhat differently apparently because they seem to represent quite different social and ecclesiastical perspectives. Anglo-Irish readers were likely to have complex feelings about institutional authority and social injustice—more mixed than even Langland's. The surviving ecclesiastical satire in Middle Hiberno-English is perhaps the most vicious extant in a medieval English vernacular, and the antimendicant satire is especially cruel. Of course, Ireland was the home of the most prominent fourteenth-century antimendicant polemicist, Richard FitzRalph, and the animosities between secular clergy and friars there were exacerbated by ethnic tensions, but this satire was also mitigated at times by public awareness of real poverty among (especially Franciscan) friars.[34] Sympathy for poverty generally was unusually vigorous in Anglo-Irish literature; poverty was endemic in the colony and was again exacerbated by interethnic tensions. Moreover, colonial views on reformist ecclesiastical issues and social issues (such as begging and bastardy) were pronounced. While many looked to English colonial traditions as the civilizing force that had tamed the "wilde Yrisshe" (to quote the undiplomatic *Richard the Redeless* author, who was quoting Richard himself),[35] native Irish traditions had affected the colonizers as well as the colonized. All of these issues surface in the Douce readings, which are in many respects as provocative and creative as any of the Langlandian "sequels," including John Ball's, so eloquently discussed by Steven Justice.[36] In the range and perceptiveness of its response, Douce can be treated as a Langlandian "sequel" itself, and as such it provides many points of comparison with the texts of the *Piers Plowman* tradition.

Perhaps most important, the Douce manuscript reveals a passionate and uncensored response to a poem that had become more radical with each passing decade of its existence.[37] Some of what Langland had felt able to say openly in his B text had to be suppressed in C, which was being revised and rapidly disseminated during the period immediately after the Rising of 1381 and the repressive legislation of the Blackfriar's Council of 1382.[38] By the late 1380s, when C was "finished" (as finished, that is, as Langland was ever to be able to make it), there was increasing official censorship in England of reformist and prophetic writings.[39] By the 1390s the Lollard-sympathetic *Pierce the Ploughman's Crede* had been written, and by the time of Arundel's *Constitutions* in 1409 Langland's poem must have looked quite dangerous—at least at this point, as Ian Doyle has shown, it stops being "a leading article of commerce" in London bookshops.[40] By 1427, the same year that Douce was made, the abbot of Saint Albans, John Whethamstede, claimed that the cause of contemporary heresy was "the possession and reading of books in our vulgar tongue."[41] Ideas perilous to discuss, or indeed illustrate, in London at this time, however, received less reticent treatment in colonial Ireland: in the hands of a provocative lay illustrator and a clerical annotator working in the Dublin-Pale district in 1427, Langland's vision retains some of the spiritual, intellectual, and ethical urgency that drew the rebels to it in 1381.

Medieval Reading, Scribe-Illustrators, and the "Utility-Grade" Manuscript

Medieval reading, as Stephen Nichols has argued, was not necessarily linear; manuscripts, he says, may present "systemic rivalries" of focus and interpretation among text, illustration, annotations, emendations, and even rubrications.[42] In this book we will try to reconstruct instances of the sometimes competing, or at least divergent, readings of *Piers Plowman* offered by the illustrator (or perhaps the patron) and the annotator. The illustrator (whether on behalf of the patron or not) seems more involved with social and reformist issues, and the annotator with clerical and intellectual concerns; some sort of rivalry is suggested by the fact that the annotator often impatiently writes directly on the illustrations and, less certainly, by the fact that the rubricator (who sometimes at least appears to be the scribe) can't seem to resist highlighting or otherwise meddling with pictures that intrigue him. The narrative of *Piers Plowman* was far from "linear" in the first place, and the Douce manuscript epitomizes for modern readers the kinds of competitive technologies that the medieval reader was much more adept at negotiating than we are today. To read Douce is to read *Piers Plowman* in the nonlinear, associative, and more fluid form that characterized reading in a manuscript culture, and also to be surprised by how the illustrations are frequently able to "cut to" the moral and social level of Langland's allegory more swiftly and uncompromisingly than the poetry, with all its complexity, digression, and qualification. These starker, quicker connections (e.g., Hunger, fol. 38, glaring triumphantly and menacingly back across the facing page at Wastor, fol. 37v [figure 12]—a pictorial epitome of cause and effect) give some sense of the underlying moral and social grid systems that were Langland's raw material.

Medieval reading could be *meditative, mnemonic, performative, self-reflexive,* and even, as Paul Saenger has shown with the growth of silent reading,⁴³ *dissenting*. The relations between text and image in Douce 104 illustrate all these aspects of the medieval reading process quite vividly. The pictures of Douce were placed against the bare vellum of the margins with no contextualizing frame or backdrop partly to economize, but also partly, as demonstrated in chapters 5 and 6, to emphasize the meditative potential of the images. This, along with their placement to highlight what we call visionary *ordinatio*, is closely related to the way the manuscript's makers understood the self-reflexive function of the medieval reading process, examined in chapter 5. What Paul Piehler describes as the participatory element in dream-vision narratives,⁴⁴ the tendency for the reader to identify with the "I" speaker in the poem, is brilliantly realized by the illustrator, who subtly links Langland's ambiguous self-portraiture (even more prominent, of course, in C) with the figure of every spiritual wanderer in the poem's cast of characters. The performative aspect of medieval reading is foregrounded in the illustrator's and the annotator's obsessive (and independent) concern with identifying and interpreting the poem's speakers, both as an act of charity for manuscript readers confronting this more than usually fluid text and as an expression of their own attitudes toward social concerns, as suggested in chapters 3 and 4. *Piers Plowman* was potentially explosive for its first audience (in fact, judging by the response of the rebels of 1381, more explosive than Langland wished) precisely because it allowed those without privilege a voice. The Douce illustrator is extremely alert to this aspect of the poem (see chapters 1 and 2), not only in his persistent foregrounding of socially inferior speakers, but also in his use of what we have called "silent witnesses" (representations of the illiterate or otherwise socially marginalized, who are shown as listening intently or even *reading* the text beside which they are placed, often at controversial points in the poem). Chapter 3 is devoted exclusively to the annotator's work, and in the conclusion we briefly examine both professional readers at work in Passus IX and X. These two passus were particularly influential with Langland's initial audience in England (whether as A.VIII and XI or B.VI and VIII or C.IX and X), as the recurrent allusions to them in Langlandian sequels — from the Ball letters to *Pierce the Ploughman's Crede* and *Mum and the Sothsegger* — suggest.

In the very little attention the manuscript received prior to the publication of Derek Pearsall and Kathleen Scott's facsimile, it was considered a crude and amateurish production.⁴⁵ In fact, we argue, it belongs to a particular (and neglected) class of manuscripts: the scribe-illustrated codex. Such manuscripts are often visually unimpressive and therefore are usually ignored by art historians; however, close examination of the paleographical evidence can show, as with Douce, that workshop professionalism is not the issue here: economics is, and this is the next problem we must address.

The question of manuscript readership, illustration, and social class is complex and will be explored and contextualized gradually throughout this study; however, a few points by way of introduction are necessary here. Douce 104 was economically produced for a client of (one assumes) relatively modest means.[46] It is not an objet d'art, but a working manuscript, or, to use J. B. Allen's delightful metaphor, a "utility-grade manuscript."[47] The client who commissioned it apparently could not afford the extra vellum—even of the poor quality he had already selected—required to place the illustrations in the usual framed boxes within the text. Even the copying of the text was done as cheaply as possible (there is not so much as a single line's space between passus divisions). But the Douce artist was skillful enough to find inspiration in what could have been a serious limitation—a need to save vellum so rigorous as to push all illustrations but the initial one into the narrow, eventually to be cropped, margins of the text. In fact, the format may have been his suggestion, because it so clearly echoes Exchequer-style drawing, which, as we will see, he must have known. He created characters that touch words or point to words with their eyes, hands, and other body parts; he frequently aligns the mouth of a speaking figure precisely with the first line spoken in the text, and the rubricator (who may or may not be the same man) also plays a role in highlighting such "interactive" body parts. Although working within limitations imposed by tight margins, misshapen vellum, and unpredictable line lengths, he managed to place figures so as to create striking visual puns (as mnemonics), such as the barefoot Franciscan with his foot on the word "stond" (figure 20); or the angry Envy, whose clenched fist rises to meet the line "he wrothe his fyst a pon wrathe..." (fol. 25). The reasons we believe that the Douce cycle was (chiefly) the conception of a single scribe-illustrator are detailed in chapter 4. However, the general characteristics of scribe-illustrators at work should be mentioned at this point. This is not a topic that has received much scholarly attention, so the observations gathered here are—to our knowledge—the first attempt to generalize on this complex and elusive subject (an attempt fraught with all the dangers of generalization, as well).

While we have found some analogues to the Douce illustrations in more lavishly produced manuscripts, a telling feature of the research for this study is the extent to which a certain kind of manuscript has been most persistently relevant, notably the kind in which the scribe is also the illustrator or in which the author or compiler himself takes on the role of scribe and/or illustrator. Throughout this study we will return time and again for comparison to a particular group of manuscripts that were scribe illustrated and that contain, like Douce, unframed marginal pictures or pictorial annotation. These manuscripts range from the thirteenth to the fifteenth centuries in date, and they have not been considered (some would say for obvious reasons) as a group before. They include manuscripts illustrated in the Giraldian tradition (for example, Oxford,

Introduction

Bodleian Library, MS Laud Misc. 720, and Cambridge, University Library, MS Ff. 1.27), that is, later descendants of the original, written and probably initially sketched by the historian and travel writer Giraldus Cambrensis (d. 1223), whose works on Ireland were so influential in the colony and in England as well. They also include manuscripts written and illustrated by Matthew Paris (d. 1259), such as Cambridge, Corpus Christi College, MSS 16 and 26. Matthew was himself indebted to Giraldus as both historian and artist. Also included in this group is a work written, supervised, and sporadically marginally illustrated by James le Palmer (d. 1375), a clerk of Edward III's Exchequer, who compiled the unique copy of the *Omne bonum* (London, British Library, MS Royal 6.E.VI–VII), an ecclesiological encyclopedia with an unusual blend of spiritual, legal, and polemical (antimendicant) material.[48] Both Matthew Paris and James le Palmer came in constant contact with legal documents, especially Exchequer materials, and both show an intimate knowledge of the marginal illustrations used in such documents. The (Westminster) *Red Book of the Exchequer* was likely Matthew's "main source" of documentary material, and "the system of [marginal] *signa* which Matthew uses is very similar to that used in the Exchequer, and was probably copied from it."[49] This may suggest one of the reasons we find so many parallels with Douce, whose scribe-illustrator knew documentary formats, too, as we shall see. In fact, the illustrated manuscript closest to Douce in style is the apparently early-fifteenth-century Dublin *Red Book of the Exchequer* (represented in our frontispiece), and another collection of Anglo-Irish legal documents, the Waterford Charter Roll,[50] is also remarkably similar to Douce in its penchant for vigorous realism and single-figure illustration. Two further manuscripts, Lincoln Cathedral Library, MS 218, and London, British Library, MS Add. 37049, both fifteenth-century English *collectanea spiritualia*, are close to Douce in appearance and date and are almost certainly also scribe-illustrated productions. With the exception of contemporary Anglo-Irish documentary and literary illustration and (descendant copies of) the manuscripts now extant in the Giraldian tradition, it is unlikely that the Douce artist would have known these specific manuscripts, but clearly he knew something quite like them, and methodologically and iconographically they provide revealing parallels to his work. The text-image relations in this group highlight heuristic questions (such as orality, meditation, and mnemonics), and they also highlight political questions through innovative social realism (especially in the historical and legal drawings of Gerald, Matthew, and the Anglo-Irish documents) and ecclesiological polemics (especially in Matthew's chronicles, in the *Omne bonum*, and in Lincoln). These in fact represent important (although not fully appreciated) areas of Langland's own reading, so it is likely no accident that one finds affinities between the Douce illustrations and scribe-illustrated works on these subjects.⁵¹ And this also raises interesting new questions about Langland's early audiences, especially those on the interface of the "lay" and "clerical" reading communities, particularly those in civil service positions.

Scribe-illustrated manuscripts are often utility-grade manuscripts — they can have, at first glance, a "homemade" appearance, but in most cases they are in fact professional or at least semiprofessional productions.⁵² These books are especially interesting for text-image scholarship because the scribe-illustrator was often the person who conceived the manuscript (and sometimes even composed or compiled the text in it) as well as the person who executed much of it. Such manuscripts display a certain *intimacy* between text and illustration, a certain *familiarity* with their (implied) audience, and a certain *freedom* of choice, of expression, and of eclecticism not found in the conventional formality of more impersonally produced workshop books (in which the tasks of production were so rigidly specialized as to preclude much spontaneity and interplay between text and image).

Frustrating for modern scholars in search of medieval reader response has been the unwelcome evidence that many medieval illustrators had not even read the texts they illustrated; instructions provided by a supervisor or patron or the existence of a previous cycle from which to copy often made reading on the part of the executing artist unnecessary, even when he (or she) was literate in the language of the text.⁵³ As Denise Despres has demonstrated in her study of the features that scribe-illustrated manuscripts tend to have in common, their pictures usually show (and not surprisingly) an *intimate knowledge of the text*, the illustration of which may then be more textually subtle and the interpretation more easily patron-customized.⁵⁴ *Emphasis on the performative* (what we call the "voicing" of the text, in which the image "dramatizes," often using iconographic convention, the character in speech) is especially possible when the scribe is the illustrator. In this type of manuscript, medieval concern with orality emerges, almost comically obvious in manuscripts like Add. 37049 (with text placement akin to modern cartoon balloons emanating from the mouths of speaking figures [figure 59]), more subtly in Douce. One also finds that the all-too-common *subordination of image to word is reversed or modified* in scribe-illustrated manuscripts. Whereas a book of hours provides illustration for narrative or devotional purposes in a carefully designated space, Douce 104, like other scribe-illustrated contemporaries, is experimental in its picture placement, with figures (or their limbs) bracketing key passages, pushing into corners, and spanning the *bas de page* and both left and right margins.⁵⁵ The spatial relationships between word and image are thus more innovative and less systematic in the manuscript of a scribal illustrator, who is able to diminish the systemic rivalry of text-image relations. Such manuscripts also show a startling degree of *innovation in ordinatio*. Normally there was little opportunity for such innovation by the time a manuscript reached the illuminator.[56] In Douce the visionary *ordinatio* actually *diminishes* or blurs the transitions between formal (e.g., passus) divisions in the narrative and deliberately creates a sense of dreamlike confusion at moments of the poem through dense illustration.[57]

In scribe-illustrated manuscripts there is also a pronounced *stylistic eclecticism*. The Douce cycle contains both the kinds of images that one would find in an artist's pattern book and others that are technically inferior or just stylistically incongruent with the pattern-book types.[58] Since the cycle would likely have been prepared from scratch,[59] some of the latter were probably drawn in response to life experience, especially some of the pictures of the poor and of characters peculiar to the poem, all of which reflect the social realism of Giraldian tradition. Most intriguing is the Douce illustrator's tendency to favor images that present socio-religious commentary where he might have simply opted for pattern-book clichés.[60] This is a trait of illustrators who, like Matthew Paris and James le Palmer, had had experience working with legal manuscripts, ecclesiastical texts, and chronicles. Moreover, his pictorial decisions neglect—or deliberately reject or satirize—most of the subjects common in books of hours and other "high-class" book illustration.[61] Scribe-illustrators also tend to make much more use of *visual mnemonics:* their pictorial choices suggest careful, even minute, reading and recognition of the need for signposting at conceptually difficult moments (not simply at high points in the narrative). Thus the Douce illustrator has littered the margins with images of busts, coins, sealed documents, boats, and other explicitly mnemonic images, such as one finds in, for instance, Matthew Paris's work and in legal illustration.[62] Finally, one of the strongest indications of a scribe-illustrator is *the range of genre-markers* of which such artists are capable. One thinks of the way that the Douce illustrator is able to shift gears easily between, say, chronicle imagery and ecclesiological or legal iconography.[63] A "formalist" workshop professional would be less likely to make the kind of generic pictorial distinctions that abound in encyclopedic scribe-illustrated works, like Matthew Paris's *Chronica majora,* for instance. As later chapters will show, the Douce cycle throws into visual relief the various genres Langland himself drew upon—*as they were recognized by medieval readers*—and some of these genres (e.g., the persistent pictorial allusion to chronicles and legal treatises) may surprise modern readers who think of Piers as largely biblically and devotionally generated.

Scribe-illustrated manuscripts, especially those containing unframed marginal illustrations, like Douce, are a unique group, and as a group they can tell us a great deal about the nonlinear nature of medieval reading habits and about what medieval book illustration was like at its most "democratic." As Malcolm Parkes has pointed out, an illustrated book must have been a comparatively rare thing in the experience even of many literate medieval people;[64] illustrations were expensive and to many book owners and readers an unaffordable (or in the case of the clergy, unnecessary) luxury. Cheaply produced scribe-illustrated manuscripts offered new visual and educational possibilities to groups who, it was thought, most needed such aids: literate laity and "functionally literate" clergy. It is these two aspects of Douce (its power to demonstrate the nonlinear quality of medieval reading and a new accessibility in book production) that, when studied alongside other scribe-illustrated manuscripts, make possible ramifications far beyond those of a single manuscript study, or even beyond those of a study in the reception of *Piers Plowman*.

Finally, there are some polemical points that any reception study, even, to our surprise, one published in the late 1990s, must apparently still address. During the course of our work we have been impressed and sometimes stunned by the diversity and sophistication of the medieval reading process. This does not mean that we advocate medieval readings in preference to modern ones. We hope it will be clear as the book progresses that we are not in the business of championing medieval responses, nor do we confuse them (indeed we would not be capable of confusing them) with modern reading. But this book is not primarily about modern readings of Langland; there are plenty such books already. Rather, it is about how medieval people read him. And this, we concede and we warn, can be surprising, even alienating. Some may find our democratizing of the usual text-image hierarchy annoying and heretical. (We don't use Langland's text as a measure of whether the Douce illustrator "got it right" — and in this we depart sharply from the working assumptions of most studies of literary illustration.)[65] One press reviewer has been exasperated by our suggestions that sometimes the Douce illustrator sees a passage of the poem with a clarity that even (or especially) Langland could not, and also by the fact that in our study "often what the poem is doing is perfectly unrecognizable." But surely this tells us something about our twentieth-century orthodoxies (and superiorities). The sanguine assumptions of New Criticism evident in such comments (that a poem "does" anything on its own, in the absence of a reader; that *we* know what it does; and that any mere scribe or artist or annotator could never be more astute on *any* given point than an author of great genius) may be pleasantly comforting, but they are not unshakable truths. We are interested, here, in understanding reception *historically*, and if we sometimes uncover different readings and come to different conclusions than modern criticism of the poem has, we don't apologize for that. Nor do we apologize for the fact that this is a book about the C text and not about B; to quote the B text for the first and last time in this study, there are, as Imaginatif says, "bokes y[n]owe" on Langland's second version (B.XII.17).[66] C's turn is long overdue, and the caprice of manuscript survival has obligingly ensured, for once, that the last shall be made first.

PART I

✜

Visual Politics
Kathryn Kerby-Fulton

CHAPTER 1

⁜

Visual Literacy and the Iconography of Reformist Polemics

The task of the next two chapters will be to try to understand why the margins of the Douce manuscript contain so many unexpected pictorial challenges to ecclesiastical and political authority. It is the very nature of medieval book illustration (given that most commissions came from the wealthy and the powerful, whether for personal or institutional use) that visual images of authority are usually unequivocal, flattering, and ubiquitous. But the Douce artist explicitly challenges these norms through the manipulation of reader expectations, and in this he relies heavily on the visual literacy—or rather, *literacies*—of his audience. Like other scribe-illustrators, he was master of a startling range of iconographical genres, but it would have required an unusual level of sophistication in both visual and polemical literacy to catch all the iconographic allusion and satire embedded in these pictures. In this context the character of the patron who commissioned Douce begins to emerge a little from the shrouds of historical oblivion, as does the ideological perspective of its artist. All these considerations bring us closer to a sense of audience for the manuscript, while raising intriguing questions about what was considered appropriate to a reading audience at the interface between lay and clerical cultures (an audience we distinguish as "clericist") and living in the Dublin-Pale region of early-fifteenth-century Ireland. The term "clericist," as we use it in this study, refers to those with clerical training who make their livings, for the most part, outside of ecclesiastical employment, especially legal scribes, civil service clerks, text writers, and other learned professionals who work outside the institutional structure of the church (a good example would be Thomas Hoccleve, a lifelong employee of the Privy Seal, who waited much of his life for a church appointment that never came). For reasons that will become clear, this group was crucial to Langland's audience and to Douce's.

That it was an Anglo-Irish audience is of special significance. The reception of *Piers Plowman* in Anglo-Ireland might seem an obscure topic at first, but there are many reasons why it should command the attention both of Langland scholars and of those interested in clerical satire and polemics (and the reading communities who followed them). It provides a striking instance of how a text sufficiently alternative to attract the most radical English readers of the 1380s became, in the colonial set-

Kathryn Kerby-Fulton

ting of Anglo-Ireland, provocatively and politically "progressive" nearly fifty years later.[1] Langland apparently had a following very early among Hiberno-English speakers. Reasons for this are *ecclesiological* (Ireland had been the home of the antimendicant propagandist Richard FitzRalph and of three other important antimendicant agitators active in England);[2] *geographical* ("the linguistic character of MHE resembles that of the ME dialects of the south-west counties and the south-west midlands,"[3] owing to patterns of settlement); *historical* (the Despensers, of whom Langland's father was apparently a tenant, in fact had property and political connections in Anglo-Ireland, and copies of *Piers Plowman* were owned by others in the colony);[4] and *cultural* (the Butlers, to whom the Despensers' Irish properties passed in 1393, became important patrons of English vernacular literature and book production in the decades to follow, as did other Anglo-Irish readers).[5] The colonial and interethnic tensions that, scholars now believe, made FitzRalph's response to the friars more vehement than that of nearly any other activist in fourteenth-century Europe also made a poem like Langland's more welcome on Anglo-Irish soil.[6] Issues of poverty, mendicancy, and clerical, papal, and royal authority were all flash points for the Anglo-Irish, and Langland's poem had much to say on all these subjects. This chapter and the next are about the antiauthoritarian sentiments of the Douce manuscript, their local context, and their visual message.

Clericist Iconography and the Civil Service Scribe

One of Langland's most overt portrayals of challenge to authority is the attack of the slothful, secularized "proud priests" who form part of the vanguard of Antichrist's siege on Unity (Holy Church). Dressed in the latest, foppish fashions, they actually join in the effort to bring the church down:

> Sleuthe with his slynge an hard sawt he made.
> Proute prestes cam with hym—passyng an hundred
> In paltokes and pikede shoes and pissares longe knyues
> Comen aȝen Consience; with Couetyse they helden.
> "By þe Marie," quod a *mansed* prest, was of þe march of *Ireland*,
> "Y counte no more Consience, by so y cache suluer,
> Then y do to drynke a drauht of goed ale!"
> And so sayde syxty of þe same contreye,
> ....
> And hadden almost Vnite and holynesse adowne.
> (Pearsall, *C-Text*, XXII.217–27; emphasis added)

The Douce scribe-illustrator's version of this passage is largely faithful to the received text, except that line 221 reads, "By mary quode a *mased* prest: was of þe march of *wales*" (fol. 109v; emphasis added). He has introduced two variants into the line, one rather comically and obviously the result of national sensitivities (Ireland was too close to home, but Wales wasn't), the other a mitigation of Langland's "mansed" (meaning "cursed"; Douce's "mased" simply means "confused" or "frustrated"). If this latter change is deliberate (and not merely the paleographical loss of a minim abbreviation), it fits a recurring pattern in this scribe-illustrator's treatment of the poem—an ambivalence about the church and about orthodox attitudes on a variety of subjects, and a sympathy for those who oppose it. His preference for relocating the rabble-rousing priest in Wales tells us a great deal about his political allegiances: he was (as his dialect would suggest) a native-born Anglo-Irishman, not, like many scribes of his time, an Englishman resident in Ireland (the Irish Chancery, for instance, was often staffed by English scribes).[7] In the eyes of an Anglo-Irish reader Langland's choice of Ireland must have appeared a depressing slur:[8] the Gaelic-Irish clergy had a Europe-wide reputation for concubinage and nepotism,[9] but the Anglo-Irish were fiercely proud of their history as the reformers and "civilizers" of Ireland.[10] This suggests both why Langland would have chosen Ireland as the home of his Proud Priest, and why the Anglo-Irish scribe would have been so sensitive to it. But Langland's choice is likely based in part on his discomfort with the image he was using: the idea of clerics attacking a church is rather shocking, even by Langlandian standards, and not the kind of complaint much vernacularized when he first wrote it, so the poet found it convenient to distance (literally) the English church from this scene ("Ireland" is not, one notes, a word chosen for alliteration; it is a metrically free choice, and a politically expedient one).

Nor, perhaps more surprising, did the Douce artist find the visual iconography for this passage in a vernacular text. He chose to illustrate it with his proud priest, posed in a *declamatio* gesture that, along with his tonsure, satirically represents the last vestiges of what was once priestly authority (figure 37). Now the closest extant contemporary iconographic analogue to this picture is not, as one might expect, to be found in an "anticlerical" vernacular source; it turns up in a copy of the *Oculus sacerdotis*, Hatfield House, Cecil Papers, MS 290 (figure 56),[11] which shows a similar priest in a fashionably short jacket, with the same motif of the sword dangling suggestively in front of the genital area. In both Douce and Hatfield, the figures epitomize the enormity of priestly secularization, but even more striking, the Hatfield figure gazes into a framed illustration that shows other similarly dandified priests engaged in *bringing down a church*—precisely the activity that the corresponding figure in Douce highlights in the lines of Langland's poem.

What we have in the *Oculus* is not simply an iconographic source for the Douce illustration (although that in itself would be interesting enough), but also, first, an indication of the likely source for Langland's own conception of the priests' attack on Unity; second, a strong indication of one important reading community to which Langland's poem spoke most urgently; and, third, an unmistakable indication of Anglo-Irish sensitivity and "professional" editorializing on behalf of the local reader. All these points deserve closer examination.

The Hatfield illustration appears at the opening of the *Oculus sacerdotis*, a manual for priests composed sometime between 1320 and 1321 by a master of theology and the parish priest of Winkfield, Berkshire, William of Pagula.[12] The *Oculus* was one of the most consulted Latin manuals of conduct for priests in medieval England; it survives in thirty manuscripts, and there is every likelihood that Langland—whose interest in the problems of the secular clergy is quite clear in the poem—knew it himself.[13] William wrote the *Oculus* to combat clerical ignorance and laxity, especially about confession, which is, of course, the Achilles' heel of Holy Church in Langland's final passus. In his prologue, William of Pagula complained of being, as Leonard Boyle succinctly puts it, "appalled to find how many parish priests seemed to have no inkling where the jurisdiction that they exercised over consciences in the confessional began or ended. Some were absolving from sins and censures over which they had no control, while others were denying absolution and referring penitents [to other authorities]." What this state of affairs suggested to William of Pagula was a fundamental "ignorance of the penitential canons of the Church."[14] The treatise was directed, then, at those priests conscientiously concerned with improving their administration of penance and interested in some of the more technical issues in the related ecclesiology. Most important, it deals in serious issues of church authority, both the broad, urgent kind familiar to all readers of Langland and the more particular ones of diocesan pastoral care (William included a catalog of excommunications and censures from provincial constitutions).[15] One sees the former concern in the opening passage (immediately beside the illustration in the Hatfield manuscript), which delivers an uncompromisingly harsh judgment on the detriment caused by those who are set in authority over others and whose ignorance can lead those in their charge to hell ("et frequenter suos subditos per suam necgligenciam ad infernum deducunt"; fol. 13).[16] Here was Langland's cue for putting priests in the vanguard of Antichrist's siege (XXII.215–16).

Clearly Langland himself had seen something like the Hatfield manuscript illustration of the priests destroying Ecclesia. By dramatizing in his final passus this vision of clerical anarchy from a Latin conduct manual for priests, Langland was daringly vernacularizing a clerical professional (that is, internal) concern. He was thus crossing a boundary that church officials had tried to make impermeable (most notoriously, although not for the first time, in Archbishop Arundel's reaffirming of the principle that the problems of the clergy ought not to be preached before the laity, in 1409).[17] In choosing this iconography, metonymically and economically reduced to a single figure, the Douce artist was dropping a visual allusion for those sophisticated enough to catch it. In doing so, he, too, was making a radical iconographical choice, especially since he was illustrating a vernacular book. (Illustrations, after all, were intelligible to the wholly illiterate and could be powerfully anticlerical propaganda.) In both instances—the choice made initially by Langland and the choice subsequently made by the Douce illustrator of his poem—there is a compliment to the discriminating reader's literacy, both literal and visual.

The Hatfield manuscript contains information on exactly the kinds of issues that concerned Langland and at least one stratum of his readers, to judge from the evidence of several *Piers* manuscripts that also contain just this kind of material, in both Latin and English.[18] The fact that the majority of Langland's nonbiblical Latin quotations, including his canon law quotations, come from pastoral manuals[19] (that is, books on priestly conduct and lay instruction) suggests that one important component of his audience was made up of secular clergy and those hoping to be secular clergy (that large army of the unbeneficed). The Hatfield manuscript is a good example of the kind of miscellany that contains a mixture of treatises on priestly conduct and legalities, penance, personal eschatology, self-knowledge, and visionary narrative—precisely the kind of potent and composite brew that one finds in Langland's own thought.[20] That Langland's audience was an educationally stratified and socially diverse one has long been known, but the exact nature of these strata has never been carefully investigated, nor has the possibility of a select (perhaps initially coterie) readership been given much thought.[21] The precise overlap between Hatfield's and Douce's iconography gives us a window on the kind of reading community capable of appreciating Langland's allusive agility—as well as that of the Douce illustrator.

In fact, many of the contemporary manuscripts that best parallel the Douce illustrator's choice of iconography are surprisingly consistent in being anthologies specifically targeted for pastorally minded clergy and clerks in minor orders, many of whom, we should note, were active pieceworkers and moonlighters (working as both scribes and illustrators) in the book trade.[22] These kinds of clergy matters of priestly behavior, interclerical controversy, and apocalypticism (fields of discourse that were closely related for those of reformist bent) were of special interest. Douce shares, for instance, with three other contemporary manuscripts (BL, Add. 37049, Lincoln 218, and the *Omne bonum*), in which the scribes were also intimately involved with the illustration, the distinction of having the only recorded portraits of Antichrist in fourteenth- and fifteenth-century Insular books.[23] It is a subject the Douce artist handled with a real psychological subtlety (figure 35). Antichrist's head appears neatly framed between the line immediately following Will's disconcerting encounter with Need ("Whan nede had me vndir nome: þus a none I fel a sclep") and the line lamenting that Antichrist "made fals spryng and spred: & spede mannes nedis." The illustrator's realistic and roguishly handsome bust of Antichrist looks for all the world like the man in the street—any man in the street. And this is precisely the illustator's point (and his apocalyptic caveat). Moreover, the bust is deftly placed so as to highlight the word "nedis," which acts almost as an inscription to the picture (fol. 107r; cf. Pearsall XXII.55)—the artist apparently agreed with Langland's polemical view that the *need* of the friars was the root of corruption among them and the cause of current crisis in the church, and in fact the means by which Antichrist "ouer tulde þe rote." He visually emblematizes Langland's point that need was a dangerously alluring concept. Iconographically startling in its simplicity, the Douce artist's Antichrist, with seductively wavy blond hair, draws attention to the intersection of polemical antimendicantism and apocalypticism, and would have surprised the reader familiar with the more sensational, devil-ridden portraits such as one sees in British Library, Add. 37049, and Lincoln 218, or even in the *Omne bonum*[24] (whose maker had a more sophisticated eschatology).[25] All these manuscripts show the eclecticism, freedom of iconographic choice, and intimacy of text-image relations common to medieval books in which the scribe has played a dual and/or supervisory role in the illustration. But the Douce artist's pictorial choices stand out as particularly ideologically distinctive and naturalistic (the latter being, as we shall see, a feature of late medieval Anglo-Irish art). His choices are closest to those of the *Omne bonum*'s maker, James le Palmer, in range and in ecclesiological polemicism, but there are important differences even here, and these differences all revolve thematically around issues of authority.

The *Omne bonum* shares more iconography with Douce than any other single manuscript, and it serendipitously provides us with a textbook instance of how a medieval artist visualized the concept of authority itself: James le Palmer's encyclopedia entry "Autoritas" (figure 64) is accompanied by an opening initial in which a young man in secular dress kneels before an older seated and mitered cleric (apparently a pope), who holds a sealed document in one hand and has his other hand raised in the conventional announcing gesture (highlighted against the dark backdrop) used for indicating authoritative speech.[26] The Douce artist knew such iconography, but usually used it to undermine it: his rendering of the infamous confrontation between Piers and the Priest in the Pardon scene appears on 44v (figure 19), where he has a *very* young priest holding a sealed document (the pardon) in one hand and making an indefinite announcing gesture with the other (here markedly less authoritatively set off). The priest is placed on a verso, and what the reader has *just* seen (on the recto of this leaf, fol. 44, figure 18) is a bishop shown asleep with his miter falling off, while a wolf attacks a sheep. This is a neat instance of economy, no doubt inspired by the opportunity (which the illustrator took up zealously) to illustrate the *Simon quasi dormit* passage (on negligent prelates, IX.255–81) just moments before the priest interrupts Piers. The artist has "downgraded" the iconographical authority stereotypical of the cleric holding the document by manipulating his age and gesture and making a sharp juxtaposition of images: the priest is not caricatured, and his dress is (like his character in the poem) fastidiously correct. But his boyish face and the company he keeps on this folio (bringing up the rear after the False Friar and Sleeping Bishop) don't give him or the church a chance of looking authoritative, and suggest that the illustrator's sympathies in this argument were with Piers.

The *Omne bonum* is also useful in relation to Douce because James's interests were close to Langland's own, and just as eclectic: he was unusually intrigued by visionary experience,[27] legal matters (especially canon law), ecclesiological polemics (especially antimendicantism), and church-state relations. James was a member of that growing group of clerks who were making a living as legal scribes and sometimes civil servants—jobs that required much more ecclesiastical knowledge than we might today imagine. Many of these civil service clerks probably thought of themselves vocationally as secular clergy "in waiting," a social group among whom Langland was perhaps himself numbered.[28] The book may have been created with an audience of Exchequer clerks in mind, because in some of his annotations he admonishes individual colleagues by name (rather as Hoccleve, who waited years himself for a benefice, sometimes playfully alluded to his fellow clerks at the Office of the Privy Seal, although James's annotations sound more prudish).[29] In fact, the early-fifteenth-century Anglo-Irish scribal illustration most like Douce's in style and character is also the product of an Exchequer: the fragmentary leaf from *The Red Book of the Exchequer* of Ireland, extant, since the destruction of the Dublin Public Record Office in 1922, only in a nineteenth-century copy, contains a socially revealing picture of the clerks of the Exchequer at work (see frontispiece). It sports all of the main (and so-called idiosyncratic) features of the Douce scribe-illustrator's work, including both his formal and caricatured styles, giving us a further clue to his training as a professional reader and his audience. Exchequer clerks in the fourteenth and fifteenth centuries were required to do a surprising amount of casual drawing for the production of documentary *signa* used for the storage and retrieval of documents in pictorially marked chests. An unframed picture or symbol was drawn in the upper left-hand corner of each document, which was then stored in the chest bearing the matching symbol, "doubtless to assist the operations of unlettered ushers or serjeants." The falling miter, for instance, which we have just seen the Douce artist use in the image of the negligent bishop (figure 18), is similar in kind to the grimmer image used in church reform documents of a miter being struck off with a sword, a motif that appears in Exchequer *signa* such as Public Record Office, E 36/274 (figure 69; see no. 7

on the top left).³⁰ In fact, the number of extant Exchequer documents relating to ecclesiastical matters and ecclesiastical *signa,* some of them wryly satirical, is quite large. A look through the contents of the (Westminster) *Red Book of the Exchequer* suggests how very useful a detailed knowledge of canon law would be in such a job, as James le Palmer obviously realized when he conceived his encyclopedia.³¹ The Exchequer was not only the place where the king's debtors were called to account, but also the court where cases affecting the rights and revenues of the Crown were heard—debtors and cases that were often ecclesiastical, often controversial or inquisitorial.

A summary of the main contents of the (now mostly lost) Dublin *Red Book* (made on a similar model to the Westminster *Red Book,* which influenced Matthew Paris's drawings)³² may help to give some sense of the mental and visual world of this group on the interface of clerical and lay cultures: in addition to its satirical drawing of the Court of Exchequer, the Dublin *Red Book* contained an elaboratedly rubricated calendar "interpolated with ancient memoranda," a copy of the canon of the Mass (with an illustration of the Crucifixion group),³³ copies of oaths of certain government officials, and the important statutes (including, apparently a *Magna carta hiberniae*), numerous papal bulls, and ecclesiastical enactments from the period of about 1350 to 1410.³⁴ Clearly, our modern notions of a secular civil service workplace and labor force are hopelessly anachronistic here. Members of this kind of social and vocational group in both England and Ireland were apparently fascinated by ecclesiological issues like "equal opportunity" employment (especially in relation to benefices), simony, antimendicantism, apostasy, clerical abuses, priestly codes of conduct, ecclesiastical authority, clerical privilege and secrecy, and related legal matters—all of which Langland expressed vehement interest in, especially in the C text's apologia or "autobiographical" passage.³⁵

The *Omne bonum,* for instance, contains illustrated articles on all these topics, such as the one on clerical *Ambitio* or the one on *Beneficia ecclesiastica* (fols. 87 and 189v of 6.E.VI). The latter shows a bishop leading a very secular-looking man (untonsured and suspiciously dressed in a worldly looking red jacket) into a church door. The note of cynicism (and envy), appropriate to an audience of unbeneficed clerks, some of whom were doubtless in waiting, is unmistakable and reminiscent of the bitter tone of Langland's C.V apologia on the same subject (James himself received no ecclesiastical preferments during his lifetime).³⁶ Another article on appropriate dress for priests ("De habitu clericorum et... qualis debet esse distinctio vestimentorum"; fol. 197 of 6.E.VII; see figure 66)³⁷ shows a well-tonsured priest and his companions, robed much like the impeccably correct priest of the pardon scene in Douce (figure 19), pointing to a group of priests dressed in short coats, the foremost of whom has a sword dangling obscenely between his legs, just like Douce's proud priest (and Hatfield's corrupt priest). In fact, the *Omne bonum* shares with Douce some twenty-eight pictorial subjects, a remarkable convergence of pictorial choice on the part of the two makers. Even more significant in some respects is that it also shares with Langland's *poem* many more topics that the Douce artist chose not to illustrate, topics that invariably relate to the prestige and authority of the medieval church and its standard iconographical symbols (issues more vexed for Langland and for the Douce artist than for James le Palmer, although no less interesting to him, apparently).[38] In fact, after seeing the *Omne bonum* one can turn back to Douce and see in its pages a kind of scaled-down and secularized ecclesiological encyclopedia; in other words, following the pictures in Douce, a reader could use *Piers Plowman* as a *vernacular* ecclesiological encyclopedia, a kind of layperson's *Omne bonum*. Pictures in medieval books were frequently intended, of course, as finding devices and mnemonics in just this way, and that is how many medieval readers of Langland used his poem, as the pattern of annotations in *Piers* manuscripts also suggests. However, there can be no doubt after studying Douce in relation to other illustrated works of pastoral or ecclesiological guidance that the Douce artist had a particular antiauthoritarian thrust—his is a secularized view, ecclesiastically disenchanted, and quite possibly a dissenting one, as we shall see. His dual role as scribe and illustrator gives us some clue: he clearly had enough clerical training to fulfill the former function as well as the latter (and enough to have an informed dislike of many in the profession), he obviously read Latin (and was comfortable with legal forms),[39] and his biography may well have looked like those of the few known late medieval scribe-artists documented by J. J. G. Alexander as "failed" ecclesiastics[40] or like the biography (if only we knew it) of the scribe-illustrator who so ruggedly portrayed courtroom life at the Exchequer in the *Red Book* fragment, with its strategic caricature and vigorous social realism.

Whereas in the *Omne bonum* all these images of delinquent clergy are safely displayed merely for a Latin-reading audience and are hedged about with multitudes of images of correctly behaved and accoutred clerics, in Douce they are exposed unforgivingly to a vernacular readership. The Douce artist exhibits little of the sense of allegiance to the religious clerical world that we find in the *Omne bonum*, in Lincoln 218, or in the Carthusian miscellany, Add. 37049—or even in Langland himself, for that matter.[41] (The Douce artist's allegiances are perhaps closer to those of the clericism of the *Red Book* artist, for whom literacy is more a technical trade, not a vocation.) The *Omne bonum*, by contrast, contains scores of illustrations that reinforce the power, prestige, and authority of the ecclesiastical world—the program in fact seems consciously designed to promote a pastoral-clerical view of every matter, even on subjects like marriage, sex, and family. The "Familia" entry of the *Omne bonum* (111r of 6.E.VII), for instance, is illustrated by a *cleric* teaching a family, while the comparable passage in *Piers* is illustrated by the Douce artist with the sympathetic portrait of the young bastard grieving over his illegitimacy (figure 22); the Douce artist's iconography here is closer to the social realism of secular legal illustration (as we will see in chapter 2). Such differences are everywhere evident when one begins comparing Douce with its closest iconographic contemporaries. In Douce, images of authority are strikingly absent, or ambivalent, and the illustrator seems intent on emphasizing the marginalized and socially inferior at the expense of conventional authoritative subjects. Moreover, he is a great champion of the laity and the lower-order secular clergy, perhaps confirming his links to the underpaid curates and unbeneficed "pieceworkers" of the clerical world. The manuscripts that most resemble Douce can illuminate the artist's (and Langland's) range of sources, and they can even illuminate some of his reformist concerns (such as antimendicant controversies or the laxity of priests), but they cannot match — with the exception of the lone Dublin *Red Book* fragment and some of the audaciously caricatured *signa* in London Exchequer memoranda[42] — the radicalism with which Douce manipulates the taxonomy of visual expectations that his readers might bring to the manuscript. A look at his pictorial choices over the whole range of the manuscript will suggest exactly how.

Retraining the Reader's Eye: Reform or Dissent?

One of the first things one notices about Douce's pictorial program is what *isn't* there: it contains not a single literal image of Christ, the Holy Family, the saints, or the church fathers, and virtually no biblical figures.[43] The cycle is full of visual silences on these subjects, perhaps defiant visual silences, but they would have spoken quite audibly to any medieval reader with even the most basic experience of didactic iconography — especially the iconography found in late medieval books of hours for the wealthy, but also the standard iconography that filled medieval churches, guildhalls, and private homes.[44] This section, then, is about something that should be impossible: it is about the pictorial choices of an artist who, apparently, disapproved of most of the religious pictures that were the bread and butter of a medieval artist's profession; he was, in short, an iconomach in the atelier. However unthinkable this may be, the striking absences and provocative presences of the Douce cycle do betray a radical set of aversions and sympathies that can only be called reformist. But — and this must be stressed — the word "reformist" is used here in the broadest sense, to encompass (initially) the reformist traditions that began with the great papal and monastic reforms during the eleventh and twelfth centuries and that remained an inspiration for religious reformers of various stripes (often of impeccable orthodoxy) for centuries. It is this tradition that established not only a standard language of reform — from which concepts such as simony arose — but also a set of principles for iconography, and principles for the *suppression* of iconography of certain kinds, from some quarters as well.[45] The Douce artist apparently had a wide visual experience of reformist and polemical iconography. It would be tempting to label him a Lollard, but this chapter is also a case study in the need to resist, or at least qualify, such temptation. There is much in his approach that is at least analogous to what Anne Hudson has called the "puritanical" habit of mind in Lollard thought. How widespread this habit of mind was prior to and outside of Lollardy is an important question, one that has bedeviled Langland scholarship for years and now bedevils the study of Langlandian reception. But we need to take a longer view, and a wider one: that is, we need to see reformist traditions both prior to Wyclif and concurrent with the one he initiated; we will also notice that some of what we might initially consider Wycliffite belongs to Anglo-Irish culture itself.

The Douce artist makes visual allusions to images and attitudes that had been present in ecclesiastical polemics since the Gregorian Reform and that were transmitted in writers like Bernard; he shares certain ideals on poverty and simplicity with the radical Franciscans (early Franciscan legislation prohibited art in its churches, for instance);[46] he has been unavoidably influenced by the FitzRalphian tradition of his native country — which was itself a broader reformist movement than most of us recognize — and, finally, he was heavily influenced by the antiauthoritarian and anticlerical satire for which medieval Anglo-Irish literature is best known (that is, when it *is* known). Somewhat less sensationally, he also knew the kind of mainstream reformist ideas of authors like William of Pagula and the *Elucidarium* of Honorius of Autun, a work represented in both the Hatfield manuscript and Lincoln 218. All of these "puritanical," reformist, or satirical traditions predated the Lollard movement itself, and certainly ran parallel to it throughout the period of Lollardy. Where our artist stands in relation to diverse reformist streams of varying degrees of "orthodoxy" is difficult to say; moreover, how conscious or knowledgeable he himself was of all the various traditions is also difficult to say. These questions are complicated by the fact that not all of the choices to reject certain images may have been his own. Given that the pictorial cycle was most likely to have been commissioned — a heavily illustrated manuscript even of the relative modesty of Douce is highly unlikely to have been produced "on spec" — it is probable that the manuscript's first reader (or readers) were *known* to the artist and participated in the decision making. Only some kind of intimacy between artist and patron could fully account for this rather provocative cycle.[47] There is evidence in the production of other illustrated books that patrons could have enormous influence over the decision-making process as the manuscript developed: making regular visits to the illustrator to check progress, sometimes supplying materials (especially gold leaf) and exemplars from which to copy.[48] In the case of Douce, the habit of patron visits in medias res might explain why certain drawings were never finished and some were even suppressed,⁴⁹ and the supplying of exemplars for visual models might partly explain the range of imagery in the cycle. What cannot be doubted is that the artist's own visual literacy (perhaps supplemented by the patron's) had included an eclectic assemblage of illustrated reformist texts: ecclesiastical, legal, and polemical—a field in which he was confident enough to play unreservedly with iconography.

The most noticeable visual silence in Douce—and this would even strike a reader whose only exposure to medieval art had been in the local parish church—is that there are no depictions of the life of Christ. The cycle contains no Annunciation, no scenes from the Nativity or the Passion or—with the exception of a single devil, later deliberately defaced (fol. 96)—from the Harrowing, even though the Dobest portion of the poem gives ample pretext for all these pictorial subjects, as do other shorter passages elsewhere. In extenuation of the artist's neglect, one could plead the narrowness of the marginal format, but the artist has shown elsewhere that he was quite capable of handling a multifigure subject in, for instance, his simultaneous use of the side and lower margins for the idle prelate who sleeps while a wolf attacks one of his sheep (figure 18) or in the suppressed image of the Devil and Castle of Care (fol. 5). Where a subject interested him, as the first of these did, he takes the trouble to solve the problems the marginal format poses, and we have even seen that he "spliced" this image in another direction to encompass the Pardon scene on its verso (figure 19); presumably he could have done so for any scene from the life of Christ, complex or otherwise. This subject of the negligent "pastor," with its centuries-old, reformist, and apocalyptic associations,⁵⁰ certainly did captivate him. The falling of the miter had been associated since the twelfth century with the Psalmist's dire prophecy of the falling of the crown from the head of Sion, and so is not merely an emblem of sloth, but also of decline in the church's power—and was brutally used as such in Exchequer *signa* (figure 69), as we have seen. It is cunningly and subtly associated here with the false friar above (the Douce artist does not often choose to put two different illustrations on the same page, so there must be a reason here—he understood Langland's antimendicantism and its reformist apocalyptic implications very well). Elsewhere he demonstrates remarkable cleverness, as does Matthew Paris, in selecting a single figure from a larger scene to epitomize narrative moments or in using cross-page relationships between two figures.⁵¹ So we can only assume that his omission of scenes from the life of Christ is not based on technical limitations; other medieval artists, even some known in Anglo-Ireland, worked with the same format of unframed marginal miniatures and managed quite nicely to incorporate, for instance, a crucifix into their margins.⁵² One could also attempt to exonerate the artist by arguing that Langland is not especially Christological, and certainly there is no evidence of the current pietistic fashions for devotion to the body of Christ in the poem itself, but Langland does dramatize the Crucifixion with vivid dignity, and the Douce artist proves elsewhere that he does not need large-scale textual hints for inspiration. He often chooses to illustrate figures who make only the briefest appearance in the poetry: Langland gave Tom Stowe (whom Reason counsels to fetch his wife from the stocks) a mere two lines (V.130–31), and the Douce illustrator made him the sole pictorial representative of passus V (figure 6). He similarly picked a minute reference to hanging in Langland's text (XVII.138) and made it the reason for a full and lurid gallows illustration (figure 32).[53] Why, then, depict Tom Stowe and not ever depict Christ?

One's suspicions of iconophobia are further heightened by the scarcity of biblical characters, although many are on offer in Langland's text, including major figures such as David, Saul, Moses, Adam, Isaiah, James, the four evangelists, and the Samaritan, to name a few. In fact, only one biblical figure, Caiaphas (fol. 101), can be certainly identified in the cycle.[54] The only other possible candidate is a faint, unfinished sketch (fol. 85) that was apparently meant to be Abraham.[55] The fact that the portrait was left unfinished and was probably suppressed after sketching may be significant as one of the points at which someone—possibly the patron?—might have intervened to stop a planned picture coming to fruition, or perhaps the artist himself thought better of it. Moreover, the small bust of Caiaphas (fol. 101) is an unusual choice; Kathleen Scott says that no other single figure of Caiaphas is known to survive in English book illustration. It was no doubt partly motivated (as with the negligent pastor) by the artist's sophisticated knowledge of the imagery of anticlerical polemics (bad priests fascinate him). What is so very odd about this choice is that the High Priest, like Tom Stowe, is only briefly mentioned (he arises in one line, XXI.140) as part of the Passion story at this point in the text. But if the avoidance of idolatry was a concern for the artist, Caiaphas would be preferable to any positive figure associated with the Passion story, especially Christ, because evil characters present no such temptation (the illustration can thereby still serve its mnemonic purpose in the narrative without risking idolatry). Most provocative, though, in this passus is the fact that David, who figures much more prominently, was *not* chosen for illustration, a decision that perhaps makes a social statement—that this particular illustrated book is *not* to be associated with the books of hours of the wealthy, which usually contain numerous illustrations of David in a variety of poses.

In the C text the poet had denounced idolatry in the voice of Conscience, mainly as part of his larger campaign against clerical fraud and avarice: "Ydolatrie ȝe soffren in sondrye places manye / ... Forthy y sey ȝe prestes and men of holy churche / That soffreth men do sacrefyce and worschipe maumettes, / ... God shal take vengeaunce on alle suche prestis" (Prol. 96, 118–21). Langland's objection is to clerical profiteering at the expense of the credulous laity, especially in dubious shrines, but his attitude toward images was not really unorthodox:⁵⁶ he represents the dreamer's devotion to the cross, for instance, as conventionally pious. So when Will awakens on Easter morning, he calls to his wife and daughter, "Arise, and go reuerense godes resureccioun, / And crepe to þe croes on knees and kusse hit for a iewel / And rihtfollokest a relyk, noon richore on erthe" (XX.473–75). And, new to C—perhaps even added to reinforce the orthodoxy of his visionary experience—is the passage in which the dreamer weeps for his sins beneath the cross in church, after having been overhauled by Conscience and Reason for his worthless manner of living (C.V.105–8). In neither case, however, did the Douce artist choose to depict the dreamer or anyone else praying before a cross or crucifix. When one considers how often any medieval artist would normally paint this kind of scene, the omission becomes surprising—take, for example, what we know of the portfolio of artist William Abell.⁵⁷ (In fact, among the many images of devotion to the cross in Abell's extant work is a depiction of one of the London scribes of *Piers Plowman*, John Cok [London, St. Bartholomew's Hospital, Cartulary; figure 68], so we can safely assume that not all of Langland's readers were so squeamishly iconophobic—or crucifobic—as the Douce artist appears to be.) Even the Wycliffite scribe-illustrator of Oxford, Bodleian Library, MS Bodley 978, although he would not depict *Christ* teaching from a boat at sea, preferring to depict an empty boat instead (figure 42), did choose to depict a marginal cross (figure 41) as a mnemonic device in his copy of a gospel harmony. One would expect the artist, who was likely faced with the task of creating a program of illustration for *Piers Plowman* from scratch, to have drawn on as many model-book set pieces and devotional staples as he could, but he did not. His very avoidance of devotional clichés, especially in a book otherwise so economically created, is highly unusual.

Nor do we see other kinds of stock-in-trade religious iconography: there are no saints or even church fathers in the cycle, although the poem gives a surprising amount of scope for their depiction: Francis, Dominic, Augustine,⁵⁸ Jerome, Gregory, Ambrose, Anthony, and Paul the Hermit are all mentioned favorably, to name but a few. For the Douce artist this is partly an issue of authority (spiritual versus ecclesiastical), and this was an artist willing to assert lay authority where he found ecclesiastical authority spiritually deficient. His iconomachic tendency seems to be part of the same ideology (parallels here to Wycliffite thought are striking indeed), and this becomes apparent when one compares the pictorial choices in a manuscript like Lincoln 218, part 1. Langland would have liked Lincoln: it contains the sources for a large number of the Latin quotations he actually used. It is a collection of Latin pastoral and devotional works aimed at young priests or novices; its part 1, which is most like Douce in illustration, contains, like the Hatfield House manuscript, Honorius's popular *Elucidarium*, along with the Pseudo-Bernardian *Meditationes*⁵⁹ and an anthology of hymns, prayers, and *sententiae* from the church fathers. We would expect, then, to find more iconographical overlap with Douce. It is similarly economically made, and its unframed marginal pictures do show an ecclesiologically reformist thrust similar to Douce's, but they also repeatedly represent single-figure images of saints and church fathers whose authority and superiority to the few abjectly represented laymen is unmistakably visually asserted, just as in *Omne bonum*. (The *Elucidarium*, in fact, stresses clerical elitism.) One can see why repeated exposure to such images would raise the hackles of an educated "layman" (perhaps an imprecise word in this context). The Douce artist's anti-institutional feelings were apparently very strong: even Holy Church herself, who plays a very important (and normally uncontroversial) role early in Langland's poem, is not depicted in Douce—and this despite a well-established medieval iconography of Ecclesia, who appears in other marginal programs.[60] The Douce artist's dislike or distrust or lack of interest in any symbol of church power and authority is quite unusual. In this he consistently out-Langlands Langland.

However, iconomachia is not his only obsession. Here are some further categories of his visual silence: his apparent disapproval of (1) images of entertainment, (2) fantastic creatures of any sort, and (3) the allegorical (the latter in sharp contrast to the annotator). To take the first: there are no images of dancers, musicians, minstrels, or people at play, even where the text mentions such activities (e.g., Activa Vita, XV.194–208), even positively (e.g., God's minstrels, VII.97–112, or the Four Daughters of God caroling, XX.470). This becomes the more surprising when one recalls that such activities form a conspicuous part of the marginal inventory in books of hours and other illustrated texts,[61] even in texts created for cloistered readers. His "puritanism" is even more marked than Langland's (at least in Langland, people dance in Heaven). Why these visual silences? Ideological and even legal factors are at work here. Minstrelsy is a complex subject in the C text, where Langland gives secular minstrels short shrift (Prol. 35–40), but throughout this version the poet was busy trying to reclaim and allegorize the image of the minstrel in the spirit of the primitive Franciscan ideal of the *joculatores domini*, "merye-mouthed men, munstrals of heuene" (IX.126).[62] The artist apparently liked this reclaiming strategy, but chose to give it a social "democratic" thrust: it is not the image of the minstrel that he elected to rehabilitate, or the image of the itinerant religious (although he was not especially anti-Franciscan), but the image of the *poor*. In the passage just cited, he chose to portray not a minstrel, but a ragged lunatic (figure 16, one of the "lunatic lollars"), with an unmistakable dignity that is lovingly enhanced by the delicate gold dust he reserved almost entirely for four figures, all raggedly poor. He has also given the lunatic the suggestion of a tonsure and exactly the same facial type as the one figure in Langland's poem he identified and treated, rather sympathetically, as a poor priest (the "leued" vicar, fol. 105)—whether in the Wycliffite sense or not, we cannot be sure. And iconographically he chose to dress the lunatic as a biblical figure (a reference to the fact that they "prophecy of þe peple" and that they are God's "apostles" [Douce, 42r; IX.114, 118]),[63] not as a contemporary, perhaps because, as Langland himself tells us, itinerant prophets dressed distinctively (IX.211) but had suspect reputations. So the Douce illustrator was taking no chances in his idealization of the poor lunatic. In fact, the Douce version takes very seriously Langland's comment that such lunatics prophesy: where the received text follows this comment with the relatively neutral half line, "And to oure syhte, as hit semeth" (IX.115), Douce reads, "And to honour such as hit semeþ."

The artist's penchant for realism also prevents him entirely from using the kinds of grotesques that inhabit the margins of many manuscripts: Tom Two-Tongue, with his very literally rendered two tongues (fol. 109), is perhaps the only unrealistic figure, but his "deformity" has an allegorical, not a frivolous, basis. It is very like the style of allegory used occasionally in Exchequer *signa*, such as the three-nosed usurer in figure 69. He makes little use of animals and never employs them frivolously, as one sees in manuscript margins, carved capitals, and misericords, or didactically in the Aesop-like roles acceptable even to Lollard writers.[64] His animals usually have a purely literal or, more rarely, unambiguously symbolic function.[65] Nor does he use them allegorically, even where Langland's text might be suggestive to a medieval artist (one thinks of the Belling of the Cat fable in the poem itself, or slighter suggestions like the "two grydy sowes" [VI.398] in the poet's description of Glutton).[66] The sins themselves are depicted in the most concrete fashion possible; none would look out of place on a medieval street. Again, Langland has provided the lead here (compare his sins with the much more schematic portraits, complete with animal symbols, in, for instance, misericords),[67] but the artist was quite prepared to ignore the poet when it suited him (e.g., his Pride [fol. 24] is a man wearing, significantly, the bells of a minstrel, not the woman, Purnele, whom Langland created—a change he may have made, as we shall see, in response to local cultural concerns).[68] Even the tree diagrams and other abstract paraphernalia that Langland describes and that inhabit the margins of clerically made illustrated didactic works (like those in Add. 37049) have no place in the Douce artist's vision, not even where they are *explicitly* invoked by the text: (the Tree of Charity passus, Patience's cartwheel [XV.162], the Branches of Sloth [VII.70]).[69] The Douce artist's use of mnemonics is of an entirely different sort even than Langland's in such instances; he prefers the concrete to the abstract and among explicit mnemonics chooses to illustrate, for instance, the Samaritan's Trinitarian analogy with a simple picture of a hand and orb (fol. 88). What he has actually chosen to highlight here is not Langland's complex allegory (and certainly not the standard iconography of the Trinity)[70] but the unobtrusive Latin quote at XIX.112a: "Mundum pugillo continens" (from the medieval hymn equivalent of "He's got the whole world in his hands"). This choice of illustration suggests the Latin literacy of the illustrator, and proves that he was concerned to translate *visually* the Latin text (which, wearing his scribal hat, he'd copied) for those who could not read Latin, because the image does not appear in Langland's vernacular explanation. It is also, as Denise Despres shows in part II, much like the kind of mnemonic image one finds even in the illustrated Wycliffite gospel harmony, Bodley 978 (another manuscript almost certainly scribe illustrated), which also contains unframed marginal pictures meant to function as memory aids.[71]

The Douce artist, then, has a Lollard-like distaste for iconic images of the divine or saintly or anyone else of official spiritual repute (only an angel [fol. 80v] manages to pass muster, and even this angel was never painted, perhaps having been suppressed at the patron's request); he has a Bernardian dislike of grotesquerie, frivolous bestiary, and frivolity generally; this looks like a "puritanical" streak a mile wide. But whose concepts of reform are these, and does Lollardy play any part in them? Here we arrive at two sensible questions and one speculative one: first, how pervasive were FitzRalph's reformist ideas in his native land, and what other Irish cultural factors may have been at work here? Second, how influential was Wyclif's thought in Anglo-Ireland? And finally, was there such a thing as Lollard book illustration?

To begin with the first question: although our sense of FitzRalph's reformist thought has been heavily (although hardly unjustly) skewed by his pervasive obsession with antimendicantism, it is important to realize that he attempted a variety of other kinds of reforms as archbishop of Armagh, many of which were still an important point of reference for the episcopacy and clergy in early-fifteenth-century Ireland. Especially if one examines the kinds of reform he preached to lay audiences (as opposed to clerical ones), one finds some of the ideas we've been calling "puritanical" in the Douce artist's program. For instance, in the register of FitzRalph's early-fifteenth-century successor, Archbishop John Swayne, are listed five decrees "described as having been enacted on the basis of the previous legislation of 'lord Richard,' and these pertain...to issues which [FitzRalph's] sermon diary...show[s] to have been among Fitz-Ralph's principal concerns."[72] These include his trademark concern with confession to one's parish priest (i.e., not a friar),[73] the legal protection of the powerless, and many other social injunctions, all of which are reflected faithfully in what the Douce artist chose to highlight (and satirize) in *Piers Plowman*. See, for instance, in relation to the first, Mede and the friar (fol. 11v), and to the second, the lawyer (figure 15). However, it is the extent of the social injunctions that is most surprising: there is "a series of prohibitions against various forms of entertainment and the maintenance of entertainers: forbidden were mimes, jugglers, poets, drummers [actually *tympán* players, or "tympanors"], harpers, and those who extort gifts, presumably in return for their talents and services."[74] Kathleen Walsh points out that, while one would expect to see such prohibitions served up to English clergy in synodalia, it is clear that FitzRalph meant the *laity* to be included as well, which was, according to Walsh, "somewhat unique" in its degree of stringency. In fact, as Alan Fletcher points out, FitzRalph's predecessor, David Mág Oireachtaigh, had issued similar prohibitions, and these were renewed by Archbishop John Colton sometime between 1381 and 1404: "We renew in all respects the issued statute or statutes of our predecessors the lords Richard [Fitz-Ralph] and David [Mág Oireachtaigh] against *mimi*, jesters, poets, *timpán* players or harpers, and especially against kerns and importunate and dishonest seekers after gifts or rather extortioners."[75] This passage is remarkable for a number of reasons, not just because it explicitly links poets and minstrels (a connection that sheds light on Langland's own dramatic and rather anxious C revisions on the same subject), but also *plunderers* and minstrels. FitzRalph had originally enacted his legislation in 1355, just eleven years before the notorious Statutes of Kilkenny made the same kind of ironclad prohibitions in oppressive colonial secular legislation.[76] The Statutes of Kilkenny explicitly forbid, on pain of imprisonment, "that any Irish minstrels, that is to say, tympanours, pipers, story tellers, babblers, rhymers, harpers, or any other Irish minstrels, come amongst the English; and that no English receive them or make gift to them."[77] Itinerant minstrels were repeatedly under suspicion of espionage in the English-dominated regions,[78] as were, in England itself, Irish students and begging clerks, called "chamberdeakyns" in the legislation.[79] This legislation may even account for the artist's refusal to illustrate the C.V apologia, in which the poet appears explicitly as a begging clerk. The fact that what we might call "articulate itinerants" seem to have been suspect in a variety of ways clearly had an important impact on the reading and illustration of Langland's poem, in which, of course, wanderers figure rather largely, and not only in Ireland.

Given the highly developed musical culture of medieval Ireland, which even the colonists had eagerly adopted, these prohibitions seem draconianly interventionist, and they were: their goal was to arrest the Anglo-Irish drift toward assimilation (the fact that we find both FitzRalph's constitutions and the Kilkenny statutes themselves being reenacted in the early fifteenth century suggests that little had changed by the time Douce was made).[80] Even Giraldus, longtime favorite author of the Anglo-Irish, allowed minstrelsy to be the finest accomplishment of the Irish race he otherwise so denigrates, and in older manuscripts of his *Topographia* this passage is often accompanied by an unframed marginal illustration of a harpist—iconography that virtually disappears in Anglo-Irish manuscripts after the mid–fourteenth century—in response, one might guess, to the legislation.[81] Here we have the source of at least some of the Douce artist's apparent "puritanism." While the episcopal motivation for such prohibitions may well have been overtly moral and social, political factors cannot—in this context—be ignored. It is difficult to grasp the unusual degree of legislated cultural intervention in colonial Ireland, but one can trace the effects of it even in iconographical patterns. In Douce itself such changes no doubt account as well for the artist's odd decision to portray Pride as a dandy sporting tiny minstrel's bells.

FitzRalph also established or championed other long-lasting reformist concerns that might explain pictorial choices in Douce, like his attacks on fornication and invalid marriages.[82] Despite the ecclesiastical reforms of the twelfth century and the best efforts of English kings like Henry II (still regarded as a hero among the fifteenth-century Anglo-Irish), many of the social customs of the native Irish, such as "Gaelic secular marriage," were widespread. In the upper classes marriages were frequently and easily dissolved, and the traditional hereditary privilege of the clerical profession, whereby even clergy were expected to marry under Gaelic law, added to the chaos. It is perhaps no wonder that the Douce artist emphasized Langland's teachings on the evils of bastardy, which must have been a topical subject among colonists. But his sympathetic rendering of the unfortunate young bastard (figure 22), who holds his head in the traditional iconographic gesture of grief, is likely that of a kinder lay (or laicized) perspective on an object of clerical condemnation. (One might contrast, for instance, the priest John Ball's harsh response to bastardy and, as Steven Justice has argued, this very passage in *Piers Plowman*.)[83] Also rather "puritanical" is FitzRalph's attack on the activities of guildsmen, which went beyond the usual condemnation of fraud in trading practices to include condemnation of money "wasted" on guild entertainments, even on the amount of wax "wasted" in their elaborate religious processions. Langland was to put a similar condemnation in the mouth of Conscience (Prol. 99, in his passage against idolatry, cited earlier). The Douce artist suggests this reformist stance in showing little sympathy for—indeed entirely suppressing from the cycle—any hint of the popular religious culture of the guilds, with its devotion to saints and affective piety.[84]

In fact, the attack for which FitzRalph is best known, namely, on the friars' misuse of the confessional, is perhaps the most highly developed of the anticlerical themes in the Douce artist's program. The antimendicant iconography in the manuscript is sophisticated, shows knowledge of English trends, yet has a peculiarly Irish facet, too. Walsh has shown that FitzRalph's "*volte-face* from cordial relations with the friar-scholars whom he knew at Oxford and Avignon to total opposition to the mendicant way of life" is best explained by the difficulties he encountered overseeing their pastoral care activities in an ethnically divided society.[85] For instance, local abuse of the penitential system could extend to the outrageous claims made by one Anglo-Irish friar that it was not a sin to kill a Gaelic-Irish man (this particular comment prompted the massacre by Gaelic-Irish of an entire convent of friars in Dundalk shortly thereafter).[86] Anglo-Irish antimendicantism, then, is no ordinary antimendicantism, hedged about as it is with powerful tensions; it is also immensely complex, and this complexity is reflected in the Douce artist's apparently conscious distinctions among the various orders. The interest of Langland's text for Hiberno-English speakers has much to do with the fact that the poet had digested his FitzRalph thoroughly and anticipated just such complexities in his own handling of the fraternal orders in the poem.

There are six pictures of friars in the cycle.[87] Two are Dominicans: Mede's confessor on fol. 11v, with his leering smile, and the smooth-talking "physician" who penetrates Unity at the end of the poem (figure 38). Three more are apparently Carmelites:[88] the friar at the Feast of Patience (fol. 67r),[89] the hypocritical friar whose extravagant gesture of devotion brackets the dreamer's antimendicant diatribe on the verso of the same folio, and earlier in the cycle, the generic false friar (figure 18), who stands in for all who fraudulently don clerical robes without actually having taken orders. There is only one Franciscan: a lean, barefoot, energetic-looking man whose hands are posed in a teaching gesture (figure 20); he is the friar who gives the Dreamer advice at the outset of the Vita. Although one could argue that the treatment of his nose suggests caricature, it also emphasizes his leanness, and there are no other elements of caricature in the portrait. He is the only friar shown barefoot or thin, which may reflect the historical reality of serious need among Irish Franciscans, and he is the only friar who has the distinction of having a precious metal lavished on him—his cord is silver.[90] As Despres shows in part II, the artist uses precious metals mainly as a seal of moral approval.

What are we to make of this mix of friars? First, all the Dominicans and Carmelites are indubitably morally corrupt; it may be no coincidence, then, that we have in these two orders the most avid opponents of the Wycliffites.[91] They were also, probably more important for the Douce artist, thought to be the most high-profile opponents of FitzRalph—at least in the *Omne bonum* they are the orders illustrated as disputing with him (figure 67), as Lucy Freeman Sandler notes with surprise.[92] What we seem to have in Douce (and the *Omne bonum*) is a phenomenon that has not been noticed before: an *iconography* of FitzRalph that projects as his enemies those orders of friars most associated with the repression of dissent and, in the popular mind, with courting the wealthy, rather than the orders that were historically his most prominent enemies. It is interesting to speculate on the origins of this iconography (the term is used here in the sense of an established, indeed fossilized, set of visual conventions, in this case at odds with history). Dominicans and Carmelites were frequently shown (and not always sympathetically) as confessors to the rich, a criticism about which Dominican officials were perpetually sensitive. In fact, Dominicans appeared so frequently in medieval

Crucifixion paintings (a sign of association with the wealthy in itself) as to prompt satirical verses on the subject (such as "O niger intrusor").⁹³ In many of these scenes a woman figures as the penitent: an unframed lower marginal illustration in London, British Library, MS Stowe 17 shows a Dominican hearing the confession of a woman (fol. 191) in a picture much like the one in which Mede appears with her smugly intimate Dominican confessor in Douce (fol. 11v); in Stowe there is the added hint of scandal in the accompanying picture of two men pointing at the suspicious couple from across the page (fols. 190v–191).⁹⁴ But the single Franciscan in Douce is much more sympathetically treated; his commitment to poverty is not in doubt (he is lean and barefoot). Moreover, Langland himself does not go out of his way to satirize the Franciscans and seems even to favor the poverty rigorists of the order.⁹⁵ Indeed, there are a number of reasons why an Anglo-Irish scribe-illustrator of Langland's poem might feel more favorably inclined toward the Franciscans.⁹⁶

Turning to the second question: there is little evidence for the influence of Wyclif in Ireland, but what there is seems heavily concerned—not surprisingly—with antimendicantism. Wyclif's debt to "Armachanus" was frequently acknowledged by Wyclif himself,⁹⁷ as well as by followers and opponents; in fact to Wycliffites the Irish archbishop was a kind of saint ("sanctus Richardus").⁹⁸ The most conspicuous case of Irish Fitz-Ralphianism in association with Lollardy in Ireland is that of Henry Crumpe, who was censured there for objecting to the friars' role in confession, and again on his return to Oxford for views of the Eucharist "savouring of Wycliffism."⁹⁹ Again in May 1392 an array of archbishops from York, Canterbury, and Dublin found ten of Crumpe's conclusions heretical, all ten extreme positions on the friars. Upon his return to Ireland, Crumpe attracted papal notice for his antifraternal views, despite his earlier abjuration in England.¹⁰⁰ Crumpe's obsession with the friars is very FitzRalphian (especially the conclusions of his 1392 abjurations),¹⁰¹ and his treatment by the authorities no doubt reflected—and heightened—an Anglo-Irish sense (in some quarters at least) of being embattled, alone in a small community in carrying the torch for FitzRalph's crusade.

An even more neglected instance of Lollard sympathies in Anglo-Ireland, however, is the evidence of London, British Library, MS Cotton Cleo. B.II, which contains a booklet of three Wycliffite poems (one in Latin and two in Hiberno-English). Written in a small, cramped hand of the late fourteenth or early fifteenth century on unruled paper, it contains three Wycliffite pieces, all canceled with large X's when, slightly later, the manuscript came into the hands of a more mendicant-sympathetic compiler.¹⁰² The two Hiberno-English poems are virulently antimendicant: the first, in which the narrator claims to have once been a friar who left in disgust, echoes the concern of easy penance for murder that so inflamed FitzRalph ("For had a man slayn al his kynne, / Go shryve him at a frere, / And for lesse then a payre of shoen / He wyl assoil him clene and sone, / And say the synne that he has done / his saule shal never dere" [Wright, 267]). This theme is repeated in the second poem ("Wyde are thair wonnynges, and wonderfully wroght; / Murdre and horedome ful dere has it boght" [Wright, 270]). The emphasis on murder is rather insistent in these poems, apparently disturbingly pertinent to their local setting.

The second poem is even more interesting for our purposes because it attacks not only the friars, but also their tradition of visual art, particularly the imagistic brand of affective piety that Franciscans especially preached. The poet appears to be describing the images he has seen in a Franciscan church:[103] "First thai gabben on God, that alle men may se, / When thai hangen him on hegh on a grene tre, / With leves and with blossemes that bright are of ble; / That was never Goddes son, by my leute" (269). What is being described here is the kind of typological conflation of images one so often finds in medieval (and not just in Franciscan) religious art.[104] Interestingly, this is precisely the kind of popular image that stimulated some of the brilliant allegorical conflations in *Piers Plowman*, images to which, as Elizabeth Salter pointed out, Langland did not scruple to make explicit reference. Clearly the Wycliffite poet (if that is what he is) prefers literal realism: in the next stanza he complains that "Thai have done him on a croys fer up in the skye, / And festned on hym wyenges, as he shuld flie. / This fals feyned byleve shal thai soure bye, / On that lovelych Lord so for to lye. / With an O and an I, one sayd ful stille, / Armachan distroy ham, if it is Goddes wille." These last lines are a rather poignant and apparently Anglo-Irish appeal to the "Lollard saint," FitzRalph, in the furtive but fervent voice ("one sayd ful stille") of the oppressed.[105] After the condemnation of Crumpe's conclusions, it may have appeared to earnest FitzRalphians in Ireland that their cause was under persecution; the mood is not unlike the garrison mentality of the radical Franciscans in the time of Pope John XXII (an analogy FitzRalph would have hated, by the way).

It is difficult to say exactly how Wycliffite these poems are. The poet's derisory deflating of images is reminiscent of Margery Baxter's.[106] Its searing wit turns on the literal absurdity of traditional pictorial devices, like the awkwardness of representing figures holding a chalice to catch blood from the side wound (here, of Saint Francis): "Ther I sawe a frere blede in myddes of his syde; / Bothe in hondes and in fete had he woundes wyde. / To serve to that same frer, the pope mot abyde. / With an O and an I, I wonder of thes dedes, / To se a pope holde a dische whyl the frer bledes" (269). The poet exhibits a kind of goliardic skepticism (unusual in a *vernacular* poem) directed at icons of affective piety, which is shocking by its very explicitness. (Langland, for instance, may not have personally approved of these sorts of images either — he never uses them — but neither does he overtly attack them.)[107]

There is nothing *necessarily* unorthodox about this poem, but there is a very strong objection to contemporary allegorical religious taste, mixed with FitzRalphian antimendicantism and hero worship. In fact, the impatient irreverence toward sacred iconography may in itself be Anglo-Irish, not Wycliffite, because one can find the same thing in other Anglo-Irish poetry. For instance, in a poem in the so-called Kildare manuscript (London, British Library, MS Harley 913) composed not only before Wyclif, but *even before FitzRalph*, we find a very similar irreverent satire on traditional church iconography. In the eighteenth century, the satire in this manuscript shocked Humphrey Wanley so much that he ended his description in the Harley catalog with this note: "I believe this manuscript was written in Ireland; and that the blasphemous things therein were occasioned by the envy of the Franciscans against the Monks."[108] The poet satirizes the standard iconography of Saint Christopher as he carries Christ on his shoulders[109] and, more shockingly, Mary Magdalene's promiscuity, with reference to "Seint Mari bastard, þe Maudlein is sone"; he also appears to associate her standard iconic attribute, the spice box, with the church's miserliness.[110] The white friars of "Drochda" (Drogheda) come in for criticism as robbers of churches, and, surprisingly, in a manuscript long associated with the Franciscans,[111] the birds traditionally pictured around Saint Francis become birds of prey and pride.[112] Whatever contempt for devotional images the Douce artist has, he was not alone in Anglo-Ireland in espousing it. Although the poet goes on, in a more Langlandian manner, to satirize the abuses of various professions and craftsmen (in a spirit reminiscent of the Douce artist's handling of the sins as a kind of estates satire), there is nothing in *Piers Plowman* to compare with this type of flamboyant, indeed, flagrant satire of the kinds of sacred images that adorned contemporary churches. In the Langlandian tradition, even the *Crede* author's dislike of the religious arts looks a little tame by comparison—and that is a work with overt Wycliffite sympathies.[113]

A word or two about that unpromising topic, Lollard book illustration, will bring us to the final (and speculative) question. This elusive genre has a limited variety of iconographic characteristics, some of which are shared with antimendicant book illustration: images seem restricted mainly to clerical caricature, didactic mnemonic devices, and an emphasis on author portraits;[114] it is, for obvious reasons, an iconography obsessed with questions of authority. Lollard book illustration, of course, avoids the portrayal of anyone or anything remotely iconic. It shares with antimendicant books an obsession with depicting authors, debates, and speech-acts (especially those involving documentation or the act of inscribing doctrine or polemics)—in short, a fascination with conflicting or competing voices (as one sees, for instance, on the opening page of FitzRalph's *De pauperie salvatoris* in Cambridge, Corpus Christi College,

MS 180, or in Oxford, Bodleian Library, MS Bodley 277, from a Wycliffite Bible).[115] Moreover, Lollard, antifraternal, and anti-Lollard books use marginal illustrations and historiated initials or roundels in a very suggestively polemical way (to highlight or enclose authority figures, while closing out or literally marginalizing enemies),[116] with much gesticulating between camps across the text. One sees this in the Corpus FitzRalph manuscript, for instance, and in the anti-Wycliffite manuscript, Oxford, Merton College, MS 319[117] (figure 47). The author, Netter, is represented in the roundel on the left, displaced from the central historiated initial (where one expects to see the author portrait) so as to highlight instead the massive and combined authority of the Elevation and the King. Netter points accusingly across at Wyclif (who is labeled W. H.); Wyclif's hands are raised in the gesture of guilty surprise that we sometimes see in Douce (take, for instance, the "friar" reacting to the accusation of his fraud made by the text beside him [figure 18]—a good instance, by the way, of the artist's ability to see text and image in explicit dialogue). Another illustration, in Bodley 277, a Wycliffite Bible, similarly shows a gesticulating prelate, the lower half of whose body is a grotesque hybrid with an obscenely placed long "nose"; a similar obscenity occurs in the now defaced Devil of Douce, as Maidie Hilmo has shown.[118] The Douce artist had definitely learned this visual language of reformist and interclerical polemics. This emphasis on picturing the text's polemical voices, on performative and accusative gesture, especially in scenes of confrontation, can be paralleled repeatedly throughout the manuscript (e.g., in the proud priest [figure 37], Trajan [figure 27], Recklessness [figure 25], the lunatic lollar [figure 16], the lawyer [figure 15], Wastor [figure 12], the friar physician [figure 38], Reason [fol. 19], and Conscience [figure 4]).

The issues of authority raised by such illustration (especially in view of what we will explore next of the artist's social ideology) are most clear in the iconography that was developed to counter it (as in Merton 319; figure 47). Merton is especially interesting in the way that the hierarchical preoccupations of the text are reflected in the segregation of the social and ecclesiastical classes in the illustration, with a rigidity that seems to be a deliberate response to the *perceived* Wycliffite threat to the social order.[119] (As if to emphasize the importance of hierarchy within the community, the whole scene takes place within or adjoined to the historiated *U* of "Uenite ascendamus ad montem" [figure 47], both text and image reflecting the "vertical" orientation in every sense.) For instance, Merton 319's representative "worthy" layman is placed outside the chancel, looking in, and the single working man is safely enclosed in a lower dependent roundel, obediently shoveling Lollard books into the flames. By contrast, the only digger in Douce is a comparatively well dressed man (figure 13). The Douce artist appears to have enjoyed overturning the social expectations established by Langland's text—that only "faytours" and "eremytes" would "henten hem spades" for fear of famine (VIII.179,

183)[120]—because he used his most expensive colors on this chap (who looks neither hermit nor beggar). For the Douce artist, famine was obviously (or *should* obviously be) a great social leveler.

In short, Lollard and antimendicant book illustration—and the illustration it provoked—is crucially concerned with issues of authority and their presence and absence, and so is Douce. It is broader questions of authority that we must address next, along with the related problem of possible models for his remarkable social realism. The mixture of reformist iconography and iconomachia found in the Douce cycle is owing, we believe, to the artist's extensive visual literacy in a range of illustrated (sometimes radical) polemics, among which Lollardy itself may have been the least important—or may have been filtered through the kind of peculiarly national perspective that saw Henry Crumpe as cause célèbre. (After the very public condemnation of Crumpe, no literate Anglo-Irishman could have been unaware of the ecclesiological issues at hand or the offense implied to their national hero, FitzRalph.) Arguments from visual silence are speculative at best—and visual silence is precisely, for the most part, what Lollardy offers us, so it is impossible to be conclusive here. But what we can do is be aware of the polyphony of reformist and satirical influences available to a thinking Anglo-Irishman of the fifteenth century, and make sure our labels are complex enough to do them justice.

CHAPTER 2

✥

Visual Literacy and the Iconography of Social Dissent

Legal Illustration and the Origins of Douce

There are very few certainties about the Douce manuscript, but one of them is that both the scribe and the annotator-corrector set out to translate *Piers Plowman* into Hiberno-English.[1] And, in fact, the colophon of the manuscript (fol. 112v) actually tells us this:

Explicit liber de Petro Ploughman
Anno *regni regis* henrici sexti sexto
Et fir' Iouis
ante *festu*m Michae*lis* Incept' trassup'

That is, "Here ends the book of Piers Plowman, in the sixth year of the reign of Henry VI, having been begun to be translated on the Thursday before Michaelmas" (i.e., it was begun Thursday, September 29, and finished sometime during that same regnal year of September 1, 1427–28).[2] The final two heavily abbreviated words likely stand for "Incepto transsumptione [sic]," the last word in any case being some form of *transsumptio*,[3] which normally means "translation"—and given the thorough conscientiousness of both scribe and corrector in rendering the poem in the Middle Hiberno-English (MHE) dialect, there seems no reason to assume that the word is used merely as a metaphor here for copying or transcribing.[4] Comparing it against the received C text and judging by the pattern of correction and erasure, it would appear that the scribe initially translated dialect as he went, and that it was the corrector who made final judgments on remaining items of vocabulary he thought too foreign and any other matters that disturbed him.[5]

These two professional readers, then, were apparently carrying out a commission to translate *Piers Plowman* into MHE, illustrate it, and annotate it for a patron. This was a large undertaking, and given the evidence of correction, it was (so far as these particular scribes knew) a new one. The main scribe clearly created the colophon with a sense of moment: rather unusually, he used the kind of formula for it that one would use for dating statutes and parliamentary records, a formula that always includes the date, proximity to a liturgical day (where appropriate), and the regnal year.⁶ This suggests something about the kind of texts he was used to copying and the kind of intellectual world in which he was at home, and, indeed, this suggestion is supported by the fact that the subjects of his illustrations are frequently reminiscent of those found in legal and parliamentary manuscripts, as well as other kinds of documentary and historical records. One finds parallels with legal manuscripts in four areas: in actual iconography, in his penchant for choosing legal topics for illustration, in his emphasis on orality (promulgation being a standard subject for a legal illustrator), and in his informal methods of creating illustration, which are reminiscent of those found in utilitarian documents. All of these parallels are startling and unexpected: documentary work, the bread and butter of many scribes working in the London and Dublin civil service circles, was a world not just of texts, but of images, as well.

This is a well-kept secret: legal book illustration is a genre that traditional art history has mostly neglected and legal historians have mostly ignored.⁷ Illustration in legal manuscripts tends to range from the surprisingly lavish to the very utilitarian. Take, for an instance of the former, the ostentatiously authoritative pictures in many *Statuta* manuscripts (usually showing a throned king, sometimes flanked by secular and religious advisers)⁸ or the flagrantly hierarchical tendencies of canon law illustration, such as we have seen in the *Omne bonum* and in Merton College 319. This tendency could be nicely epitomized in the instance of San Marino, Huntington Library, MS HM 19999, a copy of Gregory IX's *Decretals,* full of images of censuring, judging, and officiating prelates, including one of a priest celebrating mass while a layman is being forcibly ejected from it (fol. 122).⁹ The main subjects of formal legal book illustration are (endlessly and repetitively) the authority figures who make and maintain laws, most often kings, popes, and archbishops.¹⁰ In the more varied secular programs, one also sees those whom the law affects (such as merchants, knights, and clerics) and those whom it protects (notably forest game, widows, and orphans). These images seem to have functioned in a variety of ways; practically, they were mnemonics and finding devices, but ideologically they can be baldly didactic and even polemical, asserting social hierarchy and highlighting warning exempla through social realism. J. J. G. Alexander summarizes the programs in three fourteenth-century legal manuscripts now at Durham Cathedral in this way:

> The system, common in these Law Books, of inserting before each book small scenes illustrating the promulgation of a particular collection or the subject of a particular law is well seen in [Durham] C.I.4 where, for example, on folio 4 Justinian is shown enthroned and on folio 236v laws concerning passenger ships are prefaced with a picture of a sailing ship which looks dangerously overloaded! Such scenes are interesting in that they may represent historical events of the recent past, or contemporary scenes of secular life, and as

such they deserve further investigation as one of the strands in the development of naturalistic art in the later Middle Ages.[11]

The emphasis here on promulgation is common in legal illustration, since many laws were originally also read aloud at prescribed intervals, and the emphasis on social concerns and historical events of the recent past, which Alexander notes, suggests why these pictorial subjects tend to overlap with chronicle illustration (as one sees especially in Matthew Paris's work). The formally commissioned miniatures and historiated initials love to depict, not surprisingly, order and good government: kings sitting in judgment, hearing petitions, or pronouncing sentence are most common; lawbreakers (when they appear) are usually being judged or punished (or ejected), and this is where one most frequently sees members of the lower classes: one thinks of images such as the picture of the baker convicted of selling short weight being drawn on a sledge in a fourteenth-century copy of the *Decretals* (London, British Library, MS Royal 10.E.IV) or the picture of a prince ordering a merchant to prison in London, British Library, MS Harley 4605.[12] It is precisely this kind of iconography of authority that the Douce artist loves to play with, and sometimes to overturn, in images such as the grieving young bastard (figure 22), a plunderer (Wastor, figure 12), the uncertain king (figure 5), and a strikingly authoritative peasant (namely, Piers, figure 10)—these are just some of the legal pictorial subjects that startle the eye in Douce. But before we look at the artist's deviance, we need to know what he was deviating from.

He must have had an intimate knowledge of the styles and subjects of utility-grade legal illustration and the contents of legal texts. It is not surprising, given what we now know of Langland's own knowledge of legal and parliamentary matters, that an illustrator would turn to such iconography when faced with having to come up with a pictorial program for the poem.[13] Utility-grade marginal legal illustration seems to have been a rather casually inventive genre—often executed by the scribes themselves, who frequently dipped into the rubricator's inkpots or whatever came to hand to color their pictures. The ostensible purpose was to create visual mnemonics and finding devices, but in livelier hands these became spontaneous commentaries on the legal text. A delightful and quite unstudied instance of this is Huntington Library, MS EL 7 H 8, a canon law collection made in England in 1368 using exactly the same inkpot-happy techniques as James le Palmer himself used for his "pictorial annotations," and at exactly the same time. It contains penwork initial flourishes cleverly elaborated into human faces and figures that illustrate the subject or emotion of the decretal (e.g., a king, fol. 228, "rex"; a man grieving, fol. 202, "planctus"; and several other subjects we find in Douce).[14] These are much like the delightful little penwork scenes in which James le Palmer portrays an Exchequer clerk wagging a pointed finger (a *declamatio* gesture in sharp profile) against a fellow office mate, such as "W. de Hanley" (figure 65), in a warning that canon law forbids clerics from hunting, which flies in the face of ("facit contra") Hanley's indulgence in that sport.[15] Even more technically like Douce (especially the pictures done mainly in rubrication colors in Douce's last two quires) are the informal marginal pictures in secular legal manuscripts: Michael Camille describes the drawings in the fourteenth-century *Registrum Brevium*, Pierpont Morgan 812, as "all in brownish ink, with green and yellow wash sometimes added.... there is reason to think that these spirited drawings were the work of a talented scribe using the few colors, including rubricator's red, that were available to him, and were produced at the same time as the text was copied and not added as an afterthought."[16] Here we have precisely the Douce artist's method of working: the vagaries of text-image precedence, the heavy use of rubrication colors, and the (sometimes awkwardly realized) spontaneity of the program, appear much less odd in this context than they do amid the formal atelier procedures that art historians have been trained to recognize.[17]

Above all, this was utilitarian work. Such images often occur, for instance, in the margins of writs: since many writs start with the same type of formula, marginal images, however crude, were invaluable as finding devices—devices that became more important as the consumer demand for legal manuscripts rose and as reading audiences widened beyond the usual spectrum of chancery clerks, lawyers, and students to include merchants, knights, and the nobility.[18]

Like Douce, these informal illustrations are full of social realism and concern for social justice: in Morgan 812, there is a marginal image of a laborer cutting wood (figure 70), ostensibly a pictorial finding device to illustrate a writ about traditional right of access to forest (in this case, for repairs to a mill). But the laborer is shown in the act of simply *taking* what has been traditionally his, a surprisingly assertive and socially sympathetic form of mnemonic iconography, which sometimes erupts into social satire directed against the powerful classes.[19] Like the Douce artist's, such illustrations also show much interest in orality or in the "voicing" of the text, as for instance in Morgan 812, fol. 29, where a marginal picture of a charter appears with its incipit, "Sciant presentes" ("Let all men here present know..."). Many legal texts were originally intended for recurrent proclamation, and the Douce artist on two occasions portrays just such sealed documents to signal performative moments in the poem (the proclaiming of Mede's marriage charter [9r] and the priest's reading aloud of the Pardon [figure 19]). In manuscripts of the early fifteenth century, the iconography of the sealed charter has often shifted to suggest silent rather than performative reading, but in Douce it retains, in both instances of its occurrence, a signal of (narratively dramatic) orality.[20]

The most informal level of legal illustration occurs in the unframed pictures drawn (usually) by scribes themselves and used mundanely for document categorization, storage, and retrieval. These were common in Exchequer memoranda rolls, where they appear, as we have seen, either simply as *signa* or as more elaborate figures, sometimes interacting with the text of the document in a spirited way, often using *declamatio* gestures.[21] Some drawings of unusual social detail and polemical thrust have been preserved in these documents. For instance, H. F. McClintock found among Exchequer *signa* in the Public Record Office three unframed single-figure drawings of Irishmen with axes—figures done, in fact, in the Giraldian tradition of marginal illustration popular in England and Anglo-Ireland, giving no very flattering image of the Gaelic-Irish. McClintock describes the general purpose of Exchequer *signa* this way:

> The chests, etc., containing the documents are distinguished by signs painted on them, and these signs are repeated at the beginning of the appropriate sections in the register. Some are geometrical devices, others shields of arms, and others pictorial drawings having a symbolic reference to the subject matter of the groups of documents.[22]

We have already seen an instance of how such images could become grim pieces of house Exchequer polemic in the hands of any clerk with a rather black sense of humor, as is the case with the pictogram of the bishop losing his miter (figure 69, no. 7). In fact, McClintock thought it grim enough to have been inspired by the martyrdom of Saint Thomas à Becket. It is used to designate the controversial constitutions made by Archbishop Pecham at the Council of Reading (London, Public Record Office, Liber A, E 36/274, fol. 295), where he not only attempted reforms of the clergy, but also renewed his defense of church liberties and launched a campaign against royal policy, ordering copies of the Magna Carta to be posted in the churches. Edward I forced Pecham publicly to revoke his order, and Pecham retreated, a clash between king and archbishop that recalled, for some Exchequer scribe-illustrator who had the job of classifying the documents, the fate of Becket.[23] These pictures, then, were not simply utilitarian; they could be highly political visual statements, most daringly, perhaps, in the Exchequer penchant for visual caricature, even of historical contemporaries such as Richard II's half-brother, the earl of Holland, or Alice Perrers, Edward III's mistress (see figure 69, nos. 14 and 15).

There is also a great deal of legal illustration of a more ambitious sort, and here, too, we find several parallels with Douce, especially in manuscripts intended for private ownership. By the early fourteenth century, copies of the *Statuta angliae* were being illustrated frequently enough to have an established program.[24] D. C. Skemer says of *statuta* generally that they were a type of professional literature, a compilation of official documents and legal treatises for use by practical people who may have owned no other books. Pocket legal codices (both rolls and books) began to be produced in large numbers at the turn of the fourteenth century. They ranged from inexpensive versions carried by itinerant justices or lawyers to more elaborately decorated and illustrated versions for landowners to somewhat larger and plainer formats for courtroom use. Many of these books were similar to Douce in size,[25] iconography, and utility (even their more elaborate iconography was primarily place-finding and mnemonic in purpose). There is also a strong didactic element in these programs, and in the more elaborate, like the fourteenth-century collection in Harvard Law Library, MS 12, there is also a strong impetus toward social statement. This use of illustration is exactly what we see in Douce, notably the tendency to create single figures that gesture from the margin toward the text, such as the unframed image of the widow pointing to a statute on the rights of dowagers from the margin of Harvard 12 (figure 51) or the king energetically reaching out of the historiated *E* and into the text to grasp the first handwritten letter of the Magna Carta, in Princeton Library, MS Scheide 30, fol. 14.[26] The interface between written text and image in these manuscripts can be even more playfully treated in the tendency to use visual puns for mnemonic purposes; Adelaide Bennett cites the instance in Scheide 30 in which the Statute of the "Respite of Knighthood" opens with a historiated initial of a knight hiding behind a huge shield—in Latin, *scutum*, the root of "scutage," that is, a fine in lieu of military service—and the subject of the statute.[27]

Social didacticism in these formal legal illustrations can be pronounced, and Harvard Law 12 is an especially apt example: it is considered unusual for the number and thoughtfulness of its plates,[28] and it shares much civil service iconography with manuscripts like the *Omne bonum*, Douce, and the *Red Book*. In fact, it looks as if much of the iconography found in privately owned collections of statutes and other legal manuscripts like Harvard 12 originated in and emigrated from official civil service productions. Ironically, and contrary to what we might guess, this iconography gained rather than lost formality as it was taken up in private hands. Compare, for example, the satirical freedom of the Dublin Court of Exchequer picture (see frontispiece) with its iconographical cousin in Harvard 12 (figure 52), depicting elegant young Exchequer clerks soberly at work in the historiated initial of the statute "Delescheker." The fourteenth-century discomfort with the transition to a wholly monetary economy—so familiar to readers of *Piers Plowman*—is everywhere visually evident in the pages of Harvard 12, where images of feudal fealty appear poignantly overwhelmed by a sea of monetary and commercial images,[29] visually marking statutes that regulate merchants, trading practices, Exchequer collection, coinage, and the like, all showing figures wielding coins uncomfortably large for the scale of the drawings.[30] With just such iconography in mind, the Douce artist captured Langland's discomfort with changing economic realities and the domination of "Lady Mede." Among the most notable echoes of statute iconography are Douce's heavy preoccupations with pictures of merchants, coins, and fraudulent traders.[31]

The artist's knowledge of statute manuscripts (both their iconography and their contents) is suggested not only in his extensive commercial imagery, but also in images such as the king examining Mede (by far the single most common kind of legal illustration is the king hearing a case or pronouncing judgment),[32] and especially the image of the young bastard (figure 22). The *Summa de Bastarda* appears in statute collections of any size (with the opening lines, "Nota quod si bastardus se clamando legitimum heredem..."), and the Douce image may have been inspired by a mnemonic to this statute.[33] Harvard 12 has a similar image in a historiated initial, illustrating the statute "de Wardes et relief," also rendered with didactic pathos, of two distressed children being led as wards (figure 53).[34] But Douce's bastard youth is alone, and it is typical of the Douce illustrator to show a victimized figure *without* relief like this, while a formally and lavishly illustrated volume like Harvard provides the socially comforting view (an adult is in charge of the young wards). Moreover, the authority issues raised by images such as Harvard 12's initial for the statute "de Religion," which shows two clerics before the king, expressing horror at his judgment (fol. 32v; Michael, "Manuscript Wedding Gift," plate 21), is just the kind of image of interauthority strife that the Douce artist enjoys (the *Statutum de Viris Religiosis* was repressive legislation designed in the wake of Edward's feud with Pecham to put limits on ecclesiastical jurisdiction and endowments).[35] A tour through any standard collection of statutes suggests themes that we also see highlighted in Douce: the chance to illustrate anything of legal import, from fraudulent trading practices (fol. 27) to Tom Stowe preparing to release his wife from the stocks (figure 6) to a lawyer pleading (figure 15) to capital punishment (figure 32), seems to have captured the Douce artist's attention and provoked his memory of the kind of governmental documents and legal codices that were (to judge from his colophon) his bread and butter.

History, Social Realism, and the Giraldian Visual Tradition

A number of fourteenth- and fifteenth-century historical writings survive in illustrated copies, some of which have marginal programs, but turning the pages of Douce one is most strongly reminded of the unframed marginal images of the thirteenth-century scribe-illustrator Matthew Paris, with his paratactically spontaneous narrative style, his tongue-in-cheek irreverence toward corrupt or overweening authority figures, and his unflinching social realism.[36] But it is unlikely that a fifteenth-century Anglo-Irish artist could have directly known Matthew's thirteenth-century autographs. At least two links, however, are traceable: the first is the fact that Matthew helped himself plentifully to the tradition of legal and civil service marginal illustration that we have just been examining, and the other is a link to Giraldus Cambrensis—both Matthew and the Douce artist would have had access to the Giraldian pictorial tradition: Matthew as a historian, the Douce artist as a literate Anglo-Irishman; both as "free-form" scribe-illustrators. The similarities, then, that we see between the pages of Matthew and Douce are largely owing, apparently, to their use of shared sources. But there are two further factors worth considering: the first is that Matthew's work was imitated in some fifteenth-century chronicles and in copies of his *Chronica majora* itself (upon which later scribe-illustrators not as gifted as Matthew made periodic assaults).[37] In fact, it can be difficult to tell what to attribute to imitation of Matthew and what to attribute to the fact that certain later chroniclers themselves were connected to the Exchequer and to the Chancery.[38] Second, the mere fact that Matthew was a scribe-illustrator and that we know a good deal more about his techniques than we do about those of any other two-hatted scribe is revealing for Douce. This section will examine all these factors.

Examining the list of Matthew's illustrations in the *Chronica majora* (Cambridge, Corpus Christi College [CCCC], MSS 16 and 26), one is immediately struck by the similarity to pictorial inventories of statutes collections: Matthew copied not only the texts of a number of statutes and other documents (especially from the *Red Book of the Exchequer*) but also the accompanying illustrations and *signa*, elaborating them vivaciously and realistically as he went.[39] The parallels with Douce are tantalizing, and make the destruction of the Dublin *Red Book* in 1922 even more frustrating, but Matthew's use of minor documentary imagery itself remains to be studied in detail, something that has not been a priority for either art historians or legal historians. So it is difficult to know the source in either artist of certain iconographical parallels, although many of the images we will examine here—images of sealed charters, of authority figures losing power, of impending disasters and legal punishments, or of peasants laying claim to plunder—are almost certainly derived from legal sources. Take, for instance, Matthew's image of William of Scotland's crown falling off (CCCC 16, p. 266), to which we can compare Douce's image of the demitered bishop (figure 18) and the Exchequer symbol for church reform (figure 69). Or take Matthew's image of the pillory (CCCC 16, fol. 21v), a punishment that marks a passage he added on the assizes for bread, originally issued by royal proclamation in 1203. The same image appears in a fourteenth-century copy of the statute, which is sometimes illustrated more mildly or genteelly (as in Harvard 12) with an image of bread. But both Matthew and the Douce artist seem to have preferred the more violent and forbidding images of punishment from the legal illustrative tradition, and these have usually come from government sources: we might compare Matthew's stark pillory with the Douce artist's man on the gallows (figure 32), a subject chosen (like the image of Tom Stowe about to release his wife from the pillory [figure 6]) on the slimmest textual pretext.⁴⁰ These images call to mind Exchequer *signa* such as the one designating the obligations of the men of Chester to Edward, earl of Chester: a gallows, indicating the penalty for rebellion. Clearly, this was a world of stark visual mnemonics.⁴¹

But some of the similarities between Matthew and Douce seem to be more broadly historical than legal, and many of these are explicitly reformist. Medieval chroniclers—who had a penchant for editorializing and foreboding "on the times," recording "wonders" and disasters, and taking a dim view of the progress of Salvation History generally—constitute an important but as yet largely unexplored context for Langland's own thought.⁴² One of two marginal annotations in the entire cycle made by the Douce scribe-illustrator himself (rather than by the annotator) highlights Langland's mention of chronicles at V.178 (see appendix 2, for fol. 23v). This suggests that he had some interest in chronicles, which perhaps followed naturally from his civil service experience. The scribe of the Piers manuscript that is now in San Marino, Huntington Library, HM 143 also associated the passage with the symbolic style of marginalia used in Matthew's chronicles (and in Exchequer documents) when he drew a crown in the margin beside Langland's disendowment prophecy at V. 168.⁴³ The Douce illustrator himself used the same symbolism that Matthew did (figure 48) for disastrous flooding, the ominously empty boat on turbulent water, portrayed at the end of passus VIII (figure 14). It is not a large imaginative step from the legal illustration in the Durham, Cathedral Library, MS C.I.4 of an overloaded boat (with its implied consequences) to the idea of portraying the prophetic threat of flooding with an empty boat. Nor is it a large imaginative step from the illustration in Pierpont Morgan 812 of a peasant chopping wood (thereby asserting his traditional right of use [see figure 70]) or Matthew's socially sympathetic picture of a peasant threshing grain stolen, in Robin Hood style, from barns belonging to the Roman See⁴⁴ to Douce's Wastor (figure 12). Portrayed as violently and vociferously laying claim to Piers's meat, he is rather more sensational than the calm, silent peasants in Morgan and Matthew laying claims of a similar sort, but iconographically, he is their cousin. So is the Douce digger of the same passus (figure 13). In fact the whole of passus VIII must have reminded the Douce illustrator of contemporary accounts, such as one would find most readily in chronicles, of social unrest and coercion in the countryside (to which Anglo-Ireland was no stranger): itinerant workers, vagrancy, unemployed Breton soldiers, "Roberdesmen," famine, doom prophecies—this was the stuff of contemporary historical writing for Langland's early audiences.⁴⁵ Matthew himself frequently portrayed acts of crime, civil unrest, and natural disaster. Once one has perused Matthew, the iconography of Douce's passus VIII comes into both realistic and symbolic focus: for instance, as immediate forerunner to the apocalyptic portent of Douce's unmanned boat (figure 14), the digger's spade in the previous picture (figure 13) becomes not simply an accurately realized workman's tool, or even just the symbol of the sinning Adam (although it is both), but also, more portentously, the attribute of Cain.[46] Similarly, Matthew's image of a peasant threshing plundered grain both illustrates an instance of mob violence against the barns of the Holy See and draws upon an apocalyptic iconography to make its didactic point. In effect, as a medieval reader would recognize, the Douce artist treated narrative chunks of the poem as if they were pieces of "chronicle," with margins full of beggars, ruffians, friars, castles, kings and counselors, dreamers, portents, pagans (Trajan), and images of violent acts and violent ends — all these Douce subjects can be readily paralleled in Matthew's work.[47]

The detailed codicological analysis that Vaughan, Lewis, and others have carried out on Matthew's autographs reveal the characteristics of a scribe-artist's work habits, some of which (e.g., his habit of having figures touch or visually play upon key words) is remarkably like Douce's: for instance, Matthew's marginal picture of the stoning of Saint Stephen depicts a single surly-looking man in the act of vaulting a huge stone, his feet perched precariously upon the first word of the rubric to the next entry: "Petrus" (with a pun on the Latin for stone).[48] He also deploys subtle visual irony in order to quietly criticize wayward authority, as does the Douce artist.[49] Matthew also provides pictorial parallels for the Douce artist's interest in clerical satire and corruption (the collecting of clerical satire was virtually a Benedictine hobby). In the pages of Matthew Paris one sees a monastic mentality that Langland to some extent shared (we might note that Benedictines owned more manuscripts of the poem than any other *known* group, and that among these manuscripts all but one contains historical writing of some sort along with its text of *Piers*).[50] The pugnacious independence of the powerful Benedictine order had been a refuge for controversial writings for centuries, and Langland attracted quite a Benedictine audience.

Both in Matthew's historiography and in his use of unframed marginal illustrations, he was demonstrably influenced by the "histories" of Giraldus Cambrensis, especially the unframed marginal drawings in *Topographia hibernica* and his *Expugnatio hibernica*. Often paired in manuscripts, these two works were very popular in Anglo-Ireland (the former was fashionable enough to be translated into Hiberno-English in the fifteenth century and even — perhaps masochistically — into Irish).[51] Since so little illuminated work is extant from late medieval Ireland and even less from Anglo-Ireland itself, the Giraldian tradition of illustration is invaluable as a source for understanding the Douce artist's repertoire of techniques, images, and visual assumptions. In fact, one look at a Giraldian page, with its single-figure unframed marginal pictures and *signa* and its deceptively "amateurish" mise-en-page, is enough to confirm this connection with Douce (see, for instance, the image of the priest in Laud

Misc. 720, apparently executed before the text was written, as sometimes happened in Douce [figure 45]). Gerald's work was popular so many centuries after his death largely because, in the *Expugnatio*, he emphasized the heroism of the earliest invaders and emphasized, as Robert Bartlett puts it, "the grating discontent of a conquest aristocracy which felt itself bridled by the less than whole-hearted support it received from the English Crown."[52] This discontent remained a fact of colonial life, and by the fifteenth century Gerald was a best-seller. His *Topographia*, which had been enormously popular in the earlier years of the colony—doubtless because his view of the native Irish was none too flattering but extremely colorful—appears from the distribution of dates of the extant manuscripts to have been somewhat less popular than the *Expugnatio* after the fourteenth century. One might say that as the colony matured it was the *Expugnatio*, rather than the *mirabilia* of the *Topographia*, that spoke to their increasingly political need for a separate identity. However, both were illustrated with a cycle of unframed marginal pictures, and it would have been nearly impossible for the Douce scribe-illustrator, as a literate and visually sophisticated member of this tight-knit colonial group, not to have known these two works of Giraldus. Their illustrations would have appeared somewhat old-fashioned to him, but they must have constituted the most obvious *local* tradition of marginal illustration known to him.

Suzanne Lewis summarizes Giraldus's pictorial influence on Matthew Paris this way:

> Probably based on sketches added ca. 1190 by Gerald himself to a no longer extant autograph copy, the earliest surviving manuscripts in B.L. MS Roy. 13.B.VIII and MS 700 in the National Library, Dublin, both contain forty-five marginal tinted drawings in a vigorous style closely resembling Paris's later chronicle illustration.... In their new frequency, informal format, and spirit of pungent caricature [these]... animated scenes anticipate Matthew's earliest pictorial vignettes for the *Chronica Majora* by less than two decades.... Perhaps inspired by the popularity of such secular illustrations as those designed for...[the] *Topographia*, Matthew was moved to create similar pictorial addenda in the same improvisational mode of unframed marginal vignettes. (*Art of Matthew Paris*, 39–40)

One finds exactly and unmistakably the same vigorous style and pungent caricature in the pages of Douce.

The Giraldian tradition of social pictorial realism, which both Matthew and the Douce artist exhibit, has been noticed before by historians.[53] A good instance is the Giraldian cycle portrait of a crippled man crawling on blocks in the lower margin of the text (figure 50).[54] The Douce artist may have learned his social realism in part from such Giraldian illustrations, but his poor are treated with more dignity than Giraldus's are; none of the five beggars in Douce is represented in such an abject posture, even though all of them are posed so as to capture the bodily effect of social scorn in their physical posture.[55] The *Topographia*'s disabled man is all the more striking because Gerald's accompanying text is a harsh condemnation of bastardy—he views deformity in children as punishment for adultery in the parents, in stark contrast to the Douce illustrator, who represented the plight of the illegitimate, as we have seen, very sympathetically and without resorting to deformity (as even Matthew did). In Douce the portrait of the young bastard (figure 22), holding his head in a gesture of grief, suggests the social tragedy even more tenderly than Langland's text itself warrants.

The Giraldian illustrations also give us some sense of the pictorial taxonomy from which the Douce artist made and rejected choices. Giraldus emphasizes visions and marvels, as does Matthew, but both artists were unrestricted by the sober reformist strain in Douce, which was illustrated much later and in a center acutely aware of FitzRalph and likely even Wyclif (who was actually, like many schoolmen, quite distrustful of visions).[56] We have already seen Douce's rejection of a marginal crucifix such as the Giraldian cycle uses in depicting a miracle.[57] The Douce artist usually does reject sacred iconography and the miraculous as subjects, but his cycle shares with the *Topographia* an iconography, safely understated, for conveying a visionary moment in his simple picture (figure 24) of a scribe working at a desk. The illustration in Douce has puzzled scholars: it comes at the moment of Will's visionary crisis (precipitated by Scripture's sermon [XI.163ff.]), and there is no evident *textual* reason why anyone should be depicted at a desk beside this passage, unless the picture is merely a visual pun on the Latin *Scriptura*. But the artist is rarely content simply to pun. The reason may lie in Giraldus, where there is a visionary exemplum that no artist would miss the chance to highlight with an illustration; it tells of the inspiration an angel gave to the artist of the Kildare Gospels, in the course of which the drawings are described in some detail, and in *Topographia* cycles this moment of vision is illustrated with an image of a scribe (a cleric) at a desk.[58] By analogy with the *Topographia*, it looks as if the Douce iconography, too, is meant to indicate the onset of vision, although this is an unusual and undramatic way of doing so in *both* texts. But both artists capture the traditionally scribal nature of visionary narrative (visionaries are by nature *recorders* of revelation), and although the choice is rather imaginatively austere (we expect to see the angel in the *Topographia* and Scripture preaching in Douce, but we get neither), this is exactly the kind of illustration a *scribe-illustrator* (or author-illustrator) might choose. The self-reflexive nature of the visionary experience in both cases was perhaps especially engaging to textually oriented illustrators. The Douce artist may even be making a visual allusion to the *Topographia* here, because, although author and scribal portraits are common enough, there is nothing in the text at this point to call attention to, or indeed even to justify, Will's *authorial or scribal* activity. Rather, the artist is emphasizing the beginning anew of Will's vision: the picture, indeed the book and pen, highlight the lines in which Scripture taunts the dreamer, "And saide *multi multa sciunt et se ipsos ne sciunt* / Þo weped I for wo... / And in wynking I worÞe and wonderly I mette" (fol. 52v; C.XI.166–68). And—interestingly—he portrays him as a clerk (although the annotator has carelessly obscured this, he has a tonsure). The Douce artist seems to have approved of this restrained mode of visual handling of visionary experience, because he rejected all of the more fantastic options in the Giraldian cycle and elsewhere and—betraying his affinities with reformist thought—stuck to social realism, even here.

The Douce artist is very interested in self-reflexive reading, and this is particularly marked in his handling of authority figures, which he does with sophisticated ambiguity (he has exactly Matthew's provocative technique of having the most institutionally authoritative figures appear not to "speak" visually—that is, by giving them bemused expressions and ambiguous speaking gestures or leaving them in visual silence).[59] The best way of demonstrating this is by a comparison of four authority figures in BL, MS Add. 37049, Matthew, Douce, and the fifteenth-century chronicle of Peter of Icham. Generally speaking, the unframed marginal format of Douce is reminiscent of that of some fifteenth-century illustrated medieval chronicles and "historical" writings.[60] However, it is only after one has examined a range of these closely that the subtlety of the scribe-illustrator's technique emerges. Oxford, Bodleian Library, MS Laud Misc. 730 is Peter of Icham's *Genealogical Chronicle*; two of its five completed drawings (more were planned) have close analogues in Douce: a king, whose portrait highlights the chronicle's title (figure 46),[61] is so close to Douce's king (figure 5) that he could have come from the same model book. But the Douce artist altered the standard model-book type in one of his characteristically ambivalent treatments of authority. In the Laud picture, the king's hand is raised in the announcing gesture, his authority to command emphasized by the upright sword in his right hand.[62] In Douce, however, both the king's hands rest quietly in his lap; his scepter is clutched unassumingly, almost forgetfully, as he muses meekly on Conscience's "teneful" warning to those who take bribes (III.493ff.). The Douce text here departs from received C tradition:[63] the last half of line 492 (usually "a tixst of Treuthes makynge") reads "a text of treuÞe of a kyng," which (whether deliberately or not) emphasizes kingly responsibility even more. The illustration is highlighting Conscience's exemplum about the lady who read the text beginning "Omnia probate" (Try all things) incompletely, forgetting to turn the leaf and read "Quod bonum est tenete" (Hold fast to what is good): the artist cunningly made the king's eyes focus quite exactly on the last half of line

495, "as i haue rad: & oþer þat can rede" (18r)—the word "rede" appearing just a few millimeters from the king's eyes acts as a strikingly self-reflexive mnemonic for the parable about sloppy reading. This mode of illustration must be regarded as a deliberate choice: the Douce artist could have more easily and conventionally portrayed the king's words just a few lines below where he orders both Conscience and Mede to be silent (IV.1–3), the perfect opportunity for the ubiquitous royal announcing pose. But scribe-illustrators tend to have more scope for text-image relations and are less likely to rely on clichés like this. One could cite Matthew Paris's portrait of another similarly enthroned authority figure, the patriarch Germanus of Constantinople. Matthew had imported more than a page of forged material denouncing papal corruptions into his copying of the text of Germanus's letter to Gregory IX, including the comment "For no one can ever see anything ugly in his own face unless he looks in a mirror," creating an interesting visual irony.[64] Even though he is angry, Matthew's patriarch himself looks as bemused and reflective as the king in Douce by the scope of corruption he beholds, and clearly both scribe-illustrators thought this was a more realistic response. The scribe-illustrator of Add. 37049 also rather cunningly played off the standard kingly iconography in his Three Estates picture (figure 60) by retaining the commanding royal announcing pose, while giving him a speech scroll with a moralistic verse on death ("I wende to dede a kyng y wys"), which implicitly asserts the social leveling effect of the "kynde way" all men must go ("I wende to be cled in claye"). None of the artist's Three Estates figures on this folio can hold a candle to Douce's naturalism and polemicism: compare the realism of Douce's knight (figure 11) with the absurdly stereotypical armored knight in 37049, and note that the only bishop who appears in Douce is *losing* his miter—the Douce artist absolutely refuses to show ecclesiastical authorities ensconced in power like this. But as a scribe-illustrator, even the 37049 artist is working closely enough to the text to produce visual ironies.

   The work of these readerly artists appears in sharpest contrast to the more conventional mode of illustrating kingship in books of hours. Authoritative kings (even when they are villains) are the norm in such texts: either the monarch is shown sternly ordering that something be done (as one finds ad nauseam on nearly every page of the Queen Mary Psalter) or proudly enthroned with crossed legs, an attribute of authority (as in the De Lisle Hours). The Douce artist could have taken the former option when the king orders Wrong off to prison, and he could have taken the latter at several points in the text, but instead he focused on this passage and chose to portray a king who is an observer—not an actor—and, for the moment, a *reader,* too. The Douce artist's manipulation of standard iconography is also apparent in the second picture on the opening page in Laud 730 (figure 46), a castellated structure representing the New Troy (London). It is also very similar to Douce's Manor of Truth (fol. 34), the only unsuppressed castle or structure of any kind in the Douce cycle,[65] which typically accords visual characteristics of stability and riches only to heavenly or spiritual entities. Both the king and the castle represent the kind of stock pictures found in model books and used widely in the illustration of chronicles; as subtly adapted from this genre by the Douce artist, they signal visually to readers the historically and socially destabilizing experience of reading Langland's text. In the hands of the Douce artist, conventional legal and historical illustration is transformed to reflect social ironies and didacticisms very like the literary fascination with satire and poverty one finds in contemporary Anglo-Irish poetry.

Anglo-Irish satire was no ordinary satire. It tended to be outspoken, irreverent, politically self-defensive, and often, as we will see in manuscripts like Harley 3724,[66] goliardic, Giraldian, and apocalyptic in content. It is a product "of the middle nation," but what many Anglo-Irish productions have in common is a fierce independence of spirit, a sardonic sense of humor, and a penchant for challenging authority. And this is our next concern.

Authority and Visual Dissent:
Piers Plowman for the Anglo-Irish Reader

Speaking of the so-called Kildare manuscript, the largest extant collection of Anglo-Irish poetry, Bliss remarks: "Satire is not, of course, found only in Ireland, but the satirical element in the religious poems is of an anti-clerical and anti-establishment type which can readily be paralleled in Irish literature."[67] Less easy "to pin down," he continues, is the other most characteristic feature, a "sense of practicality" that manifests itself most obviously in "the highly developed social consciousness" of its verse (the "Kildare" poems, for instance, are unusual in medieval literature for their attention to "the effect the sins of the rich are likely to have on the lives of the poor who depend on them"). It is perhaps not surprising, then, given this cultural profile, that *Piers Plowman* would find an audience among the Anglo-Irish—in fact, the illustration of the text there even suggests something of a vogue for the poem. It seems to have suited local literary tastes in every respect; if anything, Langland's satirical edge is even a little softer than some of what we find in Ireland's vernaculars.

It is not likely just a coincidence that the only extant illustrated version of *Piers Plowman* should hail from Anglo-Ireland. The colony had originally been heavily settled by speakers of West Midlands and South West Midlands dialects, and trading connections continued to be strong with the Bristol area well into the fifteenth century; indeed, the exemplar of the Douce text itself was likely written in South West Midlands (SWM) dialect.[68] For the most part, the scribe seems to have understood SWM well enough to make appropriate semantic substitutions for his Hiberno-English speaking readers (although admittedly these played havoc with the alliteration, which he either did not understand or did not think worth preserving). Moreover, the fact that the Douce text belongs to the best family of C-text manuscripts (the "i-group") further confirms West Midlands associations.[69] Apparently, *Piers Plowman* was in circulation in Ireland long before Douce was made. The very earliest extant citation of *Piers* in *any* will occurs, in fact, in a will drawn in Ireland, and the most reliable biographical information we have about Langland himself appears in a manuscript (Dublin, Trinity College, MS 212) of Irish provenance (though not origin). These factors cannot simply be accidents: they have to do with patterns of colonial emigration, with the geographical serendipity of monastic property holdings, with the connections of powerful families like the Mortimers and the Despensers, and, finally, with the local popularity of satire and literature of social protest. All this requires detailed explanation.

Little Malvern Priory—the religious house, if any, with which Langland can be most closely associated—held lands in Ireland. It sent two monks (or a suitable layman) to Ireland twice a year to oversee its properties in Dublin and in outlying areas.[70] The extent of Little Malvern Priory's medieval holdings in Ireland is surprising, so much so that the constant demands of supervision and visitation put an unwanted stress on the small Benedictine community (records show that the monks dreaded the twice-yearly trip to Ireland),[71] but the traffic between Dublin and Malvern went on from 1199 until 1486, when the last of the properties was sold to Saint Mary's, Dublin, for three hundred pounds.[72]

The possibility that one of these representatives of the priory carried a copy of the latest work by the famous local poet in his baggage seems good; the monastic grapevine had for centuries been a key factor in the transmission of literary texts of all sorts. Moreover, the evidence of ownership for Langland's texts (at least in our current state of knowledge) shows, as already mentioned, that Benedictine houses were overwhelmingly the largest *documented* audience for Langland's text (with secular clergy and legal clerks or civil servants running a close second and third).[73] Of actual evidence for Langland's own association with the Benedictines in Malvern we have little that is concrete beyond the fact that the uncommon image Langland uses at VI.398 of "*two* grydy sowes" appears on a thirteenth-century bench-end in the choir of Little Malvern Priory, suggesting that he drew upon local iconography. (And local iconography may have drawn upon his poem: an early fifteenth-century misericord in Great Malvern Priory depicts the belling of the cat fable, possibly a gesture of local pride.)[74]

The regular traffic between Little Malvern and the Dublin-Pale district (where Douce was apparently made) may partly explain why there are at least three *Piers* manuscripts known to have been associated with Anglo-Ireland, all relatively early: Douce, dated 1427, is the latest of them, but the other two are very early indeed. The first is the mention of "unum librum vocatum Pers Plewman" in the will of Walter de Bruges, drawn at Trim, county Meath, in 1396 and proved at York, bequeathed (along with, we might note, a copy of the *Oculus* and a Bible) to John Wormyngton.⁷⁵ Walter de Bruges was second baron of the Exchequer in Ireland, and also "parson of Trim and prebendary of St. Patrick's Cathedral, Dublin... an important man and in high favour with the English authorities. He was also right-hand man of Roger de Mortimer, earl of March, lord of the liberty of Trim and heir apparent to the English throne....[De Bruges] was a pluralist on a large scale, holding prebends in the cathedrals of Hereford and York," as well as various posts and preferments throughout England.⁷⁶ Modern scholars persistently express surprise that such a man would own a copy of *Piers Plowman*, but clearly Langland's poetry, rife with burning matters of ecclesiological controversy, spoke urgently (if not comfortably) to those on both, or all, sides of such issues. (We often forget that, for the poem's initial audiences, parts of *Piers* were as current and topical as modern media editorials are today — they did not experience it in the timeless realm of literary aesthetics, as we now do.) De Bruges was obviously as interested in ecclesiological matters and issues of pastoral care as were many other members of Langland's early audience. He in fact bequeathed three pastoral manuals, along with a number of biblical commentaries, to various friends. As Brooks has shown, this manuscript must be distinct from Dublin, Trinity College, MS 212, the other *Piers* text known to have been associated with Ireland. Furthermore, de Bruges's copy stayed in Ireland because John Wormyngton was an Anglo-Irish priest (likely in county Meath); he had been associated with de Bruges as early as 1382 and was apparently still alive in 1426 (the year before Douce was made). It is significant that de Bruges's copy is the earliest mention of the poem in a will, and that he clearly owned the copy when resident in Ireland and that it stayed in Ireland. Trinty College, Dublin 212 is the manuscript of the poem that tells us all we know for certain of Langland's parentage (including the fact that his father was a tenant of the Despensers). It also contains annals of the Welsh border area, including references to the affairs of the Mortimers and the Despensers, and it likely came from the priory of Abergavenny,⁷⁷ not far from Malvern itself. How soon it came to Ireland we do not know, but it could have arrived in the early fifteenth century; it was certainly in Dublin by the mid–seventeenth century and may well have come much sooner.⁷⁸ Moreover, close connections between Ireland and the Despenser family may also account for some of the poem's circulation,⁷⁹ and it may thus be no accident that our only historical account of Langland's ties with that family occurs in a manuscript known to have been in Ireland since at least the seventeenth century.

Not only *Piers Plowman* but also other works of a socially and ecclesiastically polemical or satirical flavor were popular in Anglo-Ireland. In an earlier generation, Harley 2253 itself had been associated with both

Ireland and the Herefordshire area[80] — again with county Meath, the liberty of Trim, and the Mortimers. Moreover, the most radical early-fourteenth-century Middle English poetry on social issues generally seems to have come from Anglo-Ireland itself. The Kildare manuscript, which is much like the Harley manuscript in scope and character, is the largest collection of poems in a Hiberno-English dialect. The Kildare poems in fact bear a striking similarity to some of the poems most often associated with *Piers Plowman*. Like the Harley lyrics, they predate *Piers* itself; however, their presence and in some instances origin in Anglo-Ireland suggest why the Hiberno-English speaking community so readily embraced *Piers Plowman*. They form the centerpiece of a literature marked by antiauthoritarian and anticlerical satire (sometimes shockingly extreme, often exacerbated by colonial tensions and oppression) and an unusual, unromanticized sympathy for the poor.

The period during which *Piers* arrived in Anglo-Ireland is important in Irish literary historical terms not as a period of spontaneous creativity (such as the early fourteenth century, when the Kildare poems were written), but as a period of active transmission, translation, adaptation and transcription of materials from earlier times and other places. It was also a period of new cultural awareness. The *Secreta secretorum* was translated into Hiberno-English in 1422 by James Yonge, at the request of James Butler, the earl of Ormond and lieutenant in Ireland, member of an Anglo-Irish family known as cross-cultural patrons of the literary, legal, and visual arts as well.[81] The early fifteenth century was also the time when Giraldus's *Expugnatio* was translated into Hiberno-English as the *Conquest of Ireland*. Anglo-Irish was apparently an emergent culture at this point and was consciously exploring its colonial status and history. Alan Bliss speaks of the early-fifteenth-century fashion for Hiberno-English translations and transcriptions as feeding part of the new bourgeois and upper-class market for books in the vernacular: "No doubt [they] were aimed at such a market: the popularity of the translation of the *Conquest of Ireland* suggests that the English-speakers identified themselves more with Ireland than with England"[82] — although the fact that there is much in Giraldus that the native Irish would have found repugnant demonstrates the distinctive and complex cultural position of the Anglo-Irish.

The Anglo-Irish, then, were not simply English living in Ireland. Many families had been there for generations, and like all colonists, the Anglo-Irish were themselves colonized, taking on many things from the culture that surrounded them, much to the chagrin of English government officials at home. The famous Statutes of Kilkenny (1366, and repromulgated in 1402), oppressively anti-Irish as they are, constitute a tacit admission on the part of the English administration that the cultural colonization was working in two directions and that in many important respects Irish culture had the upper hand.[83] Those English who had been settled for any length of time in Ireland soon developed loyalties to Ireland and resentments toward the neglect or abuse perpetrated by absentee English rule. Thus it was, for instance, that when Edward Bruce invaded Ireland in 1315 he drew support not just from the Irish, but also from the Anglo-Irish.[84] It was not without cause that the Anglo-Irish called themselves "of the middle nation,"[85] and one sees this curious mix of loyalties in, on the one hand, the Douce scribe's fit of protective patriotism over the nationality of the proud priest (fol. 109; cf. Pearsall, *C-Text*, XXII.221) and, on the other hand, the popularity of the Hiberno-English translation of Giraldus's *Expugnatio*. But however much they enjoyed reading about the glorious (and now remote) deeds of Henry II, there is a strong antiauthoritarian sensibility in Anglo-Irish poetry and historical writings. They trusted the papacy even less than the English did (and that is saying something).[86] Their experience of secular lordship was too often at best one of neglect, at worst one of exploitation. Poverty was rampant in the colony. All of this can be seen in the Douce artist's ambivalent treatment of authority figures, an ambivalence even more deep-seated than Langland's. Open political satire would no doubt have been considered unsafe (indeed, even Langland himself is more cautious on this subject than he is with ecclesiastical satire). But strategic silence and ambivalence can be effective tools, and the Douce artist used them unreservedly.

Figures of unquestionable authority are in fact in very short supply in Douce, and this appears all the more noticeable when its program is compared with, for instance, Lincoln 218, where figures of church-fatherly and clerkly authority peer sternly at the viewer from every margin, or with the *Omne bonum*, in which a clerkly figure of some sort is seen waving a didactic finger at nearly every layman or woman in sight. Not in Douce. There are indeed many speakers, but those of authority (either social, institutional, or moral) are few: Conscience (figure 4), represented only once, has the model-book delicacy and dignity of the king, but also his saddened, bemused eyes. He turns away from the text, conveying the sense that the written word is not the powerhouse of authority that one sees, for instance, in Lincoln 218 or Harvard Law MS 12 or Scheide 30, where marginal figures gesture confidently toward it. Douce stands alone among its closest (unframed marginally illustrated) contemporaries as a repository of visual antiauthoritarianism. Perhaps only Reason (fol. 19) comes closest to the kind of assertive, proclamative figure one expects iconographically, seated (unusual in this cycle) on a tangible bench and squarely facing the viewer to whom he gestures in *declamatio*. Unfortunately, the figure is so poorly executed that it is difficult to say with certainty that he lacks the ambivalence that haunts his closest colleagues, Conscience and the king, in the cycle.[87] And, as Hilmo points out, his eyes are crossed and his gesture is directed toward his heart, suggesting that his focus is, in any case, inward. However, there are other types of authority in Douce: Mercy (figure 33), in a delicately swayed stance that indicates the artist's old-fashioned training, conveys the dignity of a divine or semidivine figure, but her gaze downward suggests a humility whose power is the paradoxical type of the Beatitudes, not the glory of majesty. Interestingly, there is a curious and apparently deliberate smudge across Mercy's face, which may indicate that the patron or an early owner was uncomfortable with this image and tried to obscure it because in its saintliness it came too close to the iconic or because its femininity was troublesome (a scenario that would make sense given the later, antifeminist additions on the last folio).[88] Dobet (figure 21), whom Langland's text gives leave to portray in all the splendor of a preaching bishop—an easy task with a pattern book to hand[89]—is also meekly and poignantly looking down. For the same humble expression we might compare Matthew Paris's picture of an early and saintly English Franciscan, likely drawn from life.[90] In these two Douce figures, and in the many sympathetic figures of the poor, the artist shows an acutely evangelical spirituality and a conviction that true dignity belongs only to the meek.

If this tendency is reformist, it is *not* FitzRalphian; rather, it looks very like the reformism of Franciscan spiritual ideology, a sensibility one finds expressed in Langland's C text in particular and one that Wyclif, too, picked up from the Franciscans before he parted company with them mid-career. So many potentially authoritative figures in Douce are silent witnesses (that is, they have no speaking gestures): the king (figure 5), the knight (figure 11), and Dobet (figure 21)—who is, according to the poem, supposed to be preaching from the lectern he stands in so humbly and silently. And many of the clerks, whom we would expect to see performing some kind of speech-act, are not. The only *active* use of a lectern in the manuscript is the corrupt lawyer's (figure 15); the many figures dressed in academic garb are usually shown musing (e.g., Imaginatif, figure 28), an expression of the meditative function of the manuscript. The only active scholar figure is asserting his authority (and rather brutally) over a child (fol. 52), in contrast to, say, Lincoln 218, where corporal penance is shown being inflicted on an adult in a very similarly placed unframed marginal illustration (fol. 53). Only two clerks in Douce are shown as engaged in a positive speech-act: the priest with the pardon (figure 19), although as we have seen even his speaking gesture is not given a clearly authoritative profile, and the Franciscan (figure 20).[91] The "leued" vicar (fol. 105), although not given a speaking gesture, is given an intelligent face; significantly, in view of the fact that the artist had lay sympathies and was obviously a man of reformist tendencies, all three figures, especially the two secular clerics, represent those low on the clerical ladder, those on the front lines of pastoral care. This fits the evidence we've seen elsewhere of his "clericist" stance. Most interesting is the fact that the "leued" vicar has been given *exactly* the same intelligent face and expression as the lunatic lollar (figure 16), whom Langland compares to the apostles Peter and Paul (IX.112). In fact, the lunatic lollar, despite his rags, has been given a tonsure, which, along with the spray of gold dust on his garment, is the Douce artist's most eloquent and defiant statement on the nature of true spiritual authority. The garment carelessly half covering him is inspired by the kind of biblical iconography that artists like Matthew Paris used. The "leued" vicar is, with Dobet, the most sympathetically drawn clerical figure in the manuscript, and the Franciscan has been given a *silver* cord to highlight his order's distinctive symbol of holy poverty. These are the marks of a subtle reverse discrimination at work (and fascinating interpretive choices that may stagger modern Langlandians).

Authority, wisdom, and dignity, then, do not reside where we would expect them to in Douce. And this fits a pattern established by the artist's unusually liberal attitude toward the laity. One thinks immediately of the poem's hero, Piers, whose portrait occurs on 35r (figure 10), a page that, together with its verso, forms one of the most complex leaves of the manuscript. At first it is puzzling not to encounter a picture of a man plowing, such as one sees in the Luttrell Psalter or even in the Trinity *Piers* itself (the marginal format could have accommodated enough of the plow to suggest the rest). There was in fact a long-standing iconographical tradition of showing plowmen, both real and symbolic, in the act of plowing—in fact, in an early English illustration of Augustine's *City of God*, plowing represents the activities of the godly on earth.[92] But the Douce artist makes a deliberate choice to show Piers *teaching*, and not only is he teaching, he is *seated*, so as to underline his authority; however, the artist has been unable to imagine what kind of seat a plowman teacher would be sitting upon, and so has drawn none, creating an oddly suspended effect in the portrait. He has given him other attributes of authority as well: Piers's hand is raised in a clear announcing gesture (much more authoritative, we might note, than the ambiguous one bestowed on the priest with the pardon, figure 19), and made all the more audacious by the prominence of his plowman's glove; the sense of stability is increased by the way he holds his plow-stick firmly in the other hand, and his eyes are directed down at the half line "and þe hey way tech" (cf. Pearsall, *C-Text*, VIII.4). The man he is instructing, the knight, although a social superior, is portrayed with the patient, slightly shamed expression of all laity under instruction in illustrated pastoral manuals and canon law collections; he is placed as close to Piers as he could be, in the left margin immediately overleaf, but for some reason he was never finished—not actively erased or suppressed like the first devil or Abraham, but never painted, never worked up beyond the sketch stage. Because of the marginal format, the artist had not been able to put the two figures together on the same page, but he is nonetheless relying upon— and overturning (if that pun is bearable)—the established iconographic expectations in manuscripts like Add. 37049 and the *Omne bonum*, where well-attired laymen are always shown in tandem with—and under the tongue (so to speak) of—a *cleric*. But the new "democracy" suggested by his playful allusion to these visual expectations may have simply seemed too daring to the patron, perhaps the reason the knight was left unfinished.

If we compare treatments of the same theme in, say, Add. 37049 (figure 61), we have two unframed figures, a layman and a clerk, facing each other across the text,[93] which is—and this is important—a dialogue on the active and contemplative lives. The layman is a soberly garbed man of good social class, dressed in a calf-length gown, just like the knight in Douce (figure 11). He, too, is being instructed on the duties of the active life. In Add. 37049 (which is like Douce in aligning text and image so carefully that the images "voice" the text), the text on that page opens with his question "I beseke þe reuerent doctour to inform me þe way of good lyfyng and how I sal dispose me to cum to euerlastyng lyfe" (87v). But in Douce the knight, who is asking (within the terms of the plowing allegory) much the same sort of question, is of course being instructed by Piers. In portraying a layman being taught by another layman, and a social inferior at that, the artist must have been aware of deviating from a repeatedly reinforced visual norm. How startling this must have seemed to early readers turning the pages of Douce—images of plowmen, even as plowmen were in themselves relatively rare in fifteenth-century manuscripts;[94] most artists clearly thought them beneath notice as subjects.

But this leaf of Douce (35r and v) is more complex yet: the impact of this folio is heightened by one of the artist's most explicitly polemical choices of illustration: his decision to show Contemplatif as a layman (figure 10).[95] Bearded and wearing a layman's chaperon (painted in the same unpretentious reddish-brown used for Piers), his head is thrust toward the lines he speaks in a visual gesture as sudden as his abrupt appearance in the poem ("Quod contemplacioun by cryst: þo3th I care suffer / Famy[n]e and defaute: folow i wil peres" [fol. 35r; cf. Pearsall, *C-Text*, VII.305–6]). That this head appears on the same page as Piers's picture is, of course, dictated in part by the text, but the choice to illustrate Contemplatif in the first place was not mandatory. The result is a folio that asserts *lay* authority quite unmistakably. One might compare the Additional manuscript in which—even though it was intended for outreach to the laity—images of contemplation or visionary experience are largely clerical, eremitical, or saintly: figures like Saint Anthony, Rolle, and numberless tonsured Carthusians appear in contemplative state, praying before crucifixes or in rapt adoration of a holy apparition; laymen are usually shown *being* taught (repeatedly, in fact) or in some activity of daily life, most often being tempted or victimized by evil. From a clerical perspective lay life was spiritually dangerous and largely full of tribulation and sin. Douce's is clearly not a run-of-the-mill clerical perspective. In a decision also not dictated by the text, the artist for some reason chose to conflate visually—or at least link—the figure of Contemplatif with the knight (they have the same features, the same heads, and the same headdress). This suggests the artist's familiarity with both the kind of iconography we have seen in Add. 37049 and the same kind of *textual* content (remember that the treatise being illustrated there was on the active and contemplative lives). In short—although it will strike modern readers as most unusual—it is very much the kind of visual reading a scribe-illustrator would do. Nor is it a "misreading": if plowing, iconographically, represents godly activities and the knight is willing to plow, then he, too, is a follower of Piers, and willing followers, as Contemplatif's isolation in the poem has just shown, are not thick on the ground.[96]

Other treatments of the laity in scribe-illustrated manuscripts are more like the Additional manuscript's than like Douce's. In Lincoln 218, which seems to have been made with some kind of clerical teaching context in mind, the reader is apparently to associate himself visually from the outset with the student who asks an enthroned Augustine, from a lower place on the opening page, "Magister quid est deus?"[97] Images of the laity in this manuscript are most certainly not spiritually flattering. The laity are seen (visually) as sources of financial support for priests or as beggars or, if wealthy, as needing to be taught by the clergy to stave off demonic victimization. And this attitude toward the laity prevails even though Lincoln, in the exact spirit of ecclesiological reform that Langland himself drew from such pastoral manuals, attacks corruption in those who abuse the office of pastoral care. We might note the striking image in this manuscript of the priest guilty of fornication holding his baby ("Non accipiam sacrificium de manibus uestris" [figure 58]) or the image of the unfaithful priest wrongly taking his ill-gotten tithe from the laity ("vt dicitur Pastores infideles locii furum sequuntur mun(er)a manus eorum plene rapina" [figure 57]). Even though the Lincoln artist knew a whole range of reformist iconography, which he deployed for criticizing faulty clergy, there is no sense in this manuscript of imagining a positive role in the spiritual life for the laity. It was for audacious reformers like Langland to do that through a figure like Piers, but even Langland himself does not *explicitly* make Contemplation a layman; his poetry suggests the *possibility* that anyone who can suffer patiently can follow Piers, but it was the Douce artist who made a deliberate and bold choice to exemplify that follower as a layman.[98]

This is part of an impetus in Douce that we might call the sanctification of ordinary life: his habit of according the highest visual dignity to the poor and the poor in spirit extends even to his treatment of the tools of ordinary life. The social realism that he learned, apparently, from sources like the Giraldian tradition blends with this penchant for sanctification of the domestic to create a rather socially radical spirituality. Thus we have the deeply sympathetic figure of Activa Vita (figure 29), who holds not just one, but two tools: a plow-stick (because he is Piers's apprentice) and an oven-spade for bread baking (because he provides bread to the "pore and þe riche" as well as eucharistic wafers to "wel come godes gistes" [fol. 69; cf. XV.201 and 199]). Kathleen Scott says that this is the only surviving depiction of an oven-spade, and if, as Maidie Hilmo has suggested, the black appearance of the spade and the tip of the plow-stick is owing to the oxidization of, perhaps, silver, then what we have here is a graphic instance of his respect for and sanctification of the "ordinary."

These "democratizing" tendencies in the Douce artist's program can be paralleled in what we know of a few other readers of *Piers*, such as the reformist but apparently orthodox William Palmere, not to mention the most subversive of Langland's known readers, John Ball.[99] In Douce, these tendencies are most obvious in his sympathetic treatment of the poor—a sympathy all the more interesting because medieval Ireland had the same kinds of problems with "vagabonds and sturdy beggars" as medieval England had.[100] But Langland's own struggle with distinguishing between the "deserving" and "undeserving" poor, as Derek Pearsall has described the problem, is barely an issue for the Douce artist. His treatment of the poor, rather, tends to be both socially and iconographically "iconoclastic": as Scott mentions, books of hours nearly always show the poor receiving charity, but there are no handouts in Douce, even though many places in the poem could support such an illustration (e.g., the many exhortations of the wealthy to charity that litter the text). In Douce, rather, the artist exploits the marginal format to isolate his poor figures from society; he seems to delight in overturning expectations established even by Langland's own text, of which he sometimes apparently disapproves. Using the kind of visual irony that one finds in Matthew Paris, the Douce artist portrayed the huddled beggar with his back to the text on fol. 72, so that he does not seem to share Patience's enthusiasm for the fact that the poor are not prone to the sins of pride—an attitude that he may have regarded as patronizing. As we have seen, he seems to have objected, subtly and pictorially, to Langland's assumption that only false beggars and hermits would be driven to work by Hunger (and perhaps even to Langland's citing of the problematic parable of the talents)[101] through his placement of the rather well-dressed digger (figure 13). Just as the digger's foot intersects with the text, Hunger is winding up his discourse with the comment, "This aren euidences,...for hem þat wolle nat swynke / That here lyflode be lene and lyte worth here clothes" (VIII.262–63).[102] Of course, in Douce's rendering the word "swynke" (work) is written directly over the digger's spade as a stark moral mnemonic, but perhaps more sinister is the picture's deliberate overturning of the text's "and lyte worth here clothes." Douce's poor are never even shown eating a piece of bread, which would be the single-figure version of the conventional charity illustration in books of hours. The marginal format could easily have accommodated a charity-giving scene: the *Hours of Catherine of Cleves*, for example, has many such giving scenes, including one of a gratuitously tiny beggar huddled at the feet of Saint Martin and receiving his portion of the cloak in a manner that would have fit the single-figure format of Douce.[103] But the Douce artist was not interested in accommodating the sensitivities of the rich. His poor are more like the poor in illustrated historical texts (in which, on contemporary social matters, idealization gives way to realism), especially in Giraldus and Matthew Paris.

To sum up: the Douce artist's view of true authority is, like the authority of the Beatitudes or perhaps of the radical Franciscans' tradition, antihierarchical. For him, those who have suffered patiently are literally the only ones worthy of receiving reward (which the artist bestows selectively in his use of gold dust and other precious metals). All his well-intentioned authority figures (and there are not many) are puzzled or saddened rather than commanding. Figures that undermine or satirize legal, institutional, or established authority are prevalent: Mede (fol. 8), Mede and the sheriff (figure 2), Mede and the friar (fol. 11v), Liar holding the charter (fol. 9), the bishop asleep as the wolf attacks (figure 18), the bribed lawyer arguing his case (figure 15), Recklessness (figure 25) and Trajan (figure 27) challenging theological doctrine, Tom Stowe taking the (social) law into his own hands (figure 6), Wastor defying the civil law (figure 12),[104] the proud priest openly flouting ecclesiastical law (figure 37), and innumerable corrupt friars. The reader turning the pages of Douce 104, *even an illiterate reader*, sees images of a church and society in chaos. Certainly Langland's poem—along with a tradition of normally safely Latinate reformist ecclesiology—is the impetus for some of this, but even Langland cannot be fully responsible for the near anarchy visualized on these pages. The final picture in the Douce cycle is emphatically not Langland's last word; his glimmer of hope in the image of Piers as future reformer or Conscience setting out in search of Grace (XXII.380–86) is absent. Rather, in Douce the last image is of the friar "physician" (figure 38), an image associated eschatologically with the end of life for the individual, apocalyptically with the corruption of penance by the friars, socially with the fraud of medical practitioners,[105] and possibly, for this artist and his patron, ecclesiastically with the persecutors of Wyclif (the doctor is represented unequivocally as a Dominican) or, more likely, with the enemies of FitzRalph. The artist's knowledge of legal illustration may even be a factor in this complex image: documents containing ordinances for almshouses and other bequests made by the pious at death also draw upon this iconography. For instance, "Dick" Whittington's ordinances for almshouses are prefaced by a miniature done by William Abell and showing Whittington's deathbed scene, with a doctor holding a urine bottle in the background.[106] The Douce illustrator apparently looked for little consolation from political, royal, ecclesiastical, or civil officials; his was a bleaker worldview than Langland's. Where Langland could give the allegorical story of Peace's complaint against Wrong an ending in which, despite the presence of Mede, justice prevails, an early-fourteenth-century Anglo-Irish poet ended a similar allegorical tale about "mede" with the only just character being imprisoned and hung, drawn and quartered because bribery prevails over truth: "Hastilich ʒe him bind; / Al his bones ʒe to-drawe" orders the king, and the poem's narrator muses: "Also hit farith nou in lond / ... The lafful man ssal be i-bund / And i-do in strang pine."[107] If the Douce artist occasionally outdoes Langland in the bitterness and cynicism of his handling of authority, he came by it honestly and culturally.

It would be fascinating to know what discussions the artist and the patron who commissioned this text had. It looks as if they disagreed on some things—some subjects were suppressed, others simply not finished, others finished and defaced at some later point in time, whether by the same owner or another. Patron visits to the workshop during the making of this manuscript may have been a little heated at times, if our guess is right, but workshop tensions did not end here. We must now add to the mix the (mercifully) more documentable rival interpretation of the annotator—his professional reading is our next problem.

CHAPTER 3

⸭

The Professional Reader as Annotator

The Professional Reader and the Politics of Annotation

Just after Douce 104 was illustrated it was provided with a full set of marginal annotations (257 in total)—a vade mecum to the entire poem quite different from what we have seen in the illustrations, both in medium and in message. The fact that many *Piers* annotators began enthusiastically but were soon daunted by the massiveness of the job (as the petering out of annotations in some extant manuscripts suggests) or that other annotators simply made sporadic notes makes Douce's annotative witness that much more valuable.[1] But it is difficult to see what makes a cycle of annotations distinctive without some standard for comparison, so we will also be looking at the fully annotated C text manuscript closest to Douce: San Marino, Huntington Library, MS HM 143, whose notes were produced at the same time as the manuscript itself was made, circa 1400.[2] Given the full set of medieval annotations in Douce and given the circumstance of their being all, with a couple of exceptions, in the same hand, it is possible to study the annotator as a careful reader of *Piers* and to learn something of his opinions and his hermeneutics; these are often abruptly at odds with the Douce illustrator's and surprisingly different in reach and tone from the HM 143 annotator's. The Douce annotations are written, like the main text itself, in Hiberno-English,[3] and they show a homogeneity in style, method, and thematic interests, making it most likely that they are the work of a single early-fifteenth-century Anglo-Irishman—likely the scribe who copied them and also corrected the main text, but certainly *not* the scribe-illustrator.[4] HM 143's annotations are similarly in a single contemporary hand, which is also the hand of the corrector but not the hand of the main scribe either, as Carl Grindley has shown.[5] Although a casual glance at the two manuscripts side by side would cast doubts upon—indeed might provoke derisory laughter at—the "professionalism" of the Douce annotator (whose work is just plain visually sloppy), it is quite clear both from the quality of the thought in the annotations and from an error he made in placing one of them that he was not simply spontaneously annotating and that he was indeed copying from a text or rough notes *prepared in advance*.[6] Douce looks "provincial" (in the pejorative sense of the word) next to HM 143, but it is a *professional* provincialism; his job description included punctuating and correcting as well as annotating; this is not the stuff of a quill-happy owner, but real scriptorium slog-work.

In an article on late medieval reading habits, Paul Saenger and Michael Heinlen show that in a scriptorium or commercial bookshop it fell to the scribe designated as the "reader-emendator" to provide a professional reading of the work; it was he "who corrected the punctuation, added the foliation as well as [sometimes] the rubrics, and provided annotations as finding notes for the reader."[7] Saenger and Heinlen found that even incunables were often annotated, punctuated, and rubricated by hand; in fact, in their sample of eighty-two incunables, 75 percent had professionally prepared reader annotations, that is, annotation that represents "provisions for the reader, and not...as is often thought, evidence of reader use" (244). As the fifteenth century progressed, this type of professional book preparation was apparently on the rise—whether in response to consumer demand or in response to the social and interactive element of medieval readership that began to disappear only in the sixteenth century, as entirely printed texts made reading an activity of passive reception (254). The enhancing of a book's readability was seen in the Middle Ages virtually as a public duty: "the total prohibition of book annotation is a phenomenon of the epoch of printing and has only limited precedent in medieval library regulations" (254). Saenger and Heinlen cite the testimony of a fifteenth-century Italian annotator from the last leaf of an incunable printed in 1477: "I Louis, priest of Puperio presently at Pisa on 20 November 1484, according to the calendar of Florence, read and wrote the words and historical facts in alphabetically distributed series in the margins of this book to the extent that thus far I have located them in all my codices, *because notes of this sort greatly aid our memory*" ("quoniam huiusmodi modus plurimum memoriae nostrae confert") (249; emphasis added). Although Louis's annotating activity was more directly scholarly in nature than the activities of the *Piers* annotators by and large, the impetus is precisely the same: concern for the edification of future readers, with special attention to mnemonic devices. The kind of annotation one finds in *Piers* manuscripts actually derives from a scholarly tradition, however, perhaps best known from the concordantial signs of Robert Grosseteste. The *Piers* annotators look for many of the same kinds of moral and theological topics as Grosseteste did (e.g., "De paupertate," "De libero arbitrio," "De falsis religiosis," "De prophecia"), although their purpose is more practical, adapted to the reading of a vernacular text.[8] Often the job of the corrector, annotating was considered a highly responsible task, and medieval annotation appears to have been, at its best, a labor of love stimulated by the conviction of working for the corporate, social good.[9]

We are fortunate to know a fair amount about two such annotators, both apparently "publishers" of fifteenth-century English texts: John Capgrave, who copied and annotated his own works for publication, and John Shirley, who copied and/or annotated the works of others. We also know something about the annotating activities of a scribe who copied an excerpt of *Piers Plowman*, John Cok. These annotators produced much the same kind of annotation as we see in Douce: Capgrave's and Cok's clerical orientations are very like the *Piers* annotators' in mentality, although Shirley's is more obviously the orientation of a layman in whom secular and humanist tastes mingle with lay piety. All three annotators were surprisingly personal in their annotating habits (Capgrave highlighted his own birthday, Shirley used his margins to joke with his coterie, and Cok loved to sign his annotations). A quick look at their work not only illuminates the social and ecclesiastical orientations of professional readers generally, but it also reminds us that annotators were not simply anonymous technicians; there was an individual attached to the pen, most frequently a person of (sometimes surprisingly) notable social standing. To be entrusted with the job of professional reading, even of a vernacular text, one needed at least some educational credibility.

John Capgrave (1393–1464) was the author of various Latin commentaries, as well as historical and hagiographical vernacular works; we know most about his annotating with respect to his "publishing" of these.[10] He described himself as "a pore frere of þe Heremites of Seynt Austyn in þe conuent of Lenne [Lynn]," although he was actually a significant figure, rising to be prior provincial of the Augustinian order in England (1453) and writing and preparing manuscripts for numerous important patrons, including King Edward IV and Duke Humphrey. He prepared, apparently with the help of at least one scribe in the friary scriptorium, manuscripts for "publication" using his own particular *nota* mark (a marginal trefoil) and often writing verbal comments as well. Like the Douce annotator, he was particularly concerned with the deictic function of marginal annotation; that is, he felt that it was his job to *draw attention to* certain passages, often using his *nota* mark, especially in those sections where he felt an important lesson was to be learned or where his personal interests or those of his clerical order were at stake. Peter Lucas has noticed that his *nota* symbol occurs in Latin manuscripts particularly where the passage contains a form of *debere, observare, docere, facere*, and similar verbs urging notice or reponsibility (Lucas, 20). For instance, on fol. 170v of Oxford, Oriel College, MS 32, the presentation copy of his *Commentarius in Genesim* made for Duke Humphrey, Capgrave has written, "contra sacerdotes terrarios" and his *nota* mark. The highlighted passage argues that priests who manage farmlands are more likely to be priests of Pharaoh than priests of the Lord ("*Observate* ergo qui hec legitis omnes Domini sacerdotes et *videte* quid sit differencia sacerdotum ne forte qui partem habent in terra et terrenis cultibus ac studiis vacant non tam Domini quam Pharaonis sacerdotes esse videantur" [28]).

Knowing precisely how to interpret a passage thus highlighted is not always easy. As Lucas's study shows, such annotations perhaps tell us more about the annotator's agenda than about the interests of his intended reader; the above instance is actually not unusual in that the issue highlighted seems more likely to have interested Capgrave than Duke Humphrey. In fact, one is struck by the obsession with clerical interests in Capgrave's preparation of his texts for all his patrons. Lucas summarizes the pattern of annotation in manuscripts for Duke Humphrey as concerning themselves with "the Christian religion, matters of faith, morality and priestly practice." He adds, "The nature of these preoccupations is remarkable (especially in view of the fact that Duke Humphrey was primarily a politician), as is their range in terms of comparative importance, from the resurrection of Christ to the reckoning of prices" [30]. Perhaps it would be more accurate to say that such annotations tell us more about what the "publisher" *thought* the reader should be interested in. These are not simply (to modern readers, dull) "finding notes"—in fact, what one sees is that there is a polemical agenda to annotating here: for instance, Capgrave's annotations in Cambridge University Library's MS Gg. 4.12, his own Middle English chronicle prepared for Edward IV, particularly highlight "historical situations where king and clergy were opposed. Their nature and range provide a new kind of insight...into the attitude of the clergy to the new king, an attitude of respect tempered with a *desire to guide*" (Lucas, 20; emphasis added).

Clearly Capgrave felt able to use his system of *nota* marks and annotations to send his readers particular messages: in the instance of his annotations for Edward IV, the subtext of the message seems to be that the king should stay out of ecclesiastical affairs, given Capgrave's penchant for marking passages that describe confrontations between king and clergy in which the clerical side emerges triumphant. As a system for making polemical points, Capgrave's use of the marginal trefoil is a highly ingenious one; it is a model instance of what Annabel Patterson in her study *Censorship and Interpretation* has called "functional ambiguity." Patterson explains that writers "gradually developed codes of communication, partly to protect themselves from hostile and hence dangerous readings of their work, partly in order to be able to say what they had to publicly without directly provoking or confronting the authorities."[11] Capgrave's apparently innocent marginal trefoils (which might even be mistaken for decorative doodles by a casual reader) are just functionally ambiguous enough to do the trick. Nor was this habit idiosyncratic to Capgrave (Cok, too, had a personal mark, and such marks occur, usually unnoticed, in many anonymously made late medieval manuscripts as well).

Capgrave's annotations are also interesting with respect to Douce 104 for the extent to which, if we did not know who Capgrave was, we would be able to deduce, fairly accurately, much about his social orientation and professional status, and the same is true for Shirley and Cok. Capgrave liked to highlight references to the Augustinian friars, issues that might concern a convent administrator (like price-fixing), clerical reformist matters, and pious *mirabilia*.[12] Capgrave's example, then, demonstrates the relevance of modern reception theory to medieval texts, both Wolfgang Iser's view of the influence that anticipation of potential reader response has upon a writer (the "implied reader") and Hans Robert Jauss's view of the influence that reader expectations have upon how a text is received (the "horizon of expectations").[13] The medieval annotator, then, as "professional reader" mediates between these two perspectives; he is not simply responding to the text, but shaping the prospective reception of the text according to his own sense of reader expectations and "needs" (moral and polemical). Of course, in the case of Douce 104 (and HM 143) we are not dealing with an author annotating his own text, but we are certainly dealing with a manuscript produced explicitly to package a very political poem in a consciously polemical fashion. Thus, the complementary concerns of modern reception theory are crucial to understanding the intentions of the Piers annotators, who are both audience and mediators.

From the subtle polemicism of author-"publisher" Capgrave we turn to a "publisher" who provided annotations to the works of other writers out of what appears to be a mixture of literary entrepreneurialism and a genuine passion for the authors he championed. John Shirley (1366–1456) held secretarial and civil service posts during his long life and seems to have taken up his role as scribe and man of letters somewhat late in his career. To what extent his copying and publishing activities were prompted by commercial motives is still open to question: Eleanor Hammond and Aage Brusendorff both held the view that he was the manager of a commercial scriptorium (thus explaining his rental of four shops in Smithfield). But although this theory, along with the extent of his publishing activity, has been questioned recently, it seems certain that at least in the case of Lydgate, he actually collected, copied, "advertised," and promoted his authors' works.[14] Modern scholars are indebted to Shirley for much of what is known of and about certain Middle English authors, especially Chaucer and Lydgate. Shirley is perhaps best known for his versified tables of contents or "kalundares"; he composed these for some of his anthologies, like Add. 16165, which is in his own hand. These "kalundares" tell us a great deal about his motives as a publisher, about the way fifteenth-century people read, and a little about his motives for annotating.[15] The world he evokes is one of courtly love interests: "God sende hem Ioye / of hir ladye / And euery womman of hir loue" (Hammond, 196, lines 103–4; from Add. 16165), very different from the world of the men of affairs for which Capgrave was preparing manuscripts. Shirley says that he prepares his manuscripts for the pleasure and edification of his readers, and always asks that they be returned "Hoome to Shirley" afterward, which has led scholars to speculate that he may have run a kind of lending library or that his books may have been samples of his wares, available for a trial period, as it were.[16]

Most interesting, for our purposes, is his characterization of the medieval reading process: "And whane ye haue þis booke ouerlooked / ... / And þe sentence / vnderstonden / With Inne youre mynde hit fast ebounden / Thankeþe þauctoures þat þeos storyes / Renoueld haue / to youre memoryes / and þe wryter [i.e., the scribe] / for his distresse" (Hammond, 196, lines 81–95). The role of a medieval author, for Shirley, was not to create, but to "renouel" stories; the role of the reader was to bind the "sentence" within his or her memory. His annotations were meant to help in this process. The notes he provided for reader guidance show a wide-ranging concern for reader comprehension and include a wide variety of categories of annotation. Like the annotators of Douce 104 and HM 143, he provides summary annotations (like the note to *Canterbury Tales* A 747 in London, British Library, MS Harley 7333: "Howe þe oste sette þe pylgrimes to þe soper"), but he goes beyond them in providing linguistic glosses, like the note to *Canterbury Tales* A 586 ("sette þeyre aller cappe": ".i. deceyvid hem"), and source glosses, like the note to *Canterbury Tales* A 1940 ("nought was forgeten þe porter ydilnesse": ".i. of þe Romaunce of þe Roose"). Like the *Piers* annotators, he also provides ethical pointers (such as his notes to Lydgate's *Fall of Princes* in London, British Library, Harley 2251: "Take þis in mynde ye that ben juges" [fol. 140v]).[17] Perhaps most entertaining for the modern reader, however, are his "polemical" annotations, like the delightful set in Harley 2251 that testifies to Shirley's annoyance (or perhaps mock annoyance) with Lydgate's antifeminism, in notes like "Yit holdith your pees or ye wilbe shent" (fol. 146r) or "Ye have no cause to say so" (fol. 144r) or, best of all, "Be pees or I wil rende this leef out of your booke" (fol. 147), perhaps an adroit allusion to the Wife of Bath.[18]

However, the most common kind of note (functioning like Capgrave's trefoil) is the simple "nota per Shirley," which is ubiquitous in his manuscripts, occurring, for example, throughout Chaucer's *Boece* (London, British Library, MS Add. 16165). Clearly Shirley, too, felt called upon to provide for his readers guidance as to what *ought* to be noticed in his manuscripts. Of course, we do not know how his clients responded to his paternalistic zeal for the quality of their reading experience (although this zeal does not seem to have included careful attention to textual accuracy in the modern sense).[19] Nor do we know whether annotations or glosses, when they were not part of a received textual tradition, as they are in, for instance, Gower, were usually provided by bookshops as a matter of course or whether they were usually requested by certain clients. Whether the Douce annotator was writing with his patron in mind we cannot say for certain, but this appears to have been the case: he does seem to *trust* his reader to make up his own mind on many controversial issues (as we shall see) in a way that the HM 143 annotator does not.

The annotating habits of Capgrave and Shirley give us some sense of the range of responsibilities a medieval "publisher" might feel for the edification of his readers, and this is very useful for understanding the type and tone of some of the *Piers* annotations. The proprietary air with which Shirley introduces his pieces in rubrics—for example, "Lo my lordes here begynneþe a balade of gode counseyl.... Takeþe goode heed Sirs and dames how Lydeyate daun johan. þe Munk of Bury moeued of deuocyoun haþe translated. þe salme"[20]—is reminiscent of the HM 143 annotator's master-of-ceremonies style: "hyer ȝe may se shortly rehersed þe visionis to foresayd" (XV.3) or "lo what resoun sayde" (IV.108) or "a comffessour as a frere comforted mede & sayde as ȝe may rede" (III.77). So too is Shirley's manifest awareness and encouragement of literary critical skills in his readers, as for instance in his rubric to Lydgate's "Stabilnesse," which ends "nowe Iugeþe yee þat beoþe kunnyng which yowe lykeþe þe beter þe ffrench or þenglissh."[21] As we shall see, the annotator of HM 143 has a conscious and formal sense of literary matters (which is altogether absent in Douce 104); both this concern with literary presentation and the nature of its decoration link it to other commercially produced London manuscripts, especially some of those known to have been copied by the scribes identified by Ian Doyle and Malcolm Parkes as having produced the Trinity Gower.[22] Like Shirley, he addresses his readers in the plural (usually "notate" where Douce 104 would have "nota"). This is some slight evidence (corroborated by the professional quality of the manuscript) for the possibility either that HM 143 was produced in a commercial workshop for some kind of group readership (like Shirley's) or that it was produced for a religious house and with such an audience in mind. We do know that later in the fifteenth century a monk, "dan Ihon Redbery," signed HM 143,[23] and, as we shall see, the internal evidence of the annotations points to the annotator's interest (or his client's) in monastic life. However, about the specific audience of Douce and its annotator we have no external evidence other than what can be gleaned from the presence of a hand very close to our annotator's in two Hiberno-English Rolle manuscripts.[24] This evidence and the internal suggestions of a strong interest in the affairs of *secular* clergy point to the possibility that the Douce annotator was a secular cleric, perhaps in minor orders or unbeneficed—but certainly not, like the scribe-illustrator, disenchanted with clerical life.

A third possible parallel (and perhaps a more exact one) to our annotator might be John Cok, who is known *only* as a scribe and annotator (not as an author or "publisher"). He copied a *Piers Plowman* extract and pieces by Richard Rolle for Shirley in a manuscript (Cambridge, Gonville and Cauis College, MS 669*/646) that contains Shirley's autograph inscription, motto, and marginal annotations.[25] We know that Cok copied and annotated other devotional literature, much of it for Saint Bartholomew's Hospital, which he later joined as a brother. He, too, seems to have been for a long while an unbeneficed "clerk-in-waiting." He also provided the marginal annotations in Cambridge, Corpus Christi College, MS 80, the only extant copy of the verse *Graal* and *Merlin* by Henry Lovelich. As George Russell says of him, "He is a careful scribe whose work is part of his vocation" (181). He is also (so far) the only externally identifiable clerical scribe of *Piers Plowman*, which makes his witness particularly valuable, as there were obviously many more like him of whom we know nothing. Like Capgrave, he often used a particular mark for his notes, which Ian Doyle calls "a little clef or flag."[26] There is no modern study of his annotating habits and no modern edition of his annotations. At first glance, one sees why: Cok's annotations suggest merely a pious-minded scribe and clerk, but closer examination reveals a distinctive reading personality and agenda, too. For instance, his annotations in London, British Library, Add. 10392, an anthology of devotional prose he copied in 1432, reveal a strong tendency to highlight emotional passages — he notes every place in which tears of sorrow and devotion are shed (e.g., on fol. 103v, his mark appears beside "In illo tempore. Maria stabat ad monumentum foris plorans"; this sort of passage is marked repeatedly throughout the manuscript); he also loves any passage about contemplation, vision, revelation, in short any dramatic moment or affair of the (religious) heart. This is also the pattern one sees in his *Graal* and *Merlin* copying in Cambridge, Corpus Christi College, MS Cambridge 80 (see, for instance, fols. 21v, 24, 24v). Born in 1392 and still copying in 1468, Cok was apparently a man of some stature in his religious community: as we have seen, what is apparently his portrait survives (the only surviving portrait, in fact, of a *Piers* scribe), painted by no less an artist than William Abell, in the illustrated cartulary Cok himself copied for Saint Bartholomew's (figure 68). This is suggestive: it may not be surprising that a portrait of a prolific author like Capgrave survives,[27] but Cok was (as far as we know) "only a scribe." Obviously, in order to have the authority required to annotate — to read — professionally, one had to be much more than a pool typist. One had to have learning, a basis for opinions — and a system of hermeneutics. And these things are precisely what the *Piers* annotators brought to their work.

Ethical, Polemical, and Literary Responses: Types of Annotations

How did a professional reader imagine that his patron would cope with a text of the literary and polemical complexity of *Piers*? The kind of apparatus that survives in manuscripts like Douce 104 and Huntington 143 indicates that the *ordinatio* of the poem, as transmitted in paleographical and textual markers,[28] was considered insufficient for informed reading and *rereading* of such a text. Modern readers approaching the reading-aid annotations of a manuscript like Douce 104 or HM 143 will be disappointed not to find instances of the kind of colorful, subjective reactions to the text that Charles Plummer made famous in his article on the marginalia of Gaelic-Irish scribes.[29] In his impersonalized use of the guidance annotation form the Douce annotator shows that his cultural and hermeneutical roots are likely in the "Anglo" half of the Anglo-Irish equation; however, although not brimming with local color, these are not wholly "impersonal" productions. Although he adopts a mask of objectivity, no exercise of this sort is ever purely objective. The next two sections of this chapter will be concerned with "unmasking" the professional reader's identity and agenda—getting a sense of the educational and ideological equipment such a reader brought to the poem.

There are four general types of annotations that occur in Douce 104 and HM 143 (and in many other *Piers* manuscripts, although often more sporadically): (1) *narrative reading aids* (plot or topic summaries, such as "nota houu p(e)res went apylgrimage" [D, VIII.56]);[30] (2) *ethical pointers* (such as "nota þat þer was no man þat my3th towch godes body" [D, XX.79]); (3) *polemical comments* ("be war of fals freris" [D, XV.78]); and (4) *literary responses* (ranging from simple genre markers, such as "pers plowghman-is testament" [D, VIII.94], to complex contextual irony).[31] These are modern labels, but they closely approximate the distinctions medieval readers made themselves: for instance, some manuscripts show paleographical evidence that scribes deliberately distinguished types of annotations; HM 143 itself has a system of brackets and marks for the flourisher that distinguishes, for instance, narrative reading aids from ethical pointers (parallel slashes before the former and L-shaped brackets before the latter; these marks will be reproduced in citing the annotations that follow).[32] Second, the medieval literary theories of different *modi* within the same text correlate well with the annotation types in Douce and in HM 143, which is hardly surprising, since medieval readers derived much of their sense of literary genre from the Bible. For instance, according to Alexander of Hales, the important biblical *modi* were the following:[33]

1. preceptive mode (*modus praeceptivus*), found in the Pentateuch;
2. historical and exemplifying mode (*modus historicus* and *exemplificativus*), found in the historical books;
3. exhorting mode (*modus exhortivus*), found in the sapiential books;
4. revelatory mode (*modus revelativus*), found in the prophetic books; and
5. orative mode (*modus orativus*), found in the Psalter.

These *modi* however, were different from the Aristotelian system of classifying genres of reasoning, which are also relevant to *Piers*. Langland, like Dante, consciously used both the affective and the rational modes;

they both, apparently, would have agreed with Aquinas, who disapproved of the disjunction between rational science and affective wisdom advocated by Alexander and his disciples, a view reflected in Saint Thomas's approach to exegesis in which, for instance, "the point is laboured that Job and the Apostle Paul employ the 'disputative mode' (*modus disputativus*)."[34] The annotator of HM 143, for instance, who appears to have had more formal rhetorical education than Douce's annotator had, presented the poem so as to emphasize most of the *modi* that Dante does, for instance, in his description in the *Epistle to Can Grande* of his *forma tractandi* in the *Commedia*: "The form or mode of treatment is poetic, fictive, descriptive, digressive and transumptive; and moreover it is definitive, divisive, probative, refutative and exemplificative."[35] Had Langland left us a description of his *forma tractandi*, it would likely not have been much different.

All of these categories are helpful in making sense of the massive amount of didactic annotation in Douce 104, as well as in other manuscripts. Langland's use of "preceptive" points is highlighted in notes like *D*'s: "nota to low god abow al þyngis & þi neghtbo<wr>" (XIX.96); historical or exemplifying points are found in notes such as "houu god ȝaw Salamon grace & tok hit from hym ayayn" (III.323). Exhortations are regularly both signaled and heightened by *D*: "madys wed maydis & wodous wed wodous" (virgins should wed virgins; and widows, [other] widows [X.278]); and even more often by *H*, who frequently adds a second-person pronoun (often in imitation of Langland) to stress his point: "// notate ȝe ryche" (I.175) or "// notate hyer how ȝe schull make festes" (XII.97). Prophetic material, which in Marie Claire Uhart's description of types of *Piers* annotations forms one of the largest categories, is sometimes signaled by *D*: "kyne low shall turne & consiens to-gedyr" (III.451), but more persistently and explicitly by *H*: "// lo how iewe schull conuerte for ioye" (III.454), "prophetia petri" (V.165), and "prophecia" (viii.349). Prayers are always noted ("nota de pater noster" [Douce, XV.245]), as is any *divisio*: "nota de branches þat bringyþ mane to slowyþ" (Douce, VII.70), "nota de þre þyngis þat puttyþ a man out of hys hous" (Douce, XIX.296)—here is the medieval love of dividing and enumerating in all its glory and pedantry. Finally, the disputative mode is especially noted by *H* ("Question" [XIII.182], "Responsio" [XIII.193], and "Culorum" [conclusion, XI.249]), giving the impression that he was at least aware of or mildly interested in university methods of thought. *D*'s education—or perhaps his sense of the education of his implied reader—was far less academic in every sense.

The polemical comments tell us something about the ideological climate in which *Piers* was read: specifically the social, political, and ecclesiastical comments Langland provoked. Wendy Scase has studied some of the anticlerical comments among the annotations in a variety of *Piers* manuscripts, and she concludes that many of Langland's early readers show an eagerness to participate in the language of polemic, which she calls the "new anticlericalism." Scase is interested in "the new blurring between clergy and laity" and argues that the poem's anticlerical polemic becomes a source of authority for lay readers.[36] However, it is important to underline that an annotator writing "anticlerical" comments was *not necessarily a layperson*, nor was he necessarily writing for a lay audience. Furthermore, what we have in most *Piers* manuscripts is the work not of owners (lay or otherwise) but of professional readers — and what we might call the professional literacy industry was still heavily "clericalized" even by the time Douce was made, in the sense that large numbers of scribes (and this would include many scribe-illustrators) were or had been clerks or aspiring clerks at some time. Such men, for a variety of reasons, had often not gone on to higher orders or acquired benefices, so they became members of that amorphous, middle group to which Langland himself apparently belonged. We have seen that the Douce's scribe-illustrator apparently belonged to a particular category of this amorphous group: clericist civil servants with legal training. He shows great comfort with Latin abbreviations (see, for instance, his colophon on the last folio) and obviously has some ecclesiastical training, while both annotators under discussion here, *D* and *H*, exhibit distinctively clerkly mentalities, all the while indulging in "anticlericalism." "Interclerical" is, in fact, a much better adjective for most of the satire and controversy we find in such annotations.

D notes a variety of polemical social comments (e.g., "houu pore gentill beþ refusit," i.e., for promotion in the church [V.78]) and, more platitudinously, political ones ("houu þe kyng shold lowe his co*m*myns" [V.181]). However, it is ecclesiastical comment that really interests him. Some of it is anticlerical (e.g., "nota de lewyt pres*s*tis" [VII.30]), but some of it is positive, like the "nota de monks" (VI.151), which highlights Langland's praise of the strict asceticism of monastic life. There are also comments on ecclesiological issues, like "houu sylu*er* & gold shall no3t go owr se<e>" (IV.125), referring to the passage about "Rome-rennares," those who take bribes to the papal court to procure clerical appointments.[37] In fact, this was a contentious issue in Ireland, where the Gaelic-Irish clergy were more likely to be "Rome-runners" than were the Anglo-Irish, and there may be some local pique associated with *D*'s comment here.[38] Such comments are typical of the concerns of the secular clergy, and there are also a few annotations wholly in Latin, like "nota de molle pastore" (which is, however, gleaned from the text: see IX.264a), pointing up Langland's sharply reformist diatribe against negligent bishops. None of these kinds of annotations would rule out a lay annotator, but they look clerically inspired. Indeed, much of the most virulent criticism of the clergy came from the clergy, and, as we shall see, the profile that emerges from a study of patterns of annotation *across full-length copies of the poem* suggests clerical rather than lay interests.

Educational differences are perhaps most evident in relation to literary response annotations. Above all, such annotations seem to mark levels of engagement with the text, and even "professional readers" show a keen sense of participation in such responses.[39] One marker of participation is the annotator's rare adoption of the first person (e.g., D, V.9 or XXII.346). Another indicator is the kind of fervored assent in notes like *D*'s "nota de woo of pore pepill þat wonnyth in por howsyn & haþ childyr" (IX.83), where the comment is not textually gleaned[40] and is far more specific than usual ("nota de pore" would have done). Similarly *D* often expresses enthusiastic assent with Langland on some of his most crotchety assertions: "nota de beggers & bidders beþ noght in þe bull" (IX.61), where the annotator has made Langland's harsh judgment even starker by a textual gleaning that omits the poet's careful qualifier (which was that all beggars are included in the pardon if they are *truly* needy).

Most intriguingly (and reassuringly for modern readers), *D* rarely lets a humorous passage in the poem go by without a comment: for instance, his "nota de ryghtfull rich" is placed beside the Latin of Patience's (characteristically kindly) joke that such specimens are rare (XV.281). His last note to the poem suggests unselfconscious enjoyment of Langland's satire, especially in his use of the first person, which is usually screened out: "nota how þe frer salwt *owr* women" (XXII.346; emphasis added), next to Peace's comic indignation about the amorous conquests of the friars. And again, even though the main text of Douce 104 universalizes (apparently deliberately) Will's run-in with Elde by changing "myn" to "men-*nys*" (XXII.183), the annotator is still clearly delighted by the play on receding hairlines: "nota de helde [old Age] yede [went] ower men<ys> hedys" (183).[41] This sort of note is a helpful reminder that medieval readers were not necessarily the stern moralists we have so often been told they were in twentieth-century criticism[42]—there is no moral, polemical, or even narrative purpose (given that the Douce text leaves Will out of the scene) for such a note. The only plausible reason for its existence is delight. He apparently also smiled when he annotated the Feast of Patience passage as he did: "nota de sowr lof" (XV.56), a delightful way of highlighting Will's enforced penance, or when he commented on Will's joke at Liberum Arbitrium's expense: "nota de hou mony nam*is* a byschop hath" (XVI.201)—Liberum Arbitrium was not amused, but *D* was. He also shows an appreciation of irony, as in the note about the "ryghtfull rich" quoted earlier, and in notes like the deceivingly simple one at XVI.284: "charyte," placed beside Will's bitter observation that he has lived long in London and never seen it. Both *D* and the more conservative *H* highlight such comments regularly, including the sardonic, unedifying remarks of characters like the cutpurse (VII.283) and the brewer (XXI.396). Since it is certainly not the case that speakers are always dutifully noted no matter what they are saying, one can only assume that these comic moments appealed to the annotators. And only simple curiosity or current topicality accounts for some notes—for instance, *D*'s neutral "nota de newfeyrs" at VI.376. Since "newfeyrs" are not explicitly criticized in the passage, one can only assume that *D* was as intrigued as modern readers have been by Langland's vivid account of what really went on in taverns—in England, at least.

A comparison of *D*'s and *H*'s responses to Langland's allegory and imagery is especially striking because *D* ignores the role of Will in the narrative, while *H* treats him as the organizing principle of the poem. Does this betray a difference in literary education or simply in literary temperament? *H* shows some awareness of medieval literary theory on the subject of poetic imagery, but *D* is fascinated by Langland's handling of the allegory—not theoretically, but practically. He has likely not had the same formal literary training that *H* has, but he has had extensive experience with religious allegory (a subject that, some modern readers might be pleased to hear, does not interest *H* in the slightest). Both show a keen interest in "resemblance-making" or *assimilatio* (best translated, as it is translated in Middle English, as "likening"), often associated in medieval theory with *ymaginatio*.[43] *Convenientia* is the word most often used in medieval literary theory, according to J. B. Allen, to describe well-made *assimilatio*, in which the relationship between *res* and *representatio* is considered accurate. Medieval literary theory, then, had a conscious concern with resemblance-making techniques and a standard by which to judge whether the "likening" was done well. *H* especially shows an interest in this sort of judgment, but at no point does either annotator try to explicitly *interpret* Langland's allegories, morally or otherwise—in fact, there is no evidence in these annotations (or in others of which I am aware) of what modern scholars have come to call Robertsonian readings of the text. *H*, especially, however, remarks on allegorical names when they occur (e.g., "// loke hyer what [*pers*] wyf hy3te & his sone & his do3ter" [VIII.79]), and he makes explicit reference to imagery in notes like "⌊ notate im*agine*" (XVI.253), written beside the kind of image that would hardly catch a modern reader's attention (in this passage priests are discussed as the "root" of right faith: where the root is rotten, no good fruit will grow—not one of Langland's more original observations). Even more telling is his note to XIV.166: "⌊ ymagenynge," explicitly linked to Langland's use of the Middle English term "likening" for *assimilatio*: "Ac longe-lybbyng men *lykened* men lyuynge / To briddes and to bestes, as here bokkes telleth" (168–69; emphasis added). The speaker here is Imaginatif (a figure who receives a good deal of notice from both *H* and *D*).

H was a very literary annotator, obviously a rhetorically trained reader of texts. He identified (centuries ahead of modern scholars) Will as the fictional principle of unity in the poem: in medieval theoretical terms, Will is the *actor*, and *H* never draws attention to the *auctor*.[44] *D*, however, seems to make a direct distinction between the two in the C.V "autobiographical" passage, as we shall see. His primary "literary" response is enjoyment (not analysis) of the imagery he finds memorable and a passionate concern with sociopastoral injustices and affairs, as the last section of this chapter will demonstrate.

The Annotators of Douce 104 and Huntington 143: Two Professional Readers at Work

The reading strategies of the two annotators are distinctive in a variety of literary and thematic ways, and both have their pitfalls. *H*'s policy of following Will through the text works well in sections of the poem where Will is central, but in other sections he is left clinging to scraps of the framing dream narrative like the survivor of a shipwreck, a feeling that all readers of *Piers* will identify with to some extent. *D*'s policy works well in controversial and discursive passages, especially where questions of speaker authority and provocative issues arise. Take, for example, the notes to passus XI and XII, which contain Recklessness's diatribe, probably the most doctrinally provocative section of the C text. Generally, *D*—as both corrector and annotator—gives an impression of complete confidence in his reading audience in all matters but dialect, whereas in HM 143 even the most obvious textual error is carefully flagged by *H* to prevent reader confusion,[45] and the annotations are formulated in such a way that there can be no mistake about the degree of authority the speaker has. This difference may indicate that *D* was preparing his text for someone he knew, while *H*'s audience was less individually defined (as we have seen, it may have been made for a communal, perhaps a monastic audience). In any event, in radical sections of the poem *H* makes it clear that what we are being told is *fictionalized*, while *D*'s concern is to highlight both allegorical speakers and what is being disputed. These differences are perhaps what one might expect simply by the look of the two manuscripts. *H*'s notes look and read like professional work—sophisticated in paleographical and in literary terms, safe in what they highlight doctrinally. *D*'s read more like they were intended for the private reading of a person the annotator knew well and trusted intellectually (and the fact that the manuscript is illustrated does suggest a known client). *D*'s notes are minimalist and economic on general points, keenly responsive to controversial matters without legislating orthodoxy or partisanship. (*H*, for instance, is much more virulently antimendicant, where *D* is more balanced.) *H* was most definitely a "professional reader"; *D* knew what professional reading required and managed to achieve it in all areas but the paleographical (where, to be frank, he made a bit of a mess). In any case, *D* seems to have cared intensely about his task: his enthusiasm is steady and is constantly being renewed, even during the last few passus, where *H*'s wanes obviously. (In XXI, *D* gives a whopping twenty-three notes to *H*'s six; in XXII, *D* provides twenty to *H*'s paltry two). And like the illustrator, *D* seems to have known the poem intimately and grasped it with certainty — and (judging by the variety of his ink colors) returned to it again and again, adding more notes each time.

Some of these differences can be seen in their handling of the theological audacity of Recklessness's challenge to orthodox Christian beliefs about salvation and clerical learning at the end of XI:

D:	XI.180–end	*H*: XI.167–end
171	**(Fortune's Wheel)**	167 // hyere fortune raueschid will & schewed hym a myrour þat hyȝte myddylȝerd
180	nota de youth	
190	**(Recklessness)**	
196	nota de rechles	239 // hyer hard sentence for techeres ȝif þay leue noȝt wel
213	nota de salomon	
235a	nota seld is hit sey clerkis lew as þey techyn	249 ⌊ Culorum
235a	**(Clerk)**	312 // hyer ȝougthe sette at noȝt al þis
255	nota of þe þefe þat heng on þe cros by owr lord	
295	nota ploghmen & herdis & pore commynys	

D's first three notes uncritically highlight the words of two audacious speakers (Concupiscencia Carnis and Recklessness), which the more conservative *H* has tiptoed around. *H*, by contrast, characteristically sticks to the storyline rather than the debate, efficiently and even uncontroversially summing up the whole passage with "hyere fortune raueschid will..."; shortly thereafter he puts a swift end to the passus with a reductive narrative summary note: "hyer ȝougthe sette at noȝt al þis." In *H*'s reading we are firmly reminded of the fictional status and the *un*authoritative nature of the voices and opinions in the scene (Fortune is in control and Youth has dismissed sound advice and that is that).[46]

D's notes, however, highlight not just the shock value of Concupiscencia Carnis's and Recklessness's comments, but also the downright confrontational passage in which Recklessness cites Solomon as a prime example of a godly, learned man who is now in Hell (XI.221); thus his simple "nota de salomon" at line 213 is drawing attention to — not avoiding and certainly not censoring — the kind of contentious issue that made *Piers* such an explosive text. Similarly, his note at line 255 points up Recklessness's pugnacious indignation that the thief's last-minute conversion earned him a spot in heaven denied to lifelong ascetics like John the Baptist and Isaiah. Finally, in this passus, he highlights the climax of Recklessness's diatribe in which, on the basis of Langland's strategic

Professional Reader as Annotator

misquotation of Augustine (line 290a), he announces that the learned are soonest "yraueschid" from orthodoxy, while plowmen, shepherds, and poor common people are soonest saved. *D*'s note at line 295 not only directly flags this passage, but raises a subject of passionate concern in Ireland: poverty.[47] When one compares *H*'s "hyer ʒougthe sette at noʒt al þis," there can be little doubt about which annotator was more at ease with Langland's indelicate probing of Christian doctrine of salvation and its socially subversive subtext.

The suspicion that *H* is trying not to notice the actual content of what he is summarizing becomes certitude in passus XII, where he tenders three fairly innocuous notes to *D*'s nine:

D:	XII	*H*:	XII
1	nota de elde & holynys	18	∟ notate hic freris
5	**(Elde/Will)**	73	// hyer cam a trogian & sayde baw for bokes
19	nota de wower*e*	97	// notate hyer how ʒe schull make festes
38a	nota houu scryptow*r* prechytte		
73	**(Trajan)**		
79	nota de troian þe trew hemp*erowr* & a pagan		
100	nota de me*n* þ*at* makyth festys		
118	þe lawe of lowe		
139	po(ue)rte is best yef pacie*n*s h*i*t follouu		
210	nota of rich man		
225	nota de rich lordis		

H has given up trying to follow the narrative and clearly has no intention of taking notice of Recklessness's unseemly debate about salvation. Until line 73, when Trajan appears and comes to the annotator's aid (we can hear his sigh of relief: action at last), he contents himself with a single antimendicant comment — always a safe subject — at line 18.[48] By contrast *D* annotates the opening lines of the passus, which set the allegorical stage and contain just the kind of allegorical punning he enjoys:

> nota de elde & holynys   "Alace ey" qu*o*d Elde: and holynesse boþe, / "That wit schal torne to wrachednesse for Wil hath h*i*s wille." (Douce, fol. 55; XII.1–2; modern quotation marks added)

Then in place of *H*'s antimendicant comment at line 18, *D* writes at line 19:

83

nota de wower*e*	"By my faith, frere," quod y, "ȝe fare lyke þe woware / That wilneth nat þe wedewe bote for to welde here godes." (Pearsall, *C-Text*, XII.19–20)

This is entirely typical of *D*'s nontheoretical enjoyment of "likening." Moreover, it is not that he is incapable of antimendicant comment (indeed he understands antimendicant ecclesiology very well, judging by his notes to XXII), but his is not an antimendicant agenda—as the illustrator's was. Rather, it is that here, as elsewhere, he seeks the word or image that will encapsulate a whole passage and trigger it in a reader's mind—in short, the most imagistically vivid mnemonic device. This note gives us some sense of how he intended his annotations to be used. When annotating XII.19, *D* could easily have written "nota de fals frers" or the equivalent (as *H* did) to draw attention to the literal event (a confessor deserting a confessee down on his luck), but he chose to note the image in Langland's simile. Now such an annotation would only be meaningful to a *re*reader and a ruminator—it would be no good to a topic hunter—and this makes *D*'s annotations rather distinctive among pedestrian Middle English annotators who normally create "finding device" annotations in long works. Moreover, his notes can be memorable simply because *D* enjoys homely imagery more than moral abstractions; in passus XII only two of the nine notes contain no concrete imagery. *D*'s sensitivity to the affective power of concrete imagery makes him a judicious packager of the poem. If this is not typical "professional reading," it is a good deal more thoughtful.

D's next two notes confirm his willingness to countenance some of Langland's most radical passages: "nota houu scripto*wr* prechytte" (line 38a) and "nota de troian þe trew hemp*erowr* & a pagan" (line 79). The "matter" Scripture preaches on is, of course, "Many are called, but few are chosen" (Matt. 22:14), which Langland allegorizes embryonically as "multi" and "pauci" in such a way that a *completely* non-Latin literate reader (or more likely, hearer) would not grasp the meaning. Will, however, does (the little Latin he learned in his youth evidently being enough [I.139]) and trembles with anxiety (XII.48). The dreamer is still in his Recklessness phase, and when Langland teasingly or forebodingly refuses to translate fully, as here, he is at his most provocative, but *D* is unperturbed.

Passing over Will's response, as usual, *D* next points out "troian þe trew hemp*erowr* & a pagan"—which has a very different emphasis from *H*'s "hyer cam a trogian & sayde baw for bok*es*" (line 73). *H* is again just following the narrative and apparently enjoys Trajan's anti-intellectualism (which, like antimendicantism, seems to have been a safe, ubiquitous satirical topic). Story and character are *H*'s brief, and these are safe paths through treacherous doctrinal territory. But *D*'s note, unlike *H*'s, is not simply textually gleaned—it is an attempt (slightly clumsy) at an explanatory gloss, a rarer kind of annotation in *Piers* texts than in Chaucer texts. It supplies information (that Trajan was an emperor) not given in the text, but more important, it comes out in support of Trajan as "trew." Modern readers may perhaps not realize how troubling the issue of Trajan's salvation could be. In Douce 104, the other reader response we have, the illustrator's, is entirely negative. Trajan is represented as a pagan—and therefore grotesquely, although the illustrator has at least anticipated *D*'s conscious and unusual historicism to the extent of showing Trajan in a pagan headdress (figure 27).[49] Trajan's story was a crux for theologians debating issues of grace and salvation, and discreet visionary writers seem to have avoided pronouncing upon it. For instance, when Mechtild of Hackeborn, the late-thirteenth-century German visionary, was asked by a friar to verify Trajan's salvation, she responded that God did not wish it to be known as yet.[50] But, although Langland makes him rather a forceful—indeed boisterous—character (something the illustrator has reacted to by giving him an unusually large and iconographically ironic speaking gesture),[51] he wanted him to be convincing, and *D* understood this. His enthusiastically affirming, historicizing note is placed not, like *H*'s, at Trajan's Scrooge-like entrance, but partway through his speech, beside the explanation of Saint Gregory's role in gaining Trajan his freedom from Hell. This is a good instance of rival readings: the Douce illustrator and the annotator are diametrically opposed on the problem of Trajan's authority. It is probably no accident that *D* thus emphasizes the authoritative figure behind this story, Saint Gregory, rather than the comic anti-intellectualism of Trajan's character, which is what so delighted *H*.

Finally in this passus, there is the theme of poverty, handled differently again by each of the annotators. The point that when one holds a feast one should invite not social peers but the poor caught the eye of both *D* and *H*, but only *D*, showing an interest often expressed in Anglo-Irish poetry, is captivated by the topic and closely follows the passus's 150 more lines on poverty, charity, and the need to distribute riches. He highlights the poignant little discussion of Christ traveling in a poor pilgrim's guise to Emmaus (118 ff.) and the passage that develops the view that the suffering of the poor will be rewarded (139 ff.), not to mention two angry outbursts against rich who hoard. None of this catches the eye of *H*, which is typical in itself of a certain kind of "professionalism"—"professional" slacking off on a commissioned job that the scribe sometimes apparently found tedious, especially toward the end of a passus or of the manuscript itself. Annotations were the first aspect of a text to suffer when professional boredom set in, because they were most disposable.[52] So it is even in this pejorative sense that HM 143 has indeed the look of a professional manuscript. We have seen that *H*'s notes are systematized with a series of brackets, while *D*'s are written haphazardly and unevenly

Kathryn Kerby-Fulton

(without ruling) into margins far too small (apparently even before binding)[53] and often right over top of the illustrations. But it is *D* who shows constant stamina for the text.

H and *D* were apparently both clerks, but with important differences; a comparison of the two annotators in passus V illuminates the distinctive ecclesiastical mentalities they bring to the poem:

D:	V	H:	V
9	I had noo wyll to do gode	8	// hyer concience & raysoun a ratyd wille for his lollynge
61	nota de clerkys		
78	houu pore gentill beþ refusit	35	// hyer wille answerid to rayson
112	nota de pestelens cummyþ for syne		
124	**(Tom Stowe)**	104	// hyer wente wille to churche & ful aȝen a sclepe
140	houu prechowrs shold do as þey prechyth	115	// hyer raysoun prechede
		146	⌞ notate Religiosi
169	bibil [main scribe's hand, in red]	165	prophetia petri
178	cronicil [main scribe's hand, in red]	168	(crown)
181	houu þe kyng schold lowe his commynys		

H's interest in Will and in narrative summary notes (which account for four of the six verbal notes in the passus, indicated paleographically by the double slash) hardly needs comment by now. His single ethical pointer (distinguished by the L-shaped bracket at line 146) highlights monastic issues, as do his two annotations to the prophecy that a king will come and reform the monasteries (at lines 165 and 168). Monastic concerns always pique his interest in a way that secular clerical concerns do not. Most interesting here is his use of a marginal illustration (the crown) in the style of Exchequer document *signa* (see figure 69, no. 10) or of Matthew Paris's chronicles, suggesting either legal or historical influence on his writing habits.[54] His historical leanings, of which we will see more shortly, along with his unflagging interest in monastic affairs and the evidence of a monk's name in a later fifteenth-century hand on the flyleaf,[55] point suggestively toward a monastic audience for *H*'s work.

D, on the other hand, is interested in preaching activities in the passus and does little to help the reader with the narrative. The first three annotations in both manuscripts cover the C text's unique "autobiographical" passage—but in entirely different ways. *H* sees the "I" speaker of this section the same way that he has seen him elsewhere in the poem, as Will, the dreamer. He cleverly and comically captures all the moral (and perhaps ecclesiastical) ambiguities of this confrontation with Reason and Conscience by using the word "lollynge" to describe what it is about Will's life that so irritates his interrogators.⁵⁶ *D*'s attempt to summarize this same section is also, like *H*'s, not textually gleaned, and exhibits the same kind of creativity, although characteristically he hits upon an allegorical pun: "I had noo wyll to do gode" (9). Not only does *D* play upon the dreamer's name here (the allegorical significance of Will's name, of course, would hardly escape the notice of a medieval reader)⁵⁷ in order to point up the idea that salvation depends on the motivation of the *affectus*, but he also, surprisingly, and for the only time in the notes, uses the first-person singular pronoun "I." As we have seen, he normally takes no notice of Will, and when he feels compelled to summarize a segment of the action in which Will is a key player, he often generalizes (e.g., "nota houu þey soght dowell" [X.4; emphasis added]). So this "I" is odd. There are two possible explanations: either he has been momentarily caught up in the participatory impetus of medieval visionary literature,⁵⁸ consciously or unconsciously identifying with the dreamer, or he has recognized that the passage is different in kind from Will's other self-referential passages in being (or at least consciously appearing) more explicitly autobiographical. This last possibility is of a piece with the illustrator's handling of the scribal figure (figure 24). Indeed, *D* shows such acumen in reading Langland's autobiographical passage, not just in his first note, but also in the other two, that one wonders whether he shared many of Langland's assumptions and perhaps the same socioecclesiastical background. Cut adrift from the passage that they highlight they look innocuous enough, but the "nota de clerkys" (61) and "houu pore gentill beþ refusit" (78) draw attention to a passage that most modern critics would prefer to sink into obscurity (V.61–81). This is Langland's diatribe against the upward mobility of bondmen's children, and worse (he suggests), their bastards, and although at least part of the passage (78–81) is a justifiable attack on simony and bribery generally, lines like "For sholde no clerke be crouned but yf he come were / Of frankeleynes and fre men and of folke ywedded. / Bondemen and bastardus and beggares children, / Thyse bylongeth to labory" (63–66) are stark indications of the limitations of Langland's social liberalism. While it is clear that Langland wrote these lines in the hope of counteracting the inaccurate reputation for social radicalism that the rebels of 1381 had given his poem, this can only explain, not excuse, such views for modern readers.⁵⁹ However, *D* knew no such squeamishness. Like Langland himself, *D* was capable of profound sympathy with the sufferings of the poor and great idealism about the merits of voluntary poverty, but he, too, had no quarrel with the rigid social hierarchy of his time. All of his sympathies, like Langland's, are here with the "pore gentill" that are being "refusit" as the aspirations and ready money of the lower classes change the face of society. The little we know of the socioeconomic profiles of late medieval English scribes, many of whom were temporaries and pieceworkers in the literacy trades, suggests that such resentment of those who had benefices was not uncommon. *H*, by contrast, is silent on all these prickly matters. Issues of advancement of the kind that concern secular clergy do not concern him, as well they might not if he was working on a monastic commission for a well-established London bookshop or had other monastic associations.

Both annotators exhibit clerkish mentalities in that the kinds of social issues that would interest a layperson are of little interest to them. For instance, neither annotator picks out for comment the social domestic advice that forms a considerable chunk of Reason's sermon (which immediately follows the autobiographical passage in passus V). The illustrator, by contrast and as we have seen, devotes the passus's only illustration to highlighting this advice with his portrait of Tom Stowe (figure 6), who (at lines 130–31) has been told to "fette Felyce hoem fram wyuene pyne"[60]—a bit part at best, although the legal subject was irresistible to the illustrator. The contrast here between what captures the attention of the two annotators and what has captivated the illustrator could not be more striking, and it tells us that annotation was a clerkly—or at least clerkish—activity. But whoever chose to single out Tom Stowe was thinking more as a layperson (or as a legal professional); perhaps he was also imagining (pretty successfully) what a lay audience might be interested in seeing. As always, it is difficult to know whether the Jauss model or the Iser model applies; that is, is it his own response or is it that of his "implied reader" that influences the artistic choice? The analogy with Capgrave, again, suggests the former.

By the time he reaches line 146, *H* has switched into Latin (beginning with his "⌐ notate Religiosi"), perhaps because he sees controversy on the horizon: "And sethe he radde religioun here reule to holde, / Laste þe kyng and his consayl ȝoure comunes apayre" (lines 144–45, which build toward the prophecy at 168), or simply because he feels that only the Latin literate would or should be interested in the upcoming section, which offers an idealized view of cloistered life set against a harsh condemnation of the *superbia* and *vanitas* of monks. Just before the prophecy that the king will confiscate the properties of the regular clergy, *H* drops his bracket system altogether and writes "prophetia petri" (line 165).[61] He had annotated the prophecy at the end of passus III (line 476) exactly the same way, which is intriguing because in neither instance is Piers speaking, nor does either prophecy involve the pope. As Anne Middleton has shown, many early readers thought of Piers's role as more extensive than it is,[62] but it seems unlikely that a reader as careful as *H* about following the narrative and designating speakers would mistake Piers for Conscience and Reason, the speakers of these two prophecies (indeed his preceding annotations in both cases make this implausible). Rather, it looks as if *H* strongly associated these prophecies with *Piers Plowman* (and they are both unknown to modern scholars outside of Langland's text, despite the fact that they are written in a recognizable tradition).⁶³ With the stern criticism of the possessioners (i.e., the monastic orders) that develops from line 146 to line 180 (nearly the end of the passus), it is perhaps no wonder (especially if he is working for a monastic patron) that H seeks refuge in Latin and finally in symbolism (at line 168 he simply drew a crown). In fact, this strategy may be a clever instance of functional ambiguity—Exchequer documents dealing with matters of royal financial jurisdiction and concern would be marked in exactly this way, and disendowment was *precisely* this kind of issue (the Exchequer, for instance, dealt with the king's interests in the case of the Templars, a case that Langland himself highlights). From this standpoint, the marginal crown becomes a good deal more than a "finding device"— something more like a prophetic warning in itself.⁶⁴

D has absolutely no interest in the problems of the monasteries, which may suggest that he (or his patron) was not a member of the regular clergy or concerned with disendowment issues (as H appears to be). In this and other issues (like antimendicantism) he is less polemical, more evenhanded. But the scribe, not the annotator, of Douce 104 had already attempted two primitive source glosses written in red ink beside the prophecy: "bibil" (169) and "cron*i*cil" (178). This sort of gloss, which looks decidedly clumsy next to the detailed source glosses in *Canterbury Tales* manuscripts⁶⁵ and appears nowhere else in the manuscript, is mystifying. One can only assume that the prophecy struck the scribe (-illustrator) as especially important (or especially controversial) and that he wanted to highlight its authorities as, in a different way, H did by attributing the prophecy to *Piers*. (Of course, H's attribution is perhaps just his usual conservatism at work—a controversial prophecy attributed to a fictional character seems less controversial somehow.) Although both annotators round off their treatment of the passus by highlighting the king's role, it is typical of both that H points silently to his power (with the marginal crown "annotation"), while D boldly points to his responsibilities (one is reminded of Capgrave's penchant for highlighting forms of *debere*).

These same patterns emerge again and again across the two manuscripts. For instance, the kind of interest D takes in marriage is of a social and theological kind, such as one might expect from someone trained in pastoral care. Langland's extensive discussion of marriage in passus X provokes three notes from D (and none from H whatsoever). D's notes betray no interest in property, sexuality, or romance (all topics covered by Langland), but rather in the social and moral ramifications of illegitimate children or ill-advised marriage: "nota de me*n* þat bene gatten out of matrimony" (line 208); "nota de marryagis wyt in degree" (line 248); "madys wed maydis & wodous wed wodous" (line 278). Again in the Tree of Charity passage, the levels of perfection ranged according to marital status interest D mainly theologically; his note is more interesting dialectically than it is socially: "nota de wedlok woddowot and maydenot" (XVIII.86). One would not expect a monastic annotator or an annotator working on a monastic commission (if that is what *H* is) to take an interest in practical issues surrounding marriage, and indeed *H* does not. Nor does the Tree of Charity passage attract his attention for other reasons; he supplies one note to it where *D* supplies six.

Similarly, as Langland wanders into an increasingly monastic area of concern in XVII, arguing that laity ought to withhold further endowments from monks who already have too much, and on to the warning exemplum of the fall of the Templars, *D* loses interest and *H* switches into Latin (six of his ten notes are in Latin). Always somewhat uncomfortable with controversy, *H* emphasizes Langland's authorities here: the notes "Thobi" (line 41) and "Jop contra religiosi" (line 52) take us, in Latin, through the brashest part of the passage. No doubt this tactic is strategic, because as soon as Langland quoted Job, he (Langland) wrote, rather cheekily, "Yf lewede men knewe this Latyn, a litel they wolden auysen hem / Ar they amorteysed eny more for monkes or for chanons" (lines 53–54), which may have encouraged *H* to stick to Latin. *H* took much more interest in this passus generally, perhaps because of the highly monastic content of XVII. Monastic writers and readers generally and traditionally show an interest in prophecy, marvels, dreams, Mohammed, and missions to the infidel—the stuff of countless monastic chronicles and miscellanies—and all this *H* found in passus XVII in plenty.[66]

By contrast, like most secular clerks, *D* has less taste (and perhaps less leisure) for the exotic. And *D* has less interest in purely abstract theological discussions, like the infamous fist analogy explaining the Trinity (XIX.109–66) and the torch analogy that follows it (167–223), both of which are noted by *H* but not by *D*. *D*, however, takes a keen interest in practical theology and loves enumerations of points of doctrine or instances of *divisio* (e.g., see—if one has the fortitude—his notes to XIX.296; XXI.75, 86, 88, 92; XXI.276; and XIV.205—the list could be multiplied easily). He is also rather obviously pious, as indicated in notes like the one to XX.79 (cited earlier) or his "nota de god-ys body in fowrme of bred" (XXI.385), neither of which have parallels in *H*. (*D* may even be registering sensitivity to Lollard issues here.)

In conclusion, then, it appears that Douce 104 was annotated by a secular clerk, probably unbeneficed or in minor orders, and that HM 143 was annotated by a professional London scribe, perhaps working on a commission from a monastery, or someone, like Langland himself, with strong monastic interests, or like Capgrave, with strong historical interests. *H* does not seem to share (or is unwilling to expose) the interest in political and ecclesiastical affairs that a man like Capgrave has (in this, *D* is more like Capgrave). Neither annotator has Cok's love of emotionalism and affective piety—but then, Langland did not care for them much either. *D*'s intellectual horizons were less broad; his world is one in which practical and social theology merit most attention, along with social injustices, political issues, and ecclesiological affairs (his annotation of antimendicant passages is knowledgeable and judicious, while *H* merely has venom for the subject). In *D* Langland's text found a reader much like its author, a man of intense practical spirituality. However, Langland has been well characterized by A. V. C. Schmidt as a "clerkly maker," and perhaps it takes both annotators studied here to encompass the richness of that epithet: if *D* worked to highlight the poem's "clerkly" (at least, pastoral) qualities, *H* was highly sensitive to its monastic culture and the aesthetic concerns of its "maker." The diversity between the two readings is, for us, a warning against regarding "the medieval reader" in monolithic terms—or assuming that the creating of so-called finding aids was ever an "objective" activity.

CHAPTER 4

✥

Visual Politics

The pictorial cycle in Douce 104 is, as near as we can guess, the product of a Dublin-area scribe-illustrator with Anglo-Irish civil service experience. He had powerful lay sympathies and legal interests, and he may have been preparing Douce for a patron with similar concerns, or at least a patron whom he *thought* should share his concerns (Capgrave's witness suggests that professional readers were more likely to inflict their own interests on their patrons than to work vicariously). This was a world in which the artist was apparently at home, and it was a world of reformist concerns—some, from a modern perspective, "democratizing" or even utopian, others simply moralizing or political: as we have seen, his illustrative program is frequently reminiscent of those found in legal and civil service manuscripts, chronicles, and the literature of socioecclesiastical polemics, kinds of writing that were closely associated in both London and Dublin bureaucratic circles. This chapter will briefly examine aspects of the political ideology of those circles and how the Douce artist used the informal book production techniques they employed.

The central administration of the Irish colony functioned much like Westminster. Parliament, for instance, as Art Cosgrove explains,

> normally included, as well as the leading lay and ecclesiastical magnates, representatives from the towns, liberties and shires, the commons and also, *unlike England, proctors from the clergy of the Irish dioceses.* The day-to-day administration of the colony rested, as it did in England, on the great departments of state, the chancery and the exchequer, and the whole apparatus of government and dispensation of justice was modelled closely, *though necessarily on a much smaller scale,* on that current in England.[1]

I have added emphasis here to highlight two key points: reading Irish records, one is indeed constantly struck by how the relative smallness of the English-speaking community forced a certain intimacy between ecclesiastical and political administrators. The urgency of its colonial troubles gave legal and parliamentary issues a high profile[2] and contributed toward certain "democratizing" tendencies, which, although limited, were unparalleled in Ricardian Westminster.³ In fact, perhaps the most important and enigmatically reformist parliamentary text known to Westminster in this period, the *Modus tenendi parliamentorum*, may have originated in the Irish civil service, and was certainly in use there.⁴ The colony was, *administratively speaking*, not a provincial backwater.⁵ The role of Anglo-Irish politics and reformist writings like the *Modus* is an important factor for the study of Ricardian and Lancastrian politics generally. It is not possible to do the topic justice here, but it is worth pausing for a moment to understand some of the key characteristics that might have influenced the sociopolitical ideology of the colony.⁶

First, there is the "democratizing" impetus. The proctors of the lower clergy were in place in the Irish parliament by the 1370s, giving them a voice that they did not have—at least as directly—in contemporary Westminster. Statements in the *Modus* (section 23) to the effect that, in granting the king's request for any financial aid, "the proctors of the clergy from one diocese, if they are agreed, have a greater voice in parliament than the bishop himself" and, similarly, "that two knights who come to parliament for the shire, have a greater voice in granting or denying aids to the king than the greatest earl in England" are striking instances of the kinds of "democratizing" tendencies that drew the *Modus* into political use in Anglo-Ireland.⁷ These aspects of the *Modus* have sounded implausibly utopian to historians of medieval England, but in the Irish system of taxation and parliamentary representation, they make historical sense, as G. O. Sayles has shown. In this context even a text like *Piers Plowman* might appear insufficiently reforming, especially socially, but this is exactly the context that explains the reformist tendencies and politics of the Douce artist's rendering of *Piers*, as well as his view of authority.

The combined authority of church and state is also an important theme in the Douce cycle, and the documentary history of medieval Anglo-Ireland suggests a strong association between ecclesiastical and political reformist legislation in the colony, a connection that appears even stronger in the Lancastrian period when Douce was made.⁸ The most important Anglo-Irish cultural legislation, the 1366 Statutes of Kilkenny (repromulgated in 1402), contains clauses imposing a more than usually stringent church censure on violators of these otherwise secular statutes. The impact of the statutes was not lost on the Anglo-Irish literary community: in 1422, only five years before Douce was created, James Yonge translated the *Secreta secretorum* into Hiberno-English for his patron, the lord lieutenant of Ireland, James Butler, reminding him not to hire minstrels ("Rymoris") because "Who-so ham any good yewyth brekyth the statutis of kylkeny, and he is acursid by a xj bisschopis, as the same Statutes makyth mencion."⁹ The statutes were aimed at arresting the Anglo-Irish drift toward assimilation, and they did have a powerful cultural effect: in trying to regulate and reanglicize every aspect of social, linguistic, ecclesiastical, and labor relations with the Gaelic Irish—a massively interventionist legislative experiment that created enormous bitterness on both sides—they nonetheless helped strengthen a new sense of communal identity in Anglo-Ireland. The early Lancastrian cultural productions of the Dublin-Pale region—Yonge's *Secreta,* the *Red Book,* Douce, the Irish version of the *Modus* (insofar as anyone has studied them)—reflect all of these concerns: with authority of church and state (in certain ways, monolithically conjoined)[10] and with the problems of government, labor, corruption, colonialism, dissent, and sedition. An artist setting out to illustrate *Piers Plowman* in such a situation could hardly be immune from such concerns, especially not the scribe-artist capable of composing the parliamentary-style colophon we find in Douce. Like Yonge, who borrowed from Langland for his MHE *Secreta* translation, the Douce artist cast a shrewd and politically aware eye upon the authority issues raised by *Piers Plowman* and upon the issues raised by the standard iconographic programs available to illustrate them. The result we have today is a uniquely vibrant witness to the reformist visual politics of this new neglected Middle-Anglophone culture.

Informal Book Illustration and the Anglo-Irish Civil Service

Very little illustrated work survives from fifteenth-century Anglo-Ireland, but one clear instance we have, the fragmentary scribe-illustrated picture from the *Red Book,* is so very like Douce in methodology that it forces us to reevaluate our artist's supposed "amateurish" or "idiosyncratic" working habits from a local rather than a purely aesthetic perspective. The purpose of this section is to examine his methodology more closely and to summarize some of the evidence that his work habits reflect certain aspects of late medieval Anglo-Irish illustration and culture.[11]

The present study has been able to show for the first time that there were *at least two* people involved in the making of Douce, because the scribe of the main text was not the annotator-corrector (their hands are distinct; see appendix 1). Moreover, we can be certain that the annotator-corrector was not the illustrator: he displays an utterly different response to the poem in many places, and the fact that he writes directly over the illustrations in a hand different from the main scribe's (but the same as the corrector's) may be evidence either of palpable annoyance with the illustrations (an instance of workshop "rivalry") or simply of a different agenda. But whatever it is, it is also, apparently, characteristic of a certain kind of informal Anglo-Irish book production. The single illustration surviving in the *Red Book* fragment showing the Dublin Court of Exchequer at work (frontispiece) displays exactly this same unusual, and to modern sensibilities annoying, habit of annotation right on top of pictures.[12] However, the care taken in the *Red Book* fragment to distinguish types of texts, speakers, and annotations (by the use of two different hands and three languages) and the innovative handling of speech and writing in the picture are so very like Douce as to indicate something unique to Anglo-Irish concepts of text-image relations. Particularly striking is the *Red Book* artist's concern with what we have called *voicing*; that is, each figure speaks or writes or reads something, and his words are aligned with his mouth or pen or laid out on the page before him, just as in Douce, so that the text acts as a form of speech scroll, inscription, or textual cue to the illustration—all these things point to a local style of scribe illustrating that is quite distinctive and not at all "amateurish" upon closer examination.

The language of many of the annotations and of the statute above the *Red Book* picture is one of the four active in the colony, Anglo-Norman (here Law French); the other language is Latin: the Chief Remembrancer, the Second Remembrancer, and the Clerk of the Pipe all hold or write documents with Latin incipits (these are the top three middle figures—the Chief Remembrancer, between the other two, holds up his pen for examination). The surname of the judge at the lower left side of the table is "Sharpe";[13] it provides a rare MHE intrusion into this documentary culture. He is identified in an annotation written—to a modern eye—sloppily right over the body of the figure in a larger *anglicana formata* script. This is the only use the scribe-illustrator made of this hand on this page, because all the other annotations are written in his more compact secretary-influenced document hand, next to which it looks very old-fashioned. The other annotations are also different in kind from this one; they are either Latin incipits to an illustrated "document," such as the Chief Remembrancer's "Memorandum quod x° die Maij..." (Remember that on the tenth day of May...), or they are actually spoken French words, written directly beside the mouths of the speakers, such as the crier's "A demain," spoken as he hastily dismisses the court, with one foot already comically outside the frame of the picture as he goes.

The sense of play (with voice, with social stereotype and caricature, and with the boundaries of text, frame, and image) is very reminiscent of Douce. Take, for instance, the irreverent attitude toward certain authority figures (e.g., the two upper judges, pictured on the left side, one of whom cries "Soient forfez" [Let them be forfeit!]), toward those who are greedy (the litigious suitors, heavily caricatured on the right side—the middle one cries, "Soit oughte" [Let it be owed!]), and toward those who are irresponsible (like the crier with one foot already out the "door"). The artist was clearly an Exchequer clerk, because the clerks themselves (all clustered at the top in the middle of the table) are uncaricatured. We have here all the vigor and humor of Exchequer *signa* satire (and that, as we have seen, is saying something), translated through the pen of a scribe who has enough artistic skill to deliver complex caricature. Comparing his first suitor (on the bottom right, with the phallically protruding sword handle) to Douce's lawyer (figure 15), or his judge (on the bottom left) to Douce's knight (figure 11), one sees similarities in style that suggest scribe-illustrators of shared training. In fact, the *Red Book* fragment has Douce's peculiar habit of overlining or highlighting in red. Kathleen Scott was particularly puzzled by this feature in Douce, calling it the artist's "one odd habit for the second quarter of the century... [of] outlin[ing]... in an orange-red ink or pigment."[14] These are the Douce rubrication colors and this outlining is often the work of the rubricator (in Exchequer documents, a role the scribe-illustrator also played). Moreover, this type of outlining is characteristic of (informal) Anglo-Irish "finishing" habits.[15] The *Red Book* picture is similarly subjected to highlighting in the two colors that most frequently (along with yellow) appear in Irish manuscript rubrication, red and green. So, for instance, red touches appear on lips, on folds of clothing, on some noses and eyes, and generally on (from the artist's perspective) the more important figures in the picture (e.g., on the Chief Remembrancer's arms and the judge's beard). Although not visible in our black and white plates, this is precisely how the Douce rubricator has handled the body parts he thinks most pertinent to his figures: to take just a few examples of many, Envy's mouth and fist (fol. 25, highlighted in the same red as that which underlines the Latin and merges with Envy's belt), the lawyer's oversized oratorical hands (figure 15), the beggar's grasping hand (figure 23), and the bare bottom of the unfortunate little scholar being thrashed (fol. 52).[16] Whether, as Hilmo has suggested, the sophistication of the rubricator's *choice* of elements for highlighting is such that we can attribute this work to the Douce artist himself or whether it is the work of an apprentice is impossible to say for certain.[17] But the parallels in the *Red Book* give us some sense of what to look for in understanding both the work habits and division of labor in Douce and its immediate cultural context.

This sort of illustration is really only possible when the artist is also the scribe, someone whose job it is to produce *both* text and illustrative program and who consequently develops a minute knowledge of both; his working method in Douce is much like that of other identifiable scribe-illustrators: he apparently moved back and forth between copying and drawing in a process that allowed for certain kinds of intimacy and spontaneity.[18] Second, whoever our scribe-illustrator was, he had many of the informal book production techniques and much of the political ideology of a legally trained civil service clerk, likely of the Dublin government. We know that such men were crucial (both as writers and as primary audiences) to the development of vernacular literature in Ricardian and Lancastrian England: Langland, Chaucer, Usk, Gower, and Hoccleve, for instance, were all affiliated in some way with the legal or civil service community of Westminster.[19] Moreover, a number of their earliest readers and their earliest scribes can be located in this milieu as well. It is interesting, then, to see evidence of the same kind of training and mentality in the Douce scribe-illustrator.

The Dublin government was in many respects a clone of Westminster: its Chancery and Exchequer were staffed, where possible, by Englishmen for reasons of internal security, but many of the surviving documents are written in MHE by native Anglo-Irishmen.[20] The colony had a chronic labor shortage at all levels (even the highest post in the land, that of lord lieutenant, was hard to fill at times).[21] In the Ricardian and Lancastrian periods Anglo-Ireland was bleeding emigrants at an alarming rate (we might note, for instance, the sweeping, draconian measures of the 1366 Kilkenny Statutes to control the itinerancy of laborers and their flight by sea, stridently reaffirmed in the *Red Book* statute of 1409–10, which forbids any mariner to convey a laborer out of the land without license).[22] The result was, oddly, a kind of strengthening of the Anglo-Irish culture among those willing to stay. The 1420s, when Douce was produced, was a decade, as we have seen, in which Anglo-Irish culture was beginning to find a sense of its own identity. Texts from England began to be translated into MHE, and MHE prose began to be written. At the same time one finds new, reformist legislation to help deal with the recurrent social crises in the colony.[23] The preoccupations of early-fifteenth-century Anglo-Ireland can be seen in its legislation, and many reflections of current legislation appear in the Douce cycle. Berry's chronological table of statutes for the fourteenth and fifteenth centuries shows all the major legislation of England dutifully proclaimed in Ireland: the two Statutes of Labourers, the Statute of Provisors (the Douce illustrator certainly knew the former, and the annotator likely the latter)—but one also sees that there are adaptations of all the major legislation for the Irish situation (even the Magna Carta itself had to be adapted). And there is much legislation specific to Ireland, some of it paralleling English problems, such as Irish attempts at government control of laborers and itinerant plunderers[24] (which likely accounts for our illustrator's fascination with the labor issues in *Piers*) and attempts to control the Gaelicization of the Anglo-Irish, in legislation like the Statutes of Kilkenny, which our illustrator most certainly knew. There were many such desperate bids to stop Anglo-Irish assimilation or, as it came to be termed, "degeneracy" (from *de genere*—that is, to be out of one's "*genus* or proper national place"),[25] into the Gaelic-Irish community, but the Kilkenny Statutes were the most ambitious: they covered every aspect of social life from minstrels to marriage, sports to interracial adoptions, haircuts to itinerants, and especially language issues. As we have just seen, even the lord lieutenant, the king's representative in Ireland, was being advised to fear and respect the Kilkenny penalties in the same decade in which Douce was made.

The Douce artist's choices of illustration suggest a close knowledge of these topical issues, delivered with the vigorous social realism evident both in Anglo-Irish pictorial traditions and in some of their literary and historical texts. Attempts to understand this culture are few and far between, and the present study has had to make pioneering efforts in some areas, efforts that will doubtless be superseded as more scholarship becomes available (and I hope it will be). Scholarship has been hampered by the destruction of materials and, until quite recently, by the lack of dialect study and accessible literary editions,[26] as well as the nearly total (and ongoing) neglect of medieval Anglo-Irish visual arts.[27] This study, too, has labored under these limitations.

If much of the Douce artist's visual training came, broadly, from the world of legal and historical records, many of his ideas about what to highlight in *Piers* through illustration and, even more important, what to suppress are traceable to the same source. A few instances will suffice here: we have seen that there are no minstrels in the Douce cycle, and this may be, in part at least, because the Statutes of Kilkenny legislated against them.[28] The Statutes also forbade the Anglo-Irish from playing "hurlings," a Gaelic-Irish game still (in the twentieth century) notorious for its violence: this likely accounts for why the Douce illustrator chose to portray Sle3th (Trickery) in Passus XXII with a "sling" that looks a good deal more like a hurling stick (figure 36).[29] In Douce this character ("Sleuth," that is, "Sloth" in most manuscripts) has been renamed as "Sle{3}th" by the correction over erasure of "u" to "3" in all three lines where it occurs (fol. 108v; XX.158, 159, 164). The reason for the renaming is not difficult to see: the line "Sleuth was sley of werre" in Langland's version tempted the Anglo-Irish illustrator to portray a Gaelic-Irishman. His bare feet and Irish hairstyle mark him as the cycle's one (certain) Gaelic-Irishman, and it is not a flattering role—the Kilkenny legislation had outlawed even this style of haircut for Anglo-Irishmen. The problem of Anglo-Irishmen dressing as the Gaelic-Irish had been around since at least 1297, and quoting this legislation may give a salutary sense of how important a haircut could be: the statute complains that certain Anglo-Irish, "having their heads half shaven, grow and extend the hairs from the back of the head and call them *Culan,* conforming themselves to the Irish in garb as well as in countenance, whereby it frequently happens that some Englishmen reputed as Irishmen are slain, although the killing of Englishmen and of Irishmen requires different modes of punishment."[30] This sobering quotation gives too clear a picture of a land riven by ethnic, legal, and, indeed, colonial tensions, something most Middle English scholars have glimpsed only through FitzRalph (whose extremisms were a direct product of all this). It was a world that provoked violent inequities and passionate concerns for cultural issues, social justice, and for parliamentary and ecclesiastical reformist measures. One cannot understand these passions in the Douce cycle—indeed, one can't even understand the significance of a haircut—without some sense of the culture that gave rise to them.

In Langland the Douce artist seems to have found a kindred spirit: Langland himself reflects a sophisticated grasp of the kind of reformist parliamentary ideology that interested certain members of the Westminster civil service.[31] The Douce artist was—like many of the authors of *Piers* sequels—fascinated by Langland's portrait of Westminster: We might take as examples Liar, whom he chose to portray with the marriage charter and seal (fol. 9), realizing that the charter was about to be proclaimed in the text; Mede riding on the sheriff (figure 2); Mede at Westminster (figure 3); Conscience as royal adviser (figure 4); the king hearing a case (figure 5); and Reason seated as judge (fol. 19). All these come in quick succession, and a variety of legal issues are, as we have seen, visually highlighted elsewhere in the cycle: Tom Stowe (figure 6); the lawyer (figure 15); the pardon and colored seal (figure 19); the young bastard (figure 22); the man on the gallows (figure 32); the merchant (figure 34), a strikingly unusual choice to represent all Grace's gifts; or Caiaphas (fol. 101), a figure unnoticed by most readers of *Piers*—perhaps the kind of pictorial subject only a canon lawyer could love.

But he had a wider experience of text-image work than legal or governmental copying would have given him; the very little bit of illustration of fourteenth- and fifteenth-century Anglo-Irish origin and provenance that survives suggests a variety of iconographical influences, especially English, but also Gaelic and even some European. Clearly legal work was not his only milieu; like many minor civil servants or legal scribes (if indeed that is what he was), he may have drifted in and out of various types of employment,[32] and he may also have been an itinerant scribe-illuminator: Françoise Henry and Genevieve Marsh-Micheli, speaking of the artists of contemporary Gaelic-Irish manuscripts, make the comment: "We are faced by the extreme mobility of these medieval scribes and the constantly shifting pattern of their movements. A few rolls of vellum, some ink and quills, and a few colours were easily packed in a satchel."[33] Douce is quite definitely an *anglo* Anglo-Irish production: among extant Anglo-Irish literary manuscripts, it is one of those which appears most consistently to reject nearly all Celtic influence.[34] Yet Douce does not fit comfortably among those manuscripts which historians of Irish art call "foreign" (that is, non-Gaelic-Irish), manuscripts like Bodleian Library, MS Rawl. G. 185 (made in England for a Dublin patron), for instance. There is virtually no scholarship attempting to delineate an Anglo-Irish visual tradition,[35] but despite the fact that little survives, it is distinctive.

Perhaps this is best exemplified by juxtaposition of three manuscripts of Anglo-Irish provenance, Harley 3724, Rawl. G. 185, and San Marino, Huntington Library, MS HM 129, which shed light on the Douce artist's handling of certain figures (especially the lunatic lollar and Trajan) and of satirical and mnemonic devices, especially busts and small objects.[36]

Let's look at Trajan. The Douce artist drew upon several visual traditions at once in creating Trajan: first, he chose the English (and French) iconographic tradition of giving pagans, especially those in roles antagonistic to Christians, a spiked headdress (a similar instance occurs in Matthew Paris's *Life of St. Alban,* now Dublin, Trinity College, MS 177, fol. 45). This "headgear" usually shows up in illustrations of figures with, as Ruth Mellinkoff notes, "disgraceful occupations and activities connected with the persecution of Christ and saints ... [e.g.] mockers, accusers, tormentors ... and executioners."[37] It is most certainly an attribute of pagans, the most unflattering one available in the international iconography. The Douce artist's choice of it is a rather extraordinary reading of Langland's Trajan (most modern critics would simply say it is "wrong") and one that differs sharply, as we have seen, from the positive reading that his colleague, the annotator, provides. But there are a variety of cultural pressures at work here, and it may be more important (and more interesting) to understand them rather than to protest the fact that the artist didn't understand ours. This motif was known in Anglo-Ireland, because it shows up in one of the crude unframed marginal scribe illustrations in HM 129, a fourteenth-century Northern Homily Cycle written in MHE: the bust of a man with similar headgear, although rendered without the violent caricature of Douce's Trajan, is sketched in the scribe's ink and overlined with red (again, an Anglo-Irish finishing technique) next to the opening lines of the story: "An hendy knyght heght placydas / bot hethyn man ful lange he was" on fol. 59v (figure 49).[38] Although a scribe-illustrator drew this picture in HM 129, he and the rubricator (who may be the same man wearing a different hat) share the job of coloring and highlighting the several little pictures throughout, which may not be unlike the situation in the making of Douce. The pictures are nearly all busts of the protagonists of the particular stories the scribe apparently wished to highlight.[39] And there is a great deal of use of colored manicules (marginal pointing hands) to draw further attention to the pictured passages, a deictic preoccupation this Anglo-Irish illustrator shares with the Douce artist, too, although the latter has evolved a much more sophisticated strategy. HM 129 is important, for all its crudeness, as the only other illustrated MHE *literary* text known to us. It, too, was made at the beginning of the fifteenth century, and it betrays, through the presence of a Celtic-style line drawing of a cat on folio 1, the ever-present pressures of Gaelicization.

But the Douce artist's treatment of his heathen figure is yet more complex. Trajan explodes suddenly into *Piers Plowman* at this point: "baw for bokes quod on: was broken out of hell" (figure 27), and the artist has represented him in profile (as in HM 129), but here in ugly caricature, sporting an elongated tongue to which his hand reaches up, as if to touch or signal. This gesture is ironic and indicates that the artist was also aware of the standard Psalter iconography that shows King David touching or pointing to his tongue, a mnemonic for the verse of Psalm 38: "I said I will take heed to my ways, that I sin not with my tongue [*in lingua mea*]: I will place a guard on my mouth when the sinner comes before me." This is, in its way, a very sophisticated reading of the dynamics of the Trajan passage, and it suggests, among other things, that the artist did not feel that Trajan's anti-intellectualism ought to be encouraged. An instance of this iconography occurs in Rawlinson G. 185, owned by the prior of Saint Patrick's, Dublin, in the latter part of the fourteenth century; it is a good example of the kind of "foreign" illustrated manuscript being imported into the colony from England.[40] But there is apparently even another layer of visual allusion in the Douce Trajan; like his contemporary who made HM 129, our illustrator was also aware of Celtic visual traditions, however peripherally. The Douce artist's interpretation of Trajan was not nearly so positive as the annotator's, but in fact the artist's pessimism about Trajan is rather like that of James Yonge's five years earlier, and may indicate a shared local perspective, at least with one of the few members of the contemporary Anglo-Irish literary community known to us—one who was also a reader of Langland.[41] To underline his negativity, the Douce artist invoked the tradition of "elongated tongue" marginalia, common in Gaelic-Irish manuscripts and well exemplified in another, more "cross-cultural" Anglo-Irish and Hiberno-Latin collection, Harley 3724 (see figure 63). On this folio in Harley, in a passage from the *Topographia*, we see the combination of a manicule and a bust of a man with his tongue thrust out; together they exactly bracket a passage on the wanton enormities and sacrilege of Gaelic-Irish priests. Here the marginal tongue is being quite literally stuck out to indicate disgust (a similar picture occurs on fol. 31v beside a similar passage on sacrilege).[42] The ironic thing about Harley is that the rubricator's style of decoration and illustration show heavy Celtic influence. Gaelic-Irish artists themselves were beginning to experiment with "foreign" styles in this period,[43] but Harley is a fascinating and unpublished example of influence in the other direction: made in a fiercely Anglo-Irish milieu, Harley nonetheless experiments with Gaelic-Irish style, especially in its decoration and illustration, and, like Douce, it is extremely economically made. The contents of Harley in fact could serve as an introductory guide to Anglo-Irish culture: it contains a copy of the papal bull "Laudibiliter," in which Pope Adrian had granted Ireland to the English; it contained a great deal of the ever popular and colorfully anti-Gaelic Giraldus (where our illustration occurs), along with some prophecy (which Art Cosgrove has described as the "new genre" of late medieval Ireland), the Lord's Prayer in MHE, and some extreme Latin clerical satire (one piece of which is obliterated with heavy ink Xs, apparently censored).[44] These were the standard texts in the world of the literate fourteenth-century Anglo-Irish, and they would be very much the intellectual inheritance of our artist, but by the fifteenth century some important shifts were being made: Harley was likely created in a religious house, as was most of the extant evidence of fourteenth-century Anglo-Irish literary culture.[45] By the early fifteenth century the most high-profile impetus for the creation and dissemination of literary texts seems to have shifted to more secular venues, notably, the administrative and civil service center of the emergent colony, Dublin (paralleling exactly what was happening with book production in England at the time). This shift brought with it a very different emphasis in text-image relations, and it is this we must understand next.

Voicing the Text: Representing and Remembering Voices

We have seen the special concern for "voice" and "voicing" evinced by Anglo-Irish book production and cultural context, and here we will look more closely at Douce's cunning use of picture placement to dramatize speaking voices (or what M. T. Clanchy called, in legal documentary illustration, "remembered voices").[46] We have already seen the tendency in (the few extant) Anglo-Irish illustrated manuscripts to use body parts (tongues, hands, or the conventional manicule) to gesture toward key passages in the text; we will see how the Douce artist exploited these gestures to emphasize the speaking voice. These unusually intimate relations between text and image would not have been, in our opinion, possible were it not that the scribe also wore the illustrator's hat, so the evidence that Douce's main text and marginal cycle were primarily the conception of one scribe-illustrator will form the final section of this chapter.

The extent to which what we see on the pages of Douce today represents workshop "rivalry," or at least disagreement about priorities in the text-image hierarchy, and the extent to which it simply reflects the Anglo-Irish practice evident in the *Red Book* of, for instance, annotating pictures by writing right over them is difficult to tell. The annotations tend to cut across the illustrations: physically, in that they were often written on the pictures themselves, and ideologically, in that they can also undermine the thrust of the illustrator's work at times; often they draw attention to something quite different in the passage.[47] All the evidence indicates that when examined as a group, the annotations constitute, as we have seen, an independent reading of the poem copied into the manuscript by someone who was apparently not always happy to have the illustrations in his path.

So what the *Red Book* picture really helps us to understand is that the annotator's habits are not unprofessional. It also helps us to understand the scribe-illustrator's work. He had already provided a kind of system of "inscriptions"—or better, embedded "speech scrolls"—by highlighting within the text itself key words or phrases (sometimes mnemonic, sometimes ironic, sometimes both) through picture-text alignment or through the physical intersection of the image with the text itself. What is remarkable (and suggestive of some degree of workshop collaboration, in spite of the sharply different agendas of the two Douce marginal laborers) is that both were persistently concerned *to highlight the poem's speaking voices* using the different media at their disposal.

Representation—a word that for us has lost all of its metaphorical impact—was, for medieval readers, a *re*-presenting or a showing again: the Latin *repraesentare* derives from the root *praesens*, originally suggesting an experience *of the moment*. Thus, Mary Carruthers has pointed out that when Saint Gregory writes, "What writing makes present to those reading, pictures make present [*praestat*] to the uneducated," he expresses the medieval view of representation as temporal, rather than objective or mimetic.[48] Few illustrated manuscripts offer such a vividly literal demonstration of this medieval understanding of representation as the figures in Douce 104: speakers and other figures are "made present," brought into the view of the reader—startlingly and starkly against blank vellum. Full figures or heads appear suddenly, out of nowhere, and they nearly always have not only a "representing" function, but also a "narrating" function (to use a terminology of pictorial inscriptions developed by Wallis).[49] Michael Camille, exploring the foundational role of orality in medieval English illustration, especially in the postconquest period, which Clanchy regards as transitional (that is, to 1307),[50] suggests that this period established the tendency for images to be represented as performing "speech-acts."[51] Camille traces this through the artists' use of special gestures to indicate speech pictorially and of speech scrolls emanating from the mouths of figures or held in their hands. The roots of this impetus can be found in several areas: in the development of legal documentation, in the oral reading habits of the period up to the early fourteenth century, and in the importance (especially for chroniclers) of the eyewitness account.[52]

With the development of silent reading and the increasing growth of documentary culture in the fourteenth century, many of these features had become culturally anachronistic by the early fifteenth century, when Douce was made, but they remained the foundation for iconographic traditions that the Douce artist uses and adapts, and they seem to have remained especially tenacious in the illustration of visionary texts. One might point to the tradition of portraying the dreamer *outside* the frame of the action of the vision, looking in—a commonplace in thirteenth-century Apocalypse illustration that survives even in fifteenth-century visionary illustration of texts such as Guillaume de Deguilleville's *The Pilgrimage of the Life of Man*, but is otherwise anachronistic.[53] Likewise, by the early fifteenth century, most readers read silently, which means that the kind of orality discussed by Clanchy and Camille in earlier texts no longer functions in the same way. However, as we shall see, the pictorial tradition established earlier persisted as an iconography of "voicing," although modified or elaborated and played upon as the development of silent reading made the iconographical possibilities for representing voicing more complex.

To illustrate this emphasis on oral performance in the early period, Camille cites a Romanesque manuscript of John of Worcester's chronicle (Oxford, Corpus Christi College, MS 157) that contains pictures portraying three dreams of Henry I, as recounted to the chronicler by the court physician, Grimbald.[54] That John was present at the narration is stressed both in the text and in marginal illustrations, which actually *show* Grimbald sitting outside the frame of the picture and the text, telling his tale, as Camille says, for those who still like their story told. This is precisely the type of figure engaged in the kind of speech-act that we often find in Douce 104, where it is made more complex by the development of silent reading, and the increased sophistication of "narrating" pictorial strategies generally, in the intervening centuries. Camille makes three points about these Grimbald illustrations,[55] all of which are still largely applicable to Douce, allowing for some historical differences: (1) the speaker, Grimbald, is placed against bare vellum, "in what is the space reserved for scribal amendments in the rest of the manuscript, as a distinct commentator"; (2) the Grimbald illustrations, Camille argues, were probably done before the text, since "the limits of the artist's working field have not been clearly defined" and body parts protrude into the text area, a common kind of trespassing in Douce, often for the same reason; (3) the illustrator makes use of the *declamatio* gesture (the pointing curved index finger of the right hand to indicate acoustical performance). As Camille shows, the gesture was often used by early Christian artists, especially to denote the voice of God, usually shown as a pointing hand emerging from the clouds. Camille mentions that this visual voicing is especially suited to visionary experience and illustration, since it has the effect of making the speaker or author of a text appear (Gregory's "praestat").[56] Thus, Saint John Chrysostom read the New Testament with an image of Saint Paul before him;[57] or, closer to the Douce artist's own period, one could point to the sudden appearance of Saint Paul in Chaucer's "Second Nun's Tale," momentarily *present* (literally, present*ed*) to deliver a text from Ephesians,[58] and to similar moments in *Piers Plowman* in which an authority figure, like Piers himself or Trajan, abruptly materializes to deliver a brief text. In all instances the text could simply have been quoted or cited, but for the medieval reader and visualizer, there was an obvious (and perhaps ancient) satisfaction and mnemonic clarity in having it literally "represented" as orally delivered (figures 10 and 27). As a result, Douce is full of disembodied heads that make sudden appearances in the text (a feature, as well, of meditative illustration, as will be seen in part II).

We have identified two types of marginal figures in Douce 104: *voicing figures* (roughly equivalent, in the way they relate to the text beside which they are placed, to Wallis's terminology for medieval pictorial inscriptions denoting "narrating" figures) and *silent witnesses* (roughly equivalent to Wallis's category of "representing"); these can have either *signaling* or merely *identifying* functions. The voicing figures in Douce often make use of a *declamatio* gesture or one of the less marked speaking gestures: either what Moshe Barasch calls the "announcing hand" (a raised right hand) or the "open hand speaking gesture."[59] They also use an array of indicators, including eyes, hands, mouths, and other body parts, to mark their relation to the text—and it is worth noting that these body parts are often explicitly highlighted by the rubricator, just as they are in the Dublin Exchequer illustration (frontispiece). Some show such a close relationship with the text beside which they are placed that they can function *as* speech scrolls. Scrolls were widely used up to the end of the thirteenth century and were maintained especially in didactic manuscripts (like Lincoln 218 and Add. 37049 [figure 60]) during the period in which Douce was made. The Douce artist may have felt that they looked rather out of date because their use in legal and many other kinds of manuscripts that he would have known had passed away, so he substituted his own innovative system, based in part on local artistic tradition.

The pictorial development of what we call silent witnesses seems to have occurred in the fourteenth and fifteenth centuries as a direct result of the growth of silent reading: it made possible, for instance, an illustration like the famous Chaucer portrait in Hoccleve's *Regiment*, in which Chaucer reaches out of the frame of his portrait, pointing in a mute *declamatio* gesture that silently authenticates Hoccleve's assertion of the "sothfastnesse" of this image of the poet.[60] Chaucer is not speaking in these lines, Hoccleve is:

...I have here his lyknesse
Do make, to this ende, in sothfastnesse,
That thei that have of him lest thought and mynde
By this peynture may ageyn him fynde.

The *declamatio* gesture is here an authenticating mnemonic, and we see exactly this usage in Douce, as well.

A vivid example of the Douce artist's interest in giving characters "voice" is the dramatic *declamatio* in the portrait of Wastor (figure 12). The gesture, often associated with authority figures, is here ironically associated with a bullying plunderer—or, to give him one of the names used in fourteenth- and fifteenth-century Anglo-Irish documents and poems, a "hobeler" or a "ravaynnour" (such plundering, both unofficial and "official," was a serious problem in the colony, and the illustrator seems both to have known the legislation on the subject and to have leapt with gusto upon the Wastor episode for illustration). Kilkenny Statute 17 forbids the keeping of "kerne hobellours ne hudyues gentz" who go about plundering victuals ("vitailles") or anything else, that is, "kernes, hobelers or idlemen": "kernes," deriving from a Celtic word meaning household troops, were in effect henchmen;[61] "hobelers" were troublesome vagabonds and often appear in MHE complaint literature;[62] "ravynnours" were plunderers who lived by exaction, but the word actually came to have a relatively neutral meaning in MHE, roughly equivalent to "gentleman"(!), that is, one whose "ravening" is "probably no more than the taking of subsidies from the tenantry and servile classes,"[63] as Michael Benskin has argued—although if this is so, it is hardly flattering. The Douce figure looks a little too well dressed to be a "hobeler," and may in fact be a "kerne" or one of the many bullying employees of a powerful lord against whom so much legislation was directed. He is, within the terms of the poem, actually a conflation of Wastor, who challenges Piers in the lines to which he gestures, and the Bretoner, who boasts two lines later that they will help themselves to Piers's meat (already languishing at the end of Wastor's stick). The gesturing hand is suitably proprietary, looking as if it will scoop up the lines as well, and his eyes, which bulge out aggressively toward his challenge ("And to peres þe ploughman: proferred to fiȝth"), would be sufficiently demonstrative even without the hand hovering threateningly above. With his other hand, wrapped fistlike around the stick upon which Piers's "flesch" hangs (VIII.154), it forms a frame for the two challenges. The placement of this image is not only dramatically appropriate, but also morally, as Hunger eyes him sinisterly from across the page (fol. 38), dressed in the same colors, a macabre silent witness and consequence of Wastor's blustering.

Another instance of voicing or oral performance, this time even more viciously satirical, is provided by the proud priest (figure 37), an image deriving from reformist pastoral iconography. Only his tonsure remains to mark his true profession, and as Kathleen Scott has shown, his tight hose, elaborate shoes, and obscenely dangling sword associate him with an iconography of Pride.[64] His hand, protruding distinctively between the lines, touches the word "Proud" exactly at this point in the text: "Proud prestes come wiþ hym: passing an hondered / In paltokes and pyked shoes and *pyssers* long knyues" (a rather graphic pun that makes this identifying mnemonic unforgettable). His eyes appear to be reading the line "And with antecrist helden: hard aȝenes consciens," another way of underlining his relation with Pride, one of the seven giants (XXII.215–19). But his own bragging monologue begins a few lines lower (about even with the phallically suggestive sword handle). As we have seen, this figure turns up in precisely these terms in canon law illustrations (such as Hatfield House 290 and in the *Omne bonum* [figures 56 and 66]). The Douce artist has used exactly the same iconography, but he has added the *declamatio* gesture to make this a performative figure suitable to narrative illustration (compare the silent witness, who is merely an identifying figure, in the Hatfield illustration).

Covetousness (fol. 27) is similarly portrayed quite specifically in full spate (his palm turned toward the viewer in a satirical echo of authoritative announcing gestures, perhaps).[65] This is the kind of portrait that, given the vivaciousness of Langland's own description, tends to draw criticism from modern scholars because the artist "failed" to deliver all of Langland's details. But the artist had a different agenda. He did make Covetousness "bitelbrowed and baburlipped" (VI.198), with a beard shaved like "a bondemannes bacoun" (VI.201), but the placement of the picture indicates that it was not Langland's *physical* description of the character that really interested the illustrator. The picture begins only after the description, where Covetousness *begins to speak* (his first words sit about level with the top of his hat), and his eyes are directed toward his description of his first lesson on weighing fraudulently, his hand significantly touching the word "faire" — a perfect mnemonic given its multiple meanings, and one that, together with the other hand, which clutches his purse below, frames the ensuing confession of the cheating practices indulged at fairs and markets, a serious legal and legislative issue (the subject of a number of statutes) that seems to have been what really interested the artist: "Wykedly to wey: was my fyst lesone / To wend to westmynster: i went to þe faire" (fol. 27). His dress, unlike Lechery's and Pride's, which is aristocratic, is trading class, and he is portrayed as a representative of the petty businesses he confesses to have haunted, but both the placement and the iconography suggest a satire on the kinds of portraits of merchants that turn up in illustrated legal manuscripts of statutes on fair trading practices (such as Harvard Law 12).

Not all methods of gesture in the text involve hands. Covetousness's portrait looks directly across the page at Lechery (figure 7), who is again placed precisely at the opening of his speech, which contains a graphic description of one of his lightning seductions:

For vch a maide þat I mett: i made hir assynge
Semyng to synward: & sum I can taste
A boute þe mouþe & be neþe: gan I hir gropp
To boþ our willes was on: & to þe werke we ʒeden.
       (Fol. 26v; cf. Pearsall, *C-Text*, VI.178–81)

Surely it is no accident that his sword protrudes phallically between lines 180 and 181, right into the ruled area of the text; the text area beside the left margin, unlike the right (which is of course unjustified), is rarely violated in Douce, but this must have seemed irresistible.[66]

Of the portraits of more authoritative figures, some of those we would expect to see with announcing or *declamatio* gestures do have them (among these are authority figures, like Conscience, Reason, and the Angel, who appears to prophesy doom to the Church upon Constantine's donation), but many we'd expect to see (such as the king) do not. The issue of authority in Douce is tremendously complex, as we have seen, and Mercy (fol. 94; figure 33) is typical of this complexity, sharing the attributes of a voicing figure and a silent witness, a strategy that nicely foregrounds the paradox of authoritative announcement and the religious ideal of (especially female) silence. Mercy's eyes look at XX.148, where Truth tells her, "hold þy tonge mercy" and stop telling idle tales of salvation for pre-Christian souls locked in Hell. Mercy's mute observance of the rebuke not only serves to identify her (note that the line also contains her name—the last word in the line and therefore closest to her gaze), but it is delightfully belied by the gentle way her hand signals her spoken response, in a fashion reminiscent of a speech scroll. The single word she touches is, appropriately, "saued" (highlighting her brief response: "þro3th experiens quod scho: i hopp þei schal be saued" [XX.154]). The low gesture of the speaking hand deliberately muted (compare those of the proud priest, Covetousness, or Wastor) and unnervingly like Lady Mede's (figure 3), where Mede doesn't speak at all. The illustrator may have thought this to be appropriately feminine. In the Douce text Mercy actually began speaking on folio 93v, but it would have been impossible to place her there, because the vellum is misshapen and much of the margin is missing as a consequence. The illustrator, who is deft at working within the economic restrictions of Douce, has made up for the defect brilliantly. The elegant sway of her body and her long golden hair indicate the attractiveness of the quality of mercy, but he may have made her too attractive: someone has tried to blot out her face, a quite deliberate smudging, unique in the manuscript, that appears to be a kind of censoring of female beauty and that may indicate that the manuscript eventually came into possession of a male religious house where such temptation was not appreciated. (Certainly the antifeminist poem about Tutivillis and the proverb on harlots, which were added on the last folio of the manuscript, are suggestive of some such ownership not long after it was completed.)[67]

There is an equally large category of nonspeaking figures who act in the manuscript as silent witnesses of lines spoken about them or about their type; although they are not speaking in the text beside which they are placed, they have their own eloquence, and they often serve to identify a character or person spoken *about*. The Douce artist was fascinated by the Westminster scenes in *Piers Plowman*, and he gave them a kind of unparalleled attention in the cycle: the illustration of Mede at Westminster as a silently seductive identifying witness (figure 3) betrays careful planning—he deliberately shrunk the size of the writing in order to make space for it. At this point in the narrative the unsavory crew who had gathered for her wedding to Fals have fled, leaving her weeping, to be brought before the king to answer charges (a favorite scenario, as we have seen, for legal manuscript illustration, here split into single figures). However, Westminster falls in love with her; government clerks are all chivalry toward the damsel in distress, and Langland marks the occasion with some rare uses of romance diction (III.12–15). Mede does not speak on this page, playing the helpless woman, silent in the official male world, with admirable and doubtless cunning self-restraint. The illustrator has already given us two illustrations of Mede. In the first (fol. 8), she is crowned and carries the chalices often associated with moneylending and bribery in medieval iconography, as well as with the Whore of Babylon.[68] In the other she is placed on the back of a sheriff (figure 2), who is portrayed as a younger, slightly more dandyish member of the same social group as the second *Red Book* judge (they wear the same style of hat and gown). The Douce sheriff's eyes gaze at the word "rydeth" in a visual double entendre that associates lechery and bribery in a way that Mede's sidesaddle position on top of him belies; it is a striking and cunningly placed picture and one of the artist's few attempts at a double-figure illustration in the cycle, but unfortunately the effect is obscured by the annotator, who seems to have been annoyed or at least to have had a very different agenda for the reader: he scratches "nota de soþnes..." right across the feet of the sheriff (the annotator is much more concerned to trace the progress of the allegory that follows this moment than he is with the sexual nuances that preoccupy the artist). By the time the reader sees the portrait of Mede on folio 11, then, the sharp change of strategy is surprising: the crown and chalices have disappeared, as has the male "mount," and she is naturalistically represented as a young woman of elegant fashion, good taste, and restraint. Her meekness is striking (this is the exact pose the artist will use for Mercy later). Mede's right hand indicates the line that serves as the caption to the picture, "þat wende to westmynst*er*: wher wircheped hir many" (13), which, with the curve of her other hand, creates a frame for this line and the next two, the ones most heavily studded with romance diction: "Gentely wiþ joy: þe justices summe [sic] / Busked hem to þe boure: þer þis burde dwelled" (III.13–15). Her eyes look directly at the king's line ("what man of þis world þat hir levest had"), for she is not speaking herself but, rather, being disposed of in a patriarchal world. The placement can hardly be accidental; the figure could have been situated anywhere on the page (the margin is uniformly wide, the writing having been made deliberately and unusually smaller to accommodate the illustration), she could have been shown weeping or handing out bribes, but the quiet seductiveness is a far more sophisticated and disturbing response.

Signaling figures are those whose dramatic gestures (often reaching right into the text space itself) signal an attitude or action in relation to the text, rather than simply an identification of character.[69] Many of the silent witnesses in Douce have an emotional relationship with the words they accompany; however, most moving, and most successful in that they establish an important set of cross-echoes, as Derek Pearsall has argued, are the illustrations of the poor.[70] Sympathy for the poor—and generosity even to a fault (what Langland would call "rechelessnesse")—was, according to the testimony of travelers to medieval Ireland, characteristic of the Gaelic-Irish,[71] and the Anglo-Irish seem to some extent to have shared that sympathy (at least judging from the high profile that poverty issues have in their literature). The amount of fourteenth- and fifteenth-century colonial and civic legislation (both parliamentary and ecclesiastical) that attempted to deal with the problems of poverty and begging testifies to the fertile ground on which Langland's sensitivity to these subjects (especially in C) landed. As we will see, the Douce artist wholly rejected the iconography available to him from books of hours and other standard visual souces and drew instead upon the social realism of the Giraldian tradition. But from a technical standpoint, which is what concerns us at the moment, the Douce artist's success (as Pearsall calls it) with these illustrations resides in the sophisticated grammar of gesture that they provide for the reader, a grammar that not only interprets the text, but—through visual cross-echo—*supplements* it. Take, for example, the beggar (figure 23). He is turned back toward the text in a gun-shy manner; he represents those who have been "sent hungry away," while the rich discuss theology over their plenty (XI.42–50), and his stance expresses both longing and repulsion. His eyes gaze down past the "blis" (47) he has been denied to the words "whan hem nediþ"; if the viewer's eye follows the graceful arc of his head, characteristic of many of this illustrator's poor or humble figures, it turns into the cradled arm, which doubles back upon the text, reaching up past "ryche" to "nediþ":

> Litil loueþ he þat lorde: þat lent hym al þat blis
> þat so partiþ wiþ þe pore: a parcel whan hem nediþ
> Ne wer mercy in mene men: mor þan in ry3th ryche
> Man tymes mendinaunt3: my3th go an hongered.
> (Fol. 51; XI.47–50)

The intent gaze is intelligent enough to identify this beggar as the kind of silent witness (and there are others in the cycle) who is clearly *reading* the text beside which he or she is placed. One remembers the priest's surprise that Piers could read, and the illustrator often chooses to portray members of the "nonliterate" classes penetratingly gazing at lines before them: perhaps legal or notarial work had likely given him actual experience of lower-class literacy that educated people in other professions might not even be aware of (as Steven Justice has shown, class prejudice was often stronger than empirical reality in contemporary perceptions of rural and working people).[72]

But even though the poor may read, they have no real voice—not even an artist imbued with the reformist parliamentary ideology of (one imagines) select political circles in late medieval Dublin seems to have been able to imagine them otherwise. The gesture the poor man makes with his hand is vague and has no specific rhetorical voice (and, indeed, in the accompanying text, it is the poet who speaks on their behalf), but the figure is nevertheless shown engaging in that most potentially explosive of activities, vernacular reading.[73] Just as the dreamer does at another, more famous point in the poem, the Douce artist shifts the reader's perspective to look *over* this poor man's (contorted) shoulder and share the text with him. The fact that the ends of his staff don't quite meet and that the working up of the underdrawing appears to have been "pulled" deliberately toward the text (see the exposed knee) tells us that the illustrator was *determined* to make this figure speak to and through the words at the edge of the text. Just as determined, but pulling in the opposite direction, is the annotator's much more clerical agenda, signaled in bold and unapologetic scrawl over the artist's gentle pastel colors and aimed at dragging the reader's attention away to notice what is said of "freres & faytowrs."

Perhaps it is because the poor have no voice, even pictorially, that the illustrator shows Activa Vita (figure 29), a silent witness of even his *own* words (such visual silence is rare in this cycle with an actual speaker). Burdened with the tools of his apprenticeship to Piers, he has no free hand to gesture with (also rare). His mouth is exactly aligned with "and corteysliche he saide," a tactical alignment usually used for speaking figures, but his gaze is the intense, silent one of the poor. The legislation of the colony or the artist's own reformist agenda, as we have seen, did not give him the option that the text does of rendering Activa Vita as a minstrel, but the two tools he holds and the special trouble and expense the artist went to to render them (the oven spade—an allusion to his job as baker and eucharistic waferer—is apparently made of oxidized silver) suggest a reformist agenda that quite outstrips the social imagination of most medieval visual artists and that springs from a striking generosity one sees in Anglo-Irish cultural productions.

In short, the illustrator of Douce 104 handled the visualizing, the voicing, and the signaling of Langland's text with remarkable perception and a sophisticated sense of social justice and community zeal. This intimacy strongly suggests a scribe-illustrator at work. His technique is the next and final problem this chapter aims to illuminate.

The Artisans of Douce 104 and Their Division of Labor

We have now examined a number of reasons why the main scribe of Douce is the most plausible candidate for the role of illustrator: the strikingly intimate relationship between picture and text, the socioeconomic class of the manuscript, and its utilitarian nature make it likely that Douce came from a smaller scriptorium or workshop in which the scribe played at least a dual role. The paleographical and linguistic evidence, of course (see appendixes 1 and 2), indicates that Douce was most likely created in a provincial workshop in the Dublin-Pale district of Ireland. As Scott has shown, the fashions portrayed by the illustrator are also not absolutely current, and the main scribe's hand is old-fashioned for its time[74] (although his *anglicana formata* may have been the scribe's sense of what was appropriate to *vernacular* writing, he certainly had other hands in his repertoire).[75] In a more expensively produced manuscript we might also expect to find a separation of duties between the person who conceived the picture cycle and the person who executed it, but there seems little reason to postulate that here. Notes for illustrators survive in the margins of various manuscripts in sufficient quantities to indicate that such instructions were usually written by workshop supervisors and that they were normally brief and stereotypical.[76] By contrast, whoever conceived the Douce illustrations approached the poem reflectively and knew it intimately; his response (and there is little doubt that the illustrator *was* male)[77] was not only subtle, but ideologically developed. None of this could have been achieved from the kinds of notes to illustrators that have survived to this day, unless the executing illustrator in question used such notes simply as a starting point for elaborating his own ideas by close study of the poem. (If so, the issue of supervisor's notes becomes trivial, in any case.)[78] The term "illustrator" or "artist" has been used in this book to mean the person who conceived and executed the underdrawings (or at least roughed them in), as well as most of the painting. Whether he had an assistant for some of the painting and some of the rubrication is difficult to determine at this stage of our collective knowledge. The former question is best left until the technical analyses of Jeremy Griffiths and Maidie Hilmo are published, although we can point to some evidence suggesting the possible presence of an assistant.[79] The way in which ascenders and flourishes in the script become intertwined or echoed playfully in the pictures makes it clear in any case that the main scribe and illustrator are the same man, and that for him there was no artificial barrier between text-image relations (take, for instance, the handling of the hair of the man on the gallows [figure 32] in relation to the "ur" [or sometimes in this dialect "wr"] abbreviation in the text).[80]

Whether the scribe-illustrator had help with the rubrication is a slightly more manageable question. We know that he himself sometimes handled the rubrication ink (in, for instance, his only two annotations, at V.169 and 178, which are written in his hand and in red, and in his inscription "liberum arbitrium" at the top of folio 74, now badly cropped).[81] Many of the illustrations have been finished, as we have seen, with red overlining (or with one of the other rubrication colors). The quality of interpretive thought that the highlighting often betrays, as Maidie Hilmo has observed (pointing to the number of places in which the red overlining emphasizes key body parts) is suggestive of the scribe-illustrator's hand.[82]

But sometimes the overlining appears much cruder and not especially interpretively significant, to say the least (e.g., Reason, fol. 19, or the bishop, figure 18).[83] The motivation for some of this activity is opaque, but what we do know is that it is always one of the two shades of red also being used for the ordinary rubrication business (like underlining Latin quotes, e.g., Envy, fol. 25; Mede, figure 3; Lechery, figure 7) that appears in this overlining. Moreover, the rubricator—or *a* rubricator—sometimes draws the kinds of flourishes normally reserved for the ends of text underlining *on* the figures (compare, for example, the flourish-end underneath "accepit," fol. 8, with the red doodle in Mede's hair on the same page). This kind of activity could be the idle "doodling" of an apprentice rubricator. Complicating this even further, however, is the pattern of rubrication-color use: the quality of painting is for some reason uneven across the cycle. This unevenness does correlate with rubrication color use to some extent—most noticeably, but by no means exclusively, in the last three quires (quires 12, 13, 14), where the painter rarely uses colors other than black, brown, yellow, and red (the main colors used in rubrication or highlighting throughout the manuscript); of the twelve figures in these last three quires, only three have any color other than a rubrication color. There was clearly some skimping on materials as work on the manuscript drew to a close, a factor that in itself suggests the slightly mercenary thinking of a "professional" workshop, or perhaps the end of a budget or allotment for this particular project.

A final complication in assessing the role of the rubricator(s) is that at important stages in the *ordinatio* of the poem, like the opening of Dowel on folio 45v, the four-letter initial is decorated with a blue and pink background in which white has been used for highlighting, just as it has been (for instance) in the robes of Conscience, Wrath, and Sloth above. Whether the rubricator wielding the red for ordinary Latin quotes (doing at best a mediocre job of it) and contributing his crude overlining of some of the pictures could be the same person who provided these more elaborate decorations is worth asking. As Pearsall has pointed out, if the rubricator was the main scribe, it is odd that he missed his own guide letter at the opening of passus I (fol. 4v; the guide letter is a *W* and the rubricator has painted a *T*)—although one is also tempted to say that perhaps only "the boss" would take the liberty of ignoring the guide letter and thus "improving" the text. In short, although we feel that there is evidence to support the theory of a second rubricator, it is impossible to be absolutely conclusive about it, but at least in trying to decide one is forced into an appreciation of the complexity of its making and made aware of how many times the various professional readers *went back over and over the manuscript,* highlighting, adjusting, "improving."[84]

It is difficult to say whether Douce's makers were perhaps less "professional" (say, by London standards) or whether they were simply following local procedures for less formal book production: for example, the mode of entering annotations when compared with a London production like Ellesmere looks amateurish, but looks simply characteristic next to the *Red Book* fragment. In any event, the fact that a manuscript with such an unusually high number of illustrations was the product of at least two, probably three hands is perfectly reasonable, and suggests a professional workshop situation in most senses of that concept. We have, moreover, Griffiths' suggestion that the erasures on the last folio obscure an illustrator's accounting, which is certainly evidence of "professionalism."[85] We might also note that the corrector took a very serious interest in preparing his manuscript for his Hiberno-English audience (see appendix 1). For many reasons it would be inaccurate to label this manuscript as simply an "amateur" production.

Certain of the illustrations suggest that the artist may have used a model book or another pictorial source for the initial drawing process. Some of the most *artistically* (as opposed to *interpretively*) successful fall into this category: the dreamer (figure 1), Conscience (figure 4), the king (figure 5), the pilgrim (figure 9), possibly the knight (figure 11), Elde (figure 26), and Mercy (figure 33). The males in this group all share a squarish jaw that sets them apart from the many round-chinned figures elsewhere in the cycle, but we have already seen exactly this distinction between caricatured and uncaricatured figures in the *Red Book*. In at least one instance we know that the manuscript was pricked (the devil, fol. 96r, bears prick-marks, more readily visible from the verso, and evidence of pouncing—a low-budget way of reproducing pictures): whether this is because the illustrator was using a visual source to produce the figure or, as Hilmo has suggested, because some later "artist" was *copying* Douce's devil remains uncertain. However, for much of the cycle the illustrator was likely thrown back on his own resources. We know from the way the pictures reflect or take account of various textual errors peculiar to Douce that his illustrations were likely created in response to the text he was copying from (take, for instance, the pilgrim's bell [figure 9], an oddity of the text in Douce only, and the text next to the picture of the skeleton [figure 31]).[86]

Placement is also crucial in determining whether the illustrator was the scribe. The uncanny way in which the artist has matched pictures to text so that figures hold or stand upon or look directly at key words has been noted repeatedly in this study. The fact that several illustrations were demonstrably done before the text,[87] an unusual order of events in book production, argues in itself for a scribe-illustrator. The scribe-artist seems to have moved back and forth between text and illustration, sometimes anticipating where the text would be and completing the drawing ahead of it (Glutton, Hunger, and the lawyer [figure 15], for instance, were certainly done ahead of the text), sometimes (more often, in fact) completing the text first. But likely only the underdrawing was done before text; therefore adjustments could later be made, at the painting stage, on eyes, hands, and so on (these have often been visibly slightly adjusted toward text: e.g., the "bug" eyes on Wastor [figure 12] and Hunger's strangely elongated hand and his eyes [fol. 38] were likely adjustments afterward to emphasize text-image relationships). The fact that there is no fixed number of lines per page, as there usually is in *Piers* manuscripts, and that ruling is minimal may have been helpful factors in this process: he sometimes squashed or expanded the written text as necessary (note, for instance, the markedly reduced size of the text to accommodate Lady Mede in figure 3), but he did not always see problems coming, as evidenced by the number of places that words are squashed up against figures, something that occurs as well in one of the extant Giraldian manuscripts (see figure 45). Nor did he immediately realize the potential for relating text and image so intimately; his first attempt was likely with Mede riding on the sheriff on folio 10 (figure 2), and by folio 25 he was so proficient that he was making visual puns.

Perhaps the most important evidence that his work habits are ad hoc—and not those of a large commercial workshop artist—is that he does not think (or work) in terms of bifolium structure. We have charted all the illustrations according to the quire structure of the manuscript and can find few of the relationships between pictures connected by shared bifolia that, for instance, Sylvia Huot found in her study of *Romance of the Rose* manuscripts. (There are only rarely relationships in subject or in paint color.)[88] This explains to some extent why the Douce artist's approach to the text is so very "readerly" compared with the work of illustrators in more lavish manuscripts made in large workshops. He thinks as a *scribe*, not as an illustrator, in matters of placement and layout, and his work looks deceptively "unprofessional" as a result (rather like that of another great "readerly" illustrator, Matthew Paris). Moreover, textual layout (e.g., the opening of a new passus, which required flourishing) or physical defects in the parchment often affect his placement of pictures, sometimes making it impossible to place a picture where it should be, but he is relatively ingenious in overcoming these problems, as we have seen, for instance, with Mercy (figure 33).

As more studies are made of medieval scribe-illustrators, even more sophisticated techniques for distinguishing the work of scribe-illustrators will emerge, and as more studies of manuscript "production teams" are carried out, strategies for distinguishing among artisans working on the same manuscript will develop.[89] As we learn more about the role patrons played in the process, some of the things that appear so mysterious in Douce (suppression of planned pictures, Scrooge-like budgetary measures, and paradoxically abundant quantities of illustration, all in the same manuscript) may be explicable. Extant patrons' contracts show that they sometimes dictated minute or eccentric details of production, including color and rubrication choices, as well as iconography.[90] The Douce patron himself likely made the decision to have *Piers Plowman* translated into

Hiberno-English (which suggests a certain cultural and political awareness), as well as the decision to opt for an extensive pictorial cycle balanced by severe economies elsewhere. Whoever he was, he was not rich, nor were his tastes complacently bourgeois. He was apparently a man of enviable visual literacy and distinctive sociopolitical views — and he was a man who intended to *use* the book, to use each page, as we will see, meditatively and mnemonically. Or, at least, the scribe-illustrator *believed* he was or should be, and he rose to the challenge of providing a book that would do all this. And succeeded.

For us, the close-knit relations between text and image in Douce are best explained as the work of a creative and capable scribe-illustrator. Scott found it "virtually impossible to comment on the possibility of the scribe and illustrator being the same craftsman";[91] we find it virtually impossible to imagine how a manuscript such as Douce — with the fully integrative and economical reading experience it offers — could have otherwise come into being.

PART II

✤

Visual Heuristics
Denise L. Despres

CHAPTER 5

⁜

Visualizing the Text
The Heuristics of the Page

Visualizing the Text

A cursory look at Douce 104 is bound to disappoint literary scholars accustomed to viewing the luxury manuscripts of fourteenth- and fifteenth-century English poetry as supplemental evidence for historical contextualization. In comparison with the richly illuminated manuscripts in the Gothic international style, Douce 104 can only be considered a poor imitation, produced in a colonial backwater by a scribal illustrator and rubricator (perhaps the same) influenced by decidedly old-fashioned styles. The illustrator in the provincial workshop where Douce 104 was produced opened the Prologue with the manuscript's single historiated initial; the rubricator recognized where a gold spray was appropriate and marked each subsequent passus with a Lombard capital. But none of these efforts, despite some fairly elegant character portraits, meets the standard of illustration we are accustomed to associating with productions of the works of Chaucer or Lydgate. According to the dictates of "connoisseurship-based art history," it is tempting to dismiss Douce 104 as a "utility-grade" manuscript providing scanty material evidence of a cultural milieu.[1] Although G. H. Russell, for example, admitted to "an amateur" eye, he dismissed the Douce illustrations as "unambitious" in his reception study of some C-text manuscripts, using the Ellesmere manuscript as his illustrative standard.[2] If we broaden our focus from decorative luxury manuscripts to consider the evidence of interpretation provided by professional readers (the scribes, illustrators, and annotators) of utility-grade manuscripts, we can learn to read images as a "process of performance in both production and reception."[3]

In Douce, we can reconstruct, however tentatively, a reading of *Piers Plowman* that is immediate, localized, and politicized, as opposed to static and finalized. Reading from the margins, we can comprehend a visual heuristic that constructs, directs, and even challenges textual meanings through a matrix of images, providing us with a commentary on, rather than pictures of, the narrative. With his reformist and iconomachic bent, the Douce illustrator used the margins to puzzle through the visual trajectory of *Piers Plowman*, engaged throughout by the moral issue of representation in a sacramental and incarnational world. Whatever his technical abilities, the Douce illustrator was sensitive to the tension between text and image, the plurality of meanings engendered by the layout of the manuscript page, and the space between narrator and reader inherent in any dream vision, which can only be relayed through "visual voices."[4]

Although she did not articulate her own sensitive response to *Piers Plowman* in the terms of New Historicism or the New Art History,[5] Elizabeth Salter anticipated reception studies, expressing her own doubts about evaluating *Piers Plowman* in the context of English court culture, where it shares neither the literary conventions of dream visions in the courtly love tradition nor their lavish physical production. In her 1971 essay "*Piers Plowman* and the Visual Arts," Salter identified a key element in the spatial design of this puzzling dream vision.[6] Intrigued by the unlocalized or "empty settings" of the colloquies in the poem, Salter mused that the lack of concrete landscapes resulted in an impression of visual foregrounding altogether different from emptiness. She concluded that the gold screen against which "foreground events may be seen to greater advantage" in Gothic manuscripts is not empty space, but "functions as a spiritual comment.... It is almost the reverse of emptiness." Seeking Langland's visual models, Salter eventually rejected lavishly illuminated religious manuscripts as illustrative paradigms and concluded that Langland's backgrounds are better "represented in visual terms by the plain, empty space of the manuscript page, as it appears behind and through the line drawings of humbler mediaeval book illustrators, who are similarly concerned with the essential shape of an act, or an episode, rather than all of its supporting and corroborative detail."[7] Those "bare unsubstantiated" backgrounds in the narrative, she argued, are created as if "exhibited to the eye of faith alone."[8] In attempting to place *Piers Plowman* in an iconographic tradition, Salter dislocated the poem from a courtly reading dynamic and described one of the visual strategies offered by a medieval reader, like the Douce illustrator, whose marginal illustrative program underscores a meditative reading.

The "eye" that Salter described is the curious "inner eye" of the mind that medieval devotional and mystical writers, often the most insistent voices of personal and institutional reform, used metaphorically to signal interior vision or mental showing of memory and meditation.[9] Given her own extensive study of medieval meditation, Salter recognized the way that the "inner eye" recollects events, scenes, voices, and bits and fragments of texts, while the memory forges all into purposeful, salvific patterns with the aid of imagination. This "collatio" is the process of both the *visio* and spiritual autobiography; in the Middle Ages such self-reflective processes were recognized as part of the process of composition, whether or not they produced a written text like Margery Kempe's *Book* or Augustine's *Confessions*.[10] The faculty of memory is integral to the pursuit of a moral life, enabling the penitent or pilgrim to recognize prudence as the object of all meditation.[11] Imagination is the visual faculty that coalesces meaningful, often illusive fragments of memory for recollection and examination. Taking place in the foremost cell of the mind, the imagination conjures images in prayer or sleep, shutting out "external stimuli, especially visual ones that distract the 'recollective eye.'"[12] As Mary Carruthers has noted, sleeping figures became a sign of *meditatio* in a medieval spiritual vocabulary that was simultaneously visual and oral. A plain background to foreground images became consistent in medieval memory treatises as well as in legal manuscripts, devotional works, biblical commentaries, and chronicles, precisely the corpus of manuscripts the Douce illustrator appears to have known.[13]

Viewing *Piers Plowman* as a *visio*, we have resumed Salter's line of inquiry not from the text, but with material evidence of the Douce illuminator's deliberate *creation* of "meditative space" through his reading and representation of the poem. This visionary sense of space, inviting interpretation and participation, is recreated in Douce 104 through single-figure marginal illustrations pressed against the "empty" space of the folio page, often touching or pointing to a foregrounded text. If we compare these illustrations with those in medieval secular texts, which often convey complete, framed scenes and construct "visual glosses" or "parallel" narratives, we will be disappointed.[14] While the Douce 104 illustrations, like most medieval manuscript illustrations, may sometimes serve as rubrics in dividing or emphasizing parts of the text, they primarily serve a mnemonic and meditative function, asking a different response from the manuscript reader than do ornate illustrations in secular works. Their logic is not so much narrative as homiletic—moving from spiritual point to point in a manner reminiscent of the "mnemonic techniques of the sermon, . . . of the oral transmission of images."[15] The Douce illustrator's awareness of the poem's meditative function may help us understand why "*Piers Plowman*, more predictably, is published . . . in smaller format, often with other religious or didactic pieces, and rarely with more than minimal decoration; more manuscripts come from outside London" or, presumably, areas of wealth or influence.[16]

Like most dream visions, the poem is richly visual, but the Douce 104 illustrator eschews the traditional iconography of dream visions—the narrative, allegorical, and scriptural—in favor of an original and reformist interpretation of the poem. Thus the one illustrated manuscript of *Piers Plowman* that we do have is a precious legacy, teaching us how imagery and issues of spiritual authority are linked in the fifteenth-century illustrator's perspective. The illustrator's awareness of the complex, recollective structure of the poem as a vision comprising waking and dream experiences is central to his *visionary ordinatio*. He provides a sophisticated understanding of memory as an oral and visual process—that "the ability to hear visually—to picture mentally what is heard—is as important to verbal comprehension as hearing is to visual discernment."[17] Although sufficiently knowledgeable of iconographic traditions to modify them when it suited his purpose, the Douce illustrator frequently rejected stable religious imagery to emphasize timely ethical and ideological sensibilities with a socioreligious impact.

We would be mistaken, however, in separating personal and spiritual from social or ecclesiological reform in our examination of the Douce illustrator's visual vocabulary and iconomachia. If he rejected the traditional pious imagery that we are accustomed to in vernacular books owned by men and women in fourteenth- and fifteenth-century England, it is not because he wished to sever the link between personal compunction and social reform.[18] Rather, his visual heuristic dismisses affective piety with a purely sacramental end—confession and pilgrimage—and emphasizes evangelical spirituality and social realism. The illustrations forge a visionary *ordinatio* that underscores both personal reformation and social accountability, urging a retrospective or ethical response from the reader. The Douce illustrative program interprets the text's moral content, rather than its story line, thereby arousing the emotions and moral faculties like conscience; only by doing so will the pictures help the viewer to experience, store, and retrieve the poem's meaning. As stated before, this means creating impressions, rather than mere images of narrative events. The visual heuristic of Douce 104 points to the illustrator's intention for us to remember voices, to connect speeches with images, to associate speeches and images from passus to passus. He creates a reading process in Douce 104 that is palpable, dramatic, and experiential, appealing to both eyes and ears. The placement of images on the folio page emphasizes the relationship between speakers and their words; the reader both witnesses and receives the dialogue, taking on the dreamer's role as a questioner of authority. The annotations, in turn, present the reader with a second set of responses, at times antagonistic to the illustrative program. This kind of reading process creates another narrative that we call participatory or self-reflexive reading, for the reader must negotiate his or her emotional response to the various images, be they grostesque, erotic, or affective. Far from being prescriptive, a visionary *ordinatio* invites disruption and personal reflection; the marginal pictures do not serve a purely illustrative function, but they are "exegetical and heuristic cues" marking an interior journey to self-illumination.[19] Adopting the metaphor of pilgrimage to describe monastic reading, Ivan Illich describes medieval manuscript illumination as the stimuli to evoke from the memory entire conversations (the *voces paginarum*) that take place on the journey; the illustration, in contrast, is the snapshot of the commuter or tourist. The distinction is quite appropriate for the dream vision, a synthesis of dialogues and images, which the Douce illustrator presents as disjunctive.

The Douce illustrator's iconomachia undoubtedly reflects his preference for practical reform rather than theological or speculative argumentation, but this does not mean that he understood *Piers Plowman* reductively as a "social document" or that the quest he surely illustrates is devoid of spiritual import.[20] The Douce illustrator's frequent representation of author as dreamer and pilgrim, a spiritual transient in the midst of the poor, disendowed, and corrupt, signals his location of the self within, rather than without, a community bereft of spiritual direction and reliable political authority. As in the illustrative programs of medieval Apocalypse manuscripts,

> the visual strategies that activate the spiritual self are inseparably bound up with contemporary ideological constellations of hierarchical values.... ideology is not limited to the representation of the content of John's visions, but pervades how the images work to construct spiritual experience. Thus, the ideological and spiritual... must be seen as interpenetrating components of a single *mentalité* in which the dualities between active propagandizing and devotional meditation, external social realities and the internal world of the reader, tend to dissolve.[21]

In the *visio*, we cannot divorce the personal, spiritual state of the dreamer from the larger concerns of politics, history, and eschatology. The illustrator's selection and omission of images convey his iconomachia, and thus his need to negotiate the paradox of creating imagery and representing the most self-reflexive and polysemous genre of poetry (the dream vision), despite its obvious dangers to his readers: idolatry, heresy, political misinterpretation, and spiritual reductionism. His socioreligious commentary and his deliberate avoidance of icons of any sort despite their availability in pattern books are preliminary clues to a visual heuristic that underscores the mutual instability and power of images. More pointedly, the illustrator links the typical luxury of manuscript production, such as the use of gold leaf on Pride's folly bells, as well as images of money (represented by his depiction of the merchant with a lap full of golden coins [figure 34] and the bad penny on fol. 78), with seduction; his subtle use of gold dust to illuminate figures who exemplify spiritual poverty is alternatively radically reformist. While his grudging application of gold may at first sight indicate a small budget, other evidence, such as his employment of the process of gold spray, may point instead to a deliberate rejection of those elements of book production that he associated with luxury, the spiritual complacency of rich patrons that Langland identifies with the purchase of stained glass and chantry prayers or with spiritual ease and corruption.[22] Similarly, the Douce illustrator's choice of color, his use of expensive and aristocratic pinks and blues on figures like Pride and Mede, may associate rich color with excess. His highly selective program of images and all that is entailed in image-making (color, placement in relationship to the text, placement on the page and in relation to other images) heightens the polemic of real pilgrimage (suffering and imitation of Christ) as opposed to false (merely physical) pilgrimage, genuine spirituality as opposed to hypocrisy, and visual excess as opposed to the right use of images. The illustrator challenges the reader, and seer, to experience such distinctions through a process of meditation—not upon reliable images like the crucifix, but on the all-too-familiar images of the poor, the impoverished, and the dissimulating. This is the world, after all, in which the ordinary Christian must make his or her moral choices.

In this program, the Douce illustrator is even more reformist than the Lollard illustrator of Oxford, Bodleian Library, MS Bodley 978—a Wycliffite gospel harmony (figures 40–42). This illustrator is a typical iconomach in his association of images with specific scriptural passages; they function purely as mnemonics, recalling words for meditation rather than scenes for affective devotion. Images in themselves do not present a moral problem, but rather, the worship of "dead" images instead of the "living word." The Bodleian 978 illustrator provides marginal illustrations, such as a wine cask on folio 32 beside the admonition not to put new wine in old casks, or a cup beside Christ's offer of charity, a cup of cold water, to the least in the kingdom. As if to emphasize his own literalism, the illustrator identified each object he depicted with a caption, the key word from the passage beside it, such as "an moot" beneath a rather startling picture of an eye with a mote in it or "cuppe" beside a cup of cold water. Thus he created a fairly standard iconomachic word-image relationship, in which images are permissible to teach laypersons Scripture, particularly those that serve as reminders of scriptural passages advocating apostolic life. Margaret Aston identifies such cautious use of imagery as the moderate Lollard position, reminding us of the Lollard association of rich images with clerical corruption and idolatry.[23] Indeed, the Bodleian 978 illustrator is so moderate that he actually includes a small image of a cross, rather than a crucifix, in the margin (figure 41) beside Christ's rejection of half-hearted disciples who fail to take up the cross and follow him. So clear was the distinction between "cross" as a recollective tool and *the Cross* as an object of worship that the illustrator came very close to reproducing the kind of image held problematic by Lollards. Indeed, a marginal drawing of a crucifix was added to Douce 240 (Oxford, Bodleian Library), an English Wycliffite New Testament, in the fifteenth century, further evidence of the complexity of iconomachia.[24] Clearly, there is nothing like this in the more reformist illustrative program of Douce 104, whose illustrator is equally concerned with apostolic injunctions. The Douce 104 illustrator does take a similar interpretive risk in using the gold dust on figures like Patience, the lunatic lollar, and Elde, but he clearly prefers to distinguish spiritual wealth and worldly impoverishment as Christlike without religious symbols or icons. In this, he approximates Lollard pronouncements on the proper use of images as is set forth in a late-fourteenth- or early-fifteenth-century treatise on images; images must be truthful and not too splendid if they are to teach, for "poor followers of Christ should have art that was suitable—humble and self-effacing."[25] As is his custom, the Douce illustrator provides a unique visual metaphor that legitimizes not only the spiritual principle of apostolic poverty but also his method of illustrating it without artistic transgression.

The Douce illustrator is moved by the same concern with social injustice in which Lollard iconomachia was rooted; instead of bestowing gifts of clothing upon dead images, the Christian's primary responsibility is to the poor, who exemplify Christ.[26] As poor priests, Lollards had the duty to teach that "Man, specially the man whose condition was that of Christ's own poverty, was the only true image of God."[27] The margins of Douce 104 reflect this preoccupation with social justice and the purpose of the Incarnation. The disendowed figures who inhabit the margins are citizens of a spiritual economy gone awry; the dreamer cannot become Christlike until, as Elde (figure 26), he shares their misery and their consolation. The poor blind man (figure 17) and Patience (figure 30) are identified as true pilgrims by their staves and the gold dust that marks their spiritual value, while the conventional pilgrim (figure 9), dressed in traditional garb with a broad hat, is entirely suspect, as are all the well-heeled, too appropriately costumed "actors" in Douce 104. Like a Lollard, then, the Douce illustrator connects pilgrimage with false "signs," bells and scrips and bags that do not signal genuine spiritual journey or transformation in the form of Christian service to the poor. Meditation upon the images in his margin must be distinguished from meditation upon religious statuary, just as spiritual pilgrimage must be defined apart from holiday travel. Douce 104, then, shares some of the characteristics of what Anne Hudson calls "peripheral" Wycliffite manuscripts; in its production, it reflects "individual...idiosyncratic interest," and appears to have been created for private rather than public reading.[28] In choosing a marginal format for his illustrations, however, the Douce illustrator deliberately constructed a synthetic, meditative sequence, exhibiting his familiarity with the process of reading utility-grade manuscripts—an identifiable, much neglected brand of cultural literacy—gospel harmonies, chronicles (where events assume an importance in the larger scheme of salvation that must be discerned by the reader), legal and medical compendia, and devotional works. One must ask an obvious question with a surprisingly complex answer to comprehend the nature of his imagery. *Piers Plowman* has a fairly substantial manuscript tradition, yet this is the only extant illustrated manuscript. Why choose to produce this "laicized" or illustrated version of the poem at all? And why choose *marginal* illustrations, apart from the usual exigencies of book production, such as space and economy?

Marginal Illustration and Meditative Reading

Given the more likely choice of *bas de page* unframed scenes or framed column pictures in literary compendia, as is exemplified in the Vernon manuscript (Oxford, Bodleian Library, MS English Poetry a.1), or commonly in luxury manuscripts, the marginal illustrations in Douce 104 automatically raise complex questions about the relationship between manuscript production and medieval reading processes. We cannot hastily conclude that the Douce illustrations were drawn by an artist insufficiently skilled to produce more detailed pictures. The "immediacy" of the Douce illustrations, upon first impression, may make them seem less sophisticated than the pictorial cycles from other poetic works or in manuscripts for private devotional reading, such as the fifteenth-century English verse and prose translations of the *Pèlerinage de la vie humaine*;[29] however, Kathleen Scott concluded from their originality and the skill exhibited in the artist's rendering of some difficult postures that the illustrator was both "subtle" and capable.[30] The choice of marginal illustration for a lengthy poem like *Piers Plowman* was deliberate and unusual, for while "the principle of placing figures and scenes in margins and borders had been well established in the fourteenth century... there was virtually no fourteenth-century tradition for placing pictorial subjects relevant to the text in a marginal position."[31] Scott thus determined that they serve a largely "emphatic function" and that they do not suggest interest in narrative scenes so much as "choice of speakers, personifications, allusions, and objects mentioned in a passage."[32] Undoubtedly, such visual pointers function mnemonically to reconstruct the dream vision. Since every speaker is not granted such distinction, however, a process of selection and thus interpretation is clearly at work in providing the most significant characters and passages for emphasis.

Precedents for marginal illustration of vernacular works may be found in Scott's useful "List of Late Fourteenth- and Fifteenth-Century English Manuscripts with Marginal Illustrations," countering the notion that Douce 104 is eccentric or anomalous.[33] Of the twenty-six works listed, at least fourteen are ethical, penitential, or devotional in nature, those titles including some of the most influential works of the Late Middle Ages, such as *Cursor Mundi*, the *South English Legendary*, and *The Pilgrimage of the Life of Man*, as well as writings by Richard Rolle, Michael de Massa's *Writings on the Passion* (Oxford, Bodleian Library, MS Bodley 758 [see figures 43–44]), and more explicitly practical volumes, such as a book of prayers (London, British Library, MS Add. 22720) and a "religious miscellany" (London, BL, MS Add. 37049 [see figures 59–61]).³⁴ In addition, those texts on the list we often think of as "secular" works of counsel, such as Lydgate's *Troy Book* and Thomas Hoccleve's *De Regimine Principium*, are meditative in that they primarily seek to reform character.³⁵ All thus typify the moral and spiritual agenda that characterizes the manuscripts containing *Piers Plowman*.³⁶

As early as the thirteenth century, Anglo-Norman vernacular religious miscellany were compiled for lay patrons; a rare, illustrated manuscript of this sort, a late-thirteenth-century confessional and devotional book produced for a noblewoman, contains the very kind of instructional material for laypersons that is the fabric of *Piers Plowman*.³⁷ Princeton, Princeton University Library, MS Taylor Medieval I features marginal illustrations, diagrams of moral and theological concepts like the "Seven Vices of Corrupt Nature," and even an image of the female patron in a historiated initial, standing over a figure of a tonsured clerk who points toward the text with a pen and knife—the scribe.³⁸ Like the Douce illustrator, the illustrator of Joan Tateshal's spiritual compendia "did not rely on pictorial models from other contexts. Rather, he depended upon the text," creating vivid, dramatic, and at times startling images that suggest a high level of vernacular literacy.³⁹ Such penitential visual traditions—the Virtues and Vices, the Seven Ages of Man, illustrated exempla of the Ten Commandments, the Wheel of Fortune—are common in other vernacular devotional books that share an iconography with Douce 104, such as the illustrious Psalter of Robert de Lisle.⁴⁰ The Douce 104 illustrator was undoubtedly familiar with the visual traditions and marginal format from such ethical works; he includes familiar figures like the Wheel of Fortune and the Seven Deadly Sins among his drawings. His choice of marginal illustration, rather than being expedient, may indicate his sense of genre and function. Scott comments upon the unusual contrast between the "willingness to bear the expense of extensive illustration side by side with a decided skimpiness in the formatting of the poem."⁴¹ Marginal illustrations in the empty space tend to signal a reflective kind of reading or envisioning and thus may help us better understand a medieval reader's sense of a literary work's function through physical formatting.

Traditionally, medieval legal and religious texts were marginally glossed, preserving the integrity of the text and simultaneously inviting a nonlinear or contemplative mode of reading:⁴²

> The choreography of reading was especially important in works with complex marginal glosses, interlinear additions and subsections.... while ostensibly providing an ordered framework for the experience of linguistic meaning, the visual also acts to disrupt any linear unitary responses by providing fissures in that smooth progression.

Holes of representations, pockets of pictorial narrative, are cracks in the scribal edifice that "lead us away" from the textual hierarchy.[43]

Marginal illustrations in the empty space function like the faculty of imagination, calling *specific* images to the forefront of thought or recollection for the kind of personal, emotional response necessary to meditation and integral to composition. The Douce figures not only interpret the text, but they also become a part of the reader's memory; in doing so, they enable the reader to mesh his experience with the dreamer's. The manuscript reader engages the text, but he or she is called away from and then sent back to other sections of the text, even discrete words, resulting in a directed reading experience that approximates the dream vision—disjunctive, unsettling, comical, nightmarish.

If we accept the premise that marginal illustrations serve purposes other than illustration, we can see how cursory the attention given to them by critics has been. Russell, for example, speculates that the Douce 104 illustrator grasps "with certainty" the text he illustrates, and is thus able to insert images of speakers at the proper moment when their respective speeches occur, but he does not see them as doing more than "amplifying" or "clarifying" the text.[44] To make this assumption of textual stability, however, Russell must ignore the evidence of interpretive conflict provided by the marginal annotations. The Douce illustrator himself appears to have recognized the poem's difficulty, for he expended his greatest efforts in those very passus that modern readers find most incomprehensible: "The Ploughing of the Half Acre," "The Pardon Sent from Truth," "The Discourse of Study, Clergy, and Recklessness," and "The Coming of Antichrist" (passus VIII, IX, XI, and XXII). The narrative and thematic cruxes that have eluded *Piers* scholars for centuries—the role of Hunger, the meaning of the pardon, the function of Recklessness, and the meaning of Unity—occur in the most heavily illustrated folios.[45] In these difficult passus, constituted less of events than of a series of dialogues, the marginal illustrations naturally elucidate the oral and dialectical nature of the dream vision. Just as medieval mystical texts are largely colloquies, sometimes little more than transcribed mystical utterance, medieval meditative works feature a "hermeneutical dialogue between the mind of the reader and the absent voices which the written letters call forth."[46] The fifteenth-century illustrator clearly understood the acoustical, dialogic nature of the poem and thus marks speeches with speakers.

These figures may have a variety of functions, as their various positions in relation to the text suggest. Some appear in profile, their bodies bracketing the text, their pronounced noses or bugged eyes functioning like a manicule to indicate a specific line (Liar [fol. 9], the friar [figure 20], and Activa Vita [figure 29]). These illustrations indicate that a particular part of a speech is important or that the speech is to be *heard* out loud, even if read silently, in keeping with the dialogic nature of the dream vision. Other figures glance dubiously at the text or close their eyes and turn their backs to it altogether (the blind man [figure 17] and Patience [figure 30]). All of these images offer specific commentary from the margins, although at their most basic the figures serve as markers, enabling the reader to reconstruct dialogue for remembrance. The confessions of the sins, meant to be heard aloud in homiletic fashion, are bracketed in part by the figures who represent them, often in specific detail and sometimes against iconographic convention.[47] The Douce illustrator has also found a way to dramatize the text's disruption; in the upper right-hand corner of folio 35v (figure 10), a bearded, chaperoned Contemplatif juts his head as abruptly onto the folio page as his speech appears, a visual challenge to the complaints of those too busy to follow Piers.

While Douce 104 abounds with examples of marginal figures signaling dialogue and thus the manuscript's visionary *ordinatio*, one particular example in passus IX underscores the crisis of textual authority through performative reading. The illustrator twice has occasion to draw documents, and both pictures (the first is Liar with the marriage charter) question the credibility of written authority. The illustration of a tonsured priest, holding Truth's pardon to Piers, its authoritative seal dangling down (figure 19), is of particular interest because of its performative nature and its juxtaposition of the Latin and a vernacular translation. The priest's mouth is aligned with the line "For schal no pardon preye for ȝow there ne no princes lettres" (IX.281), and his body spans his speech, wherein he claims to find no pardon but "Dowel." Scott suggests that the figure's curiously protruding tongue may even be a sign of reading aloud.[48] What is intriguing, however, is not that the priest reads aloud the lines of the pardon—"Qui bona egerunt ibunt in vitam eternam; / Qui vero mala in ignem eternum"—for the positioning of the marginal figure suggests that this is oral performance (IX.288–89). What is clever is the manner in which the "Y" of the poem, presumably standing behind the priest and Piers, "byheld alle þe bulle / In twȯ lynes as hit lay and nat a lettre more" (IX.285–86).[49] The manuscript reader sees along with the "Y"—the dreamer—of the poem the imposing Latin passage underlined in red beside the marginal figure on the folio page. The reader's vision becomes the dreamer's for a moment in the poem, viewing the passage translated by the priest. The reader thus becomes the dreamer at the moment that the search for Dowel begins, silently witnessing the jangling between the priest and Perkyn before awakening on Malvern Hills. By calling attention to the simple lines in the poem that construct Dowel as the moral life, primarily by the pictorial representation of the pardon and by embodying the spoken English translation in the marginal figure, the illustrator has created an oral and visual mnemonic, an image

Denise L. Despres

recollecting not so much a dramatic scene as its ethical ambiguity. Further, the illustrator has not only presented to but also involved the reader in the dangerous issue of Latin and vernacular textuality and authority. In the drawings of both Liar and the priest with the pardon, the documents jut out of the margins and are juxtaposed with the text, a depiction perhaps of competing texts and meanings.

The marginal illustrations in Douce 104 help us postulate how a near-contemporary reader of Langland's poem envisioned the experiential order of the dream vision, enabling us to refine absolutist arguments about the dreamer's function and identity based solely on printed editions. Stephen Nichols has argued that manuscripts contain various "systems of representation" resulting in "systemic rivalry."[50] Annotations, glosses, rubrics, miniatures, historiated initials, and scribal emendations function together to produce "multiple forms of representation" or a multidimensional poetic experience.[51] Because the narrative of *Piers Plowman* is not linear to begin with, we ought to expect professional readers of the poem — annotators, scribes, and illuminators — already attuned to the competitive, interpretive nature of manuscript technology, to produce an equally multivalent rendition of its meaning. This does not mean, however, that they are insensitive to the "text" or language or that they are always in disagreement. If, for example, we consider how the illustrator and the annotator comprehend the role of the narrator in the poem, it is clear that they share moments of vision. One of the most striking annotations occurs on folio 21 and reads simply "I had noo wyll to do gode." The annotation is a response to the opening of passus V, the apologia, where the wakened narrator reports his life of indolence. One might expect a drawing of the narrator at this most personal moment, if the illustrations served the simple function of narrative glossing. The illustrator waits until the narrator becomes the dreamer again, instead providing a picture of Tom Stowe with his two staves, which occurs after the dreamer has once again fallen asleep. Both the annotator and the illustrator comprehend the self-reflexivity of the *visio*. The annotator is summing up the ethical import of the apologia, marking the narrator's disordered *affectus* here. But although there are many dreamer portraits in Douce 104, they are all self-portraits in the sense that they belong to the spiritually aware, self-reflexive moments within the dream vision. The illustrator understands that the poem's text is the sleeper's reconstructed remembrance of experience; the narrator's metadiscursive voice is important, but the illustrative program's purpose is to recreate the experience of the vision, and this is different from merely illustrating the "story." The dreamer portraits reflect the "Y" of the poem at various stages of his journey (the subject of the next chapter), drawing figures not so much to suggest the poem's narrative content as to reflect the manifestations of the dreamer's inner life.[52] Given that the annotator often writes aggressively over the illustrator's pictures at important moments, clearly asserting his own opinion of the poem's ethical meaning, their different responses to the apologia are evidence of their mutually careful reading but different responsibilities in the manuscript's production.

From the first folio, the artist indicates a certain knowledge of the iconographic tradition of the dreamer, perhaps from dream vision poetry or illustrated Apocalypse manuscripts, both of which feature authors as dreamers from a recollective standpoint. Suzanne Lewis's study of the "complex, transgressive figure" of John in relation to the text of Apocalypse manuscripts suggests some interesting similarities between the Douce dreamer and John:[53]

> In many thirteenth-century English manuscripts, John frequently witnesses the apocalyptic events as a spectator physically isolated from the vision. Standing outside the frame, he shares a place in the corporeal world of the reader, clearly distinguishable from the spiritual, timeless realm represented within. The frame is no longer perceived as an impermeable boundary, a perimeter conceptually disavowed or repressed, but now plays an active role in the visual semiosis of the text-image.[54]

Lewis identifies John's ability to move between the world within the frame, the vision, and without, the world of the reader, as interpretive; "Indeed, the concept of the author becomes a heuristic device created by the process of interpretation" signaled by his position "adjacent to his text-vision."[55]

John is both the subject and object of his narrative, a story without the closure that can be provided only by the seer's death and access to the ultimate vision. The Douce illustrator, like the Apocalypse artist's in the English tradition, responds to the personal narrative in *Piers,* presenting the aging dreamer at various points in his life and spiritual progress, equally sensitive to the poem's lack of closure. We need to consider images of scribes, authors, and dreamers in Douce 104 carefully, given this illustrative tradition, specifically their physical relation to the text. The first image in Douce 104, and the only image in the panoramic Prologue, is a middle-aged man in a gray gown and tan cowl on folio 1, who is undoubtedly the dreamer (figure 1). Although his eyes are open, he sits with his head in his hands, a pose indicating the illustrator's "awareness of iconography used for several previous centuries, and, in the fifteenth century, to designate a dreamer-seer" and thus vision, meditation, and reflection, as well as an alternative iconographic tradition of sloth (cf. figure 8), wanhope, and despair.[56] It is likely that the illustrator conflated deliberately these two traditions in the figure on folio 1r. The dreamer perhaps holds an agricultural implement (the image is badly worn), connecting him early on to other characters in the program of illustrations, including a digger with a shovel (figure 13) and Piers the Plowman with a plow-stick (figure 10). Both the shovel and the plow were penitential symbols of varying degrees, connecting figures to Adam and "generic figures of Mankind" in late medieval manuscript illustration.[57] Thus from the first folio we have a figure who, open-eyed and self-conscious, presents several of the poem's most difficult themes, such as the function of dream vision, the role of labor in a divine economy, and penance in the inevitable process of aging and death.

The figure of Elde (figure 26), in contrast, looks down from the text dejectedly, although his meditative posture undoubtedly signals self-recognition and illumination, or "human imaginative powers."[58] Having been reckless, adopting a life of immediate pleasures, the dreamer now assumes a consciously recollective stance in the poem. Elde is not a general allegorical character, but a specific representation of the dreamer. Thus one of the ways in which the poem may be memorized is by the progression of youth to age as a process of spiritual illumination and maturation. Elde's physical position connects him to the self-reflexive image of Imaginatif (figure 28), the next figure in the manuscript's illustrative program to appear seated, head in hand, his body spanning a speech about grace, good works, and their relationship to Dobet and Dobest.[59] Kathleen Scott likens this figure to an image of Boccaccio and a vision of Fortune that specifically connects the head-in-hand pose to authorship, as is undoubtedly the case here.[60] Like the author and seer John, Will is an author; without Imaginatif, Will could never awaken in passus XXI to write down his dreams. While Imaginatif affirms the importance of learning in the pilgrimage to truth, his role as mediator between sense experience and spiritual comprehension, through the creation of similitudes and examples, is essential to the process of spiritual autobiography.[61] Imaginatif, as many scholars have argued, derives from *vis imaginativa*, the mental faculty responsible for corporeal similitudes and abstractions from life experience, and thus of poetic activity itself.[62] In *Piers Plowman* this is a specific kind of poetic activity, aimed at spiritual reformation and thus a deliberate *collatio* of past, present, and future events from a meditative perspective. Dreams, like poetry, are not primarily intellectual, but affective.[63] John Alford argues that, as a faculty that "extrapolates from his memory of past experience what consequences his present course of behavior will have for the future... Imaginatif represents the exercise of prudence."[64] The Douce illustrator consistently signaled self-reflection by positioning the speaker's or subject's head in his hand; here, then, he rendered Imaginatif, a clerk, as a projection of the dreamer's spiritual gathering or self-recollection. As much as modern readers would like to exalt reason as the primary faculty in the reformation of human character and behavior, medieval writers insisted that feelings culled from memory by imagination, often inspired through the visual experience of meditation, took precedence. Meditation, therefore, joins memory in its dependence upon emotional stimulation and recollection.[65] Both were essential to the process of composition:

> In the teaching and practice of composition, however, the monastic cultivation of meditational prayer, itself evolving from practices in the ancient schools, remained dominant. This stressed emotion, the basis of memory, as the key to "creativity," as we can readily see from the fact that medieval *cogitatio*, translates... not as our phrase "reasoning out" (with its emphasis on logical connections) but as "mulling over," a process that depends heavily on free association and one's "feeling for" a matter.[66]

The ethical necessity of arousing compunction—or preferably Christian indignation at social injustice—in meditation results in the playful freedom with which meditative and pastoral writers were accustomed to treat scriptural themes and images; for images to elicit compunction they must be particularized as opposed to wholly generalized.[67] The same is not true, of course, of narrative illustration or the visual gloss, which merely instructs, explicates, or illustrates.[68] Attempting, then, to treat the Douce 104 illustrations as a visual gloss will work no better than efforts to read the poem in a systematic manner. From the figure of the sleeping dreamer in the initial, head in hand, to the figure of Imaginatif, head in hand, the illustrator signals his awareness of this work as an associative, ruminative work. The placement of images on the folio page emphasizes the relationship between speakers and their words; the reader both witnesses and receives the dialogue, taking on the dreamer's role as a questioner of authority. The annotations, in turn, present the reader with a second set of responses, at times antagonistic to the illustrative program. This double vision, to be compared in the Conclusion, produces a complex, multifaceted reading of the poem.

The Physical Shape of the Poem for the Medieval Reader

Students of medieval art and literature are familiar with the frequently reproduced scenes of fourteenth-century English life that appear in manuscripts like the Luttrell Psalter, or with the comical, obscene, and courtly marginalia so expertly cataloged by Lillian Randall in *Images in the Margins of Gothic Manuscripts*.[69] Only recently, however, have art historians developed sensitive heuristics to explore such images intact as an ideologically informed system of medieval visual semiotics.[70] Wrenching images out of context dislocates them from a carefully contrived system of interrelated signs:

> In this respect, marginal images are *conscious* usurpations, perhaps even political statements about diffusing the power of the text

through its unravelling (the word "text" is derived from *textus*, meaning weaving or interlacing), rather than repressed meanings that suddenly flash back onto the surface of things.... Another important aspect of the way marginal motifs work is not by reference to the text, but by reference to one another—the reflexivity of imagery not just across single pages but in chains of linked motifs and signs *that echo throughout a whole manuscript or book.*[71]

We have long regarded the margins as the locus for the profane or for personal and whimsical commentary, or as interpretive play space challenging an orthodox or universalized view inscribed by the words on the page. This is not quite the same, however, as recognizing the complex relationship between margin and center as a dynamic interplay of responses by those who created the manuscript—the scribe, the annotator, and the illustrator. The physical layout of Douce 104 exhibits a clear sense of the links between poetic making, visionary activity, and the physical reproduction of dream poetry in manuscript form on the part of its craftsmen. The poem recreates a vision for the reader, but its success in this enterprise is necessarily bound to its physical form. Of course this activity is dependent upon a wide range of variables, such as the patron's taste, wealth, and whether the manuscript was produced in a large commercial workshop in London (where the illustrator would undoubtedly have had on hand numerous model books) or in a small insular workshop, as Douce 104 surely was. The meaning of a marginal figure depends upon all of these variables, and even then some signs have multiple meanings, for the subversive nature of the margins lend themselves to polyvalence.

As an example, the figure of a young man on folio 72, poor and disheveled, sits with his back to the text that expounds on the patience of the poor.[72] The Douce illustrator is consistently sympathetic to the impoverished, and many of his most subtle and technically complex pictures are of the poor. Here, no doubt, the figure's posture is a signal of despair, dispossession, and social alienation, meant to elicit an affective response from the viewer. Even if the text failed to confirm this as the appropriate response, the illustrator's attempts to dignify the poor, who are often physically attractive, as is the case with the beggar on folio 51 (figure 23), work to this effect. But it would be inappropriate to conclude, as a result, that this posture is part of an iconography that is consistently sympathetic. The relationship between the illustration and text is critical in interpreting such figures. Michael Camille has noted the polyvalence of such figures generally and the careful contextualization required of the reader for their interpretation:

> The particular gesture of a seated figure, for example, economically indicated in the marginal direction to the illustrator is one traditionally used to signify thought or contemplation on the part of dream-

ers and visionaries like St. John, or is associated with negative ideas of sadness, sloth and melancholy.[73]

In the thirteenth-century English *De Brailes Hours* (London, British Library, MS Add. 49999), for example, Peter weeps in the margin after betraying Christ, hunched with his back to the border of a narrative frame. Peter is thus "a visual equivalent to being outside of a state of grace."[74] With the exception, then, of visionaries and dreamers (exemplified in Douce 104 by Will [figure 1] and the scribe [figure 24]), marginal figures tend to imply justly deserved exclusion from the space of approbation or authority in medieval illustrative tradition. The Douce 104 illustrator is only partially governed by iconographic tradition in his principle of selection, and, as in this example where he extends sympathy to the poor and neglected, he revises visual traditions, just as Langland's poem consistently explores and questions the ability of language to teach truth outside of an experiential context. The way in which the marginal figures touch, point at, or gaze upon the words in the text engages the reader's memory, but also encourages the reader to reflect upon the gap between writing and sensory experience, cognition and sensory impression. Sometimes the illustrations provide more pointed commentary upon the text than we have in the annotations, whose function it is to sum up, direct, and interpret. The distinctive figure of the illegitimate youth, his hands covering his ears (figure 22), elicits sympathy from the reader, even though Langland's poem at this point cites a harsh scriptural injunction against bastardy:

Out of matrimony noȝth moylo(r): mow noȝt haue þe grace
þat {we} be gatt by þe law: mowe*n* clayme
And þat my saue is soþe: þe saut*er* bereþ wittenesse.
  (Fol. 48v; cf. X.208–10) Pearsall, *C-Text*,

The shape of the poem is thus created by the illustrative program in Douce 104. If the illustrator, like most manuscript artists, had been directed to provide standard pictures of a sequential narrative, we would have less valuable evidence of contemporary reading. Instead, the scribal illustrator created a physical layout for Douce 104 that underscores the dreamlike blending of sequences typical of the *visio*. The illustrator does not place dramatic figures at the beginnings and ends of passus to mark narrative progression, but rather they appear only when they have dramatic speeches (as in the case of the king [figure 5], Contemplatif and Piers the Plowman [figure 10], and Elde [figure 26]). Sometimes the illustrator appears to span deliberately passus with marginal figures, as in the case of the king, Pride (fol. 24), and the skeleton (figure 31). In all three cases the poem itself does not provide marked divisions in themes or action, but continues in a vein of thought. The illustrator seems aware that the vision proceeds by dialogue, continuous themes, and the appearance of new speakers, who establish positions or perspectives for debate on various themes, as opposed to shifts in action.

Although the placement of marginal figures is usually determined in part by the amount of space left by the scribe, the unusual placement of speakers in Douce 104 suggests that the illustrator was moving beyond the text to interpret relationships between characters. The king, who appears enthroned in judgment on folio 18r, ought to span his speech, according to the illustrator's tendency to mark dialogue. Instead, the illustrator has chosen to begin the portrait at the conclusion of Conscience's speech about the dangers of glossing Scripture; thus the king's body spans the transition from passus III to IV, which is made visible in the text by two red lines (figure 5). Such deliberate and sensitive marking indicates that the rubricator may, in fact, be the illustrator, for they are working with the same assumptions about voicing and visualizing the text. On the king's body, the red lines mark the beginning and end of his cope, simultaneously emphasizing the textual division and separation of speakers with the tripartite composition of his body. Between the lines of his ermine cope, in the body of the text, we read the last lines of passus III, to which is appended the introduction to passus IV. The lines that are thereby distinguished from the body of the text are "Wirchep he wynneþ: þat will ʒeu mede / Ac he þat reseyueþ hir: is reseyuowr of gyle." These lines appear to belong to the king, but they actually belong to Conscience, whom the king will command to kiss the beguiling Mede at the opening of passus IV. While his eyes gaze explicitly upon and thus underscore the line "þe which þat hatte, as y have rad, and oþer þat can rede," the king visually spans the argument between himself and Conscience, underscoring the scene as a psychomachia and raising doubts about his moral authority. The figure of Reason, who appears on folio 19 and who settles the argument between Conscience and the king, is enthroned and bears a resemblance to the king that is hardly coincidental. The illustrator's choices suggest that he read the text carefully, as does the detail and originality of many drawings; these particular figures impart a clear, economical sense of the practical role of Mede in the political life of the king, resulting in an internal battle between spiritual idealism and political pragmatism mediated by Reason.

Similarly, the Bretoner, who gazes from the top left-hand margin of folio 37v upon Wastor's speech to Piers (figure 12), is placed directly across from the figure of Hunger, who leers from the top right-hand margin of folio 38. The causal connection between the looter and scavenger and starvation is underscored simply by the shared color scheme of their clothing, which is orange and green (one of the two dominant color schemes in the manuscript, the other being pink and blue). The Bretoner, who plunders the countryside freely, is a Wastor, and his activities, as Piers complains to the knight in passus VIII, can only result in hunger.

Although the poem makes this point circuitously, the illustrator extracts and simplifies this message, giving it a direct visual impact. This is merely one case of many where the illustrator seems to share Langland's own political and spiritual agenda. His keen sensitivity to the poem, shown elsewhere, and the way in which the marginal figures interact with the text (in contrast to the aggressive dismissal of the marginal figures by the annotator, who often writes deliberately over them) suggests that the scribe and illustrator are the same person. In fact, his drawings are most original and detailed in those sections of the text that still baffle readers.

The illustrator's choice of placement and selective use of detail provides us with a near-contemporary response to cruxes in the poem that reflect social anxieties and are hotly debated by modern readers — such as the nature of Recklessness. Folio 53 begins with the line in passus XI, "For y was rauysched rihte there, for Fortune me fette" (XI.169). The dreamer describes his seduction to the cupidinous life, emphasized in Douce 104 by a traditional bust of the fashionable Dame Fortune (figure 25), who gazes conspicuously upon the line "And in a myrrour þat hihte Myddelerd she made me to loke" (XI.171). The Wheel of Fortune is too common a symbol in medieval art and literature to require commentary here, but the placement of Recklessness below her in the right-hand corner of the folio page is curious. Knowing that Langland embraces patient poverty throughout *Piers Plowman*, modern readers have been puzzled about how to interpret the actions of Recklessness, a product of complex revision in the C text.[75] Recklessness, a projection of the dreamer's impatience and worldly appetites, commands him to "Folowe forth þat Fortune wole," which can be viewed as a spiritually dangerous invitation or as a rejection of solicitude for earthly provision in keeping with the apostolic life. The illustrator's interpretation of Recklessness, however, is largely violent, the figure's physical vigor connecting him with the previous illustration of Envy, who also raises his fist in defiance. Recklessness, garbed in a dagged or tattered tunic, with his legs and feet bare, grasps a foolstick and raises his arm in a gesture of angry independence that the portrait of Lady Fortune directly above belies. The iconography of the fool is well charted, as nearly every psalter had an illustration of the fool featured in Psalm 13 and 52. Recklessness appears to belong to the visual tradition of blasphemous fools who function not as childlike moral critics but as grotesque caricatures of human folly; such figures appear in medieval Crucifixion illustrations in particolor garments, especially dagged capes, and often gesture obscenely.[76] His poverty is the consequence of sloth rather than apostolic humility. Compared with the remarkable figure of the lunatic lollar (figure 16), Recklessness conveys an entirely negative assessment of appetite masquerading as a lack of solicitude.

In contrast, the lunatic lollar also dismisses authority, reverencing neither the mayor nor any other man; he waves his hand as if in gentle farewell to the authority of the text. But his garments, apostolic in appearance, lack the restless energy of Recklessness's dagged red tunic, and his demeanor is visibly peaceful. Most striking of all, the illustrator has conveyed the lollar's inner light by washing his robe in gold. We may thus have the two visual traditions of the fool—the blasphemer and the innocent moral critic—represented in Douce 104. The illustrator cannot offer us Langland's reading of narrative cruxes, but he can present us with a near-contemporary response to the poem's more difficult characters. In this particular passage the scribe has underscored the complexity of determining apostolic holiness in the poor and vagrant from appearance alone by altering important lines: "And ȝut ar ther oþere beggares, *in hele, as hit semeth* / Ac hem wanteth wyt, men and women bothe, / The whiche aren lunatyk lollares and lepares aboute" (IX.105–7) has been changed to "*unhole as hit semeþ*" (Douce, fol. 42). The revision shifts an emphasis from the legitimacy of able-bodied, albeit witless, beggars to live a wandering life to the extreme pathos of the feeble-witted poor. The illustrator's decision to idealize the lollar, the blind beggar, Dobet, and Patience by giving each an unmistakable appearance of calmness is more radical perhaps than Langland intended.

Even more pointed is the illustrator's conveying the corruption of the friars on folio 44 (passus IX). Langland's poem is hardly politic in its ecclesiastical condemnation on this point. The reign of false clergy is made possible by the laziness of the bishops, who are accountable in the end for the corruption of a misguided laity: "The cause of al this caytiftee cometh of many bischopes / That soffreth suche sottes and oþere synnes regne" (IX.255–56). The hypocrisy of the heavily shrouded friar who gazes furtively from the margins upon the lines "A bacheler or a bew-pere beste hym bysemede / And for þe cloth þat keuereth hym ykald he is a frere" (IX.248–49) is immediately apparent to the seer-reader familiar with the medieval literary tradition of clergy as false-seeming (figure 18). To put it simply, this friar is too demure and properly dressed to be counted among the virtuous. As the lines suggest, the illustrator has emphasized costume, in contrast to visible virtue, as is clear from his contrasting drawing of Dobet (figure 21). Dobet's sad, open gaze and active role as a preacher from the pulpit contrasts specifically with this image of false clergy that is positioned a few leaves before in the manuscript. The text that he gazes upon, in addition, recollects the image of the lunatic lollar and Saint Paul's injunction that the apostolic life makes men fools of God, as opposed to cautious prevaricators: "And precheþ to þe pepil: seynt poules wordis / *Libenter suffertis incipientes cum sitis vos ipsi sapientes* / ȝe worldylich wyse: vnwyse þat ȝe suffer / Lene hem & loue hem: þis latyn is to mene." Here, as elsewhere in the manuscript, the gaze functions to emphasize important words and underscore the spoken nature of the text. And once again the reader's attention is called to the issue of translation from Latin into the vernacular. In addition, Dobet's preaching of the Pauline text explicitly calls the reader to remember previous images of religious life in the poem—and this is particularly easy in view of the radically contrasting images on folios 42 and 44 (figures 16 and 18). The text about Dobet proceeds to define the life of Dobest as the bishop's life:

> Dobest bere sholde þe bisshopes crose
> And halie with þe hoked ende all men to gode,
> And with the pyk pulte adoun *preuaricatores legis.*
> (X.92–94)

The illustrator has already provided the reader with a contrary image of a corrupt bishop right below the shady-looking friar as a visual point of reference. Beneath the friar on folio 44 is a picture of a sleeping bishop, his back turned from the text, with his miter askew and his crozier tightly but impotently grasped in his sleeping hand. In the *bas de page* the illustrator has done something unusual in drawing yet another figure: a wolf gripping the exposed neck of a struggling sheep, a particularly violent image in the program of illustration. All three images work to connect visually the themes of the poem at this juncture efficiently. But they work cumulatively with the other images of corrupt religious—such as Mede confessing to the friar (fol. 11v), the venal friar (fol. 67), and the false friar (fol. 67v)—and are thus in keeping with the poem's progression. Already discussed in the context of ecclesiastical satire, the place of such images in a visionary *ordinatio* makes them important evidence of the illustrator's sense of associative patterns in the text; no doubt a scribe would be sensitive to such visual patterns from homiletic literature, where the elaboration and linking of images enabled preachers to develop a moral point through a visual process for recollection.[77]

While some of the more subtle or problematic marginal figures in Douce 104 interpret and comment upon the text, others serve a more traditional mnemonic function. The most common mnemonic medieval illustrative strategy is allegory, and the Douce illustrator understood allegory, as he so comically displays in his drawing of Mede riding the sheriff to Westminster on folio 10r. Nonetheless, he seldom chooses allegory, which is inherently visual and mnemonic, as his subject matter, preferring to explore in more dramatic, performative ways the relationship between the margins and text, between illustration and specific words, as figures touch, protrude into, or gaze upon the lines or single words of the text. Thus he rarely abandons the textual entirely to the visual: one can reconstruct important ideas from the marginal images, but one cannot "read" the images as a sequential narrative. Like the Bodleian 978 illustrator, his images tend to conjure words. In addition, he shares an interest in marginal symbols and images that signal entire constructs or concepts in the text, such as the nature of authority, justice, or prophecy, as are commonly found in medieval legal manuscripts or in chronicles, such as Matthew Paris's *Chronica majora*. Indeed, while constructing a profile for an illustrator is a tricky proposition and an admittedly speculative one, the Douce illustrator's remarkable similarity to Matthew Paris is yet another piece of evidence that he may well have been the scribe. Images like the boat in rough water (figure 14), the bad penny (fol. 78), and a hand and orb, in addition to many busts and manicules, form mnemonic indicators. Such figures are abbreviated rubrics, signaling ideas in the text ranging from prophecy (the boat) to the Trinity (the hand and orb), while they simultaneously function as place markers. The penny and the fist with the orb, for example, appear beside important theological arguments in rather difficult passages of passus XVII and XIX, but both sum up the main import of the text and, as will be discussed later, avoid idolatry. In passus XVII, Liberum Arbitrium explores the relationship between Charity and the Church, and the illustrator draws the penny next to a passage that condemns the way learned men have shunned their Christian responsibilities, with the result that "Lewed men han no byleue and lettred men erren" (XVII.87). Lettered men, the text argues, are like "a badde peny with a gode printe," for the substance is faulty, but the appearance of the penny is true as a consequence of perfect engraving (XVII.71–75). This is a typically Langlandian similitude, and the illustrator is right to call attention, once again, to the text's anxiety about the disparity between seeming and being. The image recollects an epistemological fear of "false weights" and values in a world of absolute (as opposed to shifting) worth.[78]

The fist and orb is drawn beside the beginning of the Samaritan's lengthy and complex analogy of the fist as a Trinitarian image, but it spans the lines

> For god þat al bygan in bigynnynge of the worlde
> Ferde furste as a fuste, and ʒut is, as y leue,
> *Mundum pugillo continens,*
> As with a fuste with a fynger yfolde togyderes,
> Til hym likede and luste to vnlose that fynger
> And profered hit forth as with the paume to what place hit sholde.
> (XIX.111–15)

The passage weaves an intricate theological web in response to the Latin text, commencing with the figure of God as creator and ending with the promise of Christ's birth in the fullness of time. The image thus signifies the eschatological movement of the entire passus, initiated by the speech of Spes, or Moses, and culminating in a pastoral discussion of repentance as a necessary prologue to the Lenten experience.

These marginal symbols, mnemonic devices, are not entirely unusual in theological manuscripts. Robert Grosseteste used a wide range of visual signs in the margins of his manuscripts "to build up a theological subject index.... In the margins of the manuscripts the symbols made it possible to find the passage wanted."[79] Once again, the illustrator's visionary *ordinatio* makes it possible for us to speculate about his education and thus the audience of Douce 104. R. W. Hunt, for example, notes that London, British Library, MS Royal 5.D.X, most likely owned by Simon, abbot of Ramsay (1316–42), although written slightly earlier than the mid–fourteenth century, also contains "little drawings to illustrate the subject matter of the notes."[80] The manuscript includes works by Augustine, Bede, and Jerome, as well as treatises like *De hebraicis quaestionibus* and *De mansionibus filiorum Israel* that feature precisely the kind of eschatological concerns and figural readings of the Old Testament that one finds in passus XIX of *Piers Plowman*. The annotator of this manuscript has drawn a number of pictures, such as a horse and a windmill, in the margins that are similar to mnemonic devices in Douce 104.[81] Hunt attributes this kind of indexing in English manuscripts to the influence of Franciscan and Dominican teachers and students (the professional readers of thirteenth- and early-fourteenth-century England) who were swept up in a new theological movement to return to source studies as opposed to synthesis of the patristic texts. Thus we see the kind of authoritative speakers in the margins of their manuscripts that are important to the illustrative program of Douce 104. In a thirteenth-century manuscript of the works of Anselm and Augustine (Cambridge, St. John's College, MS 17), for example, there appears on folio 9 a picture of Plato wearing a pointed hat and on folio 18 a "very curious little bust of a 'predicator.'"[82] Douce 104 is full of such busts of the vicar, Contemplatif, Caiaphas, Trajan—all apparently meaningful in visualizing the movement of the poem but equally helpful in aiding the fifteenth-century reader to hear and comprehend the significance of a passage. It is as if the illustrator recognized in Langland's synthesis of authorities a work demanding the intellectual apparatus of the theological compilation, although (as chapter 2 shows) he was deeply uncomfortable with standard authority figures. Similarly, the annotator's topic annotations signal a fifteenth-century reader's sense of the intellectually eclectic nature of the text.[83]

The best model for Douce 104 of a visionary and mnemonic system of marginal drawings integrated with text, however, may be found in the works of Matthew Paris, who was similarly influenced by the Giraldian tradition. Matthew Paris provides us with an intriguing example of a chronicler and illustrator; he is both a careful reader and a visual interpreter. Furthermore, although he appears to have learned to draw from pattern books made available to him at Saint Albans, his exposure to other kinds of manuscripts and documents influenced his program of illustration. Lewis claims that his "dependence on such practical aids outside the context of a workshop tradition would help to explain the curious stylistic eclecticism of his artistic production."[84] Douce 104, although produced by an Anglo-Irish scribe and illustrator less than two centuries later, is a similar blend of old-fashioned and curiously innovative artistic features, reflecting an independence from "the conventional constraints of style and consistency normally imposed upon scriptorium-trained artists."[85] No doubt such innovation is partly due to the provincial origins of the Douce manuscript; the trend in fifteenth-century illumination was to work increasingly from models or pattern books:

> Illustrators of surviving vernacular works of the fifteenth century often worked from standard models employed either in another text or in previous manuscripts of the same text; by contrast, the person who commissioned Douce 104 or its illustrator, apparently, lacking pictorial models for many of the allegorical figures, was forced to give a personal response to the text.[86]

Both Matthew Paris and the Douce illustrator opted for a program of marginal illustration on a clear vellum background, indicating a similar education in theological and legal manuscripts, chronicles, and meditative works. In addition to the indexing symbols and drawings in theological manuscripts previously mentioned, such marginal illustrations appear frequently in plea rolls and public documents by the end of the thirteenth century.[87] Lewis speculates that Matthew Paris's own access to such documents may have provided the artistic impulse for the pictographic symbols that appear throughout the *Chronica majora* (see, e.g., figure 48). Also, Paris's illustrations are marked by a realism that prevails in Douce 104, where the illustrator attempts to convey the bitterness of poverty, spiritual corruption, luxury, and social distinctions through figures from various estates. Some of the remarkable similarities in choice of subject matter will be discussed later; for now, it is sufficient to point out that Paris's marginal illustrative program reflects a special kind of reading that is similar to the process of reading that Douce 104 requires. Like *Piers Plowman*, the *Chronica majora* is an expansive, encyclopedic work meant to be digested slowly, ruminated upon, and recollected for moral example. The pictographic symbols and marginal illustrations in both serve a variety of functions, from constituting an index to providing a visual symbol of a complex construct. This "pictorial thesaurus," as Lewis aptly calls it, has its roots in monastic archival practice:

> Beyond serving a practical referential purpose, Matthew's illustrations in his historical works were intended more importantly to provide a reservoir of images in which a visual memory of past events could be retained, comparable to the connections of symbolic objects to be found among written documents in a monastic archive. Since it was customary to symbolize the conveyance of property

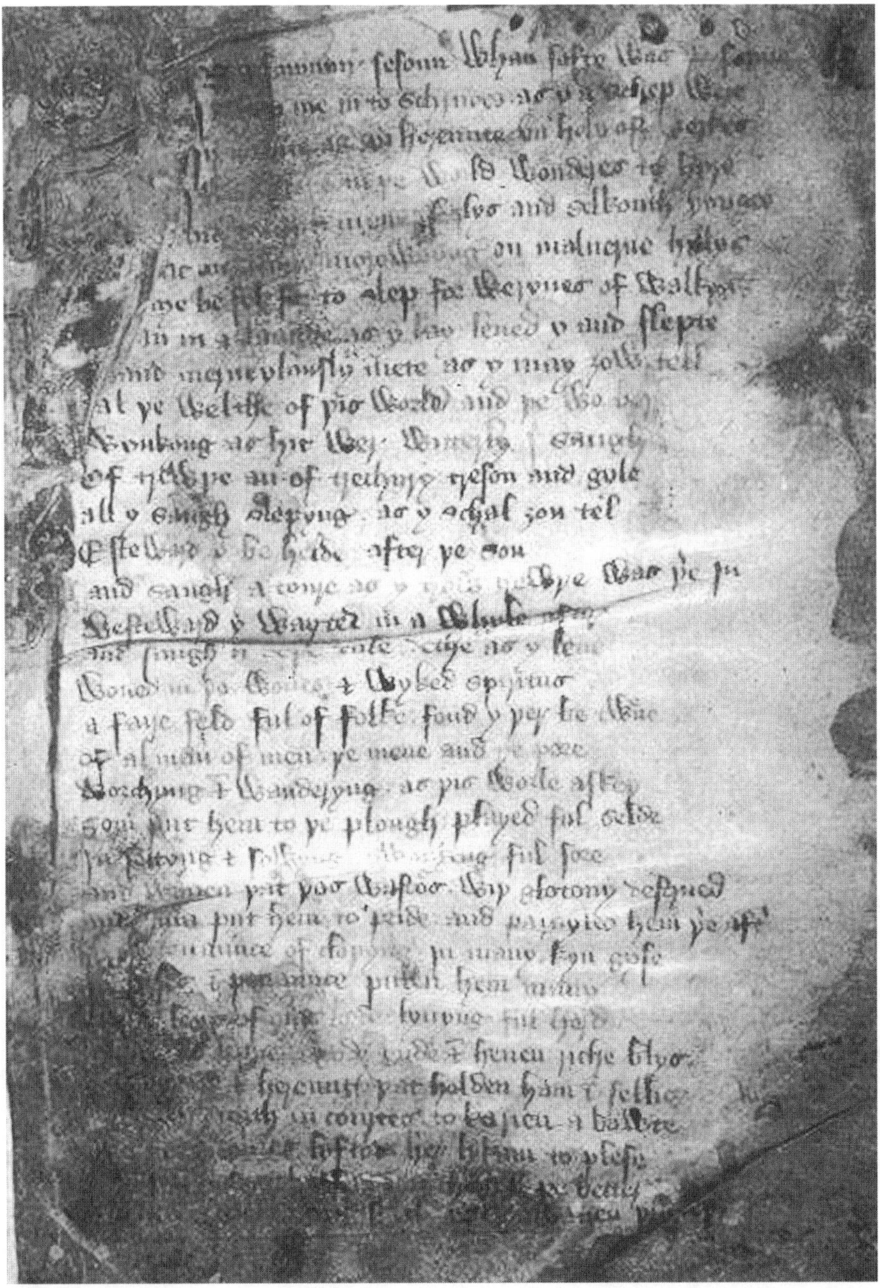

Figure 1. Will. Oxford, Bodleian Library, MS Douce 104, fol. 1, Anglo-Irish, 1427 (Damaged).

```
 1  ef: Bihold here mede  no þe med is hoþing
 2  no case to case          to gow worschip her
 3  seith sope Cason         clothing
 4  þou neuer with fist by mede
 5  : Gede and othren
 6  schuld plato come
 7  t: and Symony my felow
 8  o: I pith me anontows
 9  weo: þat priuite oft
10  w' a pelen i þe eyþes
11  r: þat supsediao takey
12  huþy: leþny up I Jydiy
13  ly me: cowey cost aftey
14  p: heý cost sthal he shall
15  teo: ou foenicatoo
16  i sobs caþt to lede al þor oþ
17  o: þat ou hey sete jyýnney
18  : jouþ forþ to gyðeyo
19  ho I al þor men aftyý
20  : þe tayl þ ham folowey
21  for mede is sake is sent aft
22  to gydyn al þor pepil
23  iý: and whý mede a bode
24  u al: and sud but litil us I symeo
25  i pacene I passed þe all þam alt
26  yes coulþe I consciens told
```

Figure 2. Mede Riding on Sheriff. Oxford, Bodleian Library, MS Douce 104, fol. 10. Anglo-Irish, 1427.

Figure 3. Mede at Westminster. Oxford, Bodleian Library, MS Douce 104, fol. 11. Anglo-Irish, 1427.

Figure 4. Conscience. Oxford, Bodleian Library, MS Douce 104, fol. 15. Anglo-Irish, 1427.

Figure 5. King. Oxford, Bodleian Library, MS Douce 104, fol. 18. Anglo-Irish, 1427.

Figure 6. Tom Stowe. Oxford, Bodleian Library, MS Douce 104, fol. 23. Anglo-Irish, 1427.

Figure 7. Lechery. Oxford, Bodleian Library, MS Douce 104, fol. 26v. Anglo-Irish, 1427.

Figure 8. Sloth. Oxford, Bodleian Library, MS Douce 104, fol. 31. Anglo-Irish, 1427.

Figure 9. Pilgrim. Oxford, Bodleian Library, MS Douce 104, fol. 33. Anglo-Irish, 1427.

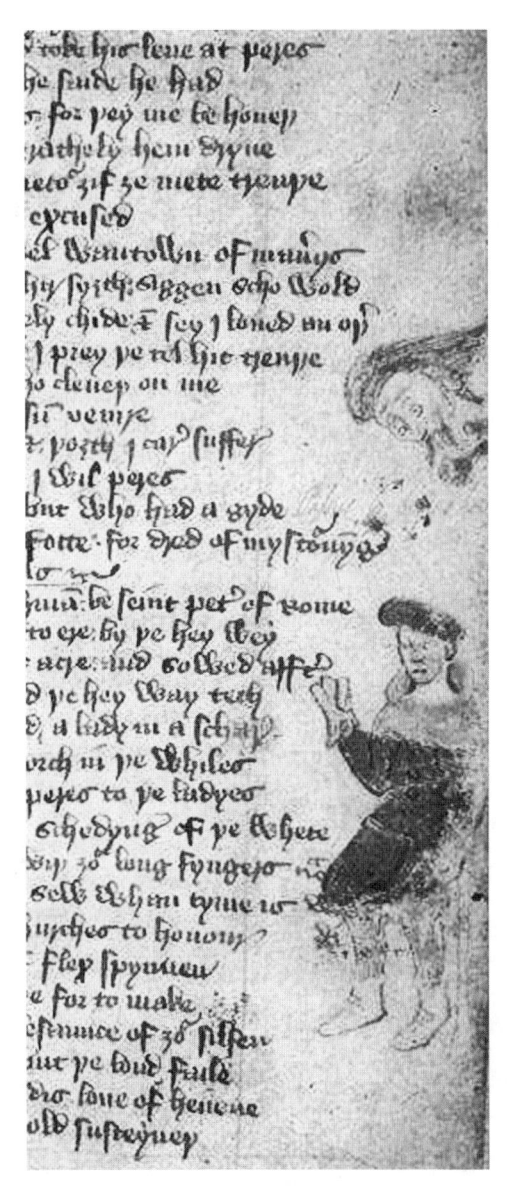

robe his leue at peres
he seide he had
= for pey me te honey
gathely hem gyue
leto zif ze mete hempe
cpcused
el Wautollu of munyo
his systi; aggen echo wold
ely chide. I sey I loued un op
I pray þe tel hir henye
to cleuep on me
hir venye
& porty I mi suffer
I wil peres
but who had a gyde
forte for dred of my stouyes
lo —
huia, be seint per of roine
to ese, by þe hey þei
age, aud colled after
d þe hey way teh
& a lady in a scha—
orch in þe whiles
peres to þe ladyes
sthedyng of þe whete
biy so long fyngers —
eth whim tyme to
i pehes to honour
flep spynnien
e for to make
esnuice of zo pilsen
uit þe bud faile
do loue of heuene
old susteyney

Figure 10. Contemplatif and Piers. Oxford, Bodleian Library, MS Douce 104, fol. 35. Anglo-Irish, 1427.

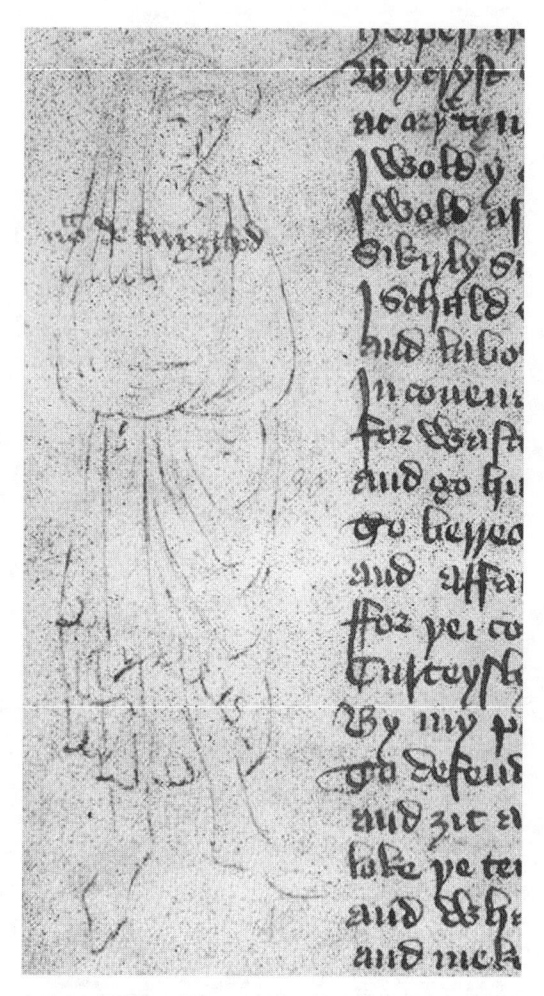

Figure 11. Knight. Oxford, Bodleian Library, MS Douce 104, fol. 35v. Anglo-Irish, 1427.

Figure 12. Wastor. Oxford, Bodleian Library, MS Douce 104, fol. 37v. Anglo-Irish, 1427.

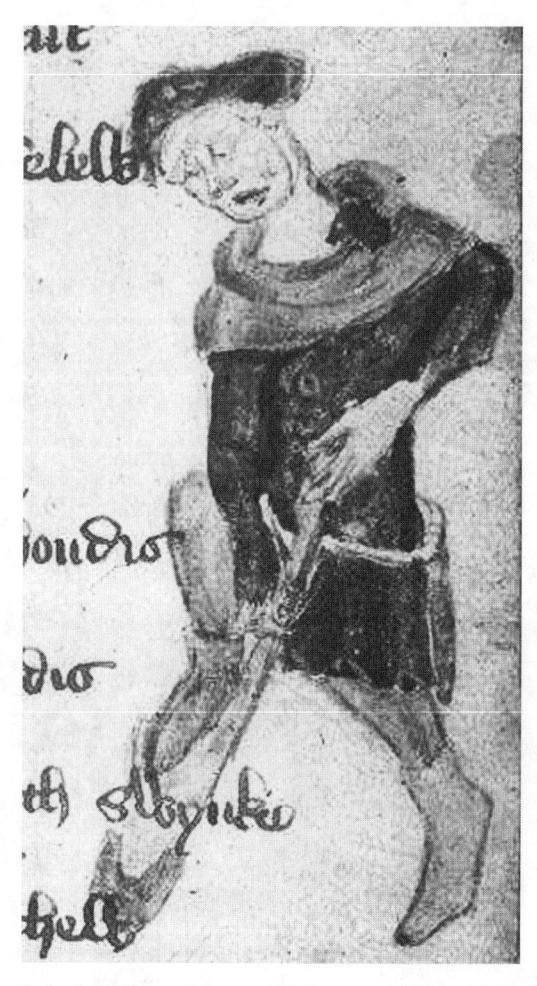

Figure 13. Digger. Oxford, Bodleian Library, MS Douce 104, fol. 39. Anglo-Irish, 1427.

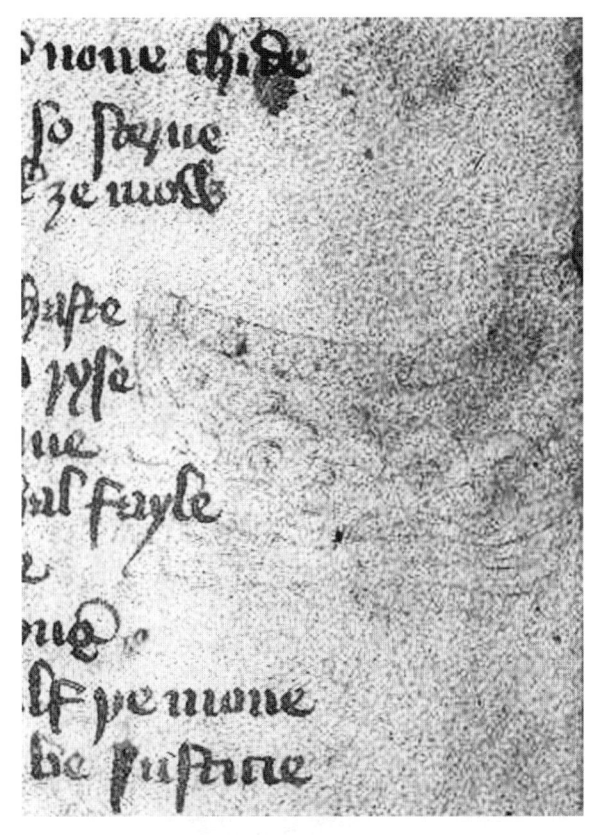

Figure 14. Boat as Flood Symbol. Oxford, Bodleian Library, MS Douce 104, fol. 40. Anglo-Irish, 1427.

Figure 15. Lawyer. Oxford, Bodleian Library, MS Douce 104, fol. 41. Anglo-Irish, 1427.

Figure 16. Lunatic Lollar. Oxford, Bodleian Library, MS Douce 104, fol. 42. Anglo-Irish, 1427.

Figure 17. Blind Man. Oxford, Bodleian Library, MS Douce 104, fol. 43. Anglo-Irish, 1427.

Figure 18. False Friar, Sleeping Bishop, and Wolf with Sheep. Oxford, Bodleian Library, MS Douce 104, fol. 44. Anglo-Irish, 1427.

Figure 19. Priest with Pardon. Oxford, Bodleian Library, MS Douce 104, fol. 44v. Anglo-Irish, 1427.

Figure 20. Franciscan Friar. Oxford, Bodleian Library, MS Douce 104, fol. 46. Anglo-Irish, 1427.

Figure 21. Dobet. Oxford, Bodleian Library, MS Douce 104, fol. 47. Anglo-Irish, 1427.

Figure 22. Young Bastard. Oxford, Bodleian Library, MS Douce 104, fol. 48v. Anglo-Irish, 1427.

Figure 23. Beggar. Oxford, Bodleian Library, MS Douce 104, fol. 51. Anglo-Irish, 1427.

Figure 24. Will Writing. Oxford, Bodleian Library, MS Douce 104, fol. 52v. Anglo-Irish, 1427.

Figure 25. Fortune's Wheel (left) and Recklessness (right). Oxford, Bodleian Library, MS Douce 104, fol. 53. Anglo-Irish, 1427.

eduesse: for well hay þ deyl
aftyr
by so þu noþe þer
 þe puo sone

o wil þe lone
z þe be seke
io to hane
pecuniouſ

zordir þeut so albeto

thy fayr be heſte
ne to be tolk
con feſſeð
ut I eilher had

Figure 26. Elde. Oxford, Bodleian Library, MS Douce 104, fol. 55. Anglo-Irish, 1427.

Figure 27. Trajan. Oxford, Bodleian Library, MS Douce 104, fol. 56. Anglo-Irish, 1427.

Figure 28. Imaginatif. Oxford, Bodleian Library, MS Douce 104, fol. 63. Anglo-Irish, 1427.

Figure 29. Activa Vita. Oxford, Bodleian Library, MS Douce 104, fol. 69. Anglo-Irish, 1427.

Figure 30. Patience. Oxford, Bodleian Library, MS Douce 104, fol. 70. Anglo-Irish, 1427.

Figure 31. Skeleton. Oxford, Bodleian Library, MS Douce 104, fol. 71. Anglo-Irish, 1427.

Figure 33. Mercy. Oxford, Bodleian Library, MS Douce 104, fol. 94. Anglo-Irish, 1427.

Figure 32. Man on Gallows. Oxford, Bodleian Library, MS Douce 104, fol. 79. Anglo-Irish, 1427.

Figure 35. Antichrist. Oxford, Bodleian Library, MS Douce 104, fol. 107. Anglo-Irish, 1427.

Figure 34. Merchant Counting Money. Oxford, Bodleian Library, MS Douce 104, fol. 102v. Anglo-Irish, 1427.

Figure 36. Sleʒth (Trickery). Oxford, Bodleian Library, MS Douce 104, fol. 108v. Anglo-Irish, 1427.

Figure 37. Proud Priest. Oxford, Bodleian Library, MS Douce 104, fol. 109v. Anglo-Irish, 1427.

Figure 38. Friar Physician. Oxford, Bodleian Library, MS Douce 104, fol. 111v. Anglo-Irish, 1427.

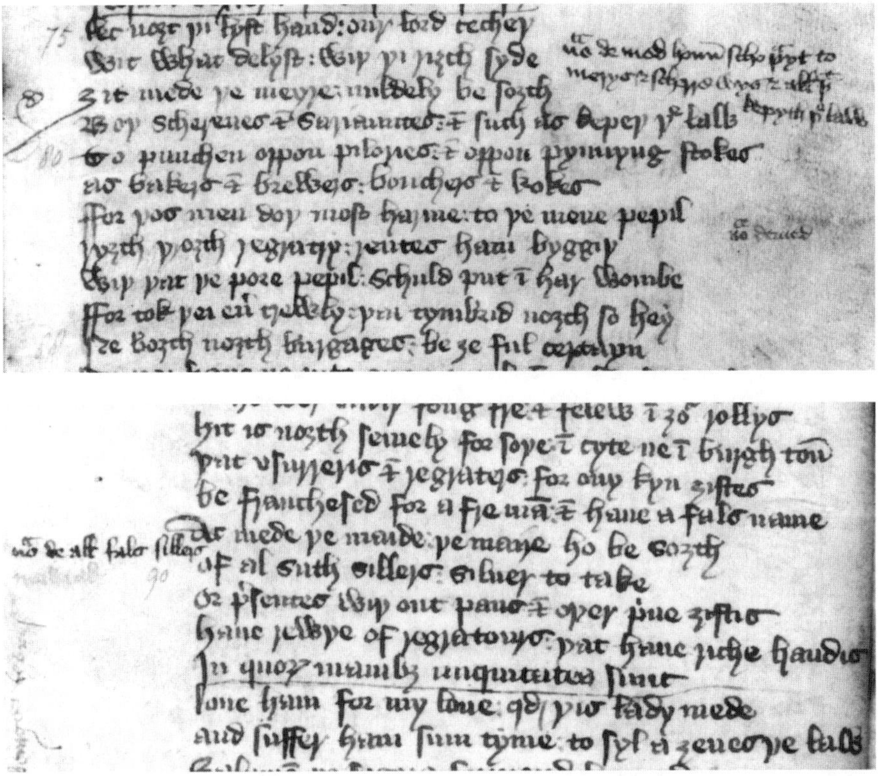

Figure 39. Text with Misplaced Annotations. Oxford, Bodleian Library, MS Douce 104, fols. 12 and 12v. Anglo-Irish, 1427.

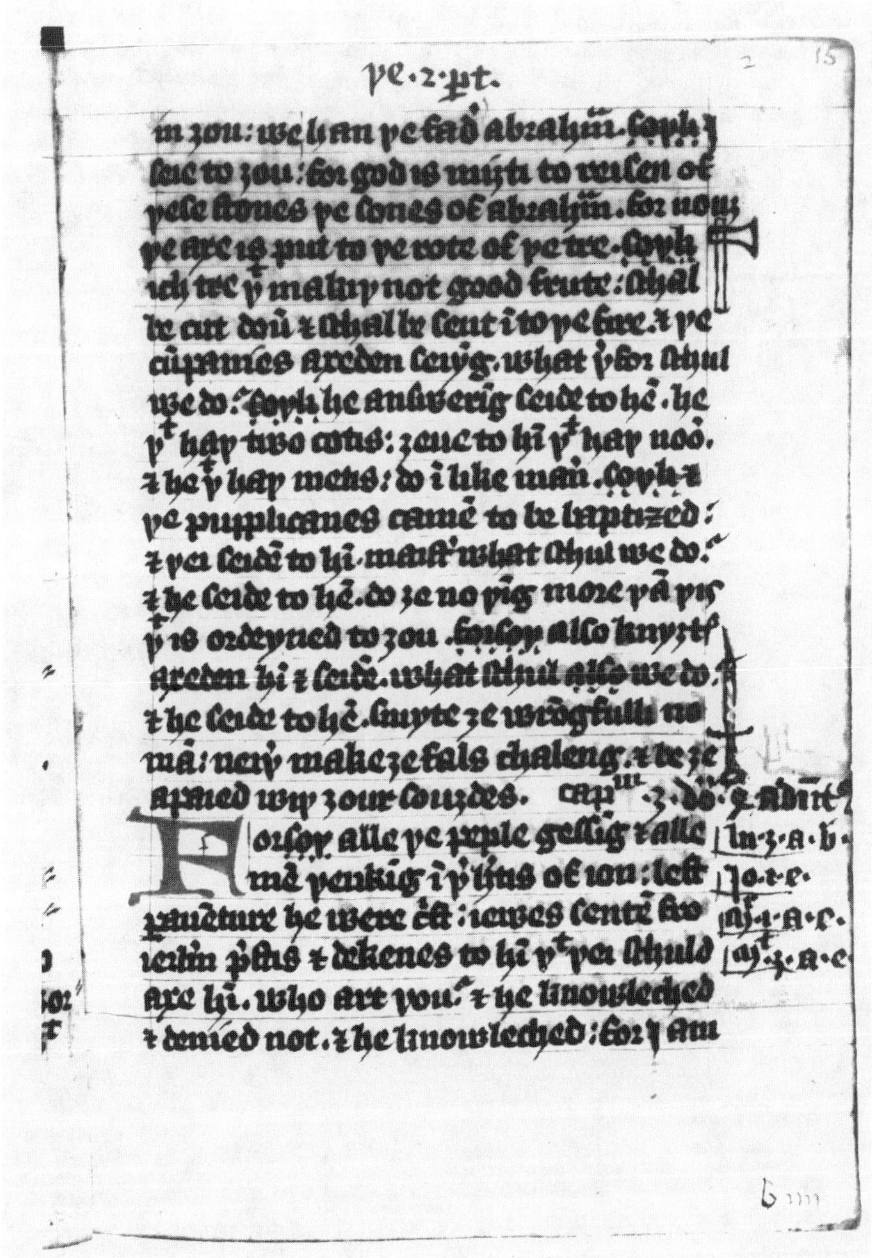

þe · 2 · pt.

in ȝou: we han þe fað abraħm. soþly I
seie to ȝou: for god is miȝti to reisen of
þese stones þe sones of abraħm. for nou
þe axe is put to þe rote of þe tre. soþly
ich tre þ makiþ not good fruite: shal
be cut doun & shal be sent into þe fire. & þe
cumpanies axeden seiyng. what þ for shul
we do? soþli he answerig seide to he. he
þt haþ two cotis: ȝeue to hi þt haþ noõ.
& he þ haþ metis: do i like man. soþli &
þe puplicanes came to be baptized:
& þei seide to hi maistr what shul we do?
& he seide to he. do ȝe no þig more þã þt
þt is ordeyned to ȝou. forsoþ also knyȝts
axeden hi & seide. what shul also we do?
& he seide to he. smyte ȝe wrogfulli no
mã: neiþ makeȝe fals chaleng. & be ȝe
apaied wiþ ȝoure couȝdes.   cap' iii · 3 · do · & admt
                                                  lu · 3 · a · b ·
Forsoþ alle þe peple gessig & alle   jo · 1 · e ·
men þenkig i þ hrtis of ion: lest   as · 1 · a · c ·
paventure he were crist: iewes sente fro   as · 3 · a · c ·
ierlm pstis & dekenes to hi þt þei shuld
axe hi. who are you? & he knowlechȝed
& denied not. & he knowlechȝed: for I am

b iiij

Figure 40. Axe and Sword, from Wycliffite adapted gospel harmony. Oxford, Bodleian Library, MS Bodley 978, fol. 15. English, c. 1400.

þe ij pt.

pees but swerd. for y cam to departe
a mā aȝés his fad' ⁊ þe douȝt' aȝen
h' mod' ⁊ þe sones wyf aȝés þe housͭ
houdẏ mod'. ⁊ þe enemies of a mā: be
his meneallis. or homli mene. he yͭ . h .
loueþ fad' or mod' more þā me is not
worþi me. ⁊ he yͭ loueþ sone or douȝt
more þā me is not worþi of me. he
yͭ takiþ not his cros ⁊ sueþ me: is not
worþi of me. he yͭ fyndeþ his lyf: schal
lesen it. ⁊ he yͭ lesiþ his lyf for me: schal
fynde it. he yͭ receyueþ ȝou receyueþ me.
⁊ he yͭ receyueþ me: receyueþ hi yͭ
sente me. he yͭ ceyueþ a pfete in þe
name of a pfete: schal take þe mede
of a pfete. ⁊ he yͭ receyueþ a iust mā
i þe name of a iust mā: schal take
þe mede of a iust mā. ⁊ who eu ȝeueþ
driṅk to oon of þe leste a cupp of cold
waͭ ouli i þe name of a disciple:
truli y seie to ȝou he schal not lese his
mede. ⁊ þei goiṅg out prechedē
castels ⁊ ȝeheden cuy where: þ me
schuldē do penaūce. ⁊ þei castedē out

þe ij pte

⁊ tabat· cured i þe sabat : seide to þe cūpa=
nie, sixe daies lxi i whiche it bihoueþ
ueþ to werken, ⁊ for come ȝe in
þese ⁊ be ȝe cured ⁊ not i þe day of
sabat, for þe lord answerig to
oxe ⁊ hi seide ypocrite whey ich of ȝou un
asse· teyeþ not i þe sabat his oxe or his
asse fro þe stalle or a naþie ⁊ ledþi
to watren, bihoueþ it not yt þis
douȝtr of abraham whō sathanas
haþ bouñden ten ⁊ eiȝte ȝeer : to be
unbouñde of þis loñd i þe day of sa
bat ? ⁊ whā he seide þes þiġs : alle his
aduersaries were shamed ⁊ al þe
ca 10· peple ioied i alle þiġs yt weren
A iiij g gloriousli don of hym·
Mt 13· eft whā bigan to techen at þe
lu 8· see ⁊ many cūpanies were gadred
to hi ⁊ haþde fro ceteris to hi so yt he
stiȝig i to a boot : satt i þe see ⁊ al þe cū
panie stood i þe brinke ⁊ he seide ma
ne yiġs to hē i publis, seiyg to hē
SQ · i his doctrine· here ȝe lo he yt sowiþ
sowige· went out to sowen his seed, ⁊ whil

Figure 43. Crucifixion, with Author, Michael de Massa, Shown Writing, from *Meditations on the Passion*. Oxford, Bodleian Library, MS Bodley 758, fol. 1. English, 1405.

Figure 44. Scribe, Radulphus de Medyltoun, from *Meditations on the Passion*. Oxford, Bodleian Library, MS Bodley 758, fol. 87. English, c. 1405.

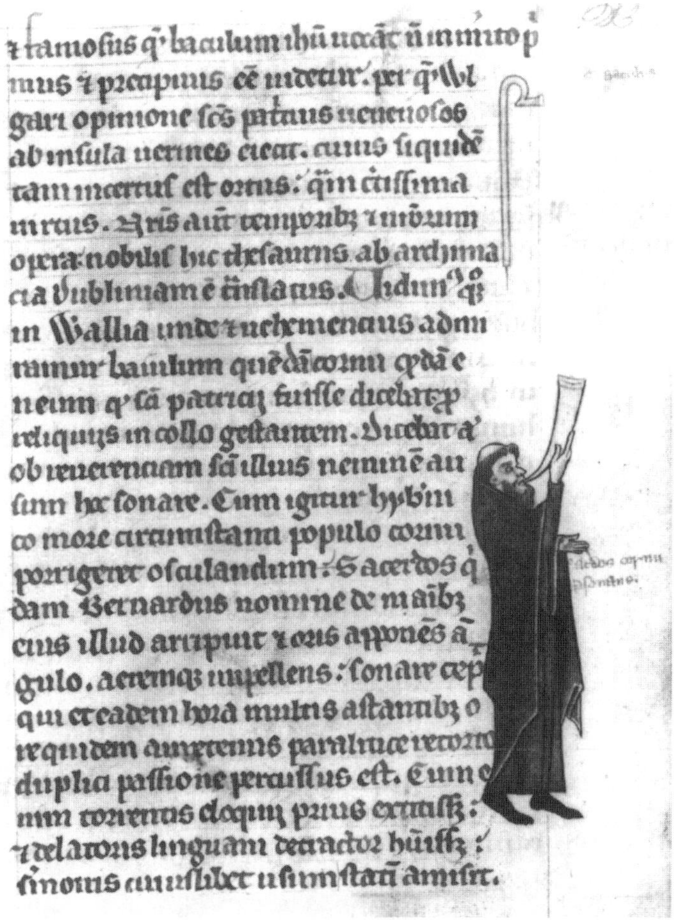

z famosius q'baculum ihu uocāt ū mīmito p
mus i pcipuis ēē uidetur: per q' ŵl
gari opinione scōs patruus uenenosos
ab insula uerines cicat. cuius siquide
tam metuus est ortus: qm ciissima
miraus. His aut temporibz i mōum
opera nobilis huic thesaurus ab archima
cia ŵublīnam ē tīnstatus. Judun' q'
in Ŵallia unde uehementius admi
ratiur baculum quēdā cornu cyda e
neum q' sā patriaz fuisse dicebat p
reliquijs in collo gestantem. Ducebat a'
ob reuerentiam sāi illius neminē au
sum hoc sonare. Cum igitur hybni
co more circumstantī populo cornu
porrigeret osculandum: Sacerdos q
dam Bernardus nomine de maibz
eius illud arripuit i oris apponēs ā
gulo. aeremq; impellens: sonare cep
qui et eadem hora multis astantibz o
requidem amptemis paraliticae recor
duplici passione perculsus est. Cum e
nim torrentis eloquij prius emisit:
i delatoris linguam detractor huius:
sinonus cuiuslibet usum stati amisit.

Figure 45. Holy Staff and Priest with Horn, showing instructions to illustrator, from Giraldus, *Topographia hiberniae.* Oxford, Bodleian Library, MS Laud Misc. 720, fol. 232. English, late thirteenth century. (See chapter 2, note 51.)

Figure 46. King and Castle, from Peter of Icham's *Chronicle*. Oxford, Bodleian Library, MS Laud Misc. 730, fol. 9. English, third quarter of fifteenth century.

Figure 47. Initial from Netter's Doctrinale. Netter in top left rondel; Wyclif in top right rondel; King present at elevation of the host in the main scene, burning of Wycliffite books in bottom left rondel. Oxford, Merton College, MS 319, fol. 41. English, mid–fifteenth century. Reprinted by permission of the Warden and Fellows of Merton College.

Figure 48. Boat as Flood Symbol, from Matthew Paris, *Chronica majora*. Cambridge, Corpus Christi College, MS 16, fol. 160v. Reprinted by permission of the Master and Fellows of Corpus Christi College, Cambridge.

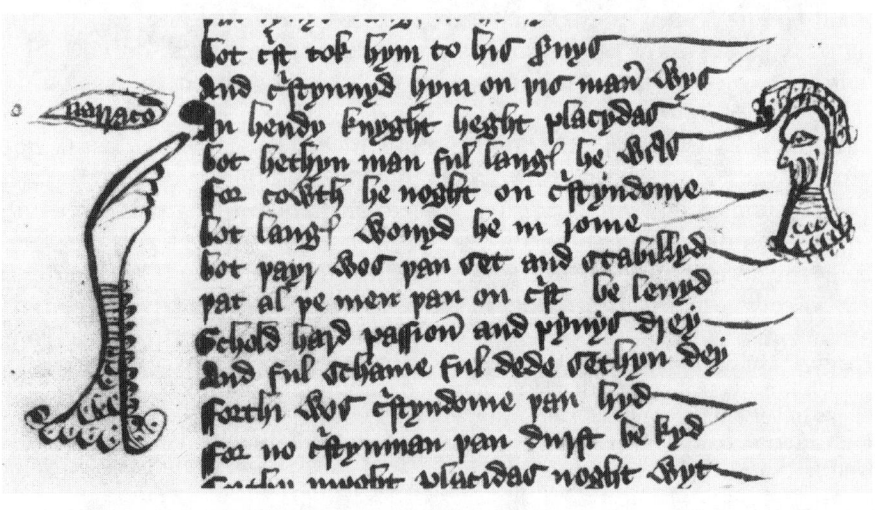

Figure 49. Heathen Knight, with Manicule, from *Northern Homily Cycle*, Huntington Library, HM 129, fol. 59v. Anglo-Irish, early fifteenth century. Reprinted by permission of Huntington Library, San Marino, California.

Figure 50. Crippled Man (Bastard), from Giraldus, *Topographia hiberniae*. Cambridge, University Library, MS Ff. 1.27, p. 344. English, second half of fourteenth century. Reprinted by permission of the Syndics of Cambridge University Library.

Figure 51. Widow Marking a Statue on Dowagers' Rights. Cambridge, Mass., Harvard Law School Library, MS 12, fol. 5. English, second quarter of fourteenth century.

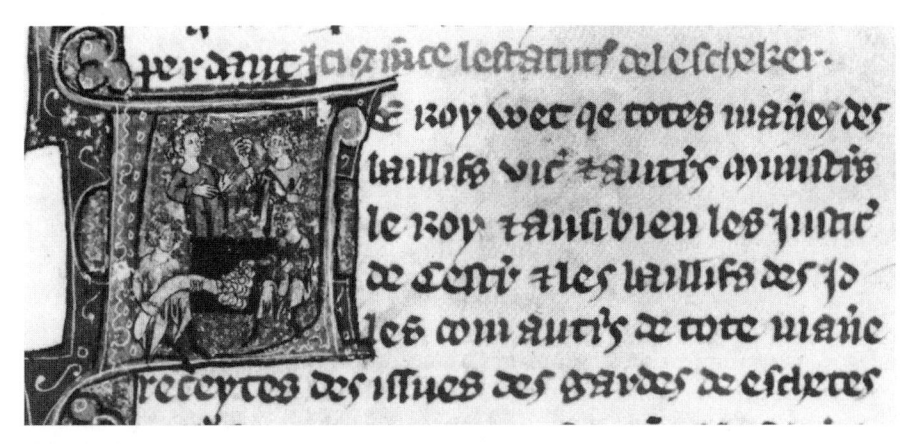

Figure 52. Exchequer at Work, Marking the Statute "Delescheker." Cambridge, Mass., Harvard Law School Library, MS 12, fol. 30v. English, second quarter of fourteenth century.

Figure 53. Children as Wards, Marking a Statute "de Wardes et Relief." Cambridge, Mass., Harvard Law School Library, MS 12, fol. 33. English, second quarter of fourteenth century.

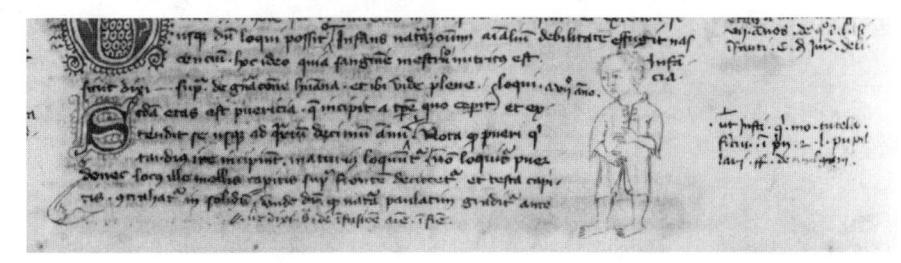

Figure 54. The Ages of Man, from Jean Raynaud's *Viridarium*. Dublin, Chester Beatty Library, MS 80, fol. 6v. French, early fifteenth century. Reproduced by kind permission of the Trustees of the Chester Beatty Library, Dublin.

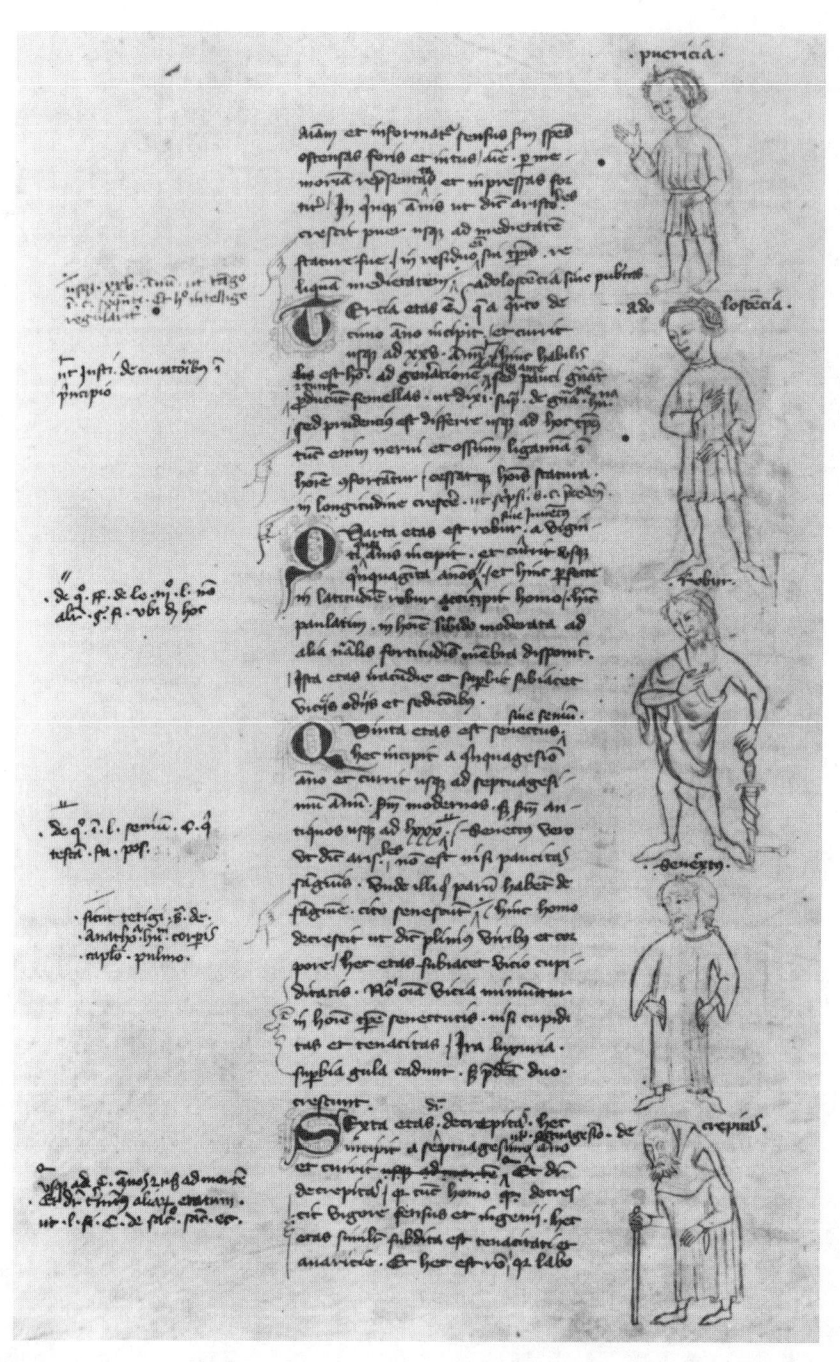

Figure 55. The Ages of Man, from Jean Raynaud's *Viridarium*. Dublin, Chester Beatty Library, MS 80, fol. 7. French, early fifteenth century. Reproduced by kind permission of the Trustees of the Chester Beatty Library, Dublin.

Figure 56. Clerics Destroying a Church, from William of Pagula, *Oculus sacerdotis*. Hatfield House, Herts., Marquess of Salisbury, MS Cecil Papers 290, fol. 13. English, second half of fourteenth century. Reproduced courtesy of the Marquess of Salisbury.

mA. De pastoribz ecclesiasticis
Aliqui cum pastores cura suscipiunt ad lata
dos subditos inardescunt pecunias ab eis ex
torquent z decipiunt z sac ordinis p omnia

Figure 57. Priest Receives Money from a Layman Bearing a Scrip, from Honorius of Autun, *Elucidarium*. Lincoln, U.K., Lincoln Cathedral Library, MS 218, fol. 17. English, c. 1400.

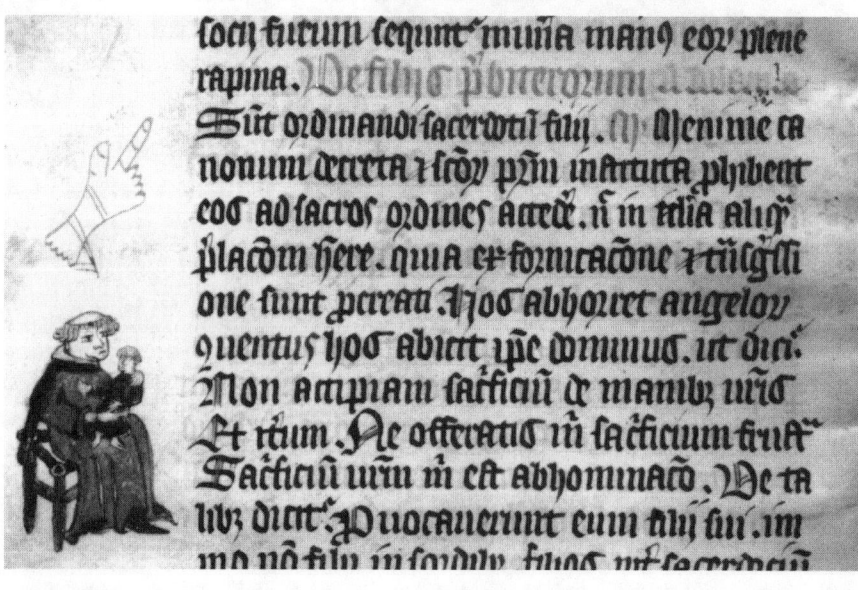

Figure 58. Seated Priest Nurses a Child, from Honorius of Autun, *Elucidarium*. Lincoln, U.K., Lincoln Cathedral Library MS 218, fol. 17v. English, c. 1400.

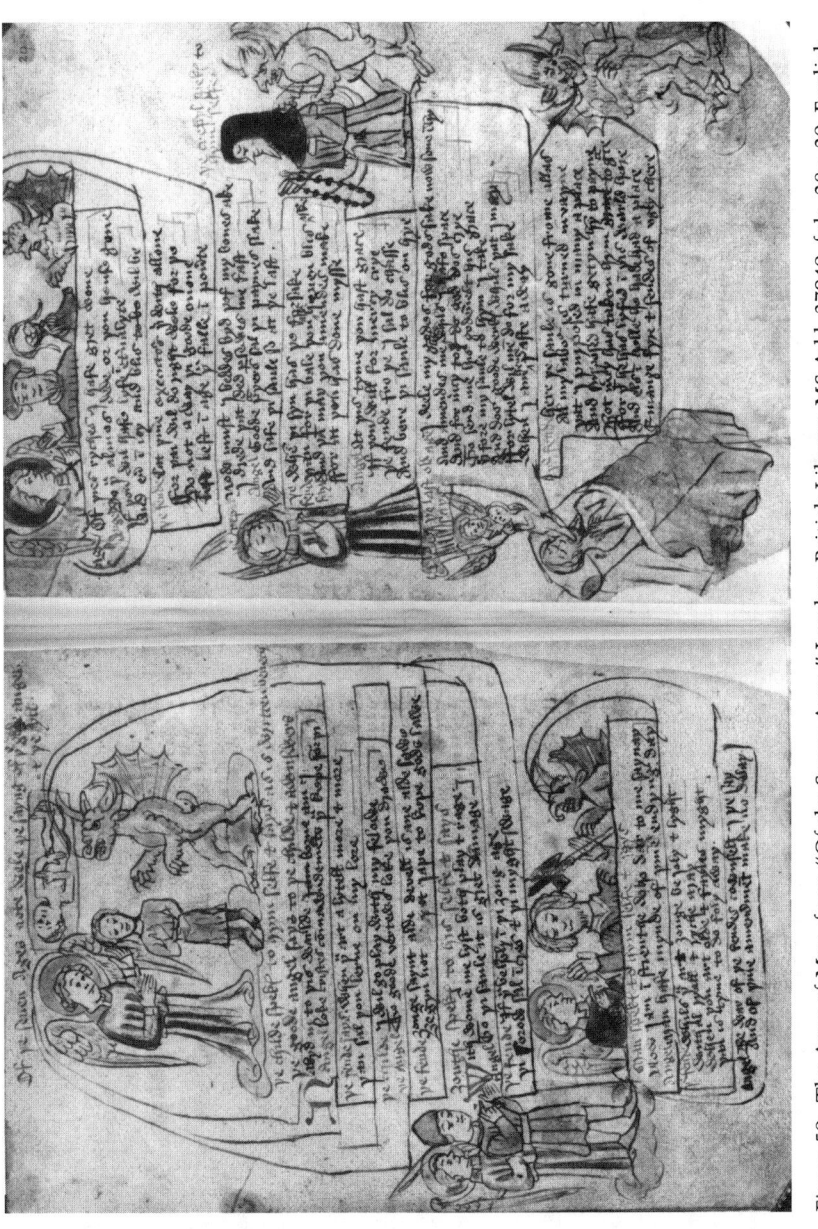

Figure 59. The Ages of Man, from "Of the Seven Ages." London, British Library, MS Add. 37049, fols. 28v–29. English, first half of fifteenth century. Reproduced by permission of the British Library.

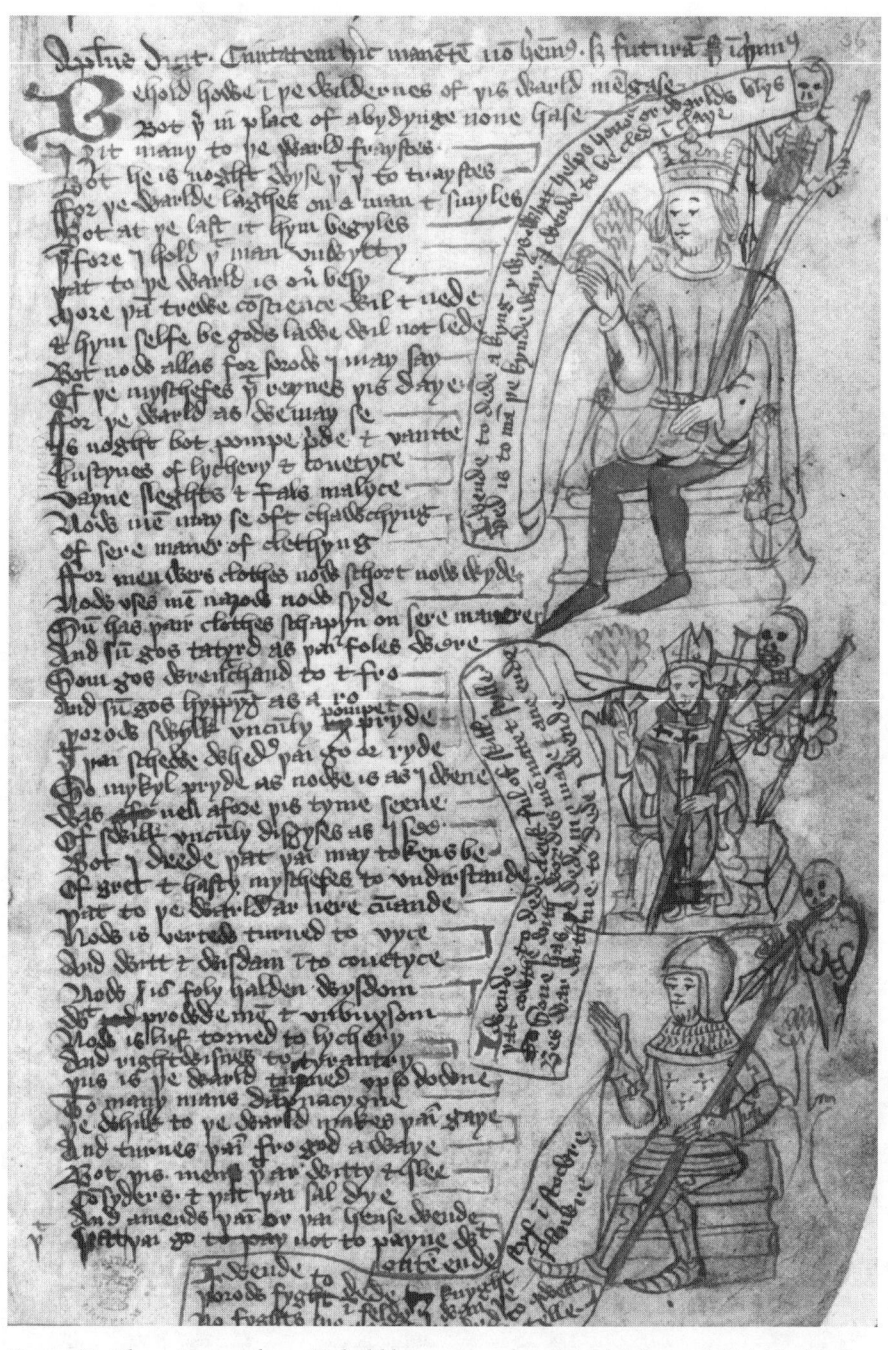

Figure 60. Three Estates, from "Behold howe," London, British Library, MS Add. 37049, fol. 36. English, first half of fifteenth century. Reproduced by permission of the British Library.

Figure 61. Clerk Teaching Knight, "Of Active and Contemplative Life." London, British Library, MS Add. 37049, fol. 87v. English, first half of fifteenth century. Reproduced by permission of the British Library.

Figure 62. The Wheel of Life, *Psalter of Robert de Lisle*. London, British Library, MS Arundel 18, fol. 126v. English, 1300–1339. Reproduced by permission of the British Library.

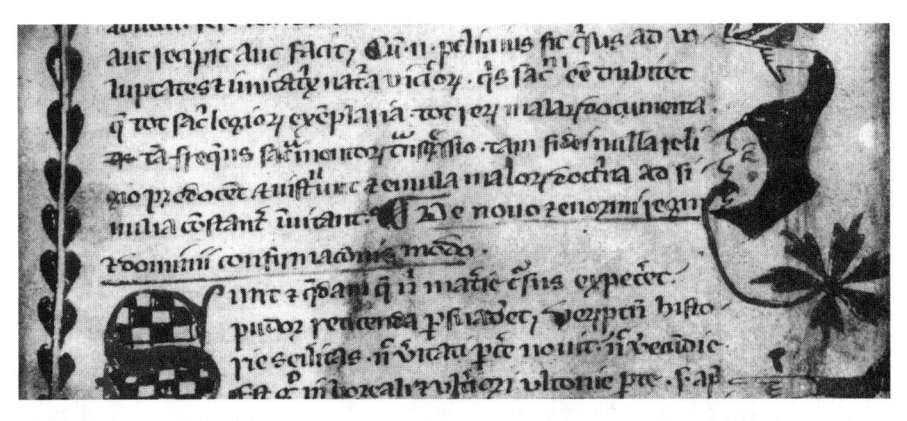

Figure 63. Elongated Tongue and Manicule Marginalia. London, British Library, MS Harley 3724, fol. 33 (new fol. 37). Anglo-Irish, early fourteenth century. Reproduced by permission of the British Library.

Figure 64. "Autoritas," from James le Palmer, *Omne bonum*. London, British Library, MS Royal 6.E.VI, fol. 158v. English, 1360–75. Reproduced by permission of the British Library.

Figure 65. James le Palmer's Marginal Drawing of Exchequer clerk, from *Omne bonum*. London, British Library, MS Royal 6.E.VI, fol. 303v. English, 1360–75. Reproduced by permission of the British Library.

Figure 66. "De habitu clericorum," from *Omne bonum*. London, British Library, MS Royal 6.E.VI, fol. 197. English, 1360–75. Reproduced by permission of the British Library.

Figure 67. FitzRalph Disputing with Dominicans and Carmelites, from *Omne bonum*. London, British Library, MS Royal 6.E.VI, fol. 528v. English, c. 1380. Reproduced by permission of the British Library.

Figure 68. John Cok, a London Scribe of *Piers Plowman*, Adoring the Cross. London, Saint Bartholomew's Hospital, Cartulary, fol. 94. Reproduced by permission of Archives Department, Saint Bartholomew's Hospital. Photo kindly supplied by J. J. G. Alexander.

Fig. 7.—Church Reform.

Fig. 8.—The Abbot of Peterborough.

Fig. 9.—A Bishop.

Fig. 10.—A Charter surrendered to the Crown.

Figure 69. Sample Exchequer Storage and Mnemonic Devices, reproduced from Hubert Hall, *The Antiquities and Curiosities of the Exchequer* (London: Elliot Stock, 1898), 56–57; fig. 7, original from Public Record Office E 36/274; fig. 13 from PRO E 36/268; fig. 14 and 15 from PRO E 36/273. English, fourteenth and fifteenth centuries.

Fig. 11.—Oath of Fealty, etc.

Fig. 12.—A Royal Marriage.

Fig. 13.—An Usurer.

Fig. 14.—John, Earl of Holland, Richard II.'s half-brother, and a fashionable Courtier.

Fig. 15.—Alice Perrers, Edward III.'s mistress.

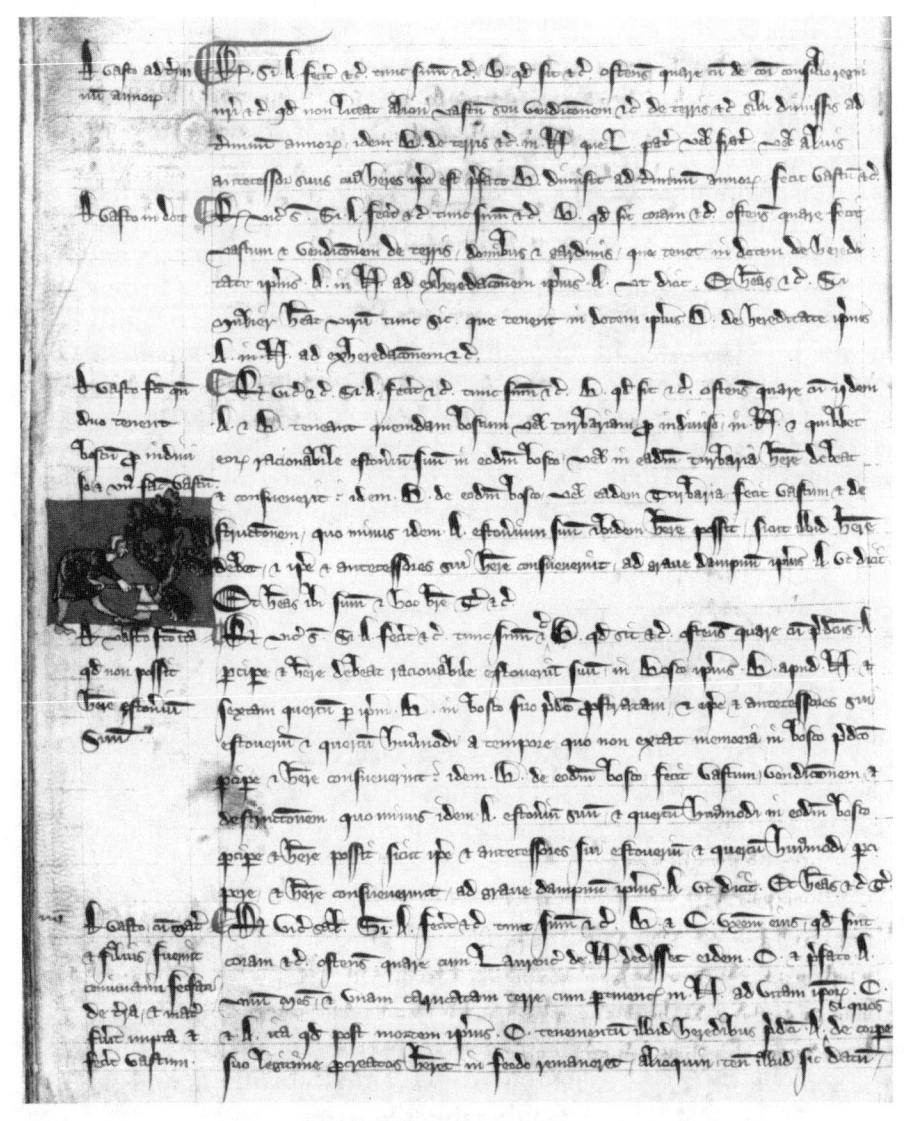

Figure 70. Peasant Chopping Tree, Mnemonic to a Writ on Timber Rights, from the *Registrum Brevium*. New York, Pierpont Morgan Library, MS 812, fol. 19v.

by an object laid upon the altar, cups, rings, staffs, knives, and other items associated in this way with past contracts were kept together with the sacred books, vessels, and relics of the abbey.... In a sense, turning the pages of Matthew's *Chronica majora* is like opening the door of a great abbey cupboard from which spills forth a rich succession of disparate images and objects, each conjuring up its own compelling story from the past, so that each event again becomes visually "present" to the viewer's eye.[88]

Discrete images are thus placed in a storehouse of memory, to be retrieved in the process of reading the written text. For this reason, Paris's illustrations, like those in Douce 104, lack an explicitly narrative *ordinatio*. Instead, Paris often used "a single isolated figure representing the major protagonist in the narrative. In other cases, Matthew illustrates his annotations in emblematic fashion, abstracting salient aspects of the episodes as isolated objects or busts of figures."[89] The result is often a kind of visual shorthand. To illustrate the Saxon king Offa's sacrifice of the crown for monastic life, for example, Paris draws a bust of King Offa, whose cowl is apparent around his neck, his crown falling off his head.[90] His loss of worldly authority is signaled in the same manner as the Douce 104 illustrator depicts the bishop's fall from spiritual authority (figure 18), perhaps both deriving from the classic image of Synagoga, with a tumbling crown and broken staff. To show the lifting of the interdict imposed upon England during the notorious reign of John, Matthew draws a marginal image in the *Historia Anglorum* of two hands pulling bells by ropes (London, British Library, MS Royal 14.C, fol. 94).[91] Paris marks ominous natural phenomena in the *Chronica majora*, such as a flood or an invasion of destructive birds who devoured the first crops in 1251, by simple images of a boat on the flooded Thames and a crossbill with fruit in its beak. In one of the prophetic and apocalyptic passages in *Piers Plowman*, Piers warns of imminent natural disasters unless the moral and social order is regenerated through honest labor (VIII.343–51). On folio 40 of Douce 104, the illustrator signals the importance of this passage with an unmanned boat uncannily like Paris's boat on the flooded Thames in Cambridge, Corpus Christi College, MS 16 (figures 14 and 48).

A close scrutiny of the relationship between language and image led to some brilliant and fanciful moments on the part of both illustrators. Homophony, in which we recall things through language or visual puns, is an ancient system of mnemonics. Manuscript technology and the potential of the margins as interpretive play space encouraged medieval scribe-illustrators not only to use puns as heuristic prompts and exegetical tools, but also to embrace the "pun as a tool of sacred wit."[92] Matthew Paris playfully indulges in such visual punning in the *Chronica majora* when he calls attention to a text in which he describes the capture of a Roman senator named Brancaleone; Paris draws a picture in the margin of a lion's claw, or *braccia leonis,* "offering the reader a far-fetched pun on his name... as well as a dramatic visual metaphor for *captus.*"[93] Medieval Apocalypse manuscripts are full of such word-image games, reminding modern readers that our disdain for puns was not shared by the most educated medieval audiences of the thirteenth century, whose reading and memorizing was governed by a different sense of leisure, a different delight in language. Suzanne Lewis warns that

> although such simple mnemonic puns are still readily accessible to the modern reader, some of the pictorial puzzles... do not lend themselves to easy solution, and upon recovery seem forced or strained to modern readers unaccustomed to the playful lexical convolutions so frequently encountered in medieval discourse.[94]

While we have nothing quite as explicit in Douce 104, or have failed to detect such oblique wordplay, there is a possible example of homophony in passus IX, folio 41. Here a handsome young lawyer in a gray gown pleads at the bar (figure 15). He is placed deliberately beside a passage that accuses lawyers of refusing to plead for the common people unless they are paid beforehand, literally "pre manibus" (IX.45). Langland undoubtedly likens this selling of legal services to simony, and warns lawyers that they will need the true pardon for salvation that comes from living by "here handes / Lellyche and lauhfollyche" (IX.58–59). The lawyer's prominent eyes gaze upon the lines "Ac he þat speneth his speche and speketh for þe pore / That innocent and nedy is and no man harme wolde," while his index finger, a sign of *declamatio,* points to the line "Shal haue grace of a good ende and greet ioye aftur" (IX.46–50). His other hand, however, which is distinctively large and fully extended, palm thrust toward the reader, must be a pun on "pre-manibus." There is no other logical reason for this peculiar gesture or the size of the hands other than to emphasize the chief sin the passage explores, and the pun is in keeping with the illustrator's tendency to undercut or underscore Latin text. Mary Carruthers speculates about the presence of other "images verborum" in Douce 104, concluding from such "odd and idiosyncratic readings" that the manuscript may have been "an entirely personal production."[95] The "personal" feeling of Douce 104 may be the consequence of a scribal illustrator who is primarily responsible for the visual interpretations that so often seem to have irritated the annotator.

The marginal drawings of another "personal production"—a manuscript in which a single individual influenced both the transmission of the text and the illustrative program—shore up the speculation that the Douce illustrator was familiar with chronicles and legal manuscripts. James le Palmer compiled his encyclopedic *Omne bonum* between 1360 and 1375 (see figures 64–67).[96] A treasurer's scribe in the Exchequer of

Edward III, James le Palmer ingeniously organized this compendium of canon law, natural history, theological exposition, and biblical and hagiographical narrative alphabetically. While a professional illustrator provided lavish pictures of the narrative within formal frames, James le Palmer freely glossed the margins with doodlings that Lucy Freeman Sandler has rightly termed "marginal notes in figural form." While many of these curious, hybrid figures function as manicules, many are more detailed visually and are specific in function. Some actually point to "verbal notes," and the details, "especially their heads and headgear, are... varied as appropriate to the written marginal text."[97] The figures reflect the particular interests of the compiler, who clearly viewed his marginal drawings as interpretive or directive apparatus with a purpose different from the illustrations created by the various artist-flourisher teams he employed. While his annotations display a clear sympathy with Langland, stringently criticizing clerics for their showy clothes and sexual mores (e.g., figure 66), his drawings (our focus here) share the Douce illustrator's selective preoccupation with the suffering of the innocent. Under the rubric of *Expositus*, for example, James has transformed the descenders of letters into "cradles or shelters for the heads of exposed, that is, abandoned infants." The Douce illustrator offers his reader a similar image of pathos on folio 48v, where a child in a green tunic holds his hands over his ears in a gesture of despair beside the previously discussed passage on children born out of wedlock (figure 22).[98]

The extraordinarily creative work of these three scribal illustrators—the Douce 104 artist, James le Palmer, and Matthew Paris—makes it clear that scholars who seek evidence of medieval reader-response should look to the margins in a wider range of manuscripts than those of secular love poetry, such as the many *Romance of the Rose* manuscripts. From the margins they may glean the kind of personal or interpretive responses that are the natural result of manuscript production in a culture that connected imagery with memory and ethical reading. The Douce 104 illustrator, a careful professional reader of the poem, appears to have been familiar with a tradition of marginal illustration that we might deem less refined than that in luxury manuscripts, but that richly served clerks, scribes, and readers for many centuries. Such textual tactics for directed reading provided manuscript makers with some means of shaping materials for a specific reader or manuscript owner, further muddying the waters of "authorial intent."[99] The poem's vehement criticism of the power of the gloss to destabilize even legal texts (XIII.116–21) comes from an author's concern for the purity of his own text; "and he was right, 'glosses,' whether verbal or visual, do alter audience response."[100] The marginal figures in Douce 104 construct a complex visionary experience for the reader, the shared product of the poem and the illustrator's reading of that poem. While the figures consistently refer the reader back to the letter of the text, the folio page's visual layout underscores the process of manuscript creation that to some extent determines reception. Nowhere does one see *artists* or *poets* in the margins, but we do see scribes, dreamers, and meditators—all reflective of the *medieval* composition process. Reading and looking at Douce 104, one is conscious of its makers at every turn.

CHAPTER 6

❖

Visual Heuristics

Performative Reading

The visionary *ordinatio*, the marginal illustrative strategy the Douce illustrator employed to invite participatory reading, thereby creating the opportunity for memory and meditation, depends upon visual voicing or the oral and performative nature of texts in a manuscript culture. The mystical colloquy, a recorded conversation reproducing (and in the process, reordering) divine experience; the dispute between the body and the soul; the dream vision recreating spiritual experience from a retrospective vantage point—a conversation with a newly authorized self—all require the reader to *listen* to voices and identify with a narrator or speaker who relays his or her unique experience to bring other Christians wisdom. Scholarship on medieval constructs of authorship is beginning to reflect upon manuscript evidence suggestive that *medieval critical editors* (scribes, illustrators, annotators) were sensitive to the complex relationship between narrators and authors.[1] Whether New Critics seeking the authentic, stable text by a historical author or deconstructionists eschewing the notion of authorship altogether, modern critics of medieval poetry, and particularly dream visions, have largely constructed their readings predicated upon notions of authorship and linguistic fixity appropriate for a print, rather than a manuscript, culture.[2] Even deconstructionism posits a "text" in the absence of an author, participating in a "metaphysics of presence" in its assumption that the critical edition, in contrast to the manuscript redaction, is recoverable and archetypal.[3] Narrators are poetic personae; authors and texts employ artifice in their stylization of motive and response, use of iconographic conventions portraying interiority, and creation of familiar psychological landscapes and narrative voices; thus the voice of the narrator in poems like *The Romance of the Rose* signal to us that they are "fiction," imaginative and "literary" in the sense that they filter emotional conflict or growth through traditional poetic formulas.[4] Chaucer's dream visions, for example, which appropriate the very language and experience of French courtly dream visions by Froissart and Machaut, are not personal or individual by modern standards, nor does the personality of his bumbling narrator accord with documentary evidence of Chaucer as the shrewd and politically astute public servant. For many years, as a consequence, we've called his "performing self" a "persona" to signal the separation of the author and the speaker in the poetry.⁵ But the complex nature of a "performing self" in a manuscript culture is largely neglected by the modern construction of the Chaucerian persona. A writer who composes to read out loud to a familiar audience creates the poem's speaker depending upon audience proximity. Under such circumstances, "clear cut divisions between the 'poet' and his 'persona' are specially unlikely."⁶ Derek Pearsall concludes, "It is not simple-minded to talk of Chaucer as the 'I' of the poem.... he is the dreamer as much and as fully as he is Chaucer.... To suppress this true memory of the experience of reading Chaucer... is to mistake 'narrative' for 'text.'"⁷

The same attention to the complex conditions for authorship and reception in a manuscript culture is enabling scholars of religious literature to question the presentation of the "performing self" in devotional, visionary, and mystical writing.⁸ Medieval writers who dared to record their spiritual colloquies were surely aware of the dangers of self-presentation and the instability of the text in a manuscript culture—particularly in the vernacular.⁹ Spiritual narratives that recount genuine experiences of conversion or revelation for the instruction and illumination of others thus reconfigure personal details through conventions of authoritative texts like Augustine's *Confessions,* even while taking into account the personal nature of spiritual experience and the needs of a specific textual community for whom the book was written. When Aelred of Rievaulx composed his *De institutione inclusarum* for anchoresses he knew, he included an Augustinian passage describing his own youthful sexual misconduct, requiring his charges to meditate on his sexual license and restoration to God's grace.¹⁰ Such an unusual and potentially dangerous topic may have been appropriate for Augustine's target audience, and even for the women in Aelred's audience, but in the fourteenth-century Middle English translation of the *Inclusarum* in the Vernon manuscript, these passages have been excerpted to conform to "social and cultural shifts in the perception of gender and sexuality in the later Middle Ages" and to provide more acceptable fare for female readers.¹¹ In other words, even when an author felt it appropriate to include personal detail, albeit through conventions, the professional readers who made the manuscript and recognized the function of literary formulas had the freedom to tailor the text according to the audience's needs. Sometimes the excision of personal material and the resultant loss of the author's identity legitimized the narrative—as is the case with Marguerite Porete and Margery Kempe, whose personal lives hampered the achievement of any literary authority they claimed by spiritual distinction.¹² Surely Langland was thinking about such authorial strategies and the difficult problem of controlling reception when he transformed passages from the B text in Passus XII and XV concerned with poetry as legitimate labor into the autobiographical apologia in the C text. With its untidy allusions to a shabby domestic life in a disreputable part of London, the starkly personal confession of laziness and negligence in the C text is all the more startling because there is nothing about it like the endearing ineptness in Chaucer's narrators.

We cannot here review critical disputations over the autobiographical nature of *Piers Plowman*, nor would doing so be to our purpose.[13] Instead, we wish to understand how the representation of the dreamer as author and speaker forged by both illustrator and annotator of Douce 104 functioned as a heuristic cue. Sensitive to the issue of control and reception, and in some sense determining both through physical production, the professional readers of Douce 104 were as absorbed in the issue of the speaker's identity and self-presentation as were medieval authors, implying a self-consciousness about textual production we seldom credit to scribes and illustrators. Laurence de Looze, Sylvia Huot, and others have recently pointed out that strategies of signing, of forging an authorial presence in medieval poems, were informed by the demands and exigencies of manuscript production.[14] We now interpret consciously from the vantage point that major writers of twelfth-century courtly narratives embedded their names in their texts explicitly, authorizing and authenticating their works.[15] By the thirteenth century, however, the author's signature is of secondary importance to the experience the work presents as authenticating the author's life; Langland is typical of fourteenth-century writers in seeming to deflect attention from his identity through "indirect naming," as de Looze calls it. The literary puzzles and anagrams in the C text tell us a great deal about self-presentation and the performing self in a manuscript culture, but the issue at hand is how professional readers understood these signs and integrated them into a program of reading and interpretation. The visionary *ordinatio* of Douce 104 calls the reader back to the experience of the poem and makes the oral and visual nature of its reading integral rather than secondary to the written word on the page; in the process, the professional readers present us with a distinctive "I" through their annotations and illustrations. Furthermore, the figures in Douce 104 bracketing speeches indicate that the text was voiced, and thus was dialogic and meditative; those artists and scribes who produced the manuscript recognized the conventions of voicing as integral to the process of reading and remembering. Rather than destabilizing the authority of the written text, voicing and visualizing the text underscored the dreamer's visionary experience and claims, his waking and sleeping moments, enabling the reader to participate in the dreamer's experience.[16] This participation in the vision makes the poem all the more realistic and convincing.

Placing the issue of authorial signing in the context of a specific manuscript, Douce 104, may add considerably to our comprehension of late medieval conventions of authorship, autobiography, and dream vision.

The illustrator and the annotator of Douce 104 both acknowledge the poem's speaker as "I," but did they interpret the poem as the experience of a real visionary, like the speaker in a mystical colloquy? Or did they envision the speaker as an Everyman figure, such as the dreamer in *Pèlerinage de la vie humaine*? And how did their assumptions, inasmuch as they can be determined, influence this particular redaction of *Piers Plowman*?

Similar studies of manuscript traditions reveal a fifteenth-century tendency toward autobiographical reading. John Dagenais, for example, has argued that a number of distinct versions of the *Libro de buen amor* by Juan Ruiz, archpriest of Hita, exist, each redaction reflecting its own interpretive thrust. While the fourteenth-century MS G "treats the text as source of moral exempla, signaling 'insiemplo' in the margins," it physically ignores the narrative's autobiographical frame, which Dagenais identifies as most interesting to the modern reader.[17] MS S, an early-fifteenth-century redaction, contains numerous rubrics stressing the autobiographical frame and underscores the oral nature of the text with the inclusion of a burlesque sermon prologue. Similarly, Peter Brieger's exhaustive reception study of the illustrations of the *Divine Comedy* challenges New Critical constructions of the fictive narrative persona in medieval poetry as well as poststructuralist dismissal of the authors, for apparently fourteenth-century readers accepted the notion that Dante was writing about his own otherworld experiences.[18] But, whereas readers in this "first stage" (1330–75) of Dante commentary and interpretation largely focused on the pilgrim's conversion experience (the kind of instructional interest we see in fourteenth-century *Libro de buen amor* manuscripts), readers in the "second stage" (1375–1410) indicate a growing interest in Dante as a historical personage. Early manuscript illuminations of *The Divine Comedy* are minimalist, even "abbreviated symbols" suggestive of allegorical reading and meditation; this gives way in the third period of Dante reception (1410–80) to Renaissance realism.[19] In illustrations of this period we see Dante the historical personage, the Florentine scholar and poet, as opposed to the less defined character depicted in the more spiritually, allegorically informed illustrations from the poem's early period. In carefully constructing reader reception from the illustrations, Brieger concludes that the fifteenth-century audience was interested in Dante's autobiography.

The illustrative program of Douce 104 is distinctive in wedding historical realism to visionary iconography. Rather than being mutually exclusive and thus conforming strictly to either a generalized or a particularized spiritual iconography, visionary experience and personal reflection come together in Douce 104, suggesting that the illustrator recognized both instructional and autobiographical elements in the narrative typical of a *visio*, a genre that admits the highly personal nature of religious experience even as it uses literary conventions to record and explore those same experiences. While it is customary in late medieval religious visionary literature to excise *irrelevant* personal detail in the reporting of religious experience (as do Margery Kempe and Julian of Norwich, for example), this narrative strategy does not impinge upon the validity of the experience; if anything, use of the conventions of spiritual reporting was thought to give greater credibility to visionary experience.[20] Medieval audiences may have found in those very conventions we associate with "fiction" an affirmation of truth. While we may never be able to answer fully John Burrow's "embarrassing question: Is the 'autobiography' of Passus XI–XII fact or fiction?," we will consider the representation of the dreamer in Douce 104 and the visual icons the illustrator employs to create the dreamer-poet, well advised by Burrow that "conventions, after all, represent nothing less than the forms in which reality presents itself to any age, medieval or modern."[21]

A case in point is the use of mirror imagery in late medieval dream poetry. Daniel Poirion has noted, for example, that the mirror in the "fountain of Narcissus" has "become a key text for the definition of unhappy self-consciousness in *The Romance of the Rose*."[22] Spiritual, rather than sexual, longing is signaled in the opening of the *Pèlerinage de la vie humaine*, where the dreamer envisions the Heavenly City in a mirror; in no illustration does he envision himself viewing the city, for his self-consciousness is limited to self-imaging as a pilgrim in search of the city. Thus the "mirror and its beautiful and compelling image exists elusively between the world of the poet-dreamer and that of the poet-dreamer's dream self."[23] In Margery Kempe's visual meditations, the Lord tells her that he has "Ordeynd þe to be a merowr" or a spiritual exemplar among people.[24] Each of these works uses the image of the mirror as a metaphor for interiority, memory, and self-reflection, but which work speaks of real as opposed to imagined experiences? Kempe (or her amanuensis) consciously turned to literary models to order her vita and influence the reception of her *Book*; those models and their metaphors, in turn, were selected because they signaled a particular kind of interiority to their audiences. "The Mirrors of Middle Earth" situated in *Piers* near the center of the C text remind the reader that the poem's core is introspective.[25] Since Will is both generalized and particularized in the C text, however, this interiority upsets modern critical expectations that the narrator at least be one or the other. Similarly, personal references to geographical place in *Piers Plowman* frustrate our desire to pronounce Will's "lond of longyng" (XI.170) a symbolic interiorization (like Augustine's) or a specific time of misspent youth. If this is an anagrammatic signature, as Anne Middleton suggests, what is the relationship between the dreamer's interior journey and the poet's?[26] The critical responses of the Douce illustrator and annotator help us fill in this interpretive lacuna. While this methodology may not provide us with Langland's intentions, it can inform us about cultural poetics and reading strategies. The extensive narrative programs extant in manuscripts illustrating interior journeys, such as in *The Romance of the Rose* and *The Pilgrimage of the Life of Man* (in both French and English redactions) suggest that no artist needed to turn to such a task without models. The Douce 104 illustrator's program is a curious blend of innovation and tradition sensitive to the C text's blend of personal, ecclesiological, and social reform.

The illustrator is undoubtedly familiar with the conventions of spiritual autobiography and penitential narrative, his marginal program emphasizing the double vision—the simultaneous immediacy and retrospective voice—of spiritual reporting that necessarily dramatizes the ethical awakening of narrator and reader. This would account for his decision not to illustrate the apologia, the sustained waking moment of the C text, with images that would necessarily describe the dreamer's historical life, those autobiographical details that have sent literary historians in search of the poet Langland; instead, the illustrator concentrates his energies on recreating the interior experience of spiritual illumination, much in the manner of mystical writers who avoid personal matter to focus on the substance of their texts: the interior life. Like Julian of Norwich or Margery Kempe, the illustrator is more interested in capturing the dreamer's interior or spiritual state than his external existence.

The illustrator's conceptualization of the dreamer at the outset of the poem argues for his awareness of the "distinction between the dreams, in which the narrator is an observer or actor, and the waking moments, in which the narrator describes himself as a visionary who is a wanderer and an idle vagabond."[27] While author portraits are traditional enough in fourteenth- and fifteenth-century manuscripts, the Douce 104 illustrator provides us with one at the outset of the poem that supports the distinction between the waking and sleeping narrator.[28] On folio 1 the dreamer is specifically conflated with the speaker of the poem by appearing within the historiated initial *Y*, constituting both "I" (speaker) and the first letter of the line "Yn a sommur sesoun." The dreamer is a middle-aged man in a gray gown and tan cowl, leaning his head in his hand (figure 1).[29] Manuscript readers would surely recognize this heuristic cue, a common sign of visionary experience and thus ethical reading in medieval manuscripts. In numerous illustrations of the sleeping dreamer and the mirror, the iconography of self-reflective dreaming at the opening of both English and French redactions of *The Pilgrimage of the Life of Man* from the fourteenth and fifteenth centuries, the dreamer lies with his eyes closed.[30] The illustrator of the Oxford, Corpus Christi College, MS 201 *Piers Plowman* also chose to place the dreamer, a middle-aged man with head in hand, in the initial on the first folio. Whereas this dreamer-narrator is asleep, however, the narrator in Douce 104 is awake—a significant choice on the part of the illustrator. Retrospective and self-conscious, the Douce 104 dreamer-narrator's poetic self-awareness emerges from revelations about the boundaries between sleeping and waking; the problem of retrieving, interpreting, and then practicing visionary wisdom is one of the most difficult aspects of the C text, where the focus on personal responsibility is intensified. Visionary experience in the Middle Ages was common; writing that experience down and presuming to publish it was dangerous, but it was the written word that conveyed the legitimacy of the vision.[31] Late-fourteenth- and fifteenth-century redactions of *The Pilgrimage of the Life of Man* link authorship, oral performance, and the dream vision by pairing illustrations of the poet writing or preaching, both writerly activities, with the dreamer and the mirror. The Douce illustrator, rather than use the mirror to signify self-reflection, associates the mirror with deception and false images, such as Fortune. In keeping with the familiar illustrative conventions of Gospel and Apocalypse manuscripts, the Douce illustrator presents writing figures in the margins of his manuscript to underscore the author's task in forging the inchoate substance of dreams into an orthodox pattern of meaning—a composition strategy we see most often in mystical writers; dream-vision conventions are not synonymous with artifice as that which is "fictional," then, in *Piers Plowman* and *The Pilgrimage of the Life of Man*.[32] Just as poets such as Hoccleve and Chaucer chose a mixture of literary convention and personal confession in their creation of a poetic persona, so has the illustrator in Douce 104 modified a visual convention to suggest something about the acute awareness of this particular dreamer-narrator, signaling this process to a knowing audience.[33]

The Seven Ages of Man

The Douce artist's depiction of the dreamer provides us with a preliminary sense of the larger pictorial design; he will adapt or modify iconography to the poem's purpose. Thus his program of illustration offers us a unique reading of *Piers Plowman*, while it constitutes a penetrating commentary on the shape of the dreamer's life. The illustrator selects images for the dreamer's life from the homiletic, penitential "Seven Ages of Man" iconography, with which he was familiar from utility-grade legal, clerical, and devotional manuscripts.[34] The choice of iconography underscores the poem's concern with conversion and mortality, but the way in which the illustrator applies and modifies these conventions implies an understanding of the narrator's life as particularized. John Burrow has argued convincingly that Langland assigned an autobiographical function to Imaginatif, who conceptualizes life according the Ages of Man schema and also associates "those ages with the idea of death."[35] Burrow argues that Imaginatif, a specific and personal faculty connected in medieval psychology to prudence and memory, confesses to following Will faithfully for more than forty winters (C.XV.3), meaning that Will is forty-five when this moral and visual faculty urges him to awaken to retrospective truth: he is now between middle and old age. In Douce 104, folio 63r,

Imaginatif sits with head in hand, much like the dreamer on the first folio, with his eyes open, indicating reflection, perhaps even despair (figure 28).[36] Dressed in a pale gray-blue gown with a red cowl, white hood, and black cap, this reflective figure is either "Imaginatif or a clerk."[37] But both the text and iconography insist that Imaginatif is both the narrator and a clerk and in this guise represents the author's awakening faculty, an identity underscored at this retrospective moment when the C text outlines the narrator's crises of faith prior to the Inner Dream. Here we discover that the "Dreamer elected to enter the clergy and became embroiled in a dispute with his teachers about the grounds for salvation, whereupon he abandoned 'clergye' to delight in the world."[38] Kathleen Scott argues that "there is little reason to believe here that the Douce figure is of Langland or even of the dreamer," but such distinctions between author and narrator belong to modern, rather than medieval, literary theory.[39]

The illustrator's choice to depict Imaginatif as a clerk reflects the autobiographical thrust of the C text; furthermore, the illustrator has carefully placed the figure to span those lines that most reflect the narrator's personal failures and criticisms of present authority (XIV.18a–29). Imaginatif best demonstrates the contemplative mode or *collatio* that engenders spiritual autobiography by shaping the Christian life from a retrospective position. The C text largely abandons a concern with poetic making (in B.XII) to focus on the problem of learning as the path to salvation and its relationship to good works. Imaginatif, who "sits by himself" (XIV.3), urges the dreamer against idleness and a mere book-learned knowledge of charity. He is thus the imaginative power who examines the dreamer's own *imitatio Christi*. With the aid of memory and Reason, Imaginatif reviews the dreamer's arguments, and in the end affirms Clergy's role in teaching penance. He assures the dreamer that relying on God's mercy while ignoring his law is imprudent. The dreamer awakens from this exchange with a keener sense of his misdirection and abandonment by the ephemeral Youth and Fortune. The illustrator provides the reader with representations of the dreamer at different stages of his life, but his principle of selection is based upon the dreamer's moments of crisis and self-reflection. *Collatio*, the meditative gathering of impressions and experiences from the storehouse of memory, is integral to the process of "making ideas, creating thoughts," and thus writing.[40] As Augustine's archetypal spiritual autobiography suggests, such collation or the creative reconfiguring of memory through the act of writing was intensely emotional and purgative, but this painful path of memory was the sole avenue to God. Despite his "metaphysical twist, ... his description of how invention occurs as an activity of *memoria* belongs clearly to the ordinary pedagogy of rhetoric."[41] Our distinction between writer and narrator (let alone writer, narrator, and scribe) must be refined to accommodate the process of authorship in a manuscript culture.

Medieval readers were undoubtedly aware of these subtle distinctions, as the authorial and scribal portraits in Michael de Massa's *Passion* (Bodley 758) illustrate. The manuscript was written by Ralph de Medylton in 1405 for a lay patron, Sir Miles de Stapelton in Norfolk.[42] Folio 1 presents the reader with an elaborate, framed drawing of the Passion, but it is clearly an image of *collatio,* the author's envisioning of the Passion, as the seated writing figure in the bottom right-hand corner suggests (figure 43). This friar is Michael de Massa, and we see him recording his vision of the Passion for the reader's edification, as the speech scroll protruding from the book on his lectern indicates to us by its brief text: a reproduction of the first line of the text. He is thus a part of the image he represents, an actor, however marginal, as his garment's slight protrusion from the frame suggests. But his marginality within the frame is altogether different in this manuscript from the marginality of the scribe who humbly and self-consciously draws his portrait, unframed, in the margin on the last folio page, identifying himself as Ralph de Medylton (figure 44). This sensitivity to author and scribe in devotional and utility-grade manuscripts must surely have been more acute in manuscripts of poetry.

David Hult, for example, has awakened us to the way in which the theme of authorship is consistently explored through author portraits in manuscripts of *The Romance of the Rose,* portraits that scholars have mistakenly confused as literal author portraits.[43] Figures shown writing in a book signify the authorial imaginative faculty; "the other significant variation in the authorial portrait depicts not a writer but more likely a reader seated at a desk with an open and completed book," sometimes with a manicule.[44] Hult provides a number of examples of both the scribal and reading author figures, noting that their expressions are various as they gaze upon their texts. But we need to remember the Douce illustrator's subtle refinement of illustrative traditions when we turn to narrator-scribe figures in Douce 104, which support a close reading of this redaction of the C text. The figure on folio 52v (figure 24) of Douce 104, also dressed like a clerk, gazes upon an open book, demonstrating the illustrator's familiarity with author-scribe figures. We might assume that this is *either* an author figure *or* Imaginatif, but Imaginatif need not be shown with book in hand to identify authorship to a medieval reader. As a creative faculty connected to the process of memory and authorship, his gaze upon the text itself is sufficient to signal the tradition of self-reflexivity necessarily connected to this faculty. Furthermore, he is an explicitly visual link between the actual process of visualization he signifies and the dream vision itself; as Hult explains, "Based squarely upon the model of the scribe, as well as on that of the oral performer, the medieval author-figure places himself in a communicative framework whose ultimate fruition is to be situated within the dialogue established between writer and reader."[45] Like the transgressive author and dream narrator of

Revelation, represented in medieval Apocalypse manuscripts by the figure of John within and without the frame, Imaginatif straddles the past and present, functioning to collate and compose. And also like John, the dreamer is in the odd position of being both the writer and the receiver of these retrospective truths, in turn presented to us. How more clearly could this be signaled than through the complicated portrayal of an imaginative faculty whose dress makes him an actor in the narrative but whose voice reflects retrospective self-knowledge?[46]

Representing the act of retrospection, Imaginatif is naturally mature in age. Here we can see the illustrator interpreting the particularized life in the dominant tradition of conceptualizing spiritual progress—the Ages of Man. A careful reader of Douce 104 must be impressed by the attributes of youth and age assigned to various characters and their parallels in the dreamer's own spiritual autobiography. A curious, youthful blond figure appears consistently at the most confessional moments in the poem—as Lechery (figure 7), Sloth (figure 8), the clerk seated with an open book (figure 24), and Recklessness (figure 25)—possibly the same figure who is the presentation of the dreamer-narrator in specific form. The Ages of Man iconography, which often presents such blond figures as portrayals of youth, appears most frequently in homiletic literature and devotional works, such as "The Parliament of the Three Ages" and the common illustrations of "The Three Living and the Three Dead."[47] In the fourteenth-century preacher's compendium *Fasciculus Morum*, for example, the sin of sloth is illustrated with a parable of a penny: "By the penny I understand man's life, which consists of four ages: childhood, youth, manhood, and old age." The wise man reaps the benefits of life by spending his penny wisely.[48] Such schema were purposefully set forth to outline the pilgrimage of life in works for lay meditation, as in penitential lyrics and the De Lisle Psalter, where some of the most famous examples appear.[49] By the first half of the fifteenth century, the Ages of Man iconography had moved from "Wheels of Life" diagrams to the margins of manuscripts, as is evidenced by MS Add. 37049 (figure 59).

In British Library, MS Add. 37049, the Ages of Man iconography functions much as it does in Douce 104, visualizing and voicing the psychomachia that constitutes every Christian's life.[50] At the top of folio 28v a naked infant signals both human vulnerability and potential sanctity, dramatically realized below in a scene typical of fifteenth-century morality plays, where a child stands between an angel and a devil, announcing his intent to play. These counselors follow him through his life, with the drama represented on folios 28v–29 by marginal figures bracketing speeches in balloonlike scrolls reminiscent of modern newspaper comics. The cast of characters is remarkably like the Ages of Man figures rendered in Douce 104, representative of childhood, youth, age, old age, and death. Undoubtedly, the appeal of such images was psychological: each character announces his appetites and pleasures without remorse, until the "crepil" Age, grasping rosary beads, begins the process of conversion: "Now must I beddes byd þof my bones ake; I drede þat ded persewes me fast." With the devil leering over his shoulder, Age gazes anxiously across the page to the angel who embraces his speech urging penitence. In this version of the moralized life, the penitent is redeemed on his deathbed, where, at his last exhalation, the angel grasps the child-like soul emerging from his mouth. The devil slinks away in the opposite margin, his back to the text. Undoubtedly, the illustrator of Add. 37049 recognized the dramatic possibilities of the page, making his figures interact with the text in a variety of ways familiar from Douce 104. Personifications of the Seven Ages gaze upon, touch, and point to the text with hands and noses. The page is dramatic space where figures interrupt the flow of speech, as when the character Man on folio 28v, standing between the angel and the devil, looks down upon his speech from the center of the page. Grasping an axe, he boasts, "Now I am in strenþe; who dar to me say nay?" Clearly, this dramatic portrayal of sin and redemption was used as a personal meditation, requiring the reader to identify with the characters who chart life's pilgrimage. Thus we would be mistaken in assuming that such images have only an artistic significance and did not influence writers and artists when they explored the progress of what we might call the "individual" or particular life.

Hoccleve, the most explicitly autobiographical Middle English poet, culls these visual traditions for didactic ends in his "Learn to Die" series.[51] Even more pointed is their application, however, in an obscure autobiographical schema of Opicinus de Canistris (Rome, Biblioteca Apostolica Vatican, MS Pal. Lat. 1993, fol. 11), written by a forty-year-old Italian clerk in 1336. The clerk has produced an astonishingly detailed diagram of his own life, configured simultaneously with a map of the Mediterranean and religious imagery, such as the four evangelists and the Virgin and child.[52] Scholars who doubt that there was a notion of the "self" in the Middle Ages need only look at the diagram, consisting of "40 concentric circles representing the years 1296–1336... divided radially into 366 days. The autobiography begins with Opicinus's conception on 24 March 1296, and ends on 3 June 1336."[53] As a signal of the autobiographical function of the whole, Opicinus has placed images of the Four Ages of Man at the quadrants. Clearly, the creator of the diagram saw no discrepancy between the minutiae of his life, laboriously recorded in the circles, and the generalizing symbols of age. Rather, the convention, which illustrates the edges of the diagram, reminds us of the hierarchy of human knowledge and experience. His life experience conforms to a larger cosmological plan with Mary and Christ, the exemplar whose life gives meaning to all human history, personal and collective, at the center.[54]

In Douce 104, the meshing of the Ages of Man tradition and a penitential or homiletic tradition is evident in the illustrations of the Seven Deadly Sins in passus VI and VII. The confession of the Seven Deadly

Sins is explicitly linked with the dreamer's life, following the apologia in the C text and the stern advice of Reason and Conscience.[55] The illustrator does not depict Pride (fol. 24) as the hypocritical Purnelle, weeping and begging for a hair shirt in a brief fit of attrition, but as a youthful male courtier. He illustrates the sin in a manner contrary to iconographic convention and to the iconography favored by the text itself, in order to strengthen the bond between the dreamer and images. In one sense, this is not a surprising phenomenon, as Douce 104 consistently displays a lack of interest in women, even when the poem includes them. Nonetheless, Scott has pointed to the originality of this figure as an unusual treatment of Pride, when a perfectly suitable iconography of the virtues and vices (employed, for example, by Spenser in book 1 of the *Faerie Queene*) was available.[56] In contrast to the typical association of ornamentation with female pride, the illustrator has given us an insight into the moral economy of masculine decadence in the fifteenth century, the counterpart to Margery Kempe's discussion of preconversion pride in her *Book*. In her own spiritual autobiography, Kempe turns to the Ages of Man iconography to signal the traditional nature of her conversion in terms recognizable to medieval readers.[57] Margery describes the clothing she wears after her initial, false conversion: "for sche weryd gold pypys on hir hevyd & hir hodys wyth þe typettys were daggyd. Hir clokys also wer daggyd & leyd wyth dyuers colowrs be-twen þe daggys þat it schuld be þe mor staryng to mennys sygth" (p. 9, lines 13–17). Such vainglory, in the mind of a medieval writer and reader, would naturally lead Margery to the sin of lechery, and she experiences a humiliating rejection from a would-be lover who spurns her once he gains her consent to adultery. The Douce illustrator no doubt recognized and integrated this iconography of conversion in his *Piers* illustrations. Pride wears sumptuous clothing, including parti-color tights, dagged sleeves, and minstrel's bells. Thus the illustrator has specifically associated the figure of Pride with youth and a frivolous materiality; youth, as is commonly presented in penitential lyrics, is a time of self-indulgence, lack of introspection, and, more specifically, lechery.[58]

In this respect, the figure undoubtedly identifies Pride with the dreamer's sins of materialism, sexual appetite, and frivolity. Just as in Kempe's confession, Pride is connected to sexual license; in Douce 104, Pride shares his youthfulness, his open shirt, and his dagged clothing with Lechery (figure 7), whose phallic sword illustrates his licentiousness. In the apologia in the C text, this first of the Seven Deadly Sins is clearly connected to the languorous young man who refuses to work and prefers to drink and sleep in the "hot heruest whenne y hadde myn hele / And lymes to labory with and louede wel fare" (V.7–8). With no sense of duty or future, the narrator admits to following the "Lyf þat me lykede" (V.41). Whether artists adapted the three-, six-, or seven-age schema of the life of man, youth is connected to sexual ease and material appetites.

Visual Heuristics

In Add. 37049, Youth, like Pride and Lechery in Douce 104, wears a short tunic, cap, and "fashionably pointed shoes," and claims "With women my lyst both play *and* rage"[59] (figure 59). Similarly, in the De Lisle Hours (New York, Pierpont Morgan Library, MS G. 50), owned by one of the daughters of Robert de Lisle of Yorkshire (1320–30), a figure of youth appears on folio 29 in a historiated initial. A young man with curly blond hair preens himself before a hand mirror, while a woman watches devotedly. As in the Douce 104 rendition of Pride and Margery Kempe's verbal portrait of this sin, where colorful clothes signify Pride, this young man's gown is blue with orange and white stripes.[60] This book of hours, of Sarum use, is typical in its illustrations of the Little Office of the Virgin, the Passion sequence; these devotional meditations are followed, however, by illustrations of the stages of life and reflect, no doubt, the link between Christocentric meditation and autobiographical reflection in preparation for penance. The De Brailes Psalter (Cambridge, Fitzwilliam Museum, MS 330, no. 4), illustrated circa 1240 in Oxford, connects the Ages of Man to the Wheel of Fortune, an iconography that thrived well into the next century, as is demonstrated in the famous De Lisle Psalter, illustrated by an artist at Westminster circa 1310 (figure 62). The latter image is particularly interesting for our purposes, as it connects the mirror image to the whole process of autobiographical reflection. The text for youth reads, "Vita decens seculi, speculo probatur. Non ymago speculi, set vita letatur" (A life worthy of the world is tested by the mirror. Not the mirror's image, but life itself delights).[61] The illustration shows a young man peering into his mirror while he combs his hair. Such images from devotional manuscripts may have inspired the Douce illustrator's rendition of Fortune and Recklessness on the same folio (figure 25).

Finally, the best evidence of the familiarity of this typology to a medieval audience may be found in Chaucer's *Canterbury Tales*. Chaucer depended upon his audience's recognition of typology in his creation of the visual clusters that locate the meaning of his narrative, what V. A. Kolve has described as a "learned language of visual sign" that provides room for both the general and the particular.[62] In his exploration of Chaucer's squire and Absolon, both youthful lovers with golden locks and sumptuous clothing, Kolve asserts that "in the youth who combs his hair—he occurs in a Seven Ages sequence from the De Lisle Hours as well—we have a veritable portrait of Chaucer's Absolon."[63] While other sins, such as Avarice, are widely connected with Senex, old age, and thus physical degeneration (Chaucer's January), the Douce illustrator has carefully distributed the sins across the spectrum of age. Wrath and Gluttony, although physically different in their body types, are neither young nor old. Sloth, a paralysis of the will given distinction in the C text by opening passus VII, and most responsible for Will's spiritual failure, is a young man. Fresh-faced, with a tussle of blond hair, Sloth sleeps peacefully, carelessly disheveled (figure 8). Undoubtedly, this image, placed in the upper right-hand margin on the first folio of the passus, recollects the image of Pride that begins the previous passus and Will's own admission of spiritual languor in the apologia. The reader of Douce 104 is asked to link these images spatially and conceptually to interpret their relationship. Similarly, the placement of Sloth's head in the hand on folio 31, eyes closed, recollects the portrait of the narrator in the initial on folio 1 (figure 1) and foreshadows that of Imaginatif (figure 28), although both characters are depicted with open eyes. Sloth, in contrast, is not dreaming or gazing upon the text—a sign of self-reflection in Douce 104. He is young, careless, and nonreflective, as is the dreamer himself at this point. Such carelessness is part of the Ages of Man tradition, supported by commentaries on age like the late-fourteenth-century (or early-fifteenth-century) work *The Chess of Love*, which argued that "the young are easily changeable...[because] the humors of [their] bodies are in themselves very changeable....[They] do not have by nature great sense of prudence in them."[64] Prudence, the virtue that Memory governs and that the illustration of a mature Imaginatif exemplifies, is linked with the autobiographical process. Medieval writers used this iconography to provide a universal pattern for their conversion narratives, but this does not mean that the states of ignorance and despair that typify such youthful forgetfulness are impersonal. The fifteenth-century Anglo-Irish illuminator employs these images of youth and frivolity because they function in both generalized and particularized ways, but without exception, the blond mop, dagged clothing, and pointed shoes signify self-deception, illusion, and needless consumption in Douce 104.

Will's search for Dowel, the first stage in his conversion and his intellectual crisis, becomes increasingly personalized in the C text, as E. Talbot Donaldson argued long ago.[65] A student of Clergy and Scripture, the dreamer "has elected to become a cleric.... This point is affirmed in the Dreamer's confession in the C-Text when he says that he had been called to 'clergye' and supported in his schooling by his family and friends (C.V.35–43)."[66] The dreamer's pursuit of an intellectual knowledge of Dowel proves to be both frustrating and fruitless. Passus X is illustrated with one of the few positive images of a friar in this manuscript (figure 20). Poor, barefoot, and engaged in *disputatio* with the dreamer in a waking moment, he is trying to convince him with an exemplum, a "forbisene" (C.X.32a) presenting the simple necessity for penance and restitution.[67] The dreamer, however, anxious and impatient, neglects this good advice in favor of theological inquiry well beyond his comprehension. The figure in Douce 104 (figure 24) whom Scott identifies as a scribe or Augustine or perhaps "a generalized picture of...an author in the process of writing a book" is in all likelihood another dreamer portrait. Scott notes that the picture is carefully placed beside Scripture's interruption of Clergy's speech to the dreamer (C.XI.166), but concludes that "the picture probably does not refer to any of these three characters."[68] Certainly, the lines above (XI.149–56) make reference to Augustine and the writing of "old books." As we have demonstrated in other illustrations, however, the illustrator usually places figures beside relevant speakers; if Will has indeed become a member of the clergy, even in minor orders, in his search for Dowel, this character is undoubtedly Will.[69]

Douce 104 provides pictures of a blond figure interacting with, or rejecting, the text at several points of spiritual crisis. This picture on folio 52v (figure 24), also mentioned earlier in the discussion on author images, shows a blond scribe seated with a lapboard and stylus, his back turned away from the text. The Latin quotations with which Scripture reprimands the dreamer underscore his own frustration with the lack of explicit direction to self-knowledge: "Fides non habet meritum ubi humana racio prebet experimentum" and "Multi multa sciunt et seipsos nesciunt" ("There is no merit in faith where human reason supplies proof" and "Many men know many things and know themselves not at all"). The latter admonition sends the dreamer into the reckless abandonment of his studies and clerical life, for he assumes that his free will is irrelevant to his salvation. The Douce illustrator has interpreted the dreamer's rejection of clergy as the preface to error, for right below this image of the seated writer, on the next folio, the figure of Fortune appears in elaborate headdress with her wheel, significant not only of Fortune, but also of the Ages of Man in English iconography. In Douce 104, the proximity of the images of Fortune and Recklessness connects writing, authorship, and the dreamer's self-revelation (figures 24 and 25). The lines

> Tho wepte y for wo and wrathe of here wordes
> And in a wynkynge y warth and wonderliche me mette,
> For y was rauysched rihte there, for Fortune me fette
> (XI.167–69)

span both figures, pointing toward Recklessness as an author-dreamer portrait. The Land of Longing is no doubt an anagrammatic signature in the C text, "thus the place where Fortune rules is called by his 'kynde' name."[70] Such signatures, as Anne Middleton demonstrates, occur in the poem at moments of "subjective crisis," but these moments in the C text "become critical turning points in the author's life. The moments of signature become narratively pivotal events that render biographical and poetic self-awareness synonymous."[71] The poet's references to Augustine prior to the dreamer's revisioning of his own narrative in a distorted mirror—a mirror that reflects material desire as opposed to spiritual refashioning—no doubt links both writers in their shared project of conceptualizing their life stories.[72] To signal this fine point, the illustrator used a gold wash, usually reserved for spiritually enlightened characters, on Fortune's wheel, emphasizing worldly seduction.[73] He then presents us with an identifiable figure, an author portrait, if we accept Hult's description of such seated figures as poetic makers, and specifically links the act of writing to Fortune through their physical proximity on the folio page. Abandoning his will to Fortune's handmaids, the dreamer proves that he doesn't know himself; rather, he only willfully knows his appetites: Concupiscencia carnis, Couetyse-of-eyes, and Pruyde-of-parfit lyuynge.

The dreamer is essentially back where he was in passus V, much the worse for wear. Concupiscence assures him that she will "sewe" his "wille" (XI.184), and he proceeds to live the life that he likes, with little care for approaching age and the worry that he will need to justify his actions at some future point. Recklessness (figure 25), one of the most interesting manifestations of the dreamer's consciousness and a species of sloth for this illustrator, rebukes the dreamer for any qualms: "þou hast ful fer to elde" (C.XI.197).

In Douce 104, Recklessness spans the prudent Elde's speech as well as his own, snapping his fingers at the text in careless abandonment. Placed below Fortune, Recklessness is linked to her visually; in fact, he is a consequence of her presence in the poem. Dressed in ragged robes, curiously reminiscent of Pride's short, dagged clothes, Recklessness is rendered as the same blond figure who is associated with youth or Fauntelete (C.XI.312). The illustrator has used the same physical characteristics to signify the spiritual profile of the earlier figures Sloth and Pride. The annotator, sensitive to this conflation of types, has buttressed the illustrator's point with his annotations "nota de rechles" and "nota de youth." Recklessness has been assigned various identities by modern critics as faith or as a form of patience, and these speculations may be appropriate; however, there is nothing about the illustration in Douce 104 that suggests patient poverty.[74] The artist has managed to capture the thoughtless abandonment of youth in the figure's restless stance and gestures; it is almost as if he rejects the process of self-reflection. While Langland's poem undoubtedly urges a more complex nexus of theological and historical associations, the illustrator has once again selected an Ages of Man typology suggestive of a spiritual autobiographical reading.

When we see a figure that the text identifies as the dreamer again, he is old (figure 26). At the beginning of passus XII, Elde and Holynesse warn the dreamer "þat wit schal torne to wrachednesse: for wil haþ hour wyl"—no doubt another authorial signature.[75] Elde's body spans the speech of Couetyse-of-eyes, urging Recklessness to confess to a friar while Fortune is his friend. But the dreamer fails to heed this advice:

> By wissyng of this wenche y dede, here wordes were so swete,
> Til y forȝet ȝouthe and ȝorn into elde.
> And thenne was Fortune my foo for al her fayre biheste
> And pouerte pursuede me and potte me to be lowe.
> (XII.11–14)

The figure of Elde on folio 55 is a bearded man, wrapped in a nondescript gown. Seated pensively, his head rests in his hands as he gazes at the text. Given the placement of his body next to the speech above, he may very well be in a state of despair.[76] The Douce illustrator, however, tends to use this posture in the dreamer portraits to signal a state of introspection. Ignoring the introspective and penitential process of life, the dreamer has missed altogether what medieval audiences would have deemed the age of perfect maturity, the moment when spiritual rectitude and self-knowledge meet. The sweetness of his youth can only be recalled briefly, and he is an old man. Given that *Piers Plowman* conforms to a model of spiritual autobiography rather than to our modern notion of chronological biography, it is natural that "Langland's interest in the representation of the ages is not, in fact, a narrative interest at all, but an interest in the moment of crisis when one age confronts another, for at such crisis moments a man may be urged into salutary action."[77] As Mary Dove notes, "The only man who has assuredly achieved the perfect age of manhood is Christ himself," who is the exemplar for all spiritual biography.[78] Having lost the days when he could best live in *imitatio Christi*, the dreamer cannot come to salvation without being like the thief on the cross.[79] Elde, also dressed in russet, is very much like the figure in the Y on the first folio (figure 1), as well as Imaginatif on folio 63 (figure 28). Their posture connects them as speculative figures, and all three appear at these "crisis moments" to direct or redirect the dreamer. It seems clear that the illustrator avoids a chronology, choosing to represent the dreamer in a manner reflective of the poem's abrupt, dreamlike, and self-reflexive shifts. In contrast, static figures like Conscience, the king, and the knight provide the physical type for man's perfect age.

Quire 7 in Douce 104 contains this progression of dreamer figures, and it is useful to consider whether the physical production of the manuscript can provide us with material evidence of the illustrator's deliberation. Certainly quire 7 in Douce 104, figuring Fortune, Recklessness, Elde, and the clerk, fails to exhibit the kind of sustained cross-bifolia glossing that Huot brilliantly charts through a layout of the bifolium structure of *Roman de la Rose* MS Mi.[80] However, like the *Rose* MS Mi (Paris, BN fr. 25526), which Huot concedes is a "most unusual visual response to the Rose" (285), Douce's marginal figures in this quire surpass the function of marginal illustration of literal events in the narrative to reflect an interpretive process. In both manuscripts, illustrators focus on various kinds of discourse and juxtapose authoritative with nonauthoritative speech through their selection of images. Hence, both manuscripts point self-consciously to the oral nature of reading through marginal illustration. If quire 7 of Douce were unbound, for example, the images of Fortune and Recklessness on folio 53 would be across the page from the priest on 60v. His body spans the lines:

> That yf thay trauaile treulyche and trist in god almyhty
> Hem sholde neuere lacke lyflode noþer lynnen ne wollene.
> The tytle 3e take 3oure ordres by telleth 3e ben avaunsed
> And nedeth nat to nyme siluer for masses þat 3e synge.
> (XIII.101–4)

It is possible that here the illustrator underscored Recklessness's dominant theme of a lack of solicitude for earthly goods, although we would not wish to press the case too strongly, as there are few such examples. What is intriguing is that passus XI–XIII offer numerous opportunities for illustrations of a traditional nature of Christ on Calvary, Adam and Eve, Martha and Mary Magdalen, David and Abraham—all familiar biblical figures—in addition to craftsmen and a host of other contemporary, extratextual images. All these he rejects for the narrative figures (Elde, Recklessness, the clerk) who gaze upon, gloss (the priest), or respond verbally (Trajan's "Baw") to the text at this most autobiographical point in the C text's trajectory.

As the poem moves to its conclusion in Douce 104, the figures we must link to the narrator, however, are suggestive of weariness, wandering, and self-deception. Patience, on folio 70 (figure 30), wears the costume of a pilgrim and carries the staff not only of travelers but of Senectutus in the Ages of Man tradition, exemplified in Dublin, Chester Beatty Library, MS 80 (figure 55).[81] The pen drawing of the skeleton on folio 71 is curious, as Scott notes, given the omission of those lines most clearly linked with its presence in the manuscript (XV.303–7), yet the image makes perfect sense in light of the numerous meditative and penitential images available to artists to illustrate the urgency of confession and reparation. The De Lisle Psalter features images of "The Three Living and the Three Dead," as do the Taymouth Hours (London, British Library, MS Yates Thompson 13).[82] In attempting to convince the viewer or reader of the necessity of penance, medieval artists, poets, and even medical writers focus on the psychological state of old age as a time of awakening reality. Like Will, who has followed Fauntelete blindly until the most vigorous years allotted to him are past, the figures dramatizing old age, decrepitude, and death in the De Lisle Psalter woefully lament:

> Sumo michi baculum, morti fere notus.
> Decrepitati deditus, mors erit michi esse.
> Infirmitati deditus, incipio deesse.
> Putavi quod viverem; vita me decepit.[83]

> [I take up my staff, almost acquainted with death.
> Given over to decrepitude, death will be my condition.
> Given over to sickness, I begin to fail.
> I thought I should live forever; life has indeed cheated me.]

In the Madonna Master's exemplar, Lyf's deception is illustrated by a physician peering futilely into the jordan, or urine flask, while the wasting patient watches helplessly. This is a moralized version of the doctor with jordan who frequently appears in medieval medical treatises without a sinister cast.[84] In the Guild Book of the Barber Surgeons of York, for example, a fifteenth-century illustrator draws a youthful doctor, pointing confidently to his jordan with an index finger—perhaps an image of diagnosis.[85] The image of the huckster physician, working with Lyf, is complicated and revised in Douce 104, as is usual with the Douce illustrator (figure 38):

> "Now y see," saide Lyf, "that surgerie ne fysyke
> May nat a myte avayle to medlen aȝen Elde."
> And in hope of his hele gode herte he hente
> And roed so to Reuel...
> (XXII.178–81)

Langland's notion of Lyf leading the elderly away from spiritual reformation with thoughts of life's pleasure conforms to the Ages of Man traditions. But in making the physician a friar, the illustrator conflates the bitter reality of spiritual negligence with clerical exploitation in anticipation of Sir Penetrans Domos, the false "surgien" of souls (XXII.336). The Douce illustrator's last image of the sly friar provides us with a dark conclusion.[86] We must remember, however, that it is only this illustrator who insists upon closure by depicting the prelude to physical death. This is the end we would expect, and indeed get, in medieval sermons and morality plays. *Piers Plowman* perhaps conforms better to modern than to medieval tastes in resisting such neat closure and offering, instead, another journey to seek grace.

In her preliminary evaluation of Douce 104, Scott comments that while "the selection of pictorial subjects is sometimes intelligent, comprehensive, and widely helpful," the program of illustration is "at other times idiosyncratic or inconsequential," leading to interpretive problems compounded by the lack of a systematic distribution.[87] Unlike manuscripts of courtly dream visions like the *Romance of the Rose*, which illustrate an interior journey through an allegorical system, Douce 104 punctuates Will's journey with pastoral, penitential, and meditative images. The illustrator clearly expected these images, whether of the dreamer portraits, the Seven Deadly Sins, or the Ages of Man, to provide thematic coherence at the most chaotic moments of the poem, as in passus XXII. That they do for the Douce illustrator, who takes his cue from the text and distributes these figures at the most self-conscious junctures of the poem, is evidence of a particular kind of reading. We would argue that the Douce illustrator is attempting to underscore in his original program a process of reading we can only call visionary, meditative, or autobiographical. His figures suggest that he comprehends this poem to be personal, idiosyncratic, its spiritual program less explicitly chartable at times than works like *The Pilgrimage of the Life of Man*. The illustrator has a layman's knowledge of preaching and penitential materials, a distinctive sense of the various orders Langland satirizes, and a clear sense of sympathy for the poor and neglected. Although he has the opportunity to provide us with all sorts of authoritative figures from Scripture, hagiography, and other conventional visual traditions, he rejects these in favor of depicting speaking characters and projections of the dreamer's own self—forcing the reader to assume the role of dreamer, retrospective narrator, and reader.

If we alter the traditional generic taxonomies applied to *Piers Plowman*, acknowledging that it belongs as much to a medieval tradition of visionary literature as to a literary tradition of allegorical visions, satire, sermon, and chronicle (as is clearly evidenced by the annotator's commentary in Douce 104 as well), we may see that there is a greater method to Douce's illustrations than we might expect.[88] This interpretive strategy, however, requires us to admit that the illustrator uses visual conventions that belong to the spiritual autobiographies and celebrated visionary works that were read in the fifteenth century, including Bridget's *Revelations* and Catherine of Siena's *Dialogues (The Orchard of Syon)*. Like *Piers Plowman*, these works offered readers visionary experiences to meditate upon and thus to "see." Strongly autobiographical, these writings also offered the spiritual novice the opportunity to share a spiritual dialogue with a famous personage, an expert, so to speak. Unlike the dream visions in allegories of courtly love, spiritual visionary literature, like the visions themselves, are "responses to real-life situations."[89]

This typification seems significant to us in light of Langland's revisionary activity in the C text. A dangerous poem, *Piers Plowman* is concerned throughout with the issue of writing as genuine labor and authority. In many respects, the historical Langland lacked the same authoritative stance required of authorship that a medieval woman visionary lacks, if the information provided in C.V is autobiographical. He admits to being poorly and partially educated, to living a life that does not conform in its definition to medieval notions of orthodoxy, and to a sexual status (married) that denies him the much-required authority of regular clergy. None of this, of course, discouraged the marginalized devout from having visions, or at least claiming to have them, as is evident from Margery Kempe's *Book*. However, divine inspiration for visions is imperative for credibility, as Margery well knew; women visionaries often use their very lack of authority and status as proof of not their, but God's, authority. Perhaps the apologia in the C text fulfills necessary criteria for Langland's visionary authority. Critics have tended to see this section as diminishing his authority, comparing him to contemporary clerical writers like Walter Hilton. In fact, he is far more like Richard Rolle, a man whose social ambiguity provides the space for self-definition.[90] Like Rolle, Langland seems to have inspired a cult in the region of his birth, where, no doubt, the reception of his writings was enhanced by a knowledge of his life and experience. Langland is not a mystic in the speculative sense, but, as a visionary writer, he clearly turns to methods of composition and self-projection in the C text that put him more comfortably in the category of mystical writers like Rolle and Julian of Norwich than Chaucer or the Pearl Poet. The heightened visual, auditory, and autobiographical nature of *Piers Plowman*, especially in the C text, alone suggests this.[91] Langland "looks surprisingly at home" when we place him in categories other than Middle English dream-vision tradition, specifically the Latin religious visionary tradition.[92]

This is another way to account for the stronger presence of an authorial voice in *Piers Plowman*. The function of meditative works is to provide spiritual experience for the reader, and thus a reader may focus on parts of a work, ignoring the whole in favor of those moments that provide the greatest degree of personal illumination. Rather than being works of a "purely narrative impulse," they present the reader with "a mixing of narrative with non-narrative elements; consequent separation of the narrative into distinct units; and clear use of the authorial voice as a linking device."[93] Even works as revered as Saint Bridget's *Revelations*, however, were subject to compilation and consequently revision and emendation. Such visionary writings, with their reformist agendas and often prophetic bent, appealed to readers seeking authorities for polemical purposes. Roger Ellis demonstrates, for instance, how Bridget's *Revelations* could be interpreted for both orthodox and unorthodox ends, once passages were taken out of context. Thus, one enterprising scribe of the *Revelations* "shows every readiness to remove individual sentences from their context" to support a discussion of the Eucharist for anti-Wycliffite ends.[94] Furthermore, he is even willing to tamper with "an elaborate allegory of a maiden and her nine brothers," keeping only those words that would support his argument."[95] The stronger the authorial voice, the stronger the linking device to forge the interdependency of the visions and thus discourage such quoting out of context—a device Langland may deliberately have used in his C revisions, having been all too aware of the misappropriation of his text. The Douce illustrator appears to be very sensitive to the moments of the text where the author interjects his voice, presence, and interpretive role; the author portraits are thus a linking device in themselves, joining the various parts of his long, digressive poem into a kind of coherence that is not necessarily thematic and thus open to a traditional illustrative program, but experiential. Furthermore, the illustrations sometimes span passus endings and beginnings, again blurring the divisions to produce a sense of continuity and, rather than closure, a shift in perception or consciousness. We know that extracts from longer works, as in the case of extracts from Kempe's *Book* or Marguerite Porete's writing, can create an authorial identity that is orthodox or unorthodox. Langland's extensive revisions of his poem bear witness to his anxiety about this very issue, and his narrative strategy of providing strong, authoritative speakers to link sections of his poem, interspersed with a self-conscious narrative voice, was a brilliant means of preventing the excerpting of sections of visions for polemical ends.

Ultimately, the modern reader's difficulty in accepting *Piers Plowman* as genuinely visionary is ontological, but our own epistemological limitations should not prevent us from exploring the variety of ways in which *Piers* was received in its own cultural context and the signals the illustrator was sending. If the Douce illustrator appears to depart from patternbook drawings, which he has the technical expertise to accomplish and did use at points, it is because his unique reading of the poem resisted such formulation. He creates images of authority, of the individual poised momentarily in specific ages, of the sinfulness of his dreamer—but he modifies or undercuts these traditions for his own purposeful ends. This kind of understanding depends not only on a literal *reading* of the poem but also on a sense of its performative voicing and visionary trajectory.

CONCLUSION

⁂

Reading Piers Plowman in a Manuscript Culture

Denise L. Despres

Caroline Barron has argued that "insofar as Langland's poem is rooted in time and place, it is rooted in the streets of London in the 1370's."[1] But to make sense of Douce 104, whose illustrator and annotator clearly find Langland's arguments immediate, provocative, and compelling, we have needed to dismiss temporarily London and reconstruct early-fifteenth-century Dublin culture from the material evidence the manuscript provides. We have attempted to provide a model of reception based upon the response to the poem by Douce's Anglo-Irish professional readers working somewhere in the Dublin-Pale—the latter only "a strip of land about 20 miles wide, running from Dublin to Dundalk, with a small extension inland along the Liffey."[2] This was a relatively small community, and an embattled one, but it was also the heart of Anglo-Ireland, its seat of government, and the nerve center of a community experiencing—especially during the decade in which Douce was made—a new kind of colonial identity and, as we have seen, a new though limited measure of fiscal and political stability. Middle English works of the previous century were being rapidly translated into Hiberno-English: along with Douce itself, the two Rolle manuscripts (both in a hand strikingly like our annotator's), the *Secreta secretorum* (with its borrowings from *Piers*), and, at least within the first quarter of the fifteenth century, the Northern Homily Cycle (with its crude little scribe-rubricated drawings).[3] The illustrations, emendations, and annotations of Douce suggest that there was nothing "old-fashioned" about Langland's poem from a colonial perspective. Our best (and most educated) guess throughout this study has been that Douce may have been copied and illustrated by an older (judging by his hand) scribe-illustrator, perhaps trained as an Exchequer clerk—someone in a position to know the current Dublin parliamentary and legal culture, a documentary world closely modeled on Langland's Westminster. We may be accused of having been more interested in the Anglo-Irish context of the text's reception than in *Piers Plowman*, but this is not something we find ourselves able to apologize for; in fact, at the risk of overextending the colonial metaphor in a politically incorrect way, we are pleased at having discovered in Middle Hiberno-English a fascinating new world, too long neglected by the Anglocentricism of Middle English studies.

Denise L. Despres

We have treated Douce, we believe justifiably, with the dignity that ought to be accorded to any imaginatively engaging sequel of *Piers Plowman*: the intelligence, energy, and scope of its production team's response to Langland's text merits attention alongside poetic responses like *Richard the Redeless, Pierce the Ploughman's Crede*, and *Mum and the Sothsegger*.[4] With that in mind we will close by offering a synopsis of the key points of that response as it is manifested in the key images of passus IX and X. These two passus had been particularly influential with Langland's initial audience in England. The rebel letters of 1381 had specifically cited Truth's injunction to Piers to stay home from pilgrimage (in Douce's C version, these lines occur at the opening of IX), and the rebels apparently knew Wit's teachings on bastardy (X.203–300 in Douce), teachings that would take on heightened significance in the Irish colonial setting, as we have seen.[5] Issues of authority (who says what and whose voice is most important?) were also crucial in early *Piers* reception, and not just for sensationally subversive readers like John Ball. Several early Langlandian imitations had taken as their starting point the opening of the Vita (X in C), with its portrayal of a dreamer wandering in search of Dowel, meeting two friars and daring to oppose their clerical authority. This scene inspired more than one sequel, including *Pierce the Ploughman's Crede* and *Mum and the Sothsegger*. Moreover, as Wendy Scase has shown, a large section of IX (66–281)—all new to the C text—was released into circulation before the C text was complete (whether with Langland's permission or not, we don't know).[6] This section contained some of the hottest topics of Langland's day: begging, vagrancy, evangelical lifestyle, episcopal negligence, and a reassuringly traditional explanation of the word "lollar."[7] Clearly either Langland or a member of his coterie (perhaps a scribe) judged this passage too urgent to await the completion of the poem. There can be no coincidence that the Douce annotator and the illustrator took special interest in it, too, the illustrator making some of his most dramatic socially and ecclesiastically subversive visual statements in the striking number of images he chose to cram into its mere 215 lines: the lunatic lollar, the blind man (both dusted with gold), the false friar, and the de-mitered bishop, with his attacking wolf (figures 16–18, respectively). In Douce's IX and X, the hierarchizing of voices is more radical than in most extant *Piers* tradition responses other than Ball's: as we have seen, the authority of legal and ecclesiastical institutions is deliberately undercut (in IX's parodic lawyer [figure 15], false friar, and de-mitered bishop), while the dignity of the poor, the silent, and the socially marginalized is enhanced by provocative pictorial decisions (IX's blind man, lunatic, the barefoot Franciscan, and the silent Dobet [figures 20 and 21 for the last two]).

Two of IX's key images will succinctly bring into focus the interpretive methodologies of the production team, their persistent concern with legal and clericist iconography, and the ways in which they expected the medieval reader to *read* the pages they made. In the image of the priest with the pardon (figure 19), the illustrator especially highlights the performative, as we've seen: impeccably tonsured and gesturing vociferously, the priest's mouth is precisely aligned, as so often in Douce, with his first words: "Peres quod a prest þo: þy pardoun wold I rede" (fol. 44v). His impressive-looking document (over a third the length of the priest's entire body) with a large seal emphasizes, in a slightly overbearing way, the Church's (if not Truth's) "secrete seal." M. T. Clanchy associates the use of seals with a continued desire for the physical tokens of bearing witness to a formal contract.[8] The illustrator, who we have argued was familiar with an illustrative tradition from legal manuscripts and chronicles, had undoubtedly seen such images and was fond of selectively reproducing them in Douce 104 (as he also does in the portrait of Liar holding Mede's marriage charter). He has placed the priest in the left-hand margin, creating a dramatic heuristic device: when the narrator claims on line 285 that "I be hynd hem boþ: be held al þe bull," reading the two lines in Latin that are underlined "Qui bona egerunt ibunt in vitam eternam; Qui vero mala in ignem eternum" (They that have done good shall go into life everlasting, and they that have done evil into everlasting fire), the reader becomes the narrator for a moment. The illustrator's intent is undoubtedly to draw the reader into performance and participation in the poem: the priest is speaking to us as we read, left to right, and we witness the contents of his pardon ourselves, in a typically clever exploitation of the permeable boundary of text and image and of the rubrication of the Latin. The priest's speaking gesture indicates, as we have seen repeatedly in Douce images, that the speech is to be heard out loud (even if read silently) and memorized, like one of the "remembered voices" of Clanchy's illustrated legal documents. The annotator's interest in this passage is also legalistic, but focuses on the interpretation of the pardon itself: his stark "nota de beggers & bidders beþ noght in þe bull" (fol. 41) lacks Langland's mitigating qualification and suggests, in the context of his pattern of annotation for the whole passage, that his sympathies for the poor were limited to the group that Pearsall has characterized as "the deserving poor."[9] He was less socially radical than the illustrator, who shows perhaps a more secularized and certainly quite Irish sympathy with poverty in any form; his drawings remind us that in the Middle Ages "the term 'poor' is relative, referring to such conditions as weakness in relation to power, illness in relation to good health, [as well as] lack of money."[10] The Douce illustrator might have underscored, as did the annotator, the social problems resulting from vagrants and hermits living without a rule or supervision; instead, he seems intent on eliciting compassion for marginal figures who might be confused with the idle, such as the blind man on folio 43 (figure 17). The illustrator chose to depict the blind man as physically strong; he is well proportioned and virile-looking, his hands firmly grasping the staff that is a sign of wandering or pilgrimage in Douce 104. The blind man's handsome features are also typical of a moral physiognomy in Douce. We see them reproduced in the figure of Conscience (figure 4) and perhaps most significantly (for his interpretation of Will) in the image of the dreamer in his manifestation as Elde, who sits, head in hand (figure 26). Like the lunatic lollar, the blind man (along with Elde and Patience [figure 30]) exemplifies that Langlandian virtue of patient poverty; thus the illustrator provided all four with the wash of gold dust he reserved for these characters—a social statement unparalleled in any manuscript illustration of which we are aware. We can only surmise that the illustrator was indeed reading carefully, thematically, and affectively and understood the distinctions Langland was making among reckless poverty (Recklessness [figure 25]), patient or apostolic poverty, and mere laziness (Sloth [figure 8]), and that he wished to heighten or clarify them for his patron.

Our sense is that the annotator was primarily and typically interested in pastoral and polemical issues; his responses throughout to the text produce a kind of indexing system to a vernacular ecclesiastical encyclopedia. Thus, in IX, the annotator calls attention to and even voices more poignantly Langland's concern for poor families (one thinks of the same sort of extrapolation of Langland's social sympathies made by the author of *Pierce the Ploughman's Crede*). He notes especially those who cannot fulfill their obligation to work because of poverty and physical disability, as here: "nota de woo of pore pepill þat wonnyth in por howsyn & haþ childyr." But if the annotator is alert to provide only a careful, professional indexing in many places, he sometimes reveals his own more aggressive reformist leanings, as in his description of the lax bishop on folio 44 (figure 18). Here he notes "nota de molle pastore" (note the negligent shepherd), responding directly to the *Latin* of the passage: "Sub molli pastore lupus lanam cacat, et grex / In-custoditus dilaceratur eo" (Under a weak and negligent shepherd the wolf befouls the wool, and the unguarded flock is torn to pieces by him), rather than to the vernacular language describing the bishop's negligence, or even the slightly less malevolent "Simon quasi dormit" (Simon is as it were asleep), which the illustrator chooses as the subject of his drawing. This is one of many places where we sense an interartisan rivalry or, at least, interpretive tension between the annotator and the illustrator (or sometimes between annotator and scribe). Here he appears to be emphasizing the harsher reading to counter the illustrator's rather impish depiction of a youthful, sleeping bishop, his miter falling off; the annotator for some reason writes boldly over the top of the bishop's head, as if to supplant its effect with his own. Apparently the rubricator also found this pictorial sequence compelling: after the illustrator drew the picture of the wolf carrying off the sheep, the rubricator provided the garish addition of a trickle of blood from the sheep's throat and crudely outlined the lips and some of the features of the bishop (in a style similar to the Dublin Exchequer artist's), using the same red ink that he'd used for underlining the Latin a few millimeters away. One cannot substantiate any lengthy argument about intentionality or workshop tensions from circumstantial evidence (although we've now seen a good deal of it), but clearly we have two and possibly three professional readers vying for the reader's attention here and offering interpretive, sometimes more or less conflicting, guidance.

Their treatment of passus X suggests that medieval readers were just as likely to find the movement into the Vita, as it is traditionally called, difficult and abstract. John Burrow notes that, at this point in the poem, *Piers Plowman* moves from the "dramatic and pictorial" to the "abstract and ratiocinative."[11] But the professional readers producing the manuscript were familiar with the dynamics of visionary *ordinatio*, and the meditative, mnemonic, and performative nature of the poem itself is sensitively translated by both annotator and illustrator in this passus, once again demonstrating different interests in the poem's workings and underscoring the fundamental nature of their separate tasks. In passus X the dreamer begins his individual search for Dowel, faced with the complex process of defining in practical, lived terms the lives of Dowel, Dobet, and Dobest. The annotator marks this shift in the poem's trajectory with a "nota houu þey soght dowell," ruthlessly universalizing (as he tends to do) the dreamer's experience of the inward journey by shifting the text's pronoun from "I" to "þey."[12] Will's encounter with the friars is the single, waking moment that the illustrator distinguishes with a drawing; in a late-fourteenth-century English context, the case for antifraternal satire at this point in the poem would indeed be considerable.[13] As we have seen, an even harsher antimendicant tradition existed in Ireland, most clearly exemplified by FitzRalph's reformist thought. But the Douce illustrator, as we have argued, presents apostolic poverty and suffering as redemptive, and this Franciscan is therefore, perhaps, more leniently treated (figure 20). Instead of antimendicantism, the illustrator has focused on the dramatic elements of this waking moment, producing a performative illustration that marks the oral nature of the dialogue between Will (the reader) and the friar. In many ways, this illustration best exemplifies the process of medieval reading as a " 'hermeneutical dialogue'... between the mind of the reader and the absent voices which the written letters call forth."[14] The Franciscan is carefully placed to enhance the remembrance of a text—in this case Proverbs 24:16 ("The righteous man falls seven times a day")—that is spoken aloud. Thus the figure functions as a mnemonic, creating a "remembered voice," and it is noteworthy that the annotator strove for exactly the same remembrance here: "nota houu <seue*n*> syþ<ys> <in> þe de<y> synny<*s*> þe <ryt>fol"). The friar's sharp nose points to his speech, his eyes gazing upon the lines " 'Seuene sithe,' sayth þe boek, 'synegeth day be day / The rihtfulluste reng þat regneth in erthe' " (X.22–23). But the illustrator also wanted to indicate that the friar is debating, and did so through his extended, upturned palms and the index finger of his left hand pointing in a *declamatio* gesture to the dispute in the text, a sign of "acoustical performance," as Michael Camille calls it, "expressing the oral witness within the written text,"[15] such as we have seen so often in Douce. As in the pardon scene, however, the "I" of the poem is at this moment also the reader, who is thus engaged in an argument with the friar over the nature of Dowel before he has actually begun his quest. Two bits of evidence suggest that the illustrator has taken great pains in the placement of this figure: the friar's hands hold up the word "well," and he has managed to place the friar's bare foot upon the word "stonde" (the last word of X.35). This is, as we now know, typical of the illustrator, who, whenever possible, creates a visual mnemonic by having a character touch a significant word, thereby both illustrating and interacting with the text. This marvelously effective device for making use of the jagged left margins of a narrow, utility-grade manuscript is one of the cleverest adaptations for economy in the Douce artist's repertoire.

Finally, passus X provides us with a few instances of something we've occasionally seen throughout: the illustrator's penchant not only for subverting the established iconography and ideology of his society, but also for boldy subverting Langland's text. He renders Dobet standing in a pulpit, presumably to illustrate the lines "And is ronne into religioun and hath rendered þe bible / And precheth to þe peple" (X.88–89 [see figure 21]). But his Dobet has wide, sad eyes, suggesting humility and perhaps a tinge of hopelessness as they gaze upon these lines defining the apostolic life. His head is also bent in a gesture of humility, while his hands lie still on the pulpit, creating a sense of composure or serenity — or, more disturbingly, *silence*. Dobet's face and delicate tonsure are reminiscent of the apostolically garbed lunatic lollar's (figure 16), whose gentle demeanor and sensitivity are marked by a rounded rather than square jaw as is typical of the Douce cycle's more refined figures.

Sometimes the illustrator's subversion of Langland, and conservative thought, is so radical that the annotator can't allow it to stand unmitigated. Over the head of the young bastard, a pictorial choice inspired, as we have seen, by legal iconography, the annotator scribbled "nota de me*n* þ*a*t bene gatten out of matrimony" (fol. 48v, figure 22).[16] By writing over the figure, the annotator preempts the illustrator's emphasis on the lines the figure gazes upon — lines in which Langland uses technical legal language for discussing illegitimacy, the kind of language that often catches this scribe-illustrator's attention: "Out of matrimony noȝth moylo(r):

mow noȝt haue þe grace / Þat {we} be gatt by þe law: mowen clayme" (fol. 48v), which contrasts with the received reading of the lines: "Out of matrimonye, nat moyloure, mowen nat haue þe grace / *That lele legityme by* þe law may claymen" (X.209–10). It was the corrector's and therefore the annotator's own hand that supplied the "we" over the erasure. Langland cites the Psalter as scriptural evidence for this harsh legal injunction, but the injunction has been made even more ruthlessly exclusive by the annotator-corrector's emendation to "{we} be gatt by þe law." But the illustrator's figure seems to reject these very lines by covering his ears, in a subtle but clever adaptation of the classic iconography of despair. The drawing apparently made the annotator uncomfortable enough either to reassert the moral lesson (note what happens to men who are illegitimate) or perhaps comment on the despair (note, look at, the suffering of men who are illegitimate).[17]

We've remarked repeatedly upon the tendency of the illustrator to have compassion upon the poor and dispossessed. Although Langland's example of Cain in the lines just below emphasizes cursedness, the Douce illustrator's picture leans rather toward sympathy. Elsewhere he has explicitly questioned the moral underpinnings of the law's treatment of the poor or dispossessed. His decision to illustrate the passage across the page from the bastard, describing the flood—"here aboughte þe barn the belsires gultes" (X.232)—with a very literal ram and calf, sacrificial animals, indicates that he is following Wit's argument from the Old Law carefully. Given the text, he ought to have drawn a pair of animals, and as none are specified, he had a wide range to choose from based upon his skill and experience. The illustration of the bastard may in fact anticipate the passage marked by the ram "Filius non portabit iniquitatem patris" (the Son shall not suffer for the iniquity of the father; Ez. 18:20) (X.234). Since Wit's speech ultimately rejects this "gloss" and argues in favor of a punitive legalism here, this image cluster supports the illustrator's rejection of Wit's logic. The animals, like the child, in the Douce illustrator's eyes, are innocent.

Our modern notions of the proprieties of faithfulness to Langland's text are simply anachronistic here. These artisans have repeatedly done what their job descriptions required of them: to adapt the text to their immediate audience, most likely their patron. In doing so they created a new piece of reformist art. They were certainly not the first to interpret *Piers Plowman* according to a program of social reform. Steven Justice has shown how John Ball transformed Wit's literal bastards into "elements in an ideology of rebellion."[18] Writing from the margins of power, outside of the margins of literary *auctoritas*, the English rebels appropriated the text "to underwrite their own particular course of reformist action,"[19] one entirely antithetical, however, to the humanitarian progressiveness of the Douce program. Douce's was not the first, but it may well be the most "democratic" of the Piers sequels. And that, in itself, makes it worth our time. These Anglo-Irish professional readers, whether in accordance with the reformist views of their patron or trusting in his (not quite complete) tolerance of theirs,[20] interpret Langland's vision so as to champion those who suffer most in times of ecclesiastical corruption and political oppression—a subject about which the Anglo-Irish knew far too much.

APPENDIX 1

⁕

The Hands of Douce's Main Scribe and Corrector-Annotator

Unlike its contemporary, HM 143, whose annotator gives clear paleographical evidence of his professional origins, Douce looks suspiciously amateur. This section will be devoted to the evidence for distinguishing the hands of the scribe of Douce's main text and the scribe of its corrections and annotations, and to the evidence that the marginal supply in Douce is not the work of an enthusiastic amateur scribbling annotations spontaneously, but rather the premeditated work of a "reader-emendator" who was at least aiming at a professional standard of reader guidance for his client.

The scribe of the main text of Douce 104 copied the poem in a more *formal* version of *anglicana formata* that is slightly old-fashioned for its date, and that is distinguishable from the *informal* secretary-influenced cursive form of the same script employed by the annotating scribe.[1] Some of the main features distinguishing the two hands are listed in the accompanying chart. Those which are (or are likely) attributable merely to the demands of the two different levels of formality of the script have been marked with an asterisk.

Text Hand	*Annotating Hand*
*Invariably both shafts of *w* are completely upright and the limb of the second *v* that forms the letter looks 3-shaped as a result (fig. 2, line 5, "sworen"; line 7, "felew").	*The duct of the shafts of *w* are angled rather than upright (fig. 2, top annotation, "wyrschup," "wedyng").
*Long *s* and *f* are upright with a hooked head that curves slightly downward (fig. 2, line 2, "scise"; line 3, "forpe").	*The duct of long *s* and *f* is angled, with an elongated head that curves slightly upward and outward (fig. 2, top annotation, "horsinen," "wyrschup"; fig. 23, bottom annotation, "freres").
In *d* and *g* there is no discernible influence of secretary	Influence of secretary features in *d* and *g* with broken strokes

Appendix 1

(fig. 2, line 22, "gydyn"); *d* is less upright than one might expect in a formal hand (compare fig. 2, line 5, "seyde," with Parkes, 2(i), line 2, "due").	in lobes (fig. 2, top annotation, "de," "goo").
Double *l* is uncrossed (fig. 2, line 25, "all").	Double *l* is crossed (fig. 2, lower annotation, "all").
*Minims have "feet" (fig. 2, line 1, "mede").	*Minims have no "feet" (fig. 2, top annotation, "med").
The finishing stroke of long *r* begins well below the line (fig. 2, line 13, "after").	The finishing stroke of long *r* emerges higher up (fig. 2, top annotation, "horsinen," "wyrschup").
Symbol for "and" is a cross with a bar on top (fig. 2, line 12).	Symbol for "and" is *z*-shaped (fig. 23, annotation).
*The formal version of *e* is used (fig. 2, line 1, "mede").	Both cursive and formal versions of *e* are used (fig. 2, top annotation, "med," "horsine*n*").

Although some of these differences (notably the asterisked ones) could be attributable to a single scribe handling both versions of the script (as is evident, for instance, in some of Capgrave's manuscripts), other factors in Douce suggest that this is unlikely.[2] The fact that the annotator's hand is invariably the corrector's hand (i.e., the script, ink, and idiosyncrasies are always exactly the same) suggests that the annotator is a second scribe acting as a "reader-emendator," to use Paul Saenger and Michael Heinlen's term, just like the annotator in HM 143. Douce's distinctive annotating hand can be seen intervening in the main text (often clumsily) in all kinds of places where he is concerned that the sense will be missed.[3] For instance, on folio 42, at IX.110–11 (figure 16), where he feels that Langland has too long a stretch of apposition without a verb, he adds the redundant "walkyþ" to clarify that the lunatic lollars "walke / wiþ a god wil witteles: many wide contres *walkyþ*." Most tellingly, when he made corrections in the main text he did not try to imitate the more formal hand, as one can see in the instance above and in folio 51, line 9, where he adds the received reading "in" to the text at XI.44: "Is none so hend to haue hym *in*." This latter kind of addition suggests that he also — sometimes, at least — corrects from an exemplar, as well as from his own judgment, but he does not bother to write the additions in the formal version of the script, suggesting that it was never his script originally. More dramatic instances of his concern for reader comprehension include his blatantly obvious erasure of the received reading "Fauntelete" (XI.312) on folio 55, which he replaced with "yougth"; or his erasure of the received "priueoste" (XVIII.98), replaced with "hyest" on folio 83v; or in his many instances of dialectically motivated substitution (e.g., his "los" for the received "tyne" [XI.198] on folio 53; his puzzled "roppes" for the received text's "thorpes" (Prol. 220) on folio 4, clearly not current in his dialect; and his penchant for erasing the word "leute" wherever it occurs).[4]

The level of professionalism exhibited by the corrector may indeed be open to some question. George Kane, always scathing on the subject of scribal contributions, places the Douce corrector among the "enthusiastic amateurs" he especially deplores (187). However, the evidence does not really support such a view. The Douce corrector in fact exhibits precisely those qualities that Malcolm Parkes aptly characterizes as arising from any professional corrector's concern "to elucidate the text transmitted to him according to the needs of his *own* audience" (139; emphasis added). It is clear that in many instances he understood West Midlands dialect well enough to make appropriate substitutions, and that concern for the needs of his Hiberno-English audience justifiably came before concern for the text as aesthetic object.

As the preceding instances indicate, then, the textual and paleographical evidence points toward a "reader-emendator" working together with, but *after,* the main scribe (and after the illustrator). We do not know if he was copying his annotations into the manuscript from an exemplar or from his own rough notes. At least once the annotations record a received reading not found in the main text of Douce;[5] this suggests that the annotations were composed from another text of the poem and not "off the page" of Douce, as they might appear. Despite the sometimes unprofessional look of their placement on the page, they could not have been the product of casual brainstorming; not only are the annotations much too thoughtfully and coherently conceived to support such a theory, but the annotator appears to have been copying to some extent from cue references: a small clue to his method is the misplacement of the annotation "nota daued" on folio 12 beside III.82, which really belongs at III.118a on the next folio. It was misplaced, apparently, because the scribe mistook the correct cue line (on 12v) for a very similar one (on 12r): the annotation occurs just below the fifth line down from a verse paragraph beginning "ʒit mede þe meyre: mildely be soʒth" (fol. 12; see figure 39), but it should be beside the fifth line down from a paragraph beginning "Ac mede þe maide: þe maire ho be soʒth" (fol. 12v; figure 39). Langland's repetition of these lines is owing to an unwieldy C addition imperfectly patched into B's train of thought, and might confuse any reader, even one who knew the poem as well as the Douce annotator did. In any event, the error suggests that, at this stage at least, the annotator may have been working from cue references, rather than compos-

Appendix 1

ing his notes extempore from the text in front of him. However, it is important to note that the misplaced notation is in one of the lighter-colored inks used on his earliest run through the text, and before (apparently) he really became engaged in the process. This brings us to one of the most confusing aspects of his method, which is that simpler annotations, often in a lighter ink, are frequently later replaced or augmented or retouched in a different ink. He seems to have begun with simple subject notes and quickly become dissatisfied, then he went back over the manuscript—how many times or how systematically is impossible to say—to add more, often lengthier notes. Folios 12 and 12v also demonstrate this: "nota daued" is in the lighter ink of the punctuator-corrector, and the two longer notes are in the darker ink with which he sometimes retouches the punctuation (e.g., fol. 12). This instance (and many similar ones) give the impression that he retouched or added further annotations while correcting or recorrecting. On folio 12v an annotation in the lighter ink has actually been erased in order to make way for the more elaborate note "nota de all fals sillers" in that spot.

All the evidence points toward a shift in annotating habits mid-course that seems to have prompted various returns through the manuscript, and a spiraling, even creative interest in the process. There is no known received tradition of a complete cycle of *Piers* annotations, although numerous reader-emendators and less professional annotators would reinvent the wheel many times over the decades during which the poem was actively copied.[6] Everything we know about the production of such notes points to their being created on an ad hoc basis during the final stages of a manuscript's making; moreover, the fact that the Douce annotations are in a Hiberno-English dialect, when the exemplar (for the main text) was, as Jeremy Smith has suggested, likely West Midlands,[7] would tend to support the theory of their having been composed, or at least adapted and elaborated, by the Anglo-Irish reader-emendator.[8]

APPENDIX 2

⁜

The Marginal Annotations of Douce 104
A Complete Transcription

A Note on the Transcription

The transcription that follows is set out according to the format recommended in Malcolm Parkes, *English Cursive Hands, 1250–1500*.[1] The spacing of words and syllables has been modernized, but as an aid to dialect study a hyphen is used to indicate those places where the scribe has formed (usually) a genitive by separating the word and its ending, for example, "antecrist-ys" (i.e., Antichrist's), appearing in the manuscript as "antecrist ys." Capital letters are used only where they occur in the manuscript. Latin abbreviations have usually been silently expanded (except in quotations where at least one expansion is open to other interpretations), but all expansions of Middle English abbreviations have been italicized. The spellings supplied in these expansions are based, where possible, on spellings found elsewhere in the gloss or upon McIntosh and Samuels's description of the main features of Anglo-Irish dialect.[2] The distinction between *u* and *v* has been preserved, but *j* has been transcribed throughout as *i*. Malcolm Parkes's transcription symbols have been used:[3]

> Angle brackets < > enclose letters that have been supplied in the transcription where the manuscript is deficient through damage or where letters have been hidden by the binding. Where traces of the letter are still visible in the manuscript, the supplied letter has been printed in roman type. Where no traces of the letter remain, the supplied letter has been printed in italics.
> Parentheses ( ) enclose letters that have been supplied either where the scribe has omitted them by mistake or where he has omitted them on purpose but has failed to use the appropriate mark of abbreviation. In addition, braces { } have been used to indicate words written over erasure.

Only the annotations that occur in the early-fifteenth-century hand are reproduced here;[4] this hand appears, with a few possible exceptions, to have single-handedly annotated the manuscript shortly after it was written.[5] Illustrations are indicated by brief captions in boldface type and parentheses; these captions form no part of the fifteenth-century annotations.

Appendix 2

PROLOGUE

Folio	Line	Contents
1	1	(Will)
1v	35	<nota de> my(n)stralys
1v	41	nota de beggers
1v	56	þe iiii ordris of freris prechyng
2	66	nota pardoners
2	82	nota de pers<o>nes & parech pres<tis>
2v	98	<nota de un> trewe sacri<fice>
3	138	nota de kny3thod
3	158	nota de men of law
3v	168	nota de cat
3v	176	nota de ratoun
3v	196	nota de mous
4	220	nota de al maner craftys

PASSUS I

Folio	Line	Contents
4v	27	<of> þe syn of droncnys
5	42	nota de kepers of monney
5	48	(Castle of Care and devil—unfinished)
5v	71	nota de holy church
5v	97	nota þe parfeccioun of knyghod
6v	146	nota de loue
7	176	nota for pore pep<le>
7	184	nota de prestys

PASSUS II

Folio	Line	Contents
7v	4	<nota> de falset
7v	19	nota de med þe mayd
8	41	nota de med-ys marryag<e>
8	53	nota de what men was þeryn to þe brydall
8	55	(Mede with chalices)
8v	80	<nota de> godys þat <fals> shall hawe <wyt> mede
9	110	(Liar with charter)
9	116	nota de <medys> reall <kynsmane>
9v	146	nota how med my3t kys þe kyng as for his kyn-ys woman
10	177	nota de med-is horsinen to goo wyrschup hyre wedyng
10	179	(Mede riding on sheriff)

182

Appendix 2

Folio	Line	
10	200	nota de soþnes þat saw ham all
10v	217	nota how dred stod at þe dor
10v	229	nota de pardoners

PASSUS III

Folio	Line	Contents
11	4	**(Mede at Westminster)**
11	13	houu med we\<nt\> to westmyster
11v	38	nota de frerys þat beþe confessowrs
11v	40	**(Mede confessing to friar)**
12	76	nota de med houu scho prayt to merys & scherrewys & all þat kepyth þe law
12	82	nota daued
12v	116	nota de all fals sillers
13	149	nota houu þe kyng desyret consiens to wed med
13v	190	nota where med-ys be-lowyt wyt ony lord
14	215	nota houu med mowrnyt & toll þe kynge
15	274	**(Conscience)**
15	300	nota de harlotys hors & all wasch leches
15v	323	houu god ȝaw Salamon grace & tok hit fro hym ayayn
16	377	nota houu þe commyne claymyþ iii þyngis of þe kynge
17	413	houu Saul brak god-is commandment
17v	451	kyne low shall turne & consiens to-gedyr
17v	463	de prestis & parsonnys
18	492	**(King)**

PASSUS IV

Folio	Line	Contents
18	6	houu consiens most fet reysoun to þe kyng
18v	45	houu pes come to þe par(lia)ment
19	46	**(Reason)**
19v	83	nota de pees
20	125	houu syluer & gold schall noȝt goo owr se\<e\>
20v	166	þe kynge callit to consaill consiens & reysoun

PASSUS V

Folio	Line	Contents
21	9	I had noo wyll to do gode
22	61	nota de clerkys
22	78	houu pore gentill beþ refusit

Appendix 2

Folio	Line	Contents
22v	112	nota de pestelens cummyþ for syne
23	124	**(Tom Stowe)**
23	140	houu prechowrs schold do as þey prechyth
23v	169	bibil [written in red, in scribe's hand]
23v	178	cronicil [written in red, in scribe's hand]
23v	181	houu þe kyng schold lowe his commynys

PASSUS VI

Folio	Line	Contents
24	1	nota de repentans
24	1	**(Pride)**
24	14	nota de pryd
25	63	nota de envye
25	67	**(Envy)**
25v	105	nota de wrath
26	151	**(Wrath)**
26	151	nota de mon\<ks\>
26v	170	nota de lechury
26v	170	**(Lechery)**
26v	196	nota de covetys
27	206	**(Covetousness)**
27	221	nota de webbys
27	225	nota de brewsters
28v	307	nota de esvres
29	350	nota de clotony
29	350	**(Glutton)**
29v	376	nota de newfeyrs

PASSUS VII

Folio	Line	Contents
30v	1	nota de slouth
30v	30	nota de lewyt prestis
31	32	**(Sloth)**
31v	70	nota de branches þat bringyþ mane to slowyþ
31v	83	nota for ham þat fedyþ flatres & lyers
32	102	nota de riche men whan þey festys mak
32	146	nota de synfulman
33	159	**(Pilgrim)**
33	161	nota de pylgrymys
33	182	nota ploughman
33v	198	nota whare trowþ wonnyþ
34	233	**(Manor of Truth)**

Appendix 2

34v	270	nota de vii sostris
34v	283	nota de kitpors
35	297	**(Contemplatif)**

PASSUS VIII

Folio	Line	Contents
35	1	**(Piers)**
35	9	nota de w\<*yues*\> what þey \<shall\> do
35v	19	**(Knight — unpainted)**
35v	23	nota de kny3thod
36	56	nota houu p(e)res went apylgrimag*e*
36v	94	pers plowghma*n*-is testame*n*t
37	124	houu pers spak to faytow*r*s
37	149	nota de wastow*r*
37v	150	**(Wastor)**
37v	167	nota de hongyr to wrek pers apon wastr(o)w*r*s
38	183	**(Hunger)**
38	205	houu pers bad hongyr go home
38v	223	nota de bold*e* begg*e*rs
38v	247	nota of þe man þ*at* lenyth h*i*s godys to iii man*er* of men*e*
39	254	**(Digger)**
39	266	nota de fessyk
39v	295	nota de leches
40	323	houu hongyr was fed dentesly
40	334	**(Boat as flood symbol)**

PASSUS IX

Folio	Line	Contents
40v	3	nota de pers-is p*ar*doun
41	43	nota de men of lawe
41	46	**(Lawyer)**
41	61	nota de beggers & bidders beþ noght i*n* þe bull
41v	83	nota de woo of pore pepill þ*at* wo*n*nyth i*n* por howsyn & haþ childyr
42	106	**(Lunatic lollar)**
42v	166	nota de begers þ*at* hath le*m*monys
43	175	**(Blind man)**
43v	203	nota de hermytes þ*at* wonyth by þe hey wey
43v	222	nota de lewyt men & lordis
44	246	**(False friar)**
44	264	nota de molle pastore

Appendix 2

Folio	Line	Contents
44	264	**(Sleeping bishop, and wolf with sheep)**
44v	282	**(Priest with pardon)**
44v	303	nota de sweuy⟨n⟩s
45	321	nota de do well

PASSUS X

Folio	Line	Contents
45v	4	nota houu þey soght dowell
46	21	**(Franciscan friar)**
46	37	nota houu ⟨seuen⟩ syþ⟨ys⟩ ⟨in⟩ þe de⟨y⟩ synny⟨s⟩ þe ⟨ryt⟩fol
46v	72	nota de þoȝt
47	88	**(Dobet)**
47	92	nota de dobest
47	114	nota de wyt
47v	121	nota what was dowell fro do better & do best fro hem boþ
47v	143	nota de Inwytte
48v	208	nota de men þat bene gatten out of matrimony
48v	208	**(Young bastard)**
49	225	**(Two beasts)**
49v	248	nota de marryagis wyt in degree
49v	278	madys wed maydis & wodous wed wodous

PASSUS XI

Folio	Line	Contents
50v	16	wo can disseyw & be-gyle schall be callitte to consayll
51	42	nota de pore & nakitte
51	45	**(Beggar)**
51	54	nota de freres & faytowrs
51v	94	nota de clergy
52	125	**(Schoolmaster beating child)**
52	129	nota de þeology
52v	161	nota de be-leve trowyth & low
52v	161	**(Will writing)**
53	171	**(Fortune's wheel)**
53	180	nota de youth
53	190	**(Recklessness)**
53	196	nota de rechles
53v	213	nota de salomon
54	235a	nota seld is hit sey clerkis lew as þey techyn
54	235a	**(Clerk)**

Folio	Line	Contents
54	255	nota of þe þefe þat heng on þe cros by owr lord
54v	295	nota ploghmen & herdis & pore commynys

PASSUS XII

Folio	Line	Contents
55	1	note de elde & holynys
55	5	**(Elde)**
55v	19	nota de wowere
55v	38a	nota houu scryptowr prechytte
56	73	**(Trajan)**
56v	79	nota de troian þe trew hemperowr & a pagan
56v	100	nota de men þat makyth festys
57	118	þe lawe of lowe
57v	139	po(ue)rte is best yef paciens hit follouu
58v	210	nota of rich man
58v	225	nota de rich lordis

PASSUS XIII

Folio	Line	Contents
59	9	nota houu abram-is wif was tak fro hi\<m\>
59	15	nota de Iob
59v	32	nota de marchan & messengere
60v	98	nota de prestis
60v	103	**(Priest)**
61	128	nota kynd \<wytt\> come clerge to help
61	139	**(Hand holding coins)**
61v	178	\<nota de *reyson þat folloþ all* best-*ys* save man\>
62	219	what \<is do\> well
62v	224	nota de adam why he was put out paradys

PASSUS IV

Folio	Line	Contents
62v	2	nota de ymagynatiff
63	19	**(Imaginatif)**
63	29	nota de spiritu sancto
64	87	nota of þe byrþ of owr lord
64v	101	nota de lewytt men & conyng men
65	135	nota de þef þat went to he\<uen\>
65	145	**(Thief)**
65v	189	nota de salamon & þe phylossofowrs
66	202	nota de Imagynatyf
66	205	nota of iiii follyny\<gis\>

Appendix 2

PASSUS XV

Folio	Line	Contents
66	5	nota de fortune hou<u> hyt falyth
66v	26	nota de consiens & clergy
67	39	**(Learned friar)**
67	56	nota de sowr lof
67v	76	**(Corrupt friar)**
67v	78	be war of fals freris
68v	138	nota de patiens
69	190	nota de activa vita
69	190	**(Activa Vita)**
70	239	**(Patience)**
70	245	nota de pater noster
70v	281	nota de ryghtfull rich
71	301	**(Skeleton)**

PASSUS XVI

Folio	Line	Contents
71	25	do well is contricioun [perhaps a different hand]
72	63	nota de boxumnys & bost ar euermor at were
72	67	**(Crouched poor man)**
73	120	nota what <pride> most hatyth
73	157	nota de fre will
73	182	nota de corpore
74	183	**(Liberum Arbitrium)**
74	201	nota de hou mony namis a byschop hath
74	212	nota luscifer
74v	217	nota þe man þat ettyth moch hony
75	251	nota parsonnes <&> prestes
75	264	nota de epocrysy
75v	284	**(Pointing hand)**
75v	284	charyte

PASSUS XVII

Folio	Line	Contents
77	7	nota of holy h<e>rimyts
77v	42	of men of holy church lordys men of law & marchaunys
78v	95	nota of schepmen
79	132	**(Man on gallows)**
79	141	nota de manda<tu>
79v	163	**(Pointing hand)**

Appendix 2

| 80 | 199 | nota houu rede nobill is wyrschuput |
| 80 | 200 | **(Angel — unpainted)** |

PASSUS XVIII

Folio	Line	Contents
82	1	nota de libere arbitrium
83	61	nota de appyl tre
83	73	nota de contemplacioun
83v	86	nota de wedlok woddowot & maydenot
83v	105	nota de elde
83v	113	nota de Adam & þe profettys
84	124	nota gretyn of owr lady
84v	164	nota of þe treysoun þat Iudas dede
85	182	**(Abraham — unfinished)**
85	188	nota of iii persones in trinite

PASSUS XIX

Folio	Line	Contents
87	21	nota de fayth
87	48	nota de samaritan
88	96	nota to low god abow al þyngis & þi neghtbo<wr>
88	112a	**(Hand holding ball)**
89	161	nota who synnyþ in holy gost
90	224	nota rychmen
90v	252	Nota for þeves
91	282	nota þer þe Kyng may noght pardoune
91	296	nota de þre þyngis þat puttyþ a man out of hys hous

PASSUS XX

Folio	Line	Contents
92	21	nota how ihesu schal jowst in pers-is armis
92	28	nota de deth & lyf
92v	79	nota þat þer was no man þat myȝth towch godes body
93	106	nota how Ivys be-came bonmen
93v	117	nota de mercy & trouþ
93v	145	nota de trouþ
94	153	nota de mercy
94	148	**(Mercy)**
94	168	nota de ryȝtwysnys
94v	210	nota de well & woo

Appendix 2

Folio	Line	Contents
95v	248	nota de stella comata
95v	273	nota how a woys sayde to lossyfere
96	284	**(Devil)**
96	295	nota de lussyf<ere>
96	312	nota de satan
96v	323	nota goblyn
96v	345	nota lussyfere-ys lessyngys
97	379	nota de gylowrs
97v	386	nota de lyffe & deth
97v	395	nota houu man was lost þrogh a tree
97v	409	nota of day of dome
98	422	nota of a kyng-ys power
98v	455	amor

PASSUS XXI

Folio	Line	Contents
99	15	nota de names of crist & ihesus
99	26	nota de knyʒt kyng & conquerowr
100	75	nota of þe iii kyngis of Collyn what þey offyrt
100	86	nota de sens
100	88	nota de gold
100	92	nota de myrre
100v	111	nota de wyne
101	138	**(Caiaphas)**
101	140	nota de C<a>yphas
101	157	nota de mari mavdelyn
101v	183	nota de pers ploghman-is pardon
102	201	nota de holy þo<rs>day
102	219	nota antecrist
102v	229	nota de p(re)chowrs
102v	235	nota de craftymen & labores
102v	240	**(Merchant counting money)**
103	261	**(Piers's oxen)**
103	263	nota de pers-ys plo<gh> bestys
103	276	nota de iiii sedys þat gras yaw to pers
103v	319	nota de pers-ys hows
104	330	nota de cart <to> draw pers-y<s> corne
104v	361	nota de kynd wyt
104v	370	nota de quest mangers & somnowrs
104v	385	nota de god-ys body in fowrme of bred
105	396	nota de brewesters
105	407	**(Unlearned vicar)**
105	408	nota de lewyt vykerry

Appendix 2

PASSUS XXII

Folio	Line	Contents
106v	10	<nota> de nede <h>ath no lawe
107	35	nota de ned
107	52	nota de antecryst
107	52	**(Antichrist)**
107v	69	nota de antecrist-ys herrottis of armys
107v	91	nota de herrotis of armys þat destruyt lordis
108	100	nota de deþ
108	109	nota de fortune-ys flatryng*is*
108v	131	nota hou*u* falce schold abid*e* in kyng*is* cowrt & all oþ*er* cowrt*is*
108v	150	**(Sleȝth)**
108v	157	nota de sleȝt
109	162	**(Tom Two-Tongue)**
109	169	nota de fesyk
109	176	**(Physician)**
109	183	nota de held*e* yed*e* ow*er* men<*ys*> hedys
109v	199	nota how kynd passite
109v	218	**(Proud priest)**
109v	218	nota de <*prowt*> prestis
110	242	nota de co*n*ciens
110v	257	<nota de nowmbyr>
110v	283	nota of ham þat <*b*>eþ asc<*hamed*> to be schrew*n*
111	288	nota of ham þat s<*hrewn*> to frerys
111	301	nota de ypocrysy
111v	322	nota de frer*e* flat*erre*re
111v	336	**(Friar physician)**
111v	346	nota how þe frer salwt ow*r* women

APPENDIX 3
❖
Translations

For the convenience of readers who wish to consult the C text passages in translation, we have provided translations of longer passages from *William Langland's* Piers Plowman: *The C Version: A Verse Translation,* translated by George Economou (Philadelphia: University of Pennsylvania Press, 1996); this is a complete translation based on Pearsall's C text and any line references in the present book could be found there. However, where the Douce manuscript readings differ from Pearsall's text, we have provided translations based on Douce transcriptions; these will differ somewhat from Economou's text, of course.

Chapter 1

"Sleuthe with his slynge an hard sawt he made. / Proute prestes cam with hym—passyng an hundred / In paltokes and pikede shoes and pissares longe knyues / Comen aȝen Consience; with Couetyse they helden. / 'By þe Marie,' quod a mansed prest, was of þe march of Ireland, / 'Y counte no more Consience, by so y cache suluer, / Then y do to drynke a drauht of goed ale!' / And so sayde syxty of þe same contreye, / ... / And hadden almost Vnite and holynesse adowne." ("Sloth with his sling launched a tough attack. / Proud priests came with him—more than a hundred / In cloaks and peaked shoes and packing long knives like common men / Come against Conscience, they were on Covetousness's team. / 'By the Mary,' said an excommunicate priest from the Irish frontier, / 'I credit Conscience no more, as long as I make money, / Than I do to drink a draft of good ale!' / And so said sixty from the same country, / ... / And almost took Unity and Holiness down.")

"...et frequenter suos subditos per suam necgligenciam ad infernum deducunt." ("And often, through their negligence, they lead those in their charge to hell.")

"Whan nede had me vndir nome: þus a none I fel a sclep." ("When Need had reproached me thus, I fell asleep at once.")

"...made fals spryng and spred: & spede mannes nedis" ("made falsehood spring and spread and supply men's needs")

Appendix 3

"ouer tulde þe rote" ("overturned the roots")

Simon quasi dormit. (Simon is as it were asleep.)

Beneficia ecclesiastica (church benefices)

"De habitu clericorum et...qualis debet esse distinctio vestimentorum" ("Concerning clerical dress and...what distinction of vestments there ought to be")

"Ydolatrie ӡe soffren in sondrye places manye / ...Forthy y sey ӡe prestes and men of holy churche / That soffreth men do sacrefyce and worschipe maumettes, / ...God shal take vengeaunce on alle suche prestis." ("In sundry places you allow idolatry / ...Therefore I say to you priests and men of the church / That tolerate idolatrous payment and prayers, / ...God shall get even with all such priests.")

"Arise, and go reuerense godes resureccioun, / And crepe to þe croes on knees and kusse hit for a iewel / And rihtfollokest a relyk, noon richore on erthe." ("Arise, and go reverence God's resurrection, / And creep on your knees to the cross and kiss it as a jewel / And most rightfully as a relic, none richer on earth.")

"And to oure syhte, as hit semeth" ("And in our view, as it seems")

"O niger intrusor" ("O Black Intruder")

"For had a man slayn al his kynne, / Go shryve him at a frere, / And for lesse then a payre of shoen / He wyl assoil him clene and sone, / And say the synne that he has done / his saule shal never dere." ("For if a man had slain all his kin, [he should] go confess to a friar, and for less than a pair of shoes he will absolve him cleanly and immediately, and say the sin that he has committed shall never cost his soul.")

"Wyde are thair wonnynges, and wonderfully wroght; / Murdre and horedome ful dere has it boght." ("Large are their houses, and wonderfully made; Murder and whoredom have bought it at great expense.")

"First thai gabben on God, that alle men may se, / When thai hangen him on hegh on a grene tre, / With leves and with blossemes that bright are of ble; / That was never Goddes son, by my leute." ("First they lie about God, that all men may see, when they hang him on high in a green tree, with leaves and with blossoms that are of bright hue; that was never God's son, by my loyalty.")

"Thai have done him on a croys fer up in the skye, / And festned on hym wyenges, as he shuld flie. / This fals feyned byleve shal thai soure bye, / On that lovelych Lord so for to lye. / With an O and an I, one sayd ful stille, / Armachan distroy ham, if it is Goddes wille." ("They have put him on a cross far up in the sky, and fastened wings on him as if he should fly. They will sorely pay for this false belief—to lie about that lovely Lord. With an O and an I, one said very quietly, Armachan destroy him, if it is God's will.")

"Ther I sawe a frere blede in myddes of his syde; / Bothe in hondes and in fete had he woundes wyde. / To serve to that same frer, the pope mot abyde. / With an O and an I, I wonder of thes dedes, / To se a pope holde a dische whyl the frer bledes." ("There I saw a friar bleed from the middle of his side; in both hands and feet he had wide wounds. The pope must stay to serve that same friar. With an O and an I, I wonder at these goings on, to see a pope hold a dish while the friar bleeds.")

"Uenite ascendamus ad montem." ("Come, let us climb the mountain.")

"'faytours' and 'eremytes' would 'henten hem spades' for fear of famine." ("'Fakers' and 'hermits' would 'take up spades' for fear of famine.")

Chapter 2

Nota quod si bastardus se clamando legitimum heredem..." ("Note that if a bastard, by claiming himself legitimate heir...")

"teneful" ("painful")

"...as i haue rad: & oþer þat can rede" ("as I or anyone else can read")

"I wende to dede a kyng y wys." ("I go to death a king indeed.")

"I wende to be cled in claye." ("I go to be clad in clay.")

"unum librum vocatum Pers Plewman" ("one book called *Piers Plowman*")

"I beseke þe reuerent doctour to inform me þe way of good lyfyng and how I sal dispose me to cum to euerlastyng lyfe." ("I beseech you, reverend doctor, to inform me of the way of good living and how I shall dispose myself to come to everlasting life.")

"Quod contemplacioun by cryst: þoȝth I care suffer / Famy[n]e and defaute: folow i wil peres" ("Contemplation said, 'By Christ, though I suffer care, / Famine and deprivation, I will follow Piers.'")

"Non accipiam sacrificium de manibus uestris." ("I will not accept a sacrifice from your hands.")

"vt dicitur Pastores infideles locii [sic]furum sequu[n]tur muna manus eorum plene rapina" ("how it is said that unfaithful pastors of the district follow the offices of thieves, their hands full of plunder")

"'This aren euidences,...for hem þat wolle nat swynke / That here lyflode be lene and lyte worth here clothes.'" ("'This is evidence,' said

Appendix 3

Hunger, 'for those who won't work / That their means of life will be lean and their clothes worth little.' ")

"Hastilich ȝe him bind; / Al his bones ȝe to-drawe"..."Also hit farith nou in lond / ...The lafful man ssal be i-bund / And i-do in strang pine." ("Quickly you, bind him; / Draw all his bones apart"..."Also it transpires now in the land / ...the lawful man shall be bound / and made to suffer various tortures."

Chapter 3

"De paupertate," "De libero arbitrio," "De falsis religiosis," "De prophecia" ("Concerning poverty," "Concerning free will," "Concerning false religions," "Concerning prophecy")

"a pore frere of þe Heremites of Seynt Austyn in þe conuent of Lenne" ("a poor friar of the hermits of Saint Augustine in the convent of Lynn")

debere, observare, docere, facere (to be obligated to, to pay attention to, to inform, to do)

"contra sacerdotes terrarios" ("against landowning priests")

"Observate ergo qui hec legitis omnes Domini sacerdotes et videte quid sit differencia sacerdotum ne forte qui partem habent in terra et terrenis cultibus ac studiis vacant non tam Domini quam Pharaonis sacerdotes esse videantur." ("Therefore, observe all you priests of the Lord who read these things and see what the difference may be in priests, lest by chance those who hold a part in the earth and earthly cultivations and leave off their studies may seem to be priests not so much of the Lord as of Pharaoh.")

mirabilia (wonders)

"God sende hem Joye / of hir ladye / And euery womman of hir loue." ("God send them joy of their lady and every woman of their love.")

"And whane ye haue þis booke ouerlooked / ... / And þe sentence / vnderstonden / With Inne youre mynde hit fast ebounden / Thankeþe þauctoures þat þeos storyes / Renoueld haue / to youre memoryes / and þe wryter / for his distresse." ("And when you have looked this book over... and understood the sentence [of it], bind it fast within your memory, thank the authors that have renewed these stories in your memories and the scribe for his distress.")

"Howe þe oste sette þe pylgrimes to þe soper" ("How the host set the pilgrims to supper")

"Yit holdith your pees or ye wilbe shent." ("Yet hold your peace or you will be ruined/shamed.")

Appendix 3

"Lo my lordes here begynneþe a balade of gode counseyl.... Takeþe goode heed Sirs and dames how Lydeyate daun johan. þe Munk of Bury moeued of deuocyoun haþe translated. þe salme." ("Lo my lords, here begins the ballad of good counsel.... Take good heed, sirs and ladies, how Don John Lydgate, the monk of Bury, moved by devotion, has translated the psalm.")

"hyer ȝe may se schortly rehersed þe visionis to foresayd." ("Here you may see presently repeated the aforesaid visions.")

"a comfessour as a frere comforted mede & sayde as ȝe may rede." ("A confessor who was a friar comforted Mede and said as you may read.")

"nowe Iugeþe yee þat beoþe kunnyng which yowe lykeþe þe beter þe ffrench or þenglissh." ("Now you who are knowledgeable, judge which you like better—the French or the English.")

"In illo tempore. Maria stabat ad monumentum foris plorans." ("In that time, Mary stood at the door of the tomb weeping.")

"nota houu p(e)res went apylgrimage" ("note how Piers went on pilgrimage")

"nota þat þer was no man þat myȝth towch godes body" ("note that there was no man that might touch God's body")

"be war of fals freris" ("Beware of false friars.")

"nota to low god abow al þyngis & þi neghtbo<wr>" ("note to love God above all things and your neighbour")

"houu god ȝaw Salamon grace & tok hit from hym ayayn" ("how God gave Solomon grace and took it from him again")

" // notate ȝe ryche." ("Note you rich people.")

"notate hyer how ȝe schull make festes." ("Note here how you shall make feasts.")

"kyne low shall turne & consiens to-gedyr." ("Natural love and conscience shall turn (or convert) together.")

"lo how iewe schull conuerte for ioye." ("See how the Jews shall convert for joy.")

"prophetia petri" ("the prophecy of Peter")

"nota de pater noster" ("note concerning the 'Our Father' ")

"nota de branches þat bringyþ mane to slowyþ" ("note concerning the branches that bring a man to sloth")

"nota de þre þyngis þat puttyþ a man out of hys hous" ("note concerning three things that put a man out of his house")

197

Appendix 3

"houu pore gentill beþ refusit" ("how poor gentility are refused")

"houu þe kyng shold lowe his commyns" ("how the king should love his commons")

"nota de lewyt presstis" ("note concerning lewd priests")

"houu syluer & gold shall noȝt go owr se\<e\>" ("how silver and gold shall not be sent overseas")

"nota de molle pastore" ("note concerning the weak pastor")

"nota de woo of pore pepill þat wonnyth in por howsyn & haþ childyr" ("note concerning the woe of poor people that live in poor housing and have children")

"nota de beggers & bidders beþ noght in þe bull" ("note concerning [the fact that] beggars and paupers are not in the bull")

"nota how þe frer salwt owr women" ("note concerning how the friar salutes our women")

"nota de helde yede ower men\<ys\> hedys" ("note concerning how old age goes over men's heads")

"nota de sowr lof" ("note concerning the sour loaf")

"nota de hou mony namis a byschop hath" ("note concerning how many names a bishop has")

"nota de newfeyrs" ("note concerning a game of exchanges" — literally, new fairs, markets)

"loke hyer what [pers] wyf hyȝte & his sone & his doȝter." ("Look here what Piers's wife is called and his son and his daughter.")

"Ac longe-lybbyng men lykened men lyuynge / To briddes and to bestes, as here bokkes telleth." ("But long-living men likened men's lives / To birds and beasts, as their books tell.")

"nota seld is hit sey clerkis lew as þey techyn" ("note [that] it is seldom that clerics live as they teach")

"nota of þe þefe þat heng on þe cros by owr lord" ("note of the thief that hung on the cross by our Lord")

"nota ploghmen & herdis & pore commynys" ("note plowmen and herdsmen and poor commoners")

"hyere fortune raueschid will & schewed hym a myrour þat hyȝte myddylȝerd." ("Here Fortune ravished Will and showed him a mirror that is called middle earth.")

"hyer hard sentence for techeres ȝif þay leue noȝt wel." ("Here hard sentence for teachers if they do not live well.")

Appendix 3

"hyer ȝoughte sette at noȝt al þis." ("Here Youth set all this at nothing.")

"nota de elde & holynys" ("note concerning Old Age and Holiness")

"nota de wowere" ("note concerning the wooer")

"nota houu scryptowr prechytte" ("note how Scripture preached")

"nota de troian þe trew hemperowr & a pagan" ("note concerning Trajan the true emperor and a pagan")

"nota de men þat makyth festys" ("note concerning men that make feasts")

"þe lawe of lowe" ("the law of love")

"po(ue)rte is best yef paciens hit follouu." ("Poverty is best if patience follows it.")

"hyer cam a trogian & sayde baw for bokes." ("Here came Trajan and said 'Bah!' for books.")

"notate hyer how ȝe schull make festes." ("Note here how you shall make feasts.")

"'Alace ey" quod Elde: and holynesse boþe, / 'That wit schal torne to wrachednesse for Wil hath his wille.'" ("'Aw, too bad!' said Old Age and Holiness together, / 'That wit will turn to wretchedness because Will has it all his way!'")

"'By my faith, frere,' quod y, 'ȝe fare lyke þe woware / That wilneth nat þe wedewe bote for to welde here godes.'" ("'By my faith, friar' I said, 'you act like the wooer / Who wants the widow only to get control of her wealth.'")

"I had noo wyll to do gode." ("I had no will to do good.")

"nota de pestelens cummyþ for syne" ("note concerning pestilence coming because of sin")

"houu prechowrs shold do as þey prechyth" ("how preachers should do as they preach")

"hyer concience & raysoun a ratyd wille for his lollynge." ("Here Conscience and Reason berated Will for his lolling about / laziness.")

"hyer wente wille to churche & ful aȝen a sclepe." ("Here Will went to church and fell asleep again.")

"For sholde no clerke be crouned but yf he come were / Of frankeleynes and fre men and of folke ywedded. / Bondemen and bastardus and beggares children, / Thyse bylongeth to labory." ("For no clerk should be

Appendix 3

crowned who doesn't come / From franklins and free men and married folks. / Serfs and bastards and beggars' children, / They should do the work.")

"fette Felyce hoem fram wyuene pyne" ("fetch home Felice from the wife's punishment stool")

"And sethe he radde religioun here reule to holde, / Laste þe kyng and his consayl ȝoure comunes apayre." ("Then he directed religious orders to keep their rule, / 'Lest the king and his council reduce your provisions.'")

superbia (pride)

"nota de men þat bene gatten out of matrimony" ("note concerning men begotten out of matrimony")

"nota de marryagis wyt in degree" ("note concerning marriages within degree")

"nota de wedlok woddowot and maydenot" ("note concerning wedlock, widowhood, and maidenhood")

"Yf lewede men knewe this Latyn, a litel they wolden auysen hem / Ar they amorteysed eny more for monkes or for chanons." ("If unlearned men knew this Latin they'd give a little more consideration / Before they made over any more property to monks and canons.")

"nota de god-ys body in fowrme of bred" ("note concerning God's body in the form of bread")

Chapter 4

Modus tenendi parliamentorum (How to hold parliaments)

"A demain" ("until tomorrow")

"Sleuth was sley of werre." ("Sloth was sly at warfare.")

"An hendy knyght heght placydas / bot hethyn man ful longe he was" ("A noble knight named Placidas, but he had been a heathen man for a very long time")

"I have heere his lyknesse / Do make, to this ende, in sothfastnesse, / That thei that have of him lest thought and mynde / By this peynture may ageyn him fynde." ("I have caused to be made here his likeness for this purpose, accurately, so that they who have lost him from thought and mind [memory] may find him again by this painting.")

"And to peres þe ploughman: profered to fiȝth" ("And offered to fight Piers the Plowman")

"Proud prestes come wiþ hym: passing an hondered / In paltokes and pyked shoes and pyssers long knyues." ("Proud priests came with him—

more than a hundred / In cloaks and peaked shoes and packing long knives.")

"And with antecrist helden: hard aȝenes consciens" ("who held hard with Antichrist against Conscience")

"bitelbrowed and baburlipped" ("beetle-browed and blubber-lipped")

"Wykedly to wey: was my fyrst lesone / To wend to westmynster: i went to þe faire." ("Wicked weighing was my first lesson / To go to Westminster, I went to the fair.")

"For vch a maide þat I mett: i made hir assynge / Semyng to synward: & sum I can taste / A boute þe mouþe & be neþe: gan I hir gropp / To boþ our willes was on: & to þe werke we ȝeden." ("For each maid I met I gave her a signal / Hinting toward sin, and some I tasted / Around the mouth and beneath began to grope / Till we were of one mind and went right to work.")

"þroȝth experiens quod scho: i hopp þei schal be saued." (" 'Through experience,' she said, 'I hope they'll be saved.' ")

"nota de soþnes" ("note concerning truth")

"þat wende to westmynster: wher wircheped hir many" ("that went to Westminster where many showed her great honour")

"Gentely wiþ joy: þe justices summe [sic] / Busked hem to þe boure: þer þis burde dwelled." ("Some of the judges, joyously gallant / Rushed into the chamber where this lady was.")

"what man of þis world þat hir levest had" ("which man in the world she'd most like to have")

"Litil loueþ he þat lorde: þat lent hym al þat blis / þat so partiþ wiþ þe pore: a parcel whan hem nediþ / Ne wer mercy in mene men: mor þan in ryȝth ryche / Man tymes mendinauntȝ: myȝth go an hongered." ("Little does he love the Lord who lent him all that bliss / That so shares a parcel with the poor in their need. / If there weren't more mercy in the common man than in the very rich, / Many times mendicants might go very hungry.")

Chapter 5

voces paginarum (the voices of the pages)

bas de page (bottom of the page)

"For schal no pardon preye for ȝow there ne no princes lettres." ("For there no pardon shall pray for you nor any princes' letters.")

Appendix 3

"Qui bona egerunt ibunt in vitam eternam; / Qui vero mala in ignem eternum." ("They that have done good shall go into life everlasting; and they that have done evil into everlasting fire.")

"byheld alle þe bulle / In two lynes as hit lay and nat a lettre more" ("beheld the entire bull / In two lines as it lay and not a letter more")

"I had noo wyll to do gode." ("I had no will to do good.")

"Out of matrimony noȝth moylo(r): mow noȝt haue þe grace / Þat {we} be gatt by þe law: mowen clayme / And þat my saue is soþe: þe sauter bereþ wittenesse." ("[Those born] out of wedlock, not of a lawful wife, may not have the grace / That {we} begotten by the Law may claim. / And that what I say is truth the psalter bears witness.")

"Wirchep he wynneþ: þat will ȝeu mede / Ac he þat reseyueþ hir: is reseyuowr of gyle." ("He wins honour that will give meed, / But he that receives it has been betrayed.")

"Þe which þat hatte, as y have rad, and oþer þat can rede" ("which calls out, as I or anyone can read")

"For y was rauysched rihte there, for Fortune me fette." ("For I was swept away right there, Fortune fetched me.")

"And in a myrrour þat hihte Myddelerd she made me to loke." ("And she made me look into a mirror named Middle Earth.")

"Folowe forth þat Fortune wole." ("Follow wherever Fortune wants.")

"And ȝut ar ther oþere beggares, in hele, as hit semeth / Ac hem wanteth wyt, men and women bothe, / The whiche aren lunatyk lollares and lepares aboute." ("And yet there are other beggars, in good health it seems, / But they're feeble-minded, men and women both, / Who are lunatic lollars and wandering tramps.")

"The cause of al this caytiftee cometh of many bischopes / That soffreth suche sottes and oþere synnes regne." ("The cause of all this villainy comes from many bishops / Who allow such sots and other sinners to prevail.")

"A bacheler or a bew-pere beste hym bysemede / And for þe cloth þat keuereth hym ykald he is a frere." ("A bachelor or a *beau-père* [good-father] suited him best, / And because of the cloth that covers him he's called a friar.")

"And precheþ to þe pepil: seynt poules wordis / *Libenter suffertis incipientes cum sitis vos ipsi sapientes* / Ȝe worldylich wyse: vnwyse þat ȝe suffer / Lene hem & loue hem: þis latyn is to mene." ("And preaches to the people Saint Paul's words: / 'For you gladly suffer the foolish' / 'You

Appendix 3

worldly wise, the unwise that you suffer, / Give to them and love them,' this scripture means.")

"Dobest bere sholde þe bisshopes crose / And halie with þe hoked ende all men to gode, / And with the pyk pulte adoun *preuaricatores legis.*" ("Do-best should bear the bishop's crozier / And drag with the hooked end all men to good, / And with the pike end push down those who misuse or evade the law.")

"Lewed men han no byleue and lettred men erren." ("Ignorant men lack faith and literate men err.")

"a badde peny with a gode printe" ("a bad penny with a good stamp")

"For god þat al bygan in bigynnynge of the worlde / Ferde furste as a fuste, and ȝut is, as y leue, / *Mundum pugillo continens,* As with a fuste with a fynger yfolde togyderes, / Til hym likede and luste to vnlose that fynger / And profered hit forth as with the paume to what place hit sholde." ("For God who began all in the world's beginning / Acted first as a fist, and still is, as I believe, / Holding the world in his hand, / Like a fist with a finger folded together, / Till it pleased him to open that finger / And put it forth as with the palm to whatever place it should go.")

"here handes / Lellyche and lauhfollyche" ("by their hands / Loyally and lawfully")

"Ac he þat speneth his speche and speketh for þe pore / That innocent and nedy is and no man harme wolde" ... "Shal haue grace of a good ende and greet ioye after." ("But he who spends his speech and speaks for the poor man / Who is innocent and needy and would harm no one" ... "Shall have the grace of a good end and great joy thereafter.")

Chapter 6

"Ordeyned þe to be a merowr" ("ordained thee to be a mirror")

"lond of longyng" ("land of longing")

"Yn a sommur sesoun" ("In a summer season")

"Now must I beddes byd þof my bones ake; I drede þat ded persewes me fast." ("Now I must tell my rosary beads though my bones ache; I fear that death pursues me quickly.")

"Now I am in strenþe; who dar to me say nay?" ("Now I am strong; who would dare to say no to me?")

"for sche weryd gold pypys on hir hevyd & hir hodys wyth þe typettys were daggyd. Hir clokys also wer daggyd & leyd wyth dyuers colowrs

Appendix 3

be-twen þe daggys þat it schuld be þe mor staryng to mennys sygth." ("For she wore gold pipes [a type of headdress] on her head and her hoods with the tippets were dagged. Her cloaks also were dagged and had diverse colors between the dags so that it should be the more eye-catching to men's sight.")

"hot heruest whenne y hadde myn hele / And lymes to labory with and louede wel fare" ("hot harvest when I was in good health / And had strong arms to work with but loved the good life")

"Lyf þat me lykede" ("A life that I liked")

"With women my lyst both play and rage" ("With women I desire to both play and romp")

"Tho wepte y for wo and wrathe of here wordes / And in a wynkynge y warth and wonderliche me mette, / For y was rauysched rihte there, for Fortune me fette." ("Then I wept for woe and anger at her words / And dropped off to sleep and dreamed wonderfully, / For I was swept away right there, Fortune fetched me.")

"þou hast ful fer to elde." ("you've a long way to old age.")

"þat wit schal torne to wrachednesse: for wil haþ hour wyl" ("That wit will turn to wretchedness because Will has it all his way!")

"By wissyng of this wenche y dede, here wordes were so swete / Til y forʒet ʒouthe and ʒorn into elde. / And thenne was Fortune my foo for al her fayre biheste / And pouerte pursuede me and potte me to be lowe." / ("I did just as the wench advised me, so sweet were her words, / Till I passed right through youth and ran into old age. / And then Fortune was my foe despite her fair promises / And poverty pursued me and put me down low.")

"That yf thay trauaile treulyche and trist in god almyhty / Hem sholde neuere lacke lyflode noþer lynnen ne wollene. / The tytle ʒe take ʒoure ordres by telleth ʒe ben avaunsed / And nedeth nat to nyme siluer for masses þat ʒe synge." ("That if they labor truly and trust in God almighty / They'll never lack livelihood neither linen nor woloen. / The title you take your orders by announces you've been advanced / And need not take silver for the masses you sing.")

" 'Now y see,' saide Lyf, 'that surgerie ne fysyke / May nat a myte avayle to medlen aʒen Elde.' / And in hope of his hele gode herte he hente / And roed so to Reuel..." (" 'Now I see,' said Life, 'that neither surgery nor medicine / Can usefully interfere with Old Age.' / And in hope of his health he took good heart / And rode off to Revel.")

Notes

❖

Preface

1. We have developed the term "professional reader" and use it in this sense, which is different from Malcolm Parkes's use of the term in "The Literacy of the Laity," in *Scribes, Scripts, and Readers* (London: Scolar, 1991), 275–97.
2. *Piers Plowman: A Facsimile of Bodleian Library, Oxford, MS Douce 104*, with an introduction by Derek Pearsall and a catalog of the illustrations by Kathleen Scott (Cambridge: Brewer, 1992); cited hereafter in the text as the Douce facsimile; in notes as *Facsimile*.
3. *Piers Plowman by William Langland: An edition of the C-Text*, ed. Derek Pearsall, York Medieval Texts (London: Edward Arnold, 1978); cited hereafter as *C-Text*.
4. This is the practice followed in *A New History of Ireland*, vol. 2, *Medieval Ireland, 1169–1534*, ed. Art Cosgrove (Oxford: Clarendon, 1987). See especially, in that volume, J. A. Watt, "Approaches to the History of Fourteenth-Century Ireland," 308–11.
5. See figures 10 and 34. I am grateful to Kathryn Finter for explaining that the artist would have applied the shell gold using a brush and gum arabic.
6. See Jonathan J. G. Alexander, "Preliminary Marginal Drawings in Medieval Manuscripts," in *Artistes, artisans et production artistique au Moyen Age*, vol. 3, *Fabrication et consommation de l'oeuvre*, ed. Xavier Barral i Altet (Paris: Picard, 1990), 307–19, esp. 310. These issues are discussed in detail in the third section of chapter 4 in this volume, as are the other workshop matters raised in this paragraph.
7. He does this in the two annotations in red on fol. 23v and in the cropped inscription on fol. 74.
8. I am grateful to De Lloyd Guth for helping me decipher some of the inscriptions in this picture. On the artist in relation to Douce's, see note on p. xviii.
9. For this terminology (derived from Moshe Barasch, *Giotto and the Language of Gesture* [Cambridge: Cambridge University Press, 1987], and from Michael Camille) and a fuller discussion of the "texts" being voiced in this scene, see chapter 4.
10. On patterns of rubrication in this and other legal manuscripts, see chapter 2.
11. For the results of Jeremy Griffiths' preliminary spectragraphic analysis, see Pearsall and Scott, *Facsimile*, xx–xxi); we hope that the results of his later work will still, despite his untimely death, be published by his literary executors. Maidie Hilmo will be doing a computer imaging analysis of the manuscript.
12. Derek Pearsall, "Manuscript Illustration of Late Middle English Literary Texts, with Special Reference to the Illustration of *Piers Plowman* in Bodleian Library MS Douce 104," in *Suche Werkis to Werche: Essays on* Piers Plowman *in Honour of David C. Fowler*, ed. Miceal Vaughan (East Lansing, Mich.: Colleagues Press, 1993), 191–210.

Introduction

1. Annabel Patterson, *Censorship and Interpretation: The Conditions of Writing and Reading in Early Modern England* (Madison: University of Wisconsin Press, 1984), 74.
2. The manuscript can be conveniently consulted in Derek Pearsall and Kathleen Scott, *Piers Plowman: A Facsimile of Bodleian Library, Oxford, MS Douce 104* (Cambridge: Brewer,

Notes to Introduction

1992). Kathleen Scott's catalog was initially published in *Yearbook of Langland Studies* 4 (1990): 1–86.

3. There are two other manuscripts of *Piers* that have each a single illustration related to the poem: Oxford, Corpus Christi College, MS 201 (a historiated initial of the dreamer on fol. 1r), and Cambridge, Trinity College, MS R.3.14 (a picture of a plowman and team at work, added on the blank front leaf); see Scott, in *Facsimile*, xxvii (also for a listing of the other manuscripts that contain illustrations unrelated to the poem itself).

4. The division of labor in the monastic scriptorium or commercial bookshop has always intrigued scholars in pursuit of physical evidence of manuscript production, but it is finally beginning to interest other scholars more generally, especially those interested in cultural literacies. For recent applications of codicology to the study of medieval readership and reception, see L. L. Brownrigg, ed., *Medieval Book Production: Assessing the Evidence* (Oxford: Anderson-Lovelace, 1991); Kevin Brownlee and Sylvia Huot, *Rethinking the Romance of the Rose: Text, Image, Reception* (Philadelphia: University of Pennsylvania Press, 1992); Sylvia Huot, The Romance of the Rose *and Its Medieval Reader* (Cambridge: Cambridge University Press, 1993); and Sandra Hindman, *Sealed in Parchment: Rereadings of Knighthood in the Illuminated Manuscripts of Chrétien de Troyes* (Chicago: University of Chicago Press, 1994).

5. On women illustrators and/or scribes, see J. J. G. Alexander, *Medieval Illuminators and Their Methods of Work* (New Haven, Conn.: Yale University Press, 1992), 18–21, 120; see also Huot, *Medieval Reader*, 321–22. Our reasons for believing the Douce scribe-illustrator and the annotator-corrector both to be male are discussed in chapter 4.

6. The study of medieval reader response has been often cavalierly neglected by critics who too often assume that they know how medieval readers thought; see the notable instance of counterblast to this kind of presumption in Peter Dronke, *Abelard and Heloise in Medieval Testimonies* (Glasgow: University of Glasgow Press, 1976). There have been several excellent reception studies in the area of medieval book illustration: in addition to Brownrigg, Brownlee and Huot, and Hindman, see P. Brieger, "Pictorial Commentaries to the *Commedia*," in Brieger, M. Meiss, and C. S. Singleton, *Illuminated Manuscripts of the Divine Comedy*, vol. 1 (Princeton, N. J.: Princeton University Press, 1969), 81–113.

7. On instructions to illustrators, see J. J. G. Alexander, "Programmes and Instructions for Illuminators," in *Medieval Illuminators*, 52–72; Lucy Freeman Sandler, "Notes for the Illuminator: The Case of the *Omne bonum*," *Art Bulletin* 71 (1989): 551–64; and Sandra Hindman, *Christine de Pizan's "Epistre Othea": Painting and Politics at the Court of Charles VI* (Toronto: Pontifical Institute for Mediaeval Studies [PIMS], 1986), 63–68.

8. There are also tensions evident between (we believe) the same two men in their different roles as scribe(-illustrator) and corrector(-annotator). We also discuss the possibility that the patron was involved in selecting the pictures and in deciding that some were to be left unfinished. For discussion of the possibility that the Douce scribe-illustrator may have had an assistant, apparently the rubricator (and for alternative explanations for certain distinctive styles apparent throughout the manuscript), see chapter 4.

9. On the role of correctors, see chapter 3; see also appendix 1.

10. On the habits of "correction" in Douce (often changes made to make the text readable by a Hiberno-English audience), see Pearsall's examples in the *Facsimile*, xxi; and see appendix 2 in this volume.

11. On the concept of social authorship, see Jerome McGann, *A Critique of Modern Textual Criticism* (Chicago: University of Chicago Press, 1983), 8.

12. Rosemary Woolf, "Some Non-Medieval Qualities of *Piers Plowman*," *Essays in Criticism* 12 (1962): 115.

13. Our count includes one more than Scott's, which for some reason lacks the unfinished drawing apparently representing Abraham on 85r (it may be faintly observed in the top right-hand corner of the folio, even in the facsimile). For a discussion about why this figure may have been unfinished, see chapter 1.

Notes to Introduction

14. Woolf, "Non-Medieval Qualities," 117.

15. See Leslie Lawton, "The Illustration of Late Medieval Secular Texts, with Special Reference to Lydgate's *Troy Book*," in *Manuscripts and Readers in Fifteenth-Century England*, ed. Derek Pearsall (Cambridge: Brewer, 1981), 41–69.

16. *The Life of Samuel Johnson by James Boswell*, ed. Ernest Rhys (London: Dent, 1914), 427.

17. See Scott's appendix B, which is a table of decorative analysis for the whole manuscript, giving statistics of the number of illustrations per passus (Pearsall and Scott, *Facsimile*, lxxxv).

18. See, for example, fol. 44 (figure 18), where a shepherd-prelate sleeps in the left margin, while a wolf attacks a sheep in the lower margin; or fol. 103, where Piers Plowman's team of four oxen is suggested by clever use of perspective in a space only large enough to draw one ox fully.

19. Mary Carruthers, *The Book of Memory: A Study of Memory in Medieval Culture* (Cambridge: Cambridge University Press, 1990), 228–29.

20. Elizabeth Salter, "*Piers Plowman* and the Visual Arts," in her *English and International: Studies in the Literature, Art, and Patronage of Medieval England* (Cambridge: Cambridge University Press, 1988), 256–66; see esp. plates 4, 5, 6. (This essay was originally published in *Encounters: Essays on Literature and the Visual Arts*, ed. John Dixon Hunt [London, 1971], 11–27.) Douce shares certain iconography with MS Add. 37049, as we will see, but it does not share these allegorical images, which is quite striking because clearly Langland himself, as Salter demonstrates, was quite aware of them.

21. In the poem, Liar appears with the charter and Simony reads it aloud (II.69–71), but in Douce Liar is depicted with a speaking gesture, brandishing the charter. The Douce artist's penchant for portraying speakers with legal documents to be read aloud will be discussed in chapter 2. For the definition of speech-act, see *Language, Discourse, and Literature: An Introductory Reader in Discourse Stylistics*, ed. Ronald Carter and Paul Simpson (London: Unwin Hyman, 1989), 290. I am grateful to Gordon Fulton for his advice about speech-act theory.

22. See Paul Saenger, "Silent Reading: Its Impact on Late Medieval Script and Society," *Viator* 13 (1982); M. T. Clanchy, *From Memory to Written Record: England 1066–1307* (London: Edward Arnold, 1979), 230.

23. Our use of the word is different from, and should not be confused with, the (now outdated) use of it made by J. L. Austin (for which see Katie Wales, *A Dictionary of Stylistics* [London: Longman, 1989], 344–45).

24. Michael Camille, "Seeing and Reading: Some Visual Implications of Medieval Literacy," *Art History* 8 (1985): 43. On the Ellesmere manuscript in relation to Douce 104, see Pearsall, "Manuscript Illustration."

25. See Pearsall and Scott, *Facsimile*, xxxii–xxxiii. For the concept of *ordinatio* (a term that describes the layout of a text and the way its internal divisions are marked), see M. B. Parkes, "The Influence of the Concepts of *Ordinatio* and *Compilatio* on the Development of the Book," in *Medieval Learning and Literature: Essays Presented to Richard William Hunt*, ed. J. J. G. Alexander and M. T. Gibson (Oxford: Clarendon, 1976), 115–41.

26. On an early tradition of *ordinatio* in C texts of *Piers Plowman*, see G. H. Russell, "Some Early Responses to the C-Version of *Piers Plowman*," *Viator* 15 (1984): 276.

27. The Douce rubrics do not use the term "Vita" (the scribe uses the word "visio" in rubrics for both parts of the poem; see Pearsall and Scott, *Facsimile*, xv), but we use it here in the traditional sense for convenience of reference.

28. On the technical skill of the illustrator, see Scott, in *Facsimile*, xxviii, and chapter 4 in this volume.

29. See Siegfried Wenzel, "The Pilgrimage of Life as a Late Medieval Genre," *Medieval Studies* 35 (1973): 378, on the emphasis in this kind of visionary literature on the progressive stages of the dreamer's life.

30. Ibid., 377. See also Susan K. Hagen, *Allegorical Remembrance: A Study of* The Pilgrimage of the Life of Man *as a Medieval Treatise on Seeing and Remembering* (Athens: University of Georgia Press, 1990).

31. See, for example, Derek Pearsall's note to the Prologue, line 128, in his edition of the C text.

32. On the Anglo-Irish origin and provenance, see Pearsall's discussion in Pearsall and Scott, *Facsimile,* xii–xvi.

33. The satirical character of Anglo-Irish literature is often discussed, but not in association with the reformist thrust of FitzRalphian thought; there is a small amount of evidence of Lollard sympathy in the colony. This study is, to our knowledge, the first to make these connections, which have been made possible partly by having *LALME* as a resource for listing the "canon" of extant manuscripts in the Hiberno-English dialect (Angus McIntosh, *A Linguistic Atlas of Late Mediaeval English* [Aberdeen: Aberdeen University Press, 1986]). I am grateful to Jeremy Smith for his advice about dialectal matters.

34. On poverty issues, as well as other social and ecclesiastical issues discussed in this paragraph, see chapter 2.

35. Passus I, line 10, in the edition by Helen Barr, *The Piers Plowman Tradition* (London: Dent, 1993), 101. Richard, in a letter written from Ireland in 1395, had distinguished three types of inhabitants: "sont trois maners des gentz cestassavoir Irrois Sauages nos enemis Irrois rebelx et engleis obeissantz"; see John T. Gilbert, *Facsimiles of the National Manuscripts of Ireland* (London: Longman, 1879), vol. 3, plate 22 and transcription.

36. Steven Justice, *Writing and Rebellion: England in 1381* (Berkeley: University of California Press, 1994), esp. chap. 3, "*Piers Plowman* in the Rising."

37. For the authoritative formulation of this view, see Anne Hudson, *The Premature Reformation* (Oxford: Clarendon Press, 1988), 408.

38. See Justice, *Writing and Rebellion,* 231–51; and Kathryn Kerby-Fulton, "Langland and the Bibliographic Ego," in Justice and Kerby-Fulton, *Written Work: Langland, Labor, and Authorship* (Philadelphia: University of Pennsylvania Press, 1997).

39. See Anne Hudson, "A Neglected Wycliffite Text," in *Lollards and Their Books* (London: Hambledon, 1985), 43–67 (originally published in *Journal of Ecclesiastical History* 29 [1978]: 257–79). On the dangers associated with vernacular reading more generally in the period up to and following 1409, see Nicholas Watson, "Censorship and Cultural Change in Late Medieval England: Vernacular Theology, the Oxford Translation Debate, and Arundel's Constitutions of 1409," *Speculum* 70 (1995): 822–64.

40. A. I. Doyle, "Remarks on Surviving Manuscripts of *Piers Plowman,*" in *Medieval English Religious and Ethical Literature: Essays in Honour of G. H. Russell,* ed. G. Kratzmann and J. Simpson (Cambridge: Brewer, 1986), 47–48.

41. Anne Hudson, "Lollardy: The English Heresy?" in *Lollards and Their Books,* 149.

42. See Stephen Nichols, "Introduction: Philology in a Manuscript Culture," *Speculum* 65 (1990): 7.

43. See Saenger, "Silent Reading," 399.

44. Paul Piehler, *The Visionary Landscape* (Montreal: McGill University Press, 1968), 9.

45. See, for instance, Carruthers, *Book of Memory,* 228–29.

46. See Pearsall and Scott, *Facsimile,* xxii. Douce is one of the smallest of *Piers* manuscripts, and its vellum is of poorer quality than most. On the various strategies for economy, see Scott's comments, xxx–xxxi, in ibid.

47. J. B. Allen, "Reading and Looking Things Up in Chaucer's England," *Chaucer Newsletter* 7, no. 1 (1985): 1–2.

48. The *Omne bonum* is now London, British Library, MS Royal 6.E.VI-VII (figures 64–67); for introductory discussion see chapter 1. On the Matthew Paris manuscripts, see chapter 2; on the Giraldian manuscripts (figures 45 and 50), see chapters 2 and 4. The role of both Giraldus and James le Palmer as scribe-illustrators requires some qualification. Giraldus is thought to have provided at least the initial sketches for his *Topographia hibernica,* but certainty about this is impossible as no autograph copy survives. However, the cycle

itself survives remarkably intact in several manuscripts, some very early, and gives evidence of a distinctive Giraldian tradition of illustration. The main illustrations in the *Omne bonum* were done by professional artists, not by James le Palmer himself, but James apparently planned the illustrations and provided a great deal of marginal caricature, both visual and verbal annotation (see figure 65) and directed the production of the whole book, although some of its formal illustrations were added after his death. See Lucy Freeman Sandler, "*Omne bonum: Compilatio* and *Ordinatio* in an English Illustrated Encyclopedia of the Fourteenth Century," in *Medieval Book Production*, ed. Brownrigg. See also Sandler, *Omne Bonum: A Fourteenth-Century Encyclopedia of Universal Knowledge*, 2 vols. (London: Harvey Miller, 1996).

49. Richard Vaughan, *Matthew Paris* (Cambridge: Cambridge University Press, 1958), 18.

50. Archives of the Municipal Corporation of Waterford, Ireland; see Cosgrove, *Medieval Ireland*, figs. 26a and b. Unfortunately, we were unable to reproduce those here.

51. On Langland's extensive knowledge of legal terminology, see John Alford, *Piers Plowman: A Glossary of Legal Diction* (Cambridge: Brewer, 1988).

52. On scribe-illustrated manuscripts generally, see Alexander, *Medieval Illuminators*, 6–30, 212 (for a list of illustrators, among whom many were also scribes); see also his "Scribes as Artists: The Arabesque Initial in Twelfth-Century English Manuscripts," in *Medieval Scribes, Manuscripts, and Libraries: Essays Presented to N. R. Ker*, ed. M. B. Parkes and A. G. Watson (London: Scolar, 1978), 87–116.

53. See Lawton, "Secular Texts," and Pearsall, "Manuscript Illustration."

54. This is true also of scribe-author produced manuscripts; see the discussion of John Capgrave's annotating habits in chapter 3. Denise Despres's study, "Douce 104 and the Profile of the Scribe-Illustrator," is forthcoming in *Studies in Iconography*.

55. See, for instance, fol. 44 (figure 18), where the bishop sleeps at a peculiar angle while, in the *bas de page*, a foreshortened wolf holds a sheep by the throat. In Matthew Paris's *Chronica majora*, pictorial position is equally dynamic (see Suzanne Lewis, *The Art of Matthew Paris in the* Chronica majora [Berkeley: University of California Press, 1987], 40), and in the *Omne bonum* as well, Lucy Freeman Sandler has argued for text-image relations "controlled and adjusted by the scribe-compiler" ("*Omne bonum: Compilatio*," 184).

56. Christopher de Hamel, *Scribes and Illuminators* (London: British Library, 1992), 48.

57. See, for instance, fols. 52v (figure 24) and 53 (figure 25), where images of the dreamer, Fortune, and Recklessness appear in rapid succession, mirroring the rapid and disjunctive motion of the narrative. Similarly, Sandler notes that James le Palmer "responded to the immediacy of the demand of a text as it was being copied" (192), and Lewis notes that Matthew Paris deviated from the traditionally disjunctive patterns of the annalistic chronicle by attempting to provide "a set of ideas that bind events and figures otherwise widely separated in space and time into interrelated clusters of actions and images" (*Art of Matthew Paris*, 92).

58. Compare, for instance, the image of Conscience (fol. 15; figure 4) with the image of Reason (fol. 19); see chapter 4 for further discussion.

59. At least, no other illustrated manuscript is known to have existed, although we cannot rule out the possibility, of course.

60. Take, for instance, his decision to illustrate Tom Stowe (figure 6) as the sole pictorial representative of passus V, where he could most easily have placed the ubiquitous pattern-book image of a bishop preaching.

61. See chapters 1 and 2; see Sandler, "*Omne bonum: Compilatio*," 189, and Lewis, *Art of Matthew Paris*, fig. 12, p. 34, for instances and discussion of James le Palmer and Matthew Paris, respectively, drawing upon legal book illustration.

62. Matthew Paris's work abounds in such images (e.g., Lewis, *Art of Matthew Paris*, figs. 107, 109, 110); Robert Grosseteste also indexed his books with symbols, including busts; see R. W. Hunt, "Manuscripts Containing the Indexing Symbols of Robert Grosseteste," *Bodleian Library Record* 4 (1953): 241–55; see 251 n. 2 for an instance of a bust, a

figure of Plato. In Douce see the images of Liar with the marriage charter (fol. 9) and the priest with the pardon (figure 19).

63. For examples see chapter 1.

64. I am grateful to Professor Malcolm Parkes for his advice about this and other matters.

65. For a discussion of this problem of "faithful illustration," see Richard Emmerson, "Text and Image in the Ellesmere Portraits of the Taletellers," in *The Ellesmere Chaucer: Essays in Interpretation*, ed. Martin Stevens and Daniel Woodward (San Marino, Calif.: Huntington Library, 1995), 143–70, which nevertheless includes an appendix listing "Textual details pictured" and "Textual details not pictured"—an approach we have deliberately chosen not to take in this study.

66. Cited from *Piers Plowman: The B Version*, ed. George Kane and E. Talbot Donaldson (London: Athlone, 1988).

1. Visual Literacy and the Iconography of Reformist Polemics

1. See also Kathryn Kerby-Fulton and Steven Justice, "Reformist Impulses in English and Irish Bureaucratic Culture: The *Modus tenendi parliamentum* and Its Literary Relations," forthcoming in *Traditio*, 1998.

2. The term "ecclesiological" is used in this study in the usual sense of a philosophy or doctrine of ecclesiastical manner of life and organization (as such it is more specialized than the adjective "ecclesiastical"); see Gordon Leff, "The Apostolic Ideal in Later Medieval Ecclesiology," *Journal of Theological Studies*, n.s., 18 (1967): 52–82. Kathleen Walsh notes that it is "a striking feature—unfortunately given little consideration by historians—that in the period between the mid–fourteenth and mid–fifteenth centuries four of the most notable opponents of the friars in England, and indeed in northern Europe, were Oxford-educated Anglo-Irishmen: FitzRalph, the Cistercian Henry Crumpe, the opponent of Lollardy, John Whitehead,...and the Dean of St. Patrick's Cathedral in Dublin, Philip Norreys. This concentration of mendicant opposition among the sons of Anglo-Irish colonists was scarcely pure coincidence." Walsh discusses the "elements peculiar to the nature of Anglo-Irish society" that brought this about; Walsh, *A Fourteenth-Century Scholar and Primate: Richard FitzRalph in Oxford, Avignon, and Armagh* (Oxford: Clarendon, 1981), 360.

3. Alan Bliss and Joseph Long, "Literature in Norman French and English to 1534," in *Medieval Ireland*, ed. Cosgrove, 708–36, quote at 709. Immigration to the colony was initially from the South West Midlands, a pattern that later shifted to the North West Midlands; I would like to thank Alan Fletcher for his advice about this.

4. See chapter 2; see also George Kane, *Piers Plowman: The Evidence for Authorship* (London: Athlone Press, 1965), 26, for the Despenser collection.

5. On James Butler, the fourth earl of Ormond, and his literary patronage, see Bliss and Long, "Literature," 735; see also Kathryn Kerby-Fulton and Steven Justice, "Langlandian Reading Circles in London and Dublin, 1380-1427," *New Medieval Literatures* 1 (1997): 51–83; and Kathleen Scott, "An English Illuminating Shop and Its Customers," *Journal of the Warburg and Courtauld Institutes* 31 (1968): 178–79; on the Butlers as luxury manuscript owners more generally, 179–81.

6. See Walsh, *Scholar and Primate*, on FitzRalph and ethnic tensions.

7. See McIntosh, *LALME*, 1:270, description of Dublin, Public Record Office of Ireland, Parliament Roll of 1429: "It is unclear how far the language is MHE. The Irish chancery was staffed mainly from England."

8. Not an anachronistic concept amid the interethnic tensions of medieval Ireland, on which see Walsh, *Scholar and Primate*, 10.

9. See ibid., 330: "Despite the reform movement of the twelfth century...the strongly hereditary character of the [Irish] clerical profession, whereby the clergy entered marriages which were clearly invalid under canon law, but valid in Gaelic law, then sought the nec-

essary dispensation ... and subsequently for their sons also in spite of their illegitimacy to succeed them in these benefices."

10. This is suggested, among other things, by the popularity of Giraldus's works.

11. A fuller picture, containing more of the text, is reproduced in Lucy Freeman Sandler, *Gothic Manuscripts, 1285–1385: A Survey of Manuscripts Illuminated in the British Isles*, vol. 5 (Oxford, 1986), 140, plate 333; the full shelf mark is Hatfield House, Herts., Marquess of Salisbury, MS Cecil Papers 290.

12. L. E. Boyle, "The *Oculus sacerdotis* and Some Other Works of William of Pagula," *Transactions of the Royal Historical Society*, 5th series, 5 (1955): 81–110. There is no printed edition of the *Oculus*; the Hatfield MS is cited here because it has the pictorial cycle. For a list of the manuscripts, see ibid.

13. On Langland's intellectual and ecclesiological affinities with the secular clergy, see Kathryn Kerby-Fulton, *Reformist Apocalypticism and Piers Plowman* (Cambridge: Cambridge University Press, 1990), 135ff.

14. Boyle, "*Oculus sacerdotis*," 86.

15. Ibid., 106.

16. Quotations from the *Oculus* itself are transcribed from the Hatfield MS.

17. See the third of Arundel's *Constitutiones*, ed. David Wilkins, *Concilia Magnae Britanniae et Hiberniae* (London: Gosling, 1737), 3:316: "Quod praedicator conformet se auditorio, aliter puniatur." For a discussion of these in relation to Langland, see James Simpson, "The Constraints of Satire in *Piers Plowman* and *Mum and the Sothsegger*," in *Langland, the Mystics, and the Medieval English Religious Tradition: Essays in Honour of S. S. Hussey*, ed. Helen Phillips (Cambridge: Brewer, 1990), esp. 15–19; and on earlier policies, see Watson, "Censorship," and H. Leith Spencer, *English Preaching in the Later Middle Ages* (Oxford: Clarendon, 1993), 175. I would like to thank Alan Fletcher for advice on this and for referring me to William Lyndwood's *Provinciale* (Oxford, 1679), 295, col. a, citing Hostiensis as the source of this idea.

18. For instance, London, Burlington House, Society of Antiquaries, MS 687, which contains a list of ecclesiastical censures (in English) and other items of interest to a parish priest, or San Marino, Huntington Library, MS 128, which contains material useful to a priest. Three of the four extant wills naming *Piers Plowman* were made by members of the secular clergy (two rectors and a canon): see Ralph Hanna III, *William Langland* (Aldershot, Eng.: Variorum, 1993), 35. On Langland's use of pastoral manuals as sources, see Anne Wenley Quick, "The Sources of the Quotations in *Piers Plowman*" (Ph.D. diss., University of Toronto, 1982).

19. Quick, "Sources," 21.

20. In Hatfield in particular these include the Pseudo-Bernardian *Meditationes*, Honorius of Autun's *Elucidarium*, the *Vision of Tundale*, Thomas Chabham's *De penitencia*, and Augustine's *De cognitione vere vite* (Sandler, *Gothic Manuscripts*, 140). The *Elucidarium*, for instance, was a popular synthesis in the form of a master-student dialogue on Christology (book 1); the Church, including priestly conduct (book 2); and the Last Things (book 3). Although not illustrated in Hatfield, another copy of it, in the scribe-illustrated Lincoln 218, contains a number of iconographic parallels to Douce.

21. See Kerby-Fulton and Justice, "Langlandian Reading Circles."

22. This is evident, among other things, from the legislation. Alexander notes that the Statutes of the Guild of text writers of York, entered in the city archives in 1377, show that "the Company wished to prevent lower ecclesiastics from exercising any of the crafts of writing or illumination, and from taking pupils"; Alexander, *Medieval Illuminators*, 31.

23. See Pearsall and Scott, *Facsimile*, lxxvii.

24. Compare the portrayal of Antichrist in part 1 of Lincoln 218, which is a collection of Latin devotional works and advice containing prayers, Honorius Augustudunensis's *Elucidarium* (in which the Antichrist portrait occurs at 33r, supported by devils), a collection of *sententiae* from the fathers, and the Pseudo-Bernardian *Meditationes*. Three

Notes to Chapter 1

portraits of Antichrist occur in succession in BL, Add. 37049, fols. 16r–v, all grimly tyrannical and violent; see the facsimile edition, James Hogg, *An Illustrated Yorkshire Carthusian Religious Miscellany: B.L. Additional MS 37049*, vol. 3, *The Illustrations* (Salzburg: Analecta Cartusiana, 1981). In the later Middle Ages Antichrist could be associated with one of two traditions: a more conventional Adsonian eschatological tradition in which Antichrist had a sensationalized and legendary vita, or a newer, Continental tradition of clerical polemics, antimendicantism, and reformist prophecy — a more intellectual and specialized field of discourse. The *Omne bonum* illustrations, closest to Douce's in showing Antichrist unsensationally and nonviolently as an ordinary man, nevertheless portray him and his two followers with oval-shaped distinguishing marks on their foreheads (Royal 6.E.VI, fols.100v, 102, and 103). For a full description of Lincoln 218, see R. M. Thomson, *Catalogue of the Manuscripts of Lincoln Cathedral* (Cambridge: Brewer, 1989), no. 218, p. 179. For a brief overview of Antichrist iconography, see Richard Emmerson, *Antichrist in the Middle Ages* (Manchester: Manchester University Press, 1981), 126–45; for the polemical eschatology, see Kathryn Kerby-Fulton, *Reformist Apocalypticism and Piers Plowman* (Cambridge: Cambridge University Press, 1990).

25. See Penn Szittya, *The Antifraternal Tradition in Medieval Literature* (Princeton, N.J.: Princeton University Press, 1986), 67–80, and his appendixes A and B.

26. The article is on papal authority; for a discussion of *declamatio* and the complexities of its use in Douce, see chapter 4.

27. The *Omne bonum* contains as a result some unusual subjects for illustration: the visions of Saint Benedict and Saint Paul, followed by an explanation of contemplative vision. For plates, see Sandler, *Gothic Manuscripts*, fig. 325.

28. On Langland's knowledge of legal matters, see Alford, *Piers Plowman: A Glossary of Legal Diction* (see introduction n. 51), and on Langland's relation to this group of legal scribes and civil servants, see Kerby-Fulton, "Langland and the Bibliographic Ego," and Kerby-Fulton and Justice, "Reading Circles."

29. Sandler, "Omne bonum: Compilatio," 188–89, and Sandler, *Omne Bonum*, 1:23–25.

30. The *signa* in Exchequer memoranda are further discussed in chapter 2. For the quotation, see Hubert Hall, *The Antiquities and Curiosities of the Exchequer* (London: Elliott Stock, 1898), 55 and 221. The image of the bishop in figure 69, no. 7, in fact designates Archbishop Pecham's Constitutions, attacking clerical abuses such as pluralism. H. F. McClintock thought that the drawing represented Thomas à Becket's martyrdom, which would make it grimly satirical; see McClintock, *Old Irish and Highland Dress* (Dundalk: Dundalgan Press, 1943), 19.

31. See Hubert Hall, ed., *The Red Book of the Exchequer*, R.S. 99 (London: HMSO, 1896), pt. 1, the calendar of contents, lxv–cxlviii; for further ecclesiastically related *signa*, see Hall, *Antiquities*, 55–75; for a modern survey of the kinds of documents handled by the Exchequer, see *Guide to the Contents of the Public Record Office*, vol. 1, *Legal Records* (London: HMSO, 1963), 45–113; 45 for the distinction of the two main functions of the Court of Exchequer.

32. Matthew Paris made copies from the *Red Book*; see Vaughan, *Matthew Paris*, 17–18.

33. J. T. Gilbert, ed., *Historic and Municipal Documents of Ireland, 1172–1320* (London: HMSO, 1870), xxii, xxiii; Gilbert, of course, was able to see the manuscript before it was destroyed.

34. R. Dudley Edwards, "Magna carta hiberniae," in *Essays and Studies Presented to Prof. Eoin MacNeill* (Dublin: Three Candles, 1940), 314–15.

35. Passus V.1–104; see Kerby-Fulton, "Bibliographic Ego."

36. Sandler, *Omne Bonum*, 1:23.

37. Quotations from the *Omne bonum* are cited from the manuscript itself, unless specifically noted otherwise.

38. One finds in the *Omne bonum*, for instance, illustrations for Ecclesia, Grace, the Pentecost, Mary, Christ, all the various offices and orders of the clergy — many of these

figure in Langland's poem, but none are illustrated by the Douce artist. See Sandler, *Omne Bonum*, vol. 2, for a complete list of subjects.

39. See the discussion in chapter 2 of the colophon he composed.

40. Alexander, *Medieval Illuminators*, 30–31.

41. On Langland's sense of belonging in the clerkly world, see Kathryn Kerby-Fulton, "Piers Plowman," in *Cambridge History of Medieval English Literature*, ed. David Wallace (Cambridge: Cambridge University Press, 1998).

42. For instances of lively caricature, see figure 69, no. 8, of the abbot of Peterborough; no. 14, of John, earl of Holland, Richard II's half-brother; and no. 15, Alice Perrers.

43. There is a symbolic image of the Trinity on fol. 88 (the hand and orb), but nothing like the more common "familial" image of the Trinity that Wyclif explicitly attacked in *De mandatis divinis*; for a reproduction and discussion, see Margret Aston, *Lollards and Reformers: Images and Literacy in Late Medieval Religion* (London: Hambledon, 1984) 99–100. The image on fol. 52v is not Saint Augustine (as Scott suggests); see note 58 below.

44. This point is worth stressing because, as Malcolm Parkes has suggested (in conversation), it can be dangerous to assume that medieval readers had the kind of extensive experience of *book* illustration that we readily assume today; an illustrated book may have been a rare thing in the experience of many, especially clerical readers, who, it was often assumed, needed no such aids. (Kathleen Scott suggests that roughly one in forty extant medieval books are illustrated; see her "Design, Decoration, and Illustration," in *Book Production and Publishing in Britain, 1375–1475*, ed. J. Griffiths and D. Pearsall [Cambridge: Cambridge University Press, 1989], 40.) One must therefore take the full range of visual art into account because even though, by the early fifteenth century, illustration of vernacular texts was on the rise, it is unlikely that many readers of *Piers Plowman* experienced the poem in an illustrated form (although some of the extant manuscripts of the poem do contain other illustrated works, and the poem itself refers to or assumes knowledge of a rich visual tradition found in other media besides books, and both the artist and the client who commissioned the Douce were clearly aware of this). I would like to thank Malcolm Parkes for his helpful epistolary and conversational advice.

45. On the beginnings of the Gregorian Reform movement generally, see, for instance, Uta-Renate Blumenthal, *The Investiture Controversy* (Philadelphia: University of Pennsylvania Press, 1988), 89–92; on Saint Bernard's austere attitudes toward the visual arts, see Ernst Kitzinger, "The Arts as Aspects of a Renaissance: Rome and Italy," in *Renaissance and Renewal in the Twelfth Century*, ed. Robert L. Benson and Giles Constable (Cambridge: Harvard University Press, 1982), 648; on the sources of Wyclif's iconomachia, see Aston, *Lollards and Reformers*.

46. We are grateful to Lawrence Clopper for making us aware of this; see his forthcoming book, *Wille Longland's Songs of Rechelesnesse*.

47. The word "patron" is used here in the singular for the sake of convenience, but it should be remembered that, as Christianson points out, many commissions were made by groups (religious communities, guilds, and the like), and the fact of a Latin colophon in the manuscript may suggest that it was made for (or even in) some such group (see Paul Christianson's "Evidence for the Study of London's Late Medieval Manuscript-Book Trade" in *Book Production and Publishing in Britain*, ed. Griffiths and Pearsall, 87–108; and for the colophon, see Pearsall, in *Facsimile*, ix, but see also the discussion in chapter 2 in this volume on the form of the colophon and its associations with documentary dating). Even if the manuscript were commissioned by a group, however, one would assume a single representative in charge of carrying out the commission, consulting with the illustrator, and so on, just as an individual patron would.

48. Alexander, *Medieval Illuminators*, 53, and, on patron visits to the workshop and for discussion of illustrations of such visits taking place, 32.

49. On the unfinished devil and Castle of Care illustration (fol. 5), see Scott, in *Facsimile*, xxxix. Interestingly, had this been finished it would have been one of the most

complex illustrations in the manuscript—the artist simplified his style of composition after this was drafted. On the unfinished Abraham, see n. 58 below; on the unfinished knight, see chapter 2.

50. See Kerby-Fulton, *Reformist Apocalypticism*, 35.

51. See, for instance, figure 18 or figure 12 (which appears across the page from Hunger, fol. 38).

52. See the example from the Cambridge *Topographia hibernica* of Giraldus, Cambridge, University Library, Ff. 1.27, p. 318, and Add. 37049, fol. 33.

53. Both of these are common subjects in legal book illustration, and this may explain his interest; see chapter 2.

54. Scott suggested that the figure on fol. 48v is Cain, but he has none of the iconographic attributes of Cain.

55. Scott does not mention this figure; our reason for thinking that this may have been intended as Abraham is that the locks of his hair are quite obviously shaped like leaves, which was likely intended as a visual (mnemonic) pun on the reference to Abraham as being "As hore [gray] as a haue-þrone [hawthorn tree]: and abraham he heʒte" (fol. 85; cf. Pearsall, *C-Text*, XVIII.183). The figure is placed exactly so that the eyes look at this line; the outlines of a forked beard may still be seen, such as the Douce artist uses for authoritative figures (compare Conscience, figure 4, and the king, figure 5, for beard and facial type).

56. On Lollard ideas about images, see Aston, *Lollards and Reformers*; the *Fasciculi Zizaniorum*, ed. W. W. Shirley (London: Longman, 1858), 368 (hereafter cited as *FZ*); and "Images and Pilgrimages," in *Selections from English Wycliffite Writings*, ed. Anne Hudson (Cambridge: Cambridge University Press, 1978), 83–88.

57. See J. J. G. Alexander, "William Abell 'lymnour' and Fifteenth Century English Illumination," in *Kunsthistorische Forschungen Otto Pacht zu seinem Geburtstag*, ed. Artur Rosenauer and Gerold Weber (Salzburg: Prestel, 1972), 166–72 (which reproduces the portrait he identified as Cok in fig. 3); his extant "portfolio" is listed on pp. 167–68.

58. We do not believe that the figure on fol. 52v is Augustine, because he has none of the attributes or authority of standard iconography of the saint (it would be unusual, unless the context specifically called for it, to portray Augustine as so boyish, in any case). Scott, too, seems doubtful about her identification (Pearsall and Scott, *Facsimile*, lxii).

59. On Langland's use of these sources, see Quick, "Sources."

60. See, for instance, Lillian Randall, *Images in the Margins of Gothic Manuscripts* (Berkeley: University of California Press, 1966), fig. 656, of MS Princeton University Library 44, fol. 116.

61. See Jean Leclercq, "'Ioculator et saltator': S. Bernard et l'image du jongleur dans les manuscrits," in *Translatio Studii: Manuscript and Library Studies Honouring L. Kapsner, O.S.B.* (Collegeville, Minn.: St. John's University Press, 1973), 124–28.

62. See Pearsall's notes to Prol. 35 and to IX.136 in his edition of *Piers*.

63. For exactly the same biblical iconography of a half-nude figure in Matthew Paris, see London, British Library, MS Cotton Nero D.I., fol. 156v; discussed in Lewis, *Art of Matthew Paris*, as figure 10, with other parallels.

64. As for instance in *The Plowman's Tale*, in *Six Ecclesiastical Satires*, ed. James Dean (Kalamazoo, Mich.: Medieval Institute Publications, 1991).

65. For an illuminating analysis of some of his animal images, see Maidie Hilmo, "Transcending Boundaries: Image and Text in the *Pearl* Manuscript, the Ellesmere Manuscript of the *Canterbury Tales*, and the Douce 104 *Piers Plowman*" (diss. in progress), and "Retributive Violence and the Reformist Agenda in the Illustrated Douce 104 Manuscript of *Piers Plowman*," *Fifteenth-Century Studies* 23 (1997): 21, plate 10.

66. R. E. Kaske, "*Piers Plowman* and Local Iconography," *Journal of the Warburg and Courtauld Institute* 31 (1968): 159–69.

67. See, for instance, the Norwich Cathedral misericords, cataloged in G. L. Remnant, *A Catalogue of Misericords in Great Britain* (Oxford: Clarendon, 1969), 108, nos. 18, 21.

Notes to Chapter 1

68. See chapter 4. I am grateful to Jeanne Coburn for the observation that the bells on Pride's garment indicate a minstrel's costume. Bells, according to Giraldus, *Topographia hibernica*, are particularly a fondness of the Irish, especially those which can be carried about (see chap. 108), and this may explain the Douce scribe-illustrator's peculiar textual and iconographical variant (figure 9) of having the pilgrim carry a bell.

69. See Pearsall's notes to these lines in his edition of *Piers*, and see Salter, "Visual Arts" (see introduction, n. 21).

70. See Aston, *Lollards and Reformers*, 99–100.

71. The gospel harmony in Bod. 978 is not Wychiffite in origin, but the manuscript itself definitely is; see Hudson, *Premature Reformation*, 267–68 n. 203.

72. Walsh, *Scholar and Primate*, 319–20; see *The Register of John Swayne, Archbishop of Armagh and Primate of Ireland, 1418–1439*, ed. David Chart (Belfast: HMSO, 1935), 11.

73. See Swayne's *Register*, 9.

74. Walsh, *Scholar and Primate*, 320, summarizing the passage in Swayne, for which see Swayne's *Register* (which actually associates these groups with the *kernarii* and those who extort gifts), 11; on the *kernarii*, who are relevant to Douce's portrait of Wastor, see chapter 4 in this volume. Alan Fletcher points out that the drummers in question were likely "timpanors" (to use the form of the word as it appears in the *Statutes of Kilkenny*, in *Statutes and Ordinances, and Acts of the Parliament of Ireland: King John to Henry V*, ed. Henry Berry [Dublin: HMSO, 1907], 446), and that FitzRalph's predecessor, O'Hiraghty, had also enacted similar prohibitions (see Walsh, *Scholar and Primate*, 320). It is worth noting how close Swayne's list of sanctioned forms of entertainment is to that of the *Statutes*.

75. "Statutum siue statuta dominorum predecessorum nostrorum Ricardi et dauid contra minos [*sic*, for *mimos*] ioculatores poetas timpanistas siue citharedas & precipue contra kernarios ac importunas [*sic*, for *importunos*?] & improbos donorum petitores quin uerius extortores editum vel edita per omnia renouamus"; Belfast, Public Record Office of Northern Ireland, D10 4/2/3 [fol. 151v] (unfoliated). I am deeply indebted to Alan Fletcher for transcribing and translating this passage, and for his illuminating comments upon it.

76. See Art Cosgrove, "The Emergence of the Pale, 1399–1447," in *A New History of Ireland*, ed. Cosgrove, 533–556.

77. Statute 15; the key part of the passage reads "cestascavoir Tympanors, fferdanes, skelagues, Bablers Rymors, clercz [for clarsaghours] ne nullez autres minstrells Irrois veignent entre les Engleis"; *Statutes of Kilkenny*, ed. Berry, 446. The mix of French, Irish, and English terms gives a sense of the linguistic richness and divisions in the colony. Compare the attempts at reform in Swayne's *Register* with this instance.

78. Statute 15 itself complains that the Irish minstrels "espient lez priuetz maners & Comyn des Englises"; Berry, *Statutes of Kilkenny*, 446; see Cosgrove, "Emergence of the Pale," 555, for Lancastrian legislation.

79. In a Westminster Statute of 1 Henry V, 1413 (Berry, 560).

80. See the comments on the antiminstrelsy prohibitions made by James Yonge in his 1422 MHE translation of the *Secreta*, discussed in chapter 4. Kilkenny was repromulgated in 1402.

81. Usually accompanying chapter 94 of the *Topographia*; on the illustrations in Giraldus's works, especially in Cambridge, University Library, MS Ff. 1.27; Dublin, National Library, MS 700; and London, British Library, MS Royal 13 B.VIII, see chapter 2.

82. For the sources in FitzRalph, see Walsh, *Scholar and Primate*, 330; see also Archbishop Swayne's *Register*, ed. Chart, 11, on clerical concubinage. Chapter 98 of the *Topographia* inveighs against fornication and incest among the Irish generally, a recurrent theme.

83. Justice, *Writing and Rebellion*, 104ff.

84. His attitude toward the bourgeois is interesting: while his portrayal of the sins associated with the middle class (Covetousness, fol. 27, and Envy, fol. 25) show a keen, although conventional, satire of mercantile culture, he has gone out of his way, most unusually, to depict a merchant as the sole figure highlighting Grace's speech on the different professions (fol. 102v). Given the marginal status (graphically realized in Truth's

pardon, IX.22) of merchants in the poem and in late medieval culture, this picture suggests, again, a pragmatically nonclerical attitude on the part of the illustrator, and the influence of legal iconography.

85. Walsh, *Scholar and Primate*, 5.

86. Ibid., 9–10. We might note that, outrageous as this seems, there were different legal punishments for killing an Irishman; see the discussion of the Statutes of Kilkenny on this matter in chapter 4 of this volume.

87. The cleric on fol. 47 (figure 21) who appears to represent Dobet preaching, might be a Dominican, but the color of the cloak looks distinctly brown, not black, and his garb may indicate no more than that he is a priest.

88. Scott makes this case (*Facsimile*, lvii, lxviii–lxix), although there is some doubt: it is more common (even in the Carmelite Missal, to which she refers, in *Facsimile*, lxviii) for Carmelites to be shown with a black robe underneath a white cope, but, in support of Scott's suggestion, one could cite Merton 319, on fols. 2 and 41v (figure 47), which does show, in an author portrait, the anti-Wycliffite Thomas Netter dressed entirely in white. For the Carmelite Missal, see Margaret Rickert, *The Reconstructed Carmelite Missal: An English Manuscript of the Late Fourteenth Century* (London: Faber and Faber, 1950).

89. Langland himself may have been satirizing Fr. William Jordan, a Dominican, in this scene (see Pearsall's note to XV.92 in his edition of *Piers*). If so, the Anglo-Irish artist, working some fifty years later, understandably missed the joke.

90. Maidie Hilmo, in "Transcending Boundaries," points out that its sheen is either silver or possibly "glare white" intended to look like silver. On need among friars, see M. W. Sheehan, "Franciscan Poverty in England, 1348–1538" (D.Phil. dissertation, Oxford, 1975), 328.

91. See Rickert, *Carmelite Missal*, p. 50, plate 6; J. P. H. Clark, "Late Fourteenth-Century Cambridge Theology," in *The Medieval Mystical Tradition*, Exeter Symposium, vol. 5, ed. Marion Glasscoe (Cambridge: Brewer, 1992), 1–16; on the indeterminate order of the cleric on fol. 47 (figure 21), see note 87 above.

92. See Sandler, "Notes for the Illuminator," 564.

93. On the poem, see *Piers Plowman: A Facsimile of the Z-text in Bodleian Library, Oxford, MS Bodley 851*, introduced by Charlotte Brewer and A. G. Rigg (Cambridge: Brewer, 1994), 37; for pictures of Dominicans confessing the rich, see Randall, *Images in the Margins*, 94; see also *The Catherine of Cleves Hours*, ed. John Plummer (New York: Braziller, 1966), fol. 107 (for an instance of a Carmelite); and London, British Library, MS Stowe 17, fol. 191 (reproduced in Randall, *Images in the Margins*, as fig. 112). I am grateful to Michèle Mulchahey for advice about the Dominican order generally.

94. Randall, *Images in the Margins*, fig. 112.

95. See Clopper, *Wille Longlond's Songs*, and Kerby-Fulton, *Reformist Apocalypticism*, 135–36.

96. Franciscans were closely associated with the development of Anglo-Irish literature, and that reading community must have been a fairly circumscribed one; see W. Heuser, *Die Kildare-gedichte* (Bonn: Bonner Beitrage zur Anglistik XIV, 1904); and, for a more recent discussion, see Michael Benskin, "The Hands of the Kildare Poems Manuscript," *Irish University Review* 20 (1990): 164.

97. For a list of Wyclif's agreements and disagreements (mainly philosophical) with FitzRalph, see Walsh, *Scholar and Primate*, 459.

98. See Walsh's epilogue, "Lollard Saint and the Cult of 'St. Richard of Dundalk,'" in *Scholar and Primate*, 452–68.

99. See *FZ*, 343–59; Hudson, *Premature Reformation*, 87; oddly, Crumpe had initially been a high-profile anti-Wycliffite, as a member of the Blackfriars' Council of 1382; a month later he was suspended from scholastic duties because he had called the heretics "Lollardos," a very early instance of the term (on which see Wendy Scase, *Piers Plowman and the New Anticlericalism* [Cambridge: Cambridge University Press, 1989], 154).

100. See *FZ*, 349ff, and Hudson, *Premature Reformation*, 88, 173.

Notes to Chapter 1

101. See *FZ*, 344–46.

102. Note the Franciscan contents beginning at (old foliation) fol. 71 ("Speculum prefectionis status fratrum minorum"), and note the different (but contemporary) hand, which has inserted these words between the antimendicant stanzas on fol. 62v: "Who so kepes þar reule al bone(?) in worde & dede / I am ful siker þat he shal haue heuen blis to mede." The poem is partially edited by Thomas Wright, *Political Poems and Songs*, Rolls Series (RS) (London, 1859–61), but see also Rossell Hope Robbins, *Historical Poems of the Fourteenth and Fifteenth Centuries* (New York: Columbia, 1959), no. 65. On the Latin poem, "Heu quanta desolatio," see Hudson, *Lollards and Their Books*, 7; George Rigg, *A History of Anglo-Latin Literature, 1066–1422* (Cambridge: Cambridge University Press, 1992), 281–82 (for its reference to "Pers," see 282); on all three poems, see Szittya, *Antifraternal Tradition*, 195–96. The Latin poem is also found in Oxford, Bodleian Library, MS Digby 98, and in a Hussite manuscript (Vienna 3929), but the two Hiberno-English poems are not found elsewhere, a factor that could suggest Irish origins, not simply Irish dissemination.

103. Szittya (*Antifraternal Traditions*) says that no such church is known in England, but, of course, the poem is likely Hiberno-English.

104. For an instance of such Franciscan-inspired tree imagery, see Karen Gould, *The Psalter and Hours of Yolande de Soissons* (Cambridge, Mass.: Mediaeval Academy of America, 1978), plate 37.

105. Bliss and Long suggest ("Literature," 734) that the Anglo-Irish origin of the Cotton Cleo. poems may be doubtful, but the quality of the devotion to FitzRalph (intimate and desperate) is distinctly Anglo-Irish in character, and different even from the pro-FitzRalphian attitudes of the English Wycliffites. See also Thorlac Turville-Petre, "The English in Ireland," in *England the Nation: Language, Literature, and Social Identity, 1290–1340* (Oxford: Clarendon, 1996), 155–75.

106. On Baxter, see Rita Copeland, "Why Women Can't Read: Medieval Hermeneutics, Statutory Law, and the Lollard Heresy Trials," in *Law, Literature and Feminism*, ed. S. Heinzeman and Z. Wiseman (Durham, N.C.: Duke University Press, 1994); and Steven Justice, "Inquisition, Speech and Writing: A Case from Late-Medieval Norwich," *Representations* (Fall 1994): 1–29.

107. On Langland's resounding silence in other controversial matters, see Justice, *Writing and Rebellion*, chap. 5.

108. *A Catalogue of the Harleian Manuscripts in the British Museum* (London: 1808), 1:474.

109. W. Heuser, *Die Kildare-gedichte* (Bonn: Bonner Beitrage zur Anglistik 14, 1904), 155.

110. "Seint Mari bastard, þe Maudelein is sone, / To be wel icloþid wel was þi wone! / Þou berrist a box on þi hond ipeintid al of gold, / Woned þou wer to be hend, ʒiue us sum of þi spices" (Heuser, *Kildare-gedichte*, 155). See also Angela Lucas, *Anglo-Irish Poems of the Middle Ages* (Dublin: Columbia Press, 1995), for this poem (pp. 59–65 and notes). There is just a suggestion here, perhaps, that even the saints bear some responsibility for ecclesiastical miserliness, a theme that Langland, too, comments on with some bitterness, but without implicating the saints (see I.186–92).

111. On the associations with Michael of Kildare, Franciscan, see Benskin, "Kildare Poems," 163–64, and Lucas, *Anglo-Irish Poems*, 18–19.

112. "Kites and crowis, reuenes and oules, / Fure and .XXti. wildges and a poucok!"; Heuser, *Kildare-gedichte*, stanza 5, p. 155.

113. See lines 102–218 of *Crede*, in *Six Ecclesiastical Satires*, ed. Dean.

114. An emphasis even more marked than the one that Scott has noted in late medieval English book illumination generally, see Scott, "Design," 47; for instances of the three characteristics identified here, see, respectively, Oxford, Bodleian Library, MS Bodley 277, fol. 302; Oxford, Bodleian Library, MS Bodley 978 (figures 40–42); Prague, Prague University Library, MS VIII.C.3 (1472), fol. 2 (reproduced in *Wyclif and His Followers: An Exhibition to Mark the 600th Anniversary of the Death of John Wyclif* [Oxford: Bodleian Library, 1985], cover illustration).

Notes to Chapter 2

115. Corpus 180, fol. 1r, is reproduced as a frontispiece to Walsh, *Scholar and Primate*; see also Bodley 277, fol. 302.
116. On the more usual use of roundels, see Scott, "Design," 42.
117. Reproduced and briefly described in *Wyclif and His Followers*, no. 89.
118. Reproduced from fol. 302 in *Wyclif and His Followers* as no. 89. We are grateful to Maidie Hilmo for her opinion on 277 and for allowing us to cite from her paper concerning the defaced devil in Douce; Hilmo, "The Illustrations of Mercy and the Devil in the Douce 104 MS of *Piers Plowman* and Traces of Audience Response," paper presented at the Medieval Association of the Pacific Conference, March 15, 1996.
119. It is important to stress perceptions here, because Lollard literature can be very socially conservative; see, e.g., *Crede*, lines 744–67, which echo the notorious passage in Langland's C.V apologia on the same theme. On the connections that contemporaries perceived between the preaching of John Ball and the Wycliffite movement, see *FZ*, 272–73, and Justice, *Writing and Rebellion*, chap. 2.
120. Fol. 39. He is wearing the most expensive colors in the manuscript and may have been wearing, as Hilmo has suggested, a large gold brooch to hold his cape, although only the brownish ground that would have been used to prepare the vellum for an application of gold leaf is now visible, the gold itself having flaked off (the same phenomenon is evident on fol. 1, where, in the demi-vinet border, the gold leaf is still visible on some dots, whereas on others it has worn away, leaving only the same brownish ground). See Hilmo, "Retributive Violence," note 37.

2. Visual Literacy and the Iconography of Social Dissent

1. See *LALME*, vol. 1, 277. The exemplar was apparently in a South West Midlands (SWM) dialect; see appendix 1. On the linguistic evidence, see Angus McIntosh and M. L. Samuels, "Prolegomena to a Study of Medieval Anglo-Irish," *Medium Aevum* 37 (1968): 1–11; on MHE and the surviving texts, see the extensive work of Michael Benskin, especially "Irish Adoptions in the English of Tipperary, ca. 1432," in *Words: For Robert Burchfield's Sixty-Fifth Birthday*, ed. E. G. Stanley and T. F. Hoad (Cambridge: Brewer, 1988), 37–67, and "The Style and Authorship of the Kildare Poems," ed. J. Lachlan Mackenzie and Richard Todd, *In Other Words: Transcultural Studies in Philology, Translation, and Lexicology Presented to Hans Heinrich Meier* (Dordrecht, Holland, and Providence, R.I.: Foris, 1989), 57–75. See also Angela Lucas, "Language," in *Anglo-Irish Poems of the Middle Ages* (Dublin: Columbia Press, 1995), 27–42.
2. On the regnal year, see Pearsall, in *Facsimile*, ix.
3. See Pearsall and Scott, *Facsimile*, ix n. 1, for the suggestions made by A. I. Doyle.
4. As does Pearsall, in *Facsimile*, i.
5. For some instances of correction, see Pearsall in *Facsimile*, xxi; and see appendix 1.
6. Compare the format of the colophon with those found throughout the *Rotuli parliamentorum*, III, for instance, the entry for 13 Ric.II, 1389, p. 257: "die Lune prox' post Festum S'c'i Hilarii, anno regni Regis Ricardi Secundi tertiodecimo"; or, for Ireland itself, see the similar colophons in *Statutes and Ordinances, and Acts of the Parliament of Ireland, King John to Henry V*, ed. Henry F. Berry (Dublin: Alexander Thom, 1907), for instance, p. 244 (for 1308); p. 478 (1380); or p. 514 (1402).
7. See Adelaide Bennett, "Anthony Bek's Copy of *Statuta Angliae*," in *England in the Fourteenth Century*, ed. W. M. Ormond (Woodbridge, Eng.: Boydell and Brewer, 1986), 1–27; Michael Camille, "At the Edge of the Law: An Illustrated Register of Writs in the Pierpont Morgan Library," in *England in the Fourteenth Century*, ed. Nicholas Rogers (Stamford, Conn.: Paul Watkins, 1993), 1–14. One can get a sense of the surprising frequency (though, unfortunately, not variety) of illustration in legal manuscripts by reading J. H. Baker, *English Legal Manuscripts in the United States of America: Part 1, Medieval and Renaissance* (London: Selden Society, 1985), one of the few catalogs of legal manuscripts that reliably mentions illustrations.

Notes to Chapter 2

8. See, for example, Kathleen Scott, "A Late Fifteenth-Century Group of *Nova statuta* Manuscripts," in *Manuscripts at Oxford: An Exhibition in Memory of R. W. Hunt*, ed. A. C. del la Mare and B. C. Barker-Benfield (Oxford: Bodleian Library, 1980), 103–5 and fig. 74; and Lynda Dennison, "An Illuminator of the Queen Mary Psalter Group," *Antiquaries Journal* 66 (1986): 287–314, and plates 45 and 55.

9. See C. W. Dutschke, *Guide to the Medieval and Renaissance Manuscripts in the Huntington Library* (San Marino, Calif.: Huntington Library, 1989), 622; for a similar instance of ostentatious authoritarianism, see San Marino, Huntington Library, MS HM 932, Statutes of the Archdeaconry of London made in 1447; Dutschke, *Guide*, 277–78 and fig. 16.

10. See Baker, *English Legal Manuscripts*, where nearly every illustrated collection of statutes contains the standard-issue miniature of a king (for instance, the early-fifteenth-century San Marino, Huntington Library, MS HM 19920, fol. 1 (fig. 82 in Dutschke, *Guide*); or Glasgow, Glasgow University Library, MS General 335, fol. 10, reproduced in Nigel Thorp, *The Glory of the Page* (London: Harvey Miller, 1987), catalog no. 26; see also Bennett, "Bek's Copy," 3, on the relatively simple iconography of most legal manuscripts, and n. 9 for a list of manuscripts with more complex programs, one of which is Anthony Bek's manuscript, now Princeton Library, Scheide MS 30; and M. A. Michael, "A Manuscript Wedding Gift from Phillipa of Hainault to Edward III," *Burlington Magazine* 127 (1985): 582–98, on Harvard Law MS 12.

11. J. J. G. Alexander, "An English Illuminator's Work in Some Fourteenth-Century Italian Law Books at Durham," in *Medieval Art and Architecture at Durham Cathedral* (Leeds: British Archaeological Association, 1980), 149–53, esp. 150.

12. For a reproduction of the drawing from BL, Royal 10.E.IV, see Dorothy Hartley and Margaret Elliott, *Life and Work of the People of England: The Fourteenth Century* (London: Batsford, 1928), plate 12a; for a reproduction of Harley 4605, see *Illustrated Letters of the Paston Family: Private Life in the Fifteenth Century*, ed. Roger Virgoe (New York: Weidenfeld and Nicholson, 1989), 126, from fol. 95. For other examples, see Camille, "At the Edge," 4–5.

13. See Alford, *Piers Plowman: A Glossary of Legal Diction*; Anna Baldwin, *The Theme of Government in Piers Plowman* (Cambridge: Brewer, 1981), 40–50; and Simpson, "Constraints on Satire"; for Langland's knowledge of canon law, see Quick, "Sources."

14. Cf. Douce's king (figure 5) and young bastard (figure 22); see Dutschke's description, *Guide*, 7–9, esp. 8; for the same phenomenon in the *Omne bonum*, see Sandler, "*Omne bonum*: *Compilatio* and *Ordinatio*" and accompanying plates.

15. For similar admonitions, see Sandler, *Omne Bonum*, 1:24.

16. Camille, "At the Edge of the Law," 7.

17. See chapter 4 for a detailed description of the Douce artist's methods, and *Facsimile*, xxviii–xxix, for Scott's (understandable) perplexities on the matter; for a good description of formal atelier procedures, see Robert Calkins, "Stages of Execution: Procedures of Illumination as Revealed in an Unfinished Book of Hours," *Gesta* 17, no. 1 (1978): 61–70.

18. Camille, "At the Edge," 13.

19. See Camille's discussion of the "cartoon" of the king in the Scheide Statutes, fol. 90 ("At the Edge," plate 3 and p. 7), and the satire "against the hawking and hunting nobility" in the Morgan Register, fol. 34 (plate 8 and pp. 9–11); see also Ruth Mellinkoff, "Riding Backwards," *Viator* 4 (1973): 171–72 and fig. 13, on Morgan as well.

20. Compare with Douce's priest, for instance, the iconography of the cleric (Abbot John Whethamstede) holding the charter in a sophisticated work like *The Golden Book of St. Albans*, in London, British Library, MS Cotton Nero D.VII, fol. 27; this was a benefactor's book, compiled by Thomas Walsingham, and illustrated by a layman, Alan Strayler; Whethamstede is portrayed without the speaking gestures that both the Douce priest and Liar have to accompany their charters. For a reproduction of Strayler's picture, see *The Benedictines and the Book* (London: British Library, 1980), no. 68 and cover; on *declamatio* and other speaking gestures, see chapter 4; on illustrations of the "remembered voices" in

Notes to Chapter 2

earlier benefactor's books, see Clanchy, *From Memory to Written Record*, plate 20 (see introduction, no. 22); for the charter in Morgan 812, see Camille, "At the Edge," 12 and fig. 12.

21. See, for instance, the Exchequer illustration of Edward I reproduced in Michael Prestwich, *The Three Edwards* (London: Weidenfeld, 1980), plates between pp. 176 and 177; the document is dated 1300, but for samples of similar Exchequer drawings ranging in date as late as the fifteenth century, see Hall, *Antiquities* (our figure 69); a more lavish version of the image appears in Princeton University Library, MS Scheide 30, fol. 30, reproduced in Bennett, "Bek's Copy," fig. 10.

22. McClintock, *Old Irish and Highland Dress*, 19, describing London's Public Record Office, T.R. Misc. Books 274, Liber A and Liber B, and Bishop Stapleton's Calendar, T.R. Misc. Books 268; for a plate of one of the three Irish figures, see McClintock's fig. 14, depicting a man in a horned hood and breeches wielding an axe ("Welsh, Scottish and Irish sections are denoted by drawings of figures which have generally been regarded as typical of each nation" [19]). For a further discussion of this type of classification, see Clanchy, *From Memory*, 172–77. For a photograph of one of these marginal images of a Scot, from a document concerning Anglo-Scottish relations (PRO, Liber A [E 36/274] f.38v), see E. L. G. Stones, "The Appeal to History in Anglo-Scottish Relations between 1291 and 1401," *Archives* 9 (1969–70): 11–21, plate across from 11; for further photographs of such *signa*, see Kerby-Fulton and Justice, "Bureaucratic Culture."

23. I am indebted to Josephine Matthews of the London Public Record Office for helping me trace this and other PRO images. The other images mentioned by McClintock can be found on fols. 40, 168v, and 188 respectively of PRO E 36/274. On Pecham's clash with Edward, see D. L. Douie, *Archbishop Pecham* (Oxford: Clarendon, 1952), 119. For further discussion of this pictogram, see Kerby-Fulton and Justice, "Bureaucratic Culture."

24. Bennett, "Bek's Copy," 3, on the iconography, and especially n. 9 for a lengthy list of illustrated *Statuta*.

25. At 21.5 by 15 cm, Douce is a very small *Piers* manuscript (see *Facsimile*, xii). For sample measurements, see Don C. Skemer, "From Archives to the Book Trade: Private Statute Rolls in England, 1285–1307," *Journal of the Society of Archivists* 16, no. 2 (1995): 193–206, esp. 198; Bennett, "Bek's Copy," 16; Clanchy, *From Memory*, plate 18 (see introduction n. 23); for Douce's pictorial affinities with legal rolls, especially the Waterford Roll, see chapter 1.

26. Bennett, "Bek's Copy," fig. 10; for the equivalent image in the memoranda rolls, see the plate in Prestwich, *Three Edwards*, 176–77.

27. Bennett, "Bek's Copy," 8 and fig. 12.

28. Michael, "Manuscript Wedding Gift," 598; Sandler, *Gothic Manuscripts*, 105 (for disagreement with Michael about its origins); see also Clanchy, *From Memory*, plate 18 and facing description.

29. E.g., the placement of the illustration for the statute "de homage et fauté" (fol. 33v); Michael, "Manuscript Wedding Gift," plate 13. We would like to thank Dorothy Africa, Harvard Law Library, for her advice about Harvard 12 and for her efforts on our behalf.

30. Among the several Harvard 12 miniatures in which money is the dominant pictorial theme are fol. 34, coins (Michael, plate 43, statute "de monae"); fol. 27, merchants trading (Michael, plate 39, statute "des marchants"); fol. 30v (our figure 52), four Exchequer clerks counting money (Michael, plate 40, "lestatutes delescheker"); and fol. 14, two men giving money to a third (Michael, plate 18, Statute of Gloucester). For modern editions of the texts of the statutes in question, see Michael, "Manuscript Wedding Gift" (Harvard 12 is in French, not Latin).

31. For these Douce images, see figure 34 and fols. 61, 78, 102v. Covetousness, fol. 27, is portrayed quite specifically as the epitome of corrupt trading practices that we see equitably handled in the rosier social images of Harvard 12.

32. Douce, fol. 18 (figure 5). For numerous instances of kings, see note 8 above. In Harvard 12, the artist dispensed with the usual authoritative image of a king for the Statute of Gloucester "by showing a transaction (concerning damages or costs)" instead (Michael,

Notes to Chapter 2

"Manuscript Wedding Gift," 598), striking evidence once again of this illustrator's interest in financial issues.

33. Quoted from Dutschke's transcription (*Guide*) of San Marino, Huntington Library, MS EL 34 B 23, fol. 107, "Sequitur Summa de Bastardia"; see also the same library's HM 923, fol. 104; both are fourteenth-century statute collections.

34. Douce, fol. 48v (figure 22); Harvard 12, fol. 33 (Michael, "Manuscript Wedding Gift," plate 41).

35. For the (Latin) text, see William Stubbs, *Select Charters*, rev. ed. by H. W. C. Davis (Oxford: Clarendon, 1942), 450–52.

36. See Lewis, *Art of Matthew Paris*, 51.

37. See, for instance, the crude and sporadic imitations of Matthew's drawings in the Huntington Library's copy of Matthew's *Chronica majora*, MS HM 30319; here the scribe is certainly the artist (the ink used for the text appears in the underdrawings, which have then been colored with rubrication ink). He makes an interesting attempt to closely align text and image: see, for instance, the bust of the king's head on fol. 11v, in which his crown brackets the climactic passage relating to the king; see also the crown on fol. 10v and the face of a monk (at a passage on Glastonbury Abbey) on fol. 91; for a detailed description of the manuscript, see Dutschke, *Guide*; in addition to the chronicles mentioned below, see also Cambridge, Corpus Christi College, MS 171, the fifteenth-century *Scotichronicon* of John Fordun, with its six tinted drawings (for a reproduction, see *Matthew Parker's Legacy* (Cambridge: Corpus Christi College, 1975), no. 32; and, for an earlier imitation of marginal drawing like Matthew's, see the *Annales Paulini*, in London, Lambeth Palace Library, MS 1106 (for a plate of the illustration on fol. 96v, see Antonia Gransden, *Historical Writing in England*, vol. 2 (Ithaca, N.Y.: Cornell University Press, 1982), plate 1).

38. On government clerks and chronicle authorship, see John Taylor, *English Historical Literature in the Fourteenth Century* (Oxford: Clarendon, 1987), 142; for an instance of shared iconography, compare the plate of the *Annales Paulini* in Gransden to the Exchequer image in Hall, *Antiquities*, fig. 16, p. 58.

39. For the lists of illustrations, see M. R. James, *A Descriptive Catalogue of the Manuscripts in the Library of Corpus Christi College, Cambridge* (Cambridge: Cambridge University Press, 1912), vol. 1, nos. 16, 26; see, for instance, MS 16, fol. 38, "Magna carta with seal"; fol. 39, "Charta de Foresta" (compare with the description of contents and illustrations in Princeton, Scheide 30, listed in Bennett, "Bek's Copy," or with any of the statute manuscripts cited above). For Matthew's use of material from the *Red Book*, see Vaughan, *Matthew Paris*, 18; for similarities between his drawings and those in legal manuscripts, see Lewis, *Art of Matthew Paris*, 195–96 and accompanying plates.

40. See Hilmo, "Retributive Violence." For Matthew's pillory, see Lewis, *Art of Matthew Paris*, fig. 33, of Cambridge, Corpus Christi College, MS 16, fol. 21v.

41. See F. Palgrave, *Ancient Kalenders* (London: HMSO, 1838), 1:xxvii.

42. Many *Piers* manuscripts also contain historical matter; see Anne Middleton's insightful comments in "Audience and Public of *Piers Plowman*," *Middle English Alliterative Poetry*, ed. David Lawton (Cambridge: Brewer, 1982).

43. On fol. 22v beside the line "Ac þer shal come a kyng and confess ȝow alle" (V.168), the scribe has drawn a crown just like those Matthew drew in the margins of the *Chronica majora* to indicate a passage about royal affairs (fol. 160v of Cambridge, Corpus Christi College (CCCC), MS 16, reproduced as fig. 185 in Lewis, *Art of Matthew Paris*, 43); the scribe may also have had Exchequer *signa* (Matthew's original source) directly in mind. See Kerby-Fulton and Justice, "Bureaucratic Culture."

44. For the boat image (CCCC 16, fol. 160v), see Lewis, *Art of Matthew Paris*, fig. 185; for the peasant threshing (CCCC 16, fol. 79), ibid., fig. 155.

45. See Pearsall, *C-Text*, notes to VIII.149, 158, 330.

46. For the image of the Cambridge riot, see Richard Vaughan, *The Illustrated Chronicles of Matthew Paris* (Cambridge: Alan Sutton and Corpus Christi College, 1993), 101; for the peasant thrashing his plunder, see Lewis, *Art of Matthew Paris*, 247, who notes

Matthew's vehement antipapalism; for the spade as an attribute of Cain, see her fig. 188 of the Wandering Jew.

47. Along with the illustrations from Matthew already mentioned, see Lewis's reproductions (in *Art of Matthew Paris*) from Cambridge, Corpus Christi College, MS 26 (e.g., Mohammed, fig. 53, from p. 87); from Cambridge, Corpus Christi College, MS 16 (e.g., friars, fols. 26 and 67, figs. 27 and 28; fol. 66v, fig. 201, for visionary iconography); for kings and magnates, see her chap. 3; for mirabilia, see her chap. 5. Criminals, violent acts, and deaths are ubiquitous in Matthew, and are similar to the didactic illustrations in Exchequer documents, which may explain the Douce illustrator's otherwise odd decision to portray a man on the gallows (figure 32); on this figure see Hilmo, "Retributive Violence".

48. CCCC 26, p. 36; reproduced in Lewis, *Art of Matthew Paris*, as fig. 19, but without comment on the pun; on Matthew's punning habits, see ibid. 43.

49. See ibid. 48.

50. This count is derived from Hanna's list of *Piers* manuscripts with identifiable provenance (*William Langland* [Aldershot: Variorum, 1993], 34–35); the following can be or can likely be associated with Benedictine houses: Oxford, Bodleian Library Bodley 851; (possibly) San Marino, Huntington Library, MS HM 143 and HM 128; London, British Library, Harley 6041; Dublin, Trinity College, MS 213; (probably) Cambridge University Library, Dd.i.17 and (possibly) Dublin, Trinity College, MS 212. Only Harley 6041 does not contain historical material, and its other contents are in fact associated with confession. See also Middleton, "Audience and Public," 101–23; and Kathryn Kerby-Fulton, "Langland's Reading: Some Evidence from Manuscripts Containing Religious Prophecy," in *The Uses of Manuscripts in Literary Studies: Essays in Memory of J. B. Allen*, ed. Charlotte Morse, Penelope Doob, and M. C. Woods (Kalamazoo, Mich.: Medieval Institute Publications, 1992), 237–62.

51. See *Expugnatio Hibernica: The Conquest of Ireland by Giraldus Cambrensis*, ed. A. B. Scott and F. X. Martin (Dublin: Royal Irish Society, 1978), for manuscript descriptions, and see also Robert Bartlett, *Gerald of Wales, 1146–1223* (Oxford: Oxford University Press, 1982), app. 1, for a list of the manuscripts of all Gerald's works, and p. 215 for a list of all the Hiberno-English manuscripts of the *Conquest*. Just as one finds in studying the *mise-en-page* of other marginal illustrations (like those in Matthew Paris and the Douce manuscript), there is distinct evidence in certain *Topographia* manuscripts of what Lewis calls the "improvisational mode" of the illustrations (*Art of Matthew Paris*, 70); this is more than simply an impressionistic remark on their informal style; rather, in some manuscripts there is evidence that the pictures were added before the text (a method we strongly suspect in certain parts of Douce): for instance, in Laud Misc. 720 (the making of which deserves further study because a nearly complete set of instructions to the illustrator survives) the priest's garment is uncomfortably squashed against the letters of the text in three places, while the artist has only slightly obscured the instructions "...sacerdos cornu pro sonans" (fol. 232; figure 45). Unfortunately, none of the four extant illustrated manuscripts with the *original* Giraldian cycle (the two above plus Cambridge, University Library, Ff.I.27 and Laud Misc. 720) can be firmly said to have originated in Ireland, but several of the extant unillustrated ones can. Cambridge, University Library, Ff.I.27 (fig. 50) is the latest (original cycle) copy; on paleographical grounds it appears to be from the second half of the fourteenth century. A fascinating copy, which is illustrated in a hybrid Irish style, London, British Library, MS Harley 3724, provides a clear link between reading in Hiberno-English dialect (it contains a copy of the Creed and the Lord's Prayer in MHE) and the reading of Giraldus in Latin in the fourteenth century. Harley 3724's mix of prophecy, goliardic poetry, and ecclesiastical politics is very similar to the mix in London, British Library, MS Royal 13.A.XIV. On Harley 3724, see chapter 4 and figure 63.

52. Bartlett, "Images of Conquest in the High Middle Ages," in *Gerald of Wales*, 16. See also Robert Bartlett, *The Making of Europe: Conquest, Colonization, and Cultural Change, 950–1350* (Princeton, N.J.: Princeton University Press, 1993).

53. Antonia Gransden, "Realistic Observation in Twelfth-Century England," *Speculum* 47 (1972): 27–51.

Notes to Chapter 2

54. For a reproduction from a different manuscript, see Gransden, "Realistic Observation," as fig. 2, from Royal 13.B.VIII, fol. 30v.

55. See fols. 42 (figure 16), 43 (figure 17), 51 (figure 23), and, possibly, 55 (figure 26) and 72.

56. See Kathryn Kerby-Fulton, "Hildegard and the Male Reader," in *Prophets Abroad*, ed. Rosalynn Voaden (Cambridge: Brewer, 1996).

57. The story in Giraldus is of a miracle involving the cross (in chap. 75 of the *Topographia*).

58. For an excellent instance, see Cambridge, University Library, MS Ff.I.27, p. 315. I would like to thank Steven Justice for his suggestion about the pun.

59. See Lewis, *Art of Matthew Paris*, 307.

60. Some of these occur in Scott's helpful "Preliminary List of Late Fourteenth and Fifteenth Century English Manuscripts with Marginal Illustrations" (*Facsimile*, lxxxviii). See also note 37 above.

61. "Cronice de gestis ac nominibus regum Britonum Anglorum Saxonum danorum & Normanorum" (fol. 9r).

62. For a similar instance, see the image of the king in Camille, "At the Edge," 2 (and n. 4, for other instances) and plate 1; see also the illustration of the king in the *Magna Carta* initial of the fifteenth-century manuscript, HM 19920, fol. 1; reproduced in Dutschke, *Guide*, fig. 82. For iconography of Richard II enthroned, see Margaret Rickert, *Painting in Britain: The Middle Ages* (Harmondsworth, Eng.: Penguin, 1954; 2d ed., 1965), 160–61 and figs. 159, 162.

63. Douce is a member of the "i" group of manuscripts; for the variant readings to III.492, see Russell and Kane.

64. See Lewis, *Art of Matthew Paris*, fig. 72, from CCCC 16, fol. 110, and accompanying discussion.

65. Either the patron or a supervisor (or the artist himself, on second thought) suppressed the image of the Castle of Care.

66. See chapter 4, and see also Robin Flower, "Manuscripts of Irish Interest in the British Library," *Analecta Hibernica* 2 (1931): 310–29, especially on Harley 3724.

67. Bliss cites, for instance, the Middle Irish "Vision of Mac Conglinne"; see his discussion in "Language and Literature," in *The English Medieval Ireland*, ed. James Lydon (Dublin: Royal Irish Academy, 1984), 32; see 32–33 for all the quotations in this paragraph. For similar sentiments, see Turville-Petre, "The English in Ireland." The "Kildare" poems are now known to have originated in Waterford; see Benskin, "Kildare Poems."

68. On the SWM connections, see Bliss, "Language and Literature," 39; on the dialect of the exemplar of Douce, I am indebted to Jeremy Smith's advice — on this, and on the scribe's substitutions, see appendix 1. Alan Fletcher has pointed out that by the fifteenth century settlement was coming more from the North West Midlands area, especially Cheshire (see McIntosh and Samuels, "Prolegomena," 8), and that trade with both Chester and Bristol was heavy. (I am indebted to Dr. Howard Clarke of the Department of History, University College, Dublin, for this advice on trading relations.)

69. On the "i-group," see Pearsall and Scott, *Facsimile*, ix n. 2.

70. Ronald Bryer, *Not the Least: The Story of Little Malvern* (Hanley, England: Hanley Publishing Workshops, 1993), 35, 39, and app. D for a list of the Irish holdings of the priory, many of which were in the Dublin-Pale area.

71. See especially *The Register of Thomas de Cobham, Bishop of Worcester, 1317–1327*, ed. E. H. Pearce (Worcestershire Historical Society, 1930), 140.

72. Bryer, *Not the Least*, 112–14.

73. See Hanna, 34–36. It is possible, of course, that after the events of 1381 Benedictines felt more able to identify themselves as owners (especially collectively) than individuals, and this factor may skew the statistics.

74. Bryer, *Not the Least*, 22; see also Kaske, "Local Iconography."

75. St. John Brooks, "The *Piers Plowman* Manuscripts in Trinity College, Dublin," *Library*, 5th series, 6 (1951): 141–53.

Notes to Chapter 2

76. Ibid., 151–52.
77. Ibid., 144–51.
78. As Pearsall has shown, Douce was also still in Ireland at that point (*Facsimile*, xiii).
79. The Despensers were actively involved in Irish concerns until at least 12 September 1392, when Sir Hugh le Despenser notified his tenants that he was transferring all his lands, rights, and jurisdictions in Ireland to James le Botiller, earl of Ormond; for the documentary evidence, see Gilbert, *Facsimiles of the National Manuscripts of Ireland*, vol. 3, plate 20.2; for discussion see Edmund Curtis, *A History of Medieval Ireland, 1086–1513* (London: Methuen, 1923), 256 (and 227, 255–56 on the activities of earlier Despensers in Ireland or as absentee magnates); see also Edmund Colledge, *The Latin Poems of Richard Ledrede* (Toronto: PIMS), xix–xxi, on the Despenser faction in Ireland and its Anglo-Irish adherents.
80. N. R. Ker, *Facsimile of British Museum MS Harley 2253* (London: Oxford University Press, 1965), xxii: "There are accounts from an important Irish household [the Mortimers] on one side of the binding leaves and from the ordinal of Hereford Cathedral on the other." Carter Revard has very kindly pointed out to me that Cambridge, University Library, MS Gg.1.1, which is also in Hiberno-English, overlaps a great deal in its Anglo-Norman contents with Harley 2253. I am grateful to Professor Revard for generously sharing his wealth of knowledge about Harley and its Irish connections, a matter that deserves much more attention and that, with further investigation, will ultimately give us a much better sense of what the literary relations between Anglo-Ireland and the South West Midlands were. It is interesting, for instance, in this regard that Hereford Cathedral also owned the earliest and most important extant Giraldus manuscript, now Dublin, National Library, MS 700 (see Scott and Martin, *Expugnatio Hibernica*, xliv).
81. See Scott, "Illuminating Shop." On Ormond, see Kerby-Fulton and Justice, "Langlandian Reading Circles"; see also Judith Ferster, *Fictions of Advice: The Literature and Politics of Counsel in Late Medieval England* (Philadelphia: University of Pennsylvania Press, 1996), 55–66.
82. Bliss, "Language and Literature," 35.
83. John Watt, *The Church in Medieval Ireland* (Dublin: Gill and MacMillan, 1972), 84.
84. John Watt, *The Church and the Two Nations in Medieval Ireland* (Cambridge: Cambridge University Press, 1970), 184.
85. See Watt, *Two Nations*, 187.
86. Ibid., 186.
87. The question of whether this figure was painted by an apprentice is discussed in chapter 4.
88. It is possible that the image of a beautiful woman was thought improper in the manuscript: Douce may have been made not for a single patron, but as a group commission for or within a male religious house, or, if not made for such a house, it may soon have ended up in one—the macaronic poem added on the last folio in an early-fifteenth-century hand (not the main scribe's or the annotator's), entitled "On Chattering in Church" by Brown, is quite antifeminist, as is the admonition against harlots that follows it (see C. Brown, *Religious Lyrics of the Fifteenth Century* (Oxford: Clarendon, 1939), 277. In order to make space to write this last item, the accounts on this folio from the illustrator (if that is indeed what they are) had to be erased (see *Facsimile*, xi and n. 5), which may be slight evidence that it was done by a second or later owner—or at least done after the bill was paid! Faces of attractive women may have been problematic for this owner, although if this is the case it is difficult to know why the various faces of Mede were not treated similarly, unless iconicity was indeed the concern. This is not the only instance of defacement in the manuscript: someone has made a serious effort to erase the devil (a common impulse: see, for instance, Harley 6563, an Hours of the Virgin, fol. 11v, which shows a man and woman in bed, tempted by the devil, who has been rubbed out). As Hilmo has shown, the picture of the devil in Douce was in fact obscene; the attempt at erasure fits

the "puritanical" profile discussed earlier. Moreover, the patron or someone intervened to prevent another picture of the devil (and the Castle of Care) from coming to completion on fol. 5. On both the devil and Mercy, see Hilmo, "Transcending Boundaries."

89. The "Dobest bere sholde þe bisshopes crose" (X.92) reads almost like a marginal instruction to an illustrator, but the illustrator refused to take the hint.

90. The Franciscan appears to be modeled on Brother William; see Lewis, *Art of Matthew Paris*, 63, figs. 27, 28.

91. On speaking figures (which in medieval iconography are indicated by gesture, not necessarily by showing the mouth open), see Moshe Barasch, *Giotto and the Language of Gesture* (Cambridge: Cambridge University Press, 1987), 15–39, and see the discussion of *declamatio* and other speaking gestures in chapter 4. I would like to thank Maidie Hilmo for advice about this.

92. M. W. Evans, *Medieval Drawings* (London: Paul Hamlyn, 1969), plate 47; see also Pearsall and Scott, *Facsimile*, lii.

93. This image is repeated many times throughout the manuscript.

94. Pearsall and Scott, *Facsimile*, lii.

95. On the issue of contemplation in lay life and the attitudes of contemporary mystical writers, see Nicholas Watson, "The Middle English Mystics," in *Cambridge History of Medieval English Literature*, ed. Wallace.

96. The Douce artist handled the Feast of Patience similarly: he does not bother to portray Clergy at all, and drew the gluttonous friar in half-length, stupidly eating, without any visual indication that he has the power to speak or teach (fol. 67), while he gives Patience (figure 30) a full-length portrait with hand raised in a speaking gesture, his pilgrim's walking stick and scrip suggesting an unworldly spiritual authority and supplanting the book and tonsure (or clerk's beret) that teachers in other manuscripts usually have.

97. Citations from Lincoln are transcribed from the manuscript itself. For a description of the manuscript and a list of the pictorial subjects, see R. M. Thomson, *Catalogue of the Manuscripts of Lincoln Cathedral Chapter Library* (Cambridge: Brewer, 1989), no. 218.

98. See Watson, "The Middle English Mystics," on lay contemplation.

99. On William Palmere, see R. A. Wood, "A Fourteenth-Century Owner of Piers Plowman," *Medium Aevum* 53 (1984): 83–90, and Kerby-Fulton, "Bibliographic Ego"; on John Ball, see Justice, *Writing and Rebellion*, chap. 3.

100. See T. K. Moylan, "Vagabonds and Sturdy Beggars: Poverty, Pigs, and Pestilence in Medieval Dublin," in *Medieval Dublin: The Living City* (Dublin: Irish Academic Press, 1990), 192–99; on this theme in Langland, see Derek Pearsall, "Poverty and Poor People in Piers Plowman," in E. Kennedy, R. Waldron, and J. Wittig, *Medieval English Studies Presented to George Kane* (Woodbridge, Eng.: Brewer, 1988), 167–85.

101. See Pearsall's note to VIII.247 in *C-Text*.

102. See Hilmo, "Retributive Violence."

103. See John Plummer, *The Hours of Catherine of Cleves* (New York: Braziller, 1966), plate 69.

104. His Wastor figure, one of his most attentively produced characters, is actually another instance of traditional iconography splitting, placed as he is across from Hunger. The association of lazy peasants, like Wastor, with undone agricultural work can also be found in lavish books like the *De Lisle Psalter*, but Douce's Wastor is more aggressive and no doubt reflects a real social threat. The Anglo-Irish poem from Harley 913 called by Wright "A Song on the Times" similarly complains of those "hoblurs" who take from husbandmen, and vows that they should be cast out as dogs, unfit for Christian burial. The poem goes on to condemn "hokerlich" beggars (p. 204), very like those who trouble Piers (Thomas Wright, ed., *Political Songs of England* [London: Camden Society, 1839], 195–205).

105. Physicians were often the butt of medieval visual satire, and this iconography is ubiquitous and instantly recognizable; see John B. Friedman, "The Friar Portrait in Douce: Contemporary Satire?" *Yearbook of Langland Studies* 8 (1994): 178.

Notes to Chapter 3

106. See Jean Imray, *The Charity of Richard Whittington: A History of the Trust Administered by the Mercer's Company, 1424–1966* (London: Athlone, 1968), fig. 1; it is intriguing that a scribe has written (in this case, the names of the various people in attendance) right on top of the pictures, a habit we see in Douce and in the *Red Book*.

107. Wright, *Political Songs*, 201–2. Turville-Petre ("The English in Ireland," 170) suggests that this poem may have been written in England, but he gives no reason for the suggestion. The Harley 913 satires, as he admits (173), exist only in MHE.

3. The Professional Reader as Annotator

I would like to thank Carl Grindley especially, not only for permission to cite his unpublished dissertation, "From Creation to Desecration: the Marginal Annotations of *Piers Plowman* C-Text HM 143" (M.A. thesis, University of Victoria, 1992), but also for so generously sharing the energy and enthusiasm with which he carried it out. I am also grateful to Marie Claire Uhart for permission to cite the appendixes of her unpublished dissertation ("The Early Reception of *Piers Plowman*," Ph.D. diss., University of Leicester, 1986), which contain transcriptions of the annotations of a number of *Piers* manuscripts, as well as tremendously useful descriptions of all the manuscripts.

1. For a complete transcription of the Douce annotations, see appendix 2; for analysis of the hands, see appendix 1. Instances of *Piers* manuscripts in which annotations peter out, or simply appear sporadically, include Oxford, Bodleian Library, MSS Douce 323, Rawlinson Poet. 137, and Bodley 851. For an overview of kinds of *Piers* annotations, see Uhart, "Early Reception," and Helen Barr, *Signes and Sothe: Language in the Piers Plowman Tradition* (Cambridge: Brewer, 1994), 9–11; see also G. H. Russell, "Some Early Responses to the C-Version of *Piers Plowman*," *Viator* 15 (1984): 275–300, which contains a transcription from three of the fullest sets of C-text annotations in HM 143, Douce 104, and London, British Library, MS Add. 35157. The latter's marginal supply is in a variety of sixteenth-century hands, and therefore testifies to Reformation rather than medieval reading of the poem; this is the subject of Carl Grindley's Ph.D. dissertation, "The Life of a Book: British Library MS Add. 35157 in an Historical Context" (Glasgow University, 1996). For a complete transcription of the fifteenth- and sixteenth-century annotations (the majority of which are also late) in Digby 102 and a study of the different scribal annotating patterns, see Tanya Schaap, "From Scribe to Reader: A Study of the Marginal Annotations of *Piers Plowman* C Text, Oxford, Bodleian Library Digby 102", (M.A. thesis, University of Victoria, 1996). David Benson is currently transcribing the B text annotations.

2. All citations of HM 143 are from Grindley, "From Creation to Desecration"; for the evidence that the Douce annotations are contemporary with the manuscript's production, see appendix 1.

3. I am grateful to Dr. Jeremy Smith for confirmation of this fact. In addition to his helpful observations, I have found Angus McIntosh and M. L. Samuels, "Prolegomena to a Study of Mediaeval Anglo-Irish," *Medium Aevum* 37 (1968): 1–11, to be invaluable, along with McIntosh and M. Benskin, *A Linguistic Atlas of Late Mediaeval English* (Aberdeen, 1986), vol. 1, which contains the list of Anglo-Irish manuscripts; see also the studies by Benskin cited in chapter 2, note 1.

4. See appendix 1.

5. Grindley, "From Creation to Desecration."

6. See appendix 1. For a facsimile of HM 143, see R. W. Chambers, R. B. Hazelden, and H. C. Schulz, *Piers Plowman: The Huntington Library Manuscript (HM 143) Reproduced in Photostat* (San Marino, Calif.: Huntington Library, 1936). For a plate of HM 143 showing the annotations, see Kerby-Fulton and Justice, "Bureaucratic Culture."

7. Paul Saenger and Michael Heinlen, "Incunable Description and Its Implication for the Analysis of Fifteenth-Century Reading Habits," in *Printing the Written Word: the Social History of Books, circa 1450–1520*, ed. Sandra L. Hindman (Ithaca, N.Y.: Cornell, 1991),

239. The authors also document a number of instances in which the rubricator and the reader-emendator were different people.

8. For a transcription of the topics of these signs, see S. Harrison Thomson, "Grosseteste's Concordantial Signs," *Medievalia et Humanistica* 9 (1955): 39–53; 41 and 42 for the examples given here.

9. On the goals of medieval correcting, see Mary Rouse and Richard Rouse, "Correction and Emendation of Texts in the Fifteenth Century and the Autograph of the Opus Pacis by 'Oswaldus Anglicus,'" in *Authentic Witnesses: Approaches to Medieval Texts and Manuscripts* (Notre Dame: University of Notre Dame Press, 1991), 427–47; and appendix 1 in this volume.

10. On Capgrave, see Cyril Smetana, introduction to *The Life of St. Norbert* by John Capgrave (Toronto: PIMS, 1977); and on his annotating activities, see Peter Lucas, "John Capgrave, O.S.A. (1393–1464), Scribe and Publisher," *Transactions of the Cambridge Bibliographical Society* 5 (1969). Gower, of course, also glossed his own works, but this was a very different kind of commentary from the annotations of Capgrave, which are much closer in character to the *Piers* annotations under discussion here, despite the fact that the latter are not authorial. This tells us, of course, that *Piers* was read more like the didactic religious works Capgrave was producing than like the humanist works of Gower (see Derek Pearsall, "Gower's Latin in the *Confessio Amantis*," in *Latin and Vernacular*, ed. A. J. Minnis [Cambridge: Brewer, 1988], 13–25).

11. Annabel Patterson, *Censorship and Interpretation: The Conditions of Writing and Reading in Early Modern England* (Madison: University of Wisconsin Press, 1984), 11.

12. Lucas, "John Capgrave," 30.

13. Wolfgang Iser's concept of the "implied reader" is unfortunately largely phenomenological (see the final chapter of Iser, *The Implied Reader: Patterns of Communication in Prose Fiction from Bunyan to Beckett* [Baltimore, Md.: Johns Hopkins University Press, 1974]); for discussion of some of the problems implicit in it, see Robert C. Holub, *Reception Theory: A Critical Introduction* (New York: Methuen, 1984), esp. 84–85. Iser's lack of interest in the social and historical reader is unsatisfying, and as Paul Strohm has shown, medievalists will probably derive more helpful models from Mikhail Bakhtin and his collaborators (or surrogates) V. N. Voloshinov and P. N. Medvedev, whose sociolinguistics conceives of literary reception as a two-way negotiation between author and audience (see Strohm, *Social Chaucer* [Cambridge, Mass.: Harvard University Press, 1988], 49–50); for Hans Robert Jauss's theory of the "horizon of expectations," see "Literary History as a Challenge to Literary Theory," in *Toward an Aesthetic of Reception*, trans. Timothy Bahti (Brighton, England: Harvester, 1982), 3–45.

14. See Eleanor P. Hammond, *English Verse between Chaucer and Surrey* (New York: Octagon Books, 1965), 191–97; and Aage Brusendorff, *The Chaucer Tradition* (London: Oxford University Press, 1925), 207–35 and appendixes. Richard Firth Green has recently questioned the extent of Shirley's publication activity (Green, *Poets and Princepleasers* [Toronto: University of Toronto Press, 1980], 131), to which A. S. G. Edwards has responded convincingly countering Green's skepticism, at least in the case of Lydgate (Edwards, "Lydgate Manuscripts: Some Directions for Future Research," in *Manuscripts and Readers in Fifteenth-Century England*, ed. Derek Pearsall [Cambridge: Brewer, 1981], 20). For a judicious reassessment of all the evidence concerning Shirley's book production activities, see Julia Boffey and John Thompson, "Anthologies and Miscellanies: Production and Choice of Texts," in *Book Production and Publishing in Britain 1375–1475*, ed. Jeremy Griffiths and Derek Pearsall (Cambridge: Cambridge University Press, 1989), 284–87 and the bibliography. See also A. S. G. Edwards, "John Shirley and the Emulation of Courtly Culture," in *The Court and Cultural Diversity*, ed. Evelyn Mullally and John Thompson (Cambridge: Brewer, 1997), 309–17.

15. He tells us that he put together his collections for the consumption of a reading public he addresses in characterizations l ike "all þat in this company / ben knight squyer

or lady / or other estat what euer they be" (Hammond, *English Verse*, 197, lines 91–93; from London, British Library, MS Add. 29729; hereafter cited in text by page and line number).

16. See ibid., 197, lines 83–86; from Add. 29729; and Edwards, "Lydgate Manuscripts," 20; Boffey and Thompson, "Anthologies," 287.

17. The first three examples are cited in Brusendorff, *Chaucer Tradition*, 472–73; the last in ibid., 462. Although the Douce 104 and HM 143 annotators do not provide linguistic and explanatory glosses (indeed, the Douce annotator just alters the main text when he fears linguistic incomprehension!), some *Piers* annotators did provide the former (e.g., Dublin, Trinity College, MS 212), and more rarely the latter (e.g., the annotations to London, British Library, MS Add. 35287 at VII.76 and XII.268, in Uhart's transcription, in "Early Reception," pp. 356 and 358).

18. Brusendorff, *Chaucer Tradition*, 463–64; Shirley's profeminist notes are more fully transcribed in A. S. G. Edwards, "John Lydgate, Medieval Antifeminism, and Harley 2251," *Annuale Medievale* 13 (1972): 32–44. See also Derek Pearsall, *John Lydgate* (London: Routledge, 1970), 75.

19. See Edwards in Pearsall, *Lydgate*, 21, and Boffey and Thompson, "Anthologies."

20. Cited in Brusendorff, *Chaucer Tradition*, 217, from MS Trinity R.3.20, p. 15.

21. Ibid., from Trinity R.3.20, p. 50.

22. See A. I. Doyle and M. B. Parkes, "The Production of Copies of the *Canterbury Tales* and the *Confessio Amantis*," in *Medieval Scribes, Manuscripts, and Libraries: Essays Presented to N. R. Ker* (London: Scolar, 1978), and see Kerby-Fulton, "Professional and Private Readers."

23. Grindley, 5.

24. The manuscripts in question are Longleat House, Wilts., MS 29 and Oxford, Bodleian Library, MS Bodley e Mus. 232, on which see *Richard Rolle: Prose and Verse*, ed. S. J. Ogilvie-Thomson, EETS (Oxford: Oxford University Press, 1988), xxxi–xxxiv (a plate of Longleat is reproduced as the frontispiece for that volume, which is useful for comparison with the Douce annotator's hand). The Longleat and the Bodley manuscripts are in the same hand (see ibid., xxxi), and both, like Douce, are datable to the second quarter of the fifteenth century (in fact, Longleat's *terminus a quo* is 1422, which is close to Douce's date of 1427). Close examination of the two manuscripts suggests that the main scribe of both was a scribe trained in exactly the same workshop or scriptorium as our annotator, or may even be the same man. In Longleat the scribe is using a more formal version of the script (*anglicana formata*), as of course he would be since he is copying a main text there, not annotating. The only apparent differences between the Longleat and the Douce annotator's hands are that in Longleat the flourish coming from the shoulder of the long *r*, which forms (usually) an *e* abbreviation, is somewhat more cramped; and in Bod. e Mus. the abbreviation for (usually) "us" is slightly more curved. (See, for instance, fol. 25, "Eusebius.") These are not large differences; all other abbreviations (in this comparison twelve have been checked) are handled nearly identically. Unfortunately, punctuation, which is the other feature most likely to betray idiosyncrasies, is virtually nonexistent in the annotations, so it is impossible to be certain (however, the dash, a double virgule, does occur and is handled the same way in both). Letter forms look identical. The rubricator of Bod. e Mus. signed his name, "jon Flemmyn," but unfortunately the rubrication of Douce appears to have been done by a different hand; however, there are similarities in training again (e.g., both manuscripts have a trefoil on the red flourishes of blue initials). Unless further evidence appears, we can only conclude that it is *not unlikely* that Douce and the two Rolle manuscripts emanated from the same workshop, possibly handled by the same scribe or by scribes of shared training, in the Dublin-Pale district. I would like to thank Kate Harris and Nicholas Watson for advice about Longleat.

25. A. I. Doyle, "More Light on John Shirley," *Medium Aevum* 30, no. 2 (1961): 98–99 and n. 42. See also George Russell, "As They Read It: Some Notes on Early Responses to the C-Version of *Piers Plowman*," *Leeds Studies in English*, n.s., 20 (1989): 173–87.

Notes to Chapter 3

26. Cok joined Saint Bartholomew's in 1421 at the age of twenty-nine, but he seems to have been copying manuscripts before becoming a brother, which suggests that he was an unbeneficed clerk who earned his living as a freelance scribe (see Doyle, "John Shirley," on the records of his life; quotation at 98). Many such clerks were employed as scribes or secretaries, often writing legal documents, and it has been suggested that Langland himself earned a living this way for a time; see Kerby-Fulton and Justice, "Langlandian Reading Circles."

27. See the frontispiece to Smetana for Capgrave's portrait; the portrait of Cok is not identified explicitly as such in the manuscript, but the identification seems certain from the context; see Alexander, "William Abell 'lymnour,'" 167 and fig. 3.

28. On paleographical manifestations of *ordinatio*, see M. B. Parkes, "The Influence of the Concepts of *Ordinatio* and *Compilatio* on the Development of the Book," in *Medieval Learning and Literature: Essays Presented to R. W. Hunt*, ed. J. J. G. Alexander and M. T. Gibson (Oxford: Oxford University Press, 1975), 115–41; on textual aspects, see A. J. Minnis, *Medieval Theory of Authorship* (Philadelphia: University of Pennsylvania Press, 1988), 147–48 and passim; and for *Piers* manuscripts, see Russell, "Some Early Responses" (although for correctives see Grindley, "From Creation to Desecration"); see also Pearsall's introduction to *Facsimile*. The study of annotations in Middle English literary texts, and especially in *Piers Plowman*, is still in its infancy, and the glossing of Chaucer is very different from the annotating of *Piers* (a difference that cannot be explored here), but on the latter, in addition to Brusendorff, *Chaucer Tradition*, see Susan Schibanoff, "The New Reader and Female Textuality in Two Early Commentaries on Chaucer," *Studies in the Age of Chaucer* 10 (1988): 71–108; see also note 31 below. It is interesting to note that medieval readers saw more similarities between *Troilus* and *Piers* than between *The Canterbury Tales* and *Piers*; Anne Middleton has noted the surprising fact that *Piers* and *Troilus* frequently occur together in manuscripts, as indeed they do in HM 143 (Middleton, "The Audience and Public of *Piers Plowman*," in *Middle English Alliterative Poetry*, ed. David Lawton (Cambridge: Brewer, 1982), 101–53; see further Kerby-Fulton and Justice, "Langlandian Reading Circles." These instances are taken from C. David Benson and B. A. Windeatt, "The MS Glosses to Chaucer's *Troilus and Criseyde*," *Chaucer Review* 25 (1990): 33–53; *sigla* of the manuscripts from which they come appear in brackets with the line reference when cited in the text.

29. Charles Plummer, "On the Colophons and Marginalia of Irish Scribes," *Proceedings of the British Academy* 12 (1926): 11–42. Here are a few examples of these wonderful annotations (trans. from Irish by Plummer): "That is sad, O little book" (18); "I am the man of the bad script who wrote this... to wit, John Macdonnell, and far from my home am I to-day" (22); "How is that, O pen? and methinks 'tis good" (24).

30. For a complete text of the Douce notes, see appendix 2. Hereafter, D refers to the Douce annotations, and an italicized *D* refers to the Douce annotator; H will likewise refer to the HM 143 annotations, *H* to the annotator himself.

31. This terminology was developed in collaboration with Carl Grindley, although the terms used in his work differ slightly; in his study of HM 143, Grindley also identified a category of graphic annotations (small marginal drawings). Uhart records some instances of rhetorical marking in annotations; see, for example, the notes to III.228 and 331 in Add. 35287 (Uhart, "Early Reception," 354), which are an attempt to formally mark the stages of the Conscience-Mede debate. Stephen Partridge sets out categories for distinguishing types of Chaucer glosses (which are very different from Langland glosses) in *The Manuscript Glosses to the Canterbury Tales* (Cambridge: Boydell and Brewer, forthcoming).

32. The Hengwrt manuscript, for instance, is interesting in that even though its scribe (Doyle and Parkes's Scribe B) seems not to have foreseen the extent of the marginal apparatus, he used left and right margins to distinguish "headings" that indicated subordinate topics in the text from "a Latin apparatus of citations and quotations from sources in the right-hand margin"; A. I. Doyle and M. B. Parkes, "Production of Copies," 163–210. For

Notes to Chapter 3

HM 143, see Grindley, "From Creation to Desecration," who observes that parallel lines occur before (to use Grindley's terminology) summation and personal admonition annotations in HM 143, L-shaped brackets before reading aid and comment annotations, and no bracket before certain other types, like textual notes (it should be added to his observations that Scribe B used similar parallel lines as a direction to the flourisher for the Hengwrt glosses).

33. See Minnis, *Theory of Authorship*, 124–25.
34. Ibid., 128.
35. Cited in ibid., 144–45, from *Dantis Alagherii epistolae*, ed. P. Toynbee; 2d ed., C. Hardie (Oxford: Clarendon, 1966), 175.
36. Wendy Scase, *Piers Plowman and the New Anticlericalism* (Cambridge: Cambridge University Press, 1989), 45–46, 109.
37. See Pearsall's note to this line in *C-Text*.
38. See Francis J. Cotter, *The Friars Minor in Ireland from Their Arrival to 1400* (St. Bonaventure, N.Y.: Franciscan Institute, 1994), 131.
39. See B. A. Windeatt, "The Scribes as Chaucer's Early Critics," *Studies in the Age of Chaucer* 1 (1979): 119–41.
40. Grindley's helpful label for annotations that are simply parroted from the text, instead of being "composed."
41. Compare lines 183, 184, and 185 in Pearsall to the text in Douce on fol. 109r, where consistent changes have been made to shift the force of Elde's attack from Will's first-person narrative ("myn," "me," "myn," respectively) to the neutral third person ("mennys," "men," "menys"). The changes were not made (as some changes quite obviously are, over erasure) by the annotator-corrector, but they appear smoothly in the main scribe's hand, either by his own initiative or from something he copied from his exemplar. The changes might have originally been inspired by the use of "menne" in (apparently) the received tradition at line 187, but Russell and Kane report no other instances of these readings.
42. Peter Dronke makes a similar point in his fascinating reception study of the letters of Heloise and Abelard, *Abelard and Heloise in Medieval Testimonies* (Glasgow: Glasgow University Press, 1976).
43. See J. B. Allen, *The Ethical Poetic of the Later Middle Ages* (Toronto: University of Toronto Press, 1982), 182–84, 297.
44. See M.-D. Chenu, "Auctor, actor, autor," *Bulletin du Cange* 3 (1927): 81–86.
45. Grindley, "From Creation to Desecration," 11–17.
46. He finds only two more points noteworthy in this section between lines 167 and 312 (in contrast with *D*, who found six). One, at line 249, is a formal rhetorical marker, drawing attention to the formal conclusion of one of Recklessness's arguments (that just as the wrights who worked on Noah's ark were lost in the flood, so too will be many *curatores*, "wrihtes of holy churche" [line 253], come Doomsday). The note is textually gleaned, and looks more like an eagerly snatched bit of *ordinatio* than the result of careful study of Recklessness's arguments, which continue long after this "culorum" (until line 305). The other point he finds noteworthy, at line 312, "hyer hard sentence for techeres ȝif þay leue noȝt wel" (also noted, although less judgmentally, by *D*), looks like the only other thing in this section that he was willing to tackle.
47. See Cotter, *Friars Minor in Ireland*, 129.
48. Antimendicantism was downright fashionable in literary circles in the late fourteenth century; if someone of the impeccable orthodoxy and political discretion of Chaucer could indulge in it, we assume it was very safe.
49. See Ruth Mellinkoff's interesting discussion of feathered headgear as a "derogatory attribute" for pagans in medieval illustration, a motif that seems to have originated in England or France, and her figs. 30, 32, 33 for close parallels to Douce's Trajan, in Mellinkoff, *The Devil at Isenheim* (Berkeley: University of California Press, 1987), 49; see also chap-

ter 4. For the theory that Trajan's headgear represents that worn by emperors as found on some Roman coins, see Hilmo, "Transcending Boundaries."

50. The passage is reminiscent of Langland: the friar also asks about Sampson, Solomon, and Origen, and Mechthild points out flaws in all of them(!), but reserves judgment (see the Middle English translation edited by Theresa Halligan, *The Booke of Gostlye Grace of Mechtild of Hackeborn* [Toronto: PIMS, 1979], 569ff.). For a helpful overview of medieval opinions, see Frank Grady, "Piers Plowman, St. Erkenwald, and the Rule of Exceptional Salvations," *Yearbook of Langland Studies* 6 (1992): 61–86.

51. For a more detailed discussion of this iconography and its sources, see chapter 4.

52. For a similar case, see Derek Pearsall, "The Manuscripts of Gower's *Confessio Amantis* in the British Library," paper presented at the Sixth York Manuscripts Conference, July 5–7, 1991.

53. Some of *D*'s annotations have been marred by cropping, therefore we know it was annotated before binding. Staining on outer quire leaves suggests that it lay unbound for a long time.

54. See Kerby-Fulton and Justice, "Bureaucratic Culture," and on Matthew Paris, see the lists of illustrations in M. R. James, *Catalogue of the Manuscripts in Corpus Christi College, Cambridge*, vol. 1 (Cambridge: Cambridge University Press, 1912), MSS 16 and 26, in which the image of the crown recurs frequently. See also note 64 below.

55. Grindley, "From Creation to Desecration," 3.

56. Scase, *New Anticlericalism*, 157.

57. Allen, *Ethical Poetic*, 299.

58. Paul Piehler, *The Visionary Landscape: A Study in Medieval Allegory* (Montreal: McGill University Press, 1971).

59. See Kerby-Fulton, "Bibliographic Ego."

60. See Pearsall's note to V.130, "A lesson in family discipline," despite Skeat's pious hope that the staves were intended to break up the crowd.

61. H also drops the brackets beside the "prophetia petri" note at III.476. He seems to drop brackets for his few crude source glosses (e.g., "sapience," XI.122), for textual notes, and for extremely abbreviated notes (e.g., "frer"), but none of these types occurs frequently.

62. Anne Middleton, "William Langland's 'Kynde Name': Authorial Signature and Social Identity in Late Fourteenth-Century England," in *Literary Practice and Social Change in Britain, 1390–1500*, ed. Lee Patterson (Berkeley: University of California Press, 1990), 15–16.

63. Kerby-Fulton, *Piers Plowman and Reformist Apocalypticism*.

64. For the Exchequer documents relating to the Templars, see Hall, *The Red Book of the Exchequer*, cxi. For the crown image, see PRO E/36/273, fols. 24, 31, 43v, 60v.

65. It is best exemplified (among *Piers* manuscripts) by San Marino, Huntington Library, MS HM 137, where the scribe uses a *textura* hand to highlight both the Latin quotes and, beside them, a (usually rather imprecise) source gloss, e.g., "Salamon" beside Prol. 205a.

66. See Kerby-Fulton, "Langland's Reading."

4. Visual Politics

1. Cosgrove, "Emergence of the Pale," 547 (italics added).

2. See J. A. Watt, "The Anglo-Irish Colony under Strain, 1327–99"; Cosgrove, "Emergence of the Pale"; and see the chronological table of statutes in Henry Berry, ed., *Statutes and Ordinances, and Acts of the Parliament of Ireland: King John to Henry V* (Dublin: HMSO, 1907), xix–xxv, which gives an overview (1204–1421) of successive Irish government attempts to deal with colonial disturbances, along with English legislation that had also to be incorporated into the colony.

3. See note 23 below on attempts at parliamentary reform; see also notes 4 and 6. See Ferster, *Fictions of Advice*, 58–59, on the egalitarian impetus in Yonge's *Secreta* and on Anglo-Irish politics.

4. For the English and Irish versions of the *Modus*, see Nicholas Pronay and John Taylor, *Parliamentary Texts of the Later Middle Ages* (Oxford: Clarendon, 1980), 13–116 and 117–154, respectively (Latin text and English translation in both cases). On the *Modus* and its reformist impetus, see the lucid discussion in A. L. Brown, *The Governance of Late Medieval England* (Stanford, Calif.: Stanford University Press, 1989), 32, 208–9, 228; and for the case that it originated in Ricardian Ireland and was brought to England for polemical purposes in the 1380s, see G. O. Sayles, "*Modus tenendi parliamentum*: Irish or English?", in *England and Ireland in the Later Middle Ages: Essays in Honour of Jocelyn Otway-Ruthven* (Dublin: Irish Academic Press, 1981), 122–52, esp. 144–45 on the question of when and why the *Modus* was brought to the attention of "English politicians, royalists and dissidents" in Ricardian Westminster. For the most recent discussion of the origins problem, see Kerby-Fulton and Justice, "Bureaucratic Culture."

5. See Benskin, "Irish adoptions": "The forms of the documents and their modes of script keep pace with English practice; the later medieval material wears no old-fashioned look, nor does it betray the influence of written Irish" (39).

6. On the political use of the *Modus* in England and Ireland, see Kerby-Fulton and Justice, "Bureaucratic Culture"; see also Kerby-Fulton and Justice, "Langlandian Reading Circles."

7. Citing Pronay and Taylor's translation of the earliest version of the English *Modus* in *Parliamentary Texts*, 89; for the Latin text, see 77; for Sayles's discussion of this passage, see his "Irish or English?" 134. Whether the *Modus* was written as a guide to parliamentary procedure or a piece of political polemic (or even satire) is still a subject of debate among scholars; there is no doubt, however, that it was used politically at times, especially in Ireland.

8. Compare the attempts at reform recorded in archbishop of Armagh John Swayne's *Register* (1418–39) with those in the Statutes of Kilkenny, discussed in this paragraph and in chapter 1; see also Cosgrove, "Emergence of the Pale," 541.

9. Robert Steele, ed., *Three Prose Versions of the* Secreta secretorum, EETS, o.s., 74 (London: Kegan, 1898), 157, lines 28–30.

10. There is plenty of evidence, however, especially on the local level, of anticlericalism among civic authorities: take, for instance, the dispute launched by the mayor of Dublin over church donations, which resulted in his excommunication; Margret Murphy, "*Pro anima* Bequests in Medieval Dublin," in *The Church and Wealth*, ed. W. J. Sheils and D. Wood, Studies in Church History, vol. 24 (Oxford: Blackwell, 1987), 116.

11. In addition to Giraldian manuscripts such as Harley 3724 (figure 63), another contemporary MHE instance is HM 129 (figure 49), and there are some Gaelic-Irish instances contemporary with Douce, for plates of which see Françoise Henry and Genevieve Marsh-Micheli, "Manuscripts and Illuminations, 1169–1603," in *A New History of Ireland*, ed. Cosgrove: Dublin, King's Inn, MS 17 (plate 31b of fol. 5v); Edinburgh, National Library of Scotland, MS Advocates 72.1.2 (plate 31c of fol. 3r); and, likely, Dublin, Royal Irish Academy, MS 23, *Leabhar Breac* (plate 28a of p. 16). Among these, National Library of Scotland Advocates is most like Douce: the figure of Libra actually touches the first word ("Libra") as a mnemonic and with his other hand gestures toward the text; the figure was likely sketched in just before or at the same time as the text was written, because the edges of the left margin are jagged so as to make room for protruding parts of the drawing.

12. Reproduced in Gilbert, *Facsimiles of the National Manuscripts of Ireland*, vol. 3, as plate 36; see pp. xiv–xv for Gilbert's description and transcription of some of the annotations in the picture. De Lloyd Guth has very kindly given me his opinion on the others. The Red Book has since been destroyed (in the destruction of the 1922 Dublin Public Record Office). The best description of it can be found in R. Dudley Edwards, "Magna Carta Hiberniae," *Essays and Studies Presented to Professor Eoin Mac Neil*, ed. John Ryan (Dublin: Three Candles, 1940), 313–15; Edwards suggests that the Red Book was rather informally produced: "The manuscript volume known as the *Red Book* of the Irish Exchequer appears to have contained much material similar to that of the English exchequer collec-

Notes to Chapter 4

tions of statutes of the same period...[where] there was a similar lack of order....Its copies of statutes cannot be regarded as authoritative, for there is no evidence as to the manner in which they were entered" (313–15). The Red Book was, then, a working book, a manuscript compiled, apparently, with a kind of office humor as well as utility. On the drawing, see also Bliss and Long, "Literature in Norman French and English," 713 (on the use of French in it), and, very briefly, Henry and Marsh-Micheli, "Manuscripts and Illuminations," 786, who pause only to link it to the "original, vivid quality of the Waterford [Charter Roll] drawings"—the social realism of which seems to have been a feature of fifteenth-century Anglo-Irish art—and to comment on its "plunging perspective, reminiscent of miniatures in the same perspective [and period] showing the English parliament."

13. The name above his sleeve is apparently "Huse." Many men with this name (also Husy, Hose, etc.) were associated with the English Exchequer, but I know of only one (so far) associated with the Dublin Exchequer, a Nicholas Hosse, who was a collector in 1420. See H. G. Richardson and G. O. Sayles, *Parliaments and Councils in Medieval Ireland* (Dublin: Stationery Office, 1947), 163.

14. Scott, in *Facsimile*, xxxiv; see also our preface on the identical artistic styles.

15. For a similar kind of "finishing" of a crude drawing, see, for instance, the Yellow Book of Lecan (Oxford, Bodleian Library, MS Rawl. B. 488), fol. 243, where the drawings of the banqueting house at Tara show a similar use of red and yellow rubrication colors (on the candle and lamps); reproduced in Gilbert, *Facsimiles,* as plate 24. This Anglo-Irish practice may be a technique borrowed from Gaelic-Irish artists.

16. We would like to thank Kevin Kennedy for his insightful comments about the role of the Douce rubricator.

17. The question of whether the work is the Douce artist's or that of an apprentice is discussed in this chapter's final section.

18. For a very similar instance in a contemporary Gaelic-Irish manuscript, see the discussion of the National Library of Scotland Advocates manuscript in note 11; for Scott's alternative theories of the actual working methods of the illustrator, see *Facsimile,* xxviii n. 5, although she seems to think that the illustrator worked from instructions.

19. See Kerby-Fulton and Justice, "Langlandian Reading Circles."

20. McIntosh, *LALME,* 1:270, but see also Benskin, "Irish Adoptions," 39, on the use of English documentary and administrative culture in the colony.

21. On the difficulty of filling the post in the 1370s and 1380s, see Watt, "The Anglo-Irish Colony," 364.

22. Berry, *Statutes and Ordinances,* 464–66 for the Kilkenny Statute 34, and 516 for the 1409–10 statute of 11 Henry IV.

23. See Cosgrove, "The Emergence of the Pale," 549, on the fourth earl of Ormond's attempts to reform parliament, notably by bringing in Gaelic-Irish representation.

24. In addition to those statutes mentioned earlier, see Kilkenny Statutes 17 and 18, pp. 446–48 in Berry, *Statutes and Ordinances.*

25. A concept first used in 1297: "Anglici eciam quasi degeneres modernis temporibus hybernicalibus se induunt vestimentis..."; this statute of XXV Edward I (Berry, ibid., 210) speaks of Englishmen who dress in Irish garments, these "hibernicised 'English by blood'..., straggling precariously across both cultures," as Watt calls them; he notes, "Parliament had begun the process of adding a new word to the English language," Watt, "Approaches to the History of Fourteenth-Century Ireland," in Cosgrove, *Medieval Ireland,* 310.

26. We are much indebted to the work of Michael Benskin and to Angela Lucas's *Anglo-Irish Poems of the Middle Ages.*

27. Henry and Marsh-Micheli briefly mention the remarkable realism in the Waterford Charter Rolls, a penchant for single-figure illustration we also see in Douce and in some Gaelic-Irish productions, like the cruder De Burgo Rolls at the end of the fifteenth century. See Henry and Marsh-Micheli, "Manuscripts and Illuminations," for plates of Waterford, figs. 26a and b, and discussion of the De Burgo Rolls, Dublin, Trinity College, MS 1440 (with a plate of the Passion scene, fig. 32); and, for a plate of one of the single figures, see

Notes to Chapter 4

Peter Fox, *Treasures of the Library [of] Trinity College Dublin* (Dublin: Royal Irish Academy, 1986), 68.

28. Or at least against Gaelic-Irish minstrels, although Yonge's comment in 1422 seems to suggest that all "rymours" were tarred with the same brush, because he makes no ethnic distinctions and he was writing for a man known to have hired Gaelic-Irish scribes and legal experts. On Ormond as a patron of both cultures, see Henry and Marsh-Micheli, "Manuscripts and Illuminations," 801.

29. I would like to thank Paul Nelson for advice about hurling.

30. Translated in Berry, *Statutes and Ordinances*, 211.

31. Kerby-Fulton and Justice, "Langlandian Reading Circles."

32. Thomas Usk is a good documentable instance of this; see Paul Strohm, in *Hochon's Arrow: The Social Imagination of Fourteenth-Century Texts* (Princeton, N. J.: Princeton University Press, 1992), "Usk's Appeal," 147.

33. Henry and Marsh-Micheli, "Manuscripts and Illuminations," 795. On the technique and materials of Irish itinerant artists, see ibid., 795 n. 1.

34. For Anglo-Irish manuscripts that show, unlike Douce, evidence of Celtic influence in the decoration, see Longleat 29 (especially its rubrication); Huntington Library HM 129, fol. 1; and Harley 3724 especially.

35. Henry and Marsh-Micheli come closest ("Manuscripts and Illuminations," 786), but regard it as "foreign."

36. Douce's lunatic lollar (figure 16) is much more sympathetically portrayed than the standard image of the fool in Psalter iconography for "Dixit insipiens"; contrast Rawl. G. 185's fool (reproduced in appendix 3 of vol. 4 in Gilbert, *Facsimiles*) with Douce's lunatic, fol. 42r.

37. Ruth Mellinkoff, "Demonic Winged Headgear," *Viator* 16 (1985): 367–81; fig. 5 for the illustration from Paris, 374 for the quote.

38. The text is transcribed here from the manuscript itself; there are several rough drawings by the scribe (overlined with red ink) in the manuscript, but this one has the most careful underdrawing (which is perhaps not saying much). The manuscript has been described by C. W. Dutschke, *Guide to Medieval and Renaissance Manuscripts in the Huntington Library* (San Marino, Calif.: Huntington Library, 1989), 1:166 for the incipit and 172 for a note on the drawings in the manuscript.

39. HM 129 also has pictures of an archbishop (fols. 15v and 35v); a knight who is not a pagan and who has a more muted headdress (fol. 84); a caricature(?) of a monk (fol. 103v); a picture of a coin or a round loaf(?), perhaps in reference to the charitable bishop of the accompanying story on fol. 140v; a rich man (fol. 207); a worldly prince (fol. 213v) (see plate 79 in Dutschke, ibid.).

40. Otto Pächt and J. J. G. Alexander, *Illuminated Manuscripts in the Bodleian Library, Oxford*, vol. 3, plate 653; owned by the prior, Stephen of Derby, 1349–c. 1382. For the literature on the manuscript and its style, see also Sandler, *Gothic Manuscripts*, where it is number 128. For this iconography more generally, see Carruthers, *Book of Memory*, 227 and fig. 10. A similar iconography of extended tongues may be found in Greek illustrated Psalters, where it is used to portray heretics (I would like to thank Pamela Jouris for alerting me to this): see Kathleen Corrigan, *Visual Polemics in the Ninth-Century Byzantine Psalters* (Cambridge: Cambridge University Press, 1992), 14.

41. Yonge retails the story of Trajan, possibly from Langland, but rather more cynically: in his version the angel tells Gregory not to pray for any more such requests! See Yonge's *Secreta*, ed. Steele, 169, where the story arises after a nasty anti-Semitic tale. On Yonge's use of Langland, see Kerby-Fulton and Justice, "Langlandian Reading Circles," 81.

42. The passage thus "bracketed" on fol. 33 corresponds to the passage in Chapter 29 of the *Topographia hibernica*, beginning at (about) "Sacros igitur...," page 168 in Dimock's edition; the "bracketed" passage on fol. 31v corresponds to the opening of Chapter 20, "Preterea pre omni alia...," 165 in Dimock (Giraldi Cambrensis, *Topographia hibernica et Expugnatio hibernica*, ed. James Dimock, Rolls Series vol. 21 (Weisbaden: Kraus

Reprint, 1964; originally published, London: HMSO, 1867). For the same motif in another Gaelic-Irish manuscript, see Rawl. C. 32, fols. 23 and 35, made at Mellifont in 1501.

43. Instances occur in the Book of Ballymote (Royal Irish Academy [RIA], MS 23), the (later) Saints' Island Lough Ree Manuscript (Oxford, Bodleian Library, MS Rawl. B. 505), and the Leabhar Breac (RIA, MS 24); see Henry and Marsh-Micheli, plate 29c of the Book of Ballymote, showing Noah and his family in contemporary Irish dress; plate 28a, showing a picture of Christ in the Leabhar Breac; and plate 26c, showing a canopied saint.

44. The only published description of Harley is still *A Catalogue of the Harleian Manuscripts in the British Museum* (London, 1808).

45. Most importantly the "Kildare" Manuscript, on which see Benskin, "Kildare Poems."

46. Clanchy, *From Memory to Written Record,* caption to plate 20.

47. See the instances of Trajan (figure 27), and of Tom Stowe (figure 6).

48. Carruthers, *Book of Memory,* 222, alluding to Gregory's famous statement: "Aliud est enim picturam adorare, aliud per picturae historiam quid sit adorandum addiscere. Nam quod legentibus scriptura, hoc idiotis praestat pictura cernentibus, quia in ipsa ignorantes uident quod sequi debeant, in ipsa legunt qui litteras nesciunt; unde praecipue gentibus pro lectione pictura est"; *Epist.* XI, 10, *Corpus Christianorum, series latina* (*CCSL*) 140 A:874.

49. M. Wallis, "Inscriptions in Paintings," *Semiotica* 9 (1973): 1–28; see also Allison Flett, "The Significance of Text Scrolls: Toward a Descriptive Terminology," in *Medieval Texts and Images: Studies of Manuscripts from the Middle Ages,* ed. M. M. Manion and Bernard J. Muir (Poststrasse, Switzerland: Harwood Academic, 1991), 43–46.

50. Michael Camille, "Seeing and Reading: Some Visual Implications of Medieval Literacy and Illiteracy," *Art History* 8 (1985): 26–49; Clanchy, *From Memory to Written Record.*

51. See Michael Camille, "The Book of Signs: Writing and Visual Difference in Gothic Manuscript Illumination," *Word and Image* 1 (1985): 143.

52. Along with Camille and Clanchy, see the detailed account in Paul Saenger, "Silent Reading: Its Impact on Late Medieval Script and Society," *Viator* 13 (1982): 367–414.

53. For an intriguing thirteenth-century instance, see the Saint Albans Apocalypse, MS Ludwig III 1, fol. 20 (Santa Monica, Calif., J. Paul Getty Museum), which shows Saint John looking through a slit in the frame (not unlike a medieval anchoress's window into the church) at the "action" of the vision; see also the study by Suzanne Lewis, *Reading Images: Narrative Discourse and Reception in the Thirteenth-Century Illuminated Apocalypse* (Cambridge: Cambridge University Press, 1995); for fifteenth-century examples from Deguilleville, see Hagen, *Allegorical Remembrances.*

54. Camille, "Seeing and Reading," 23–24, and plate 1 of p. 382 of Oxford, Corpus Christi College (CCC) 157.

55. Camille, "Seeing and Reading," n. 6.

56. Langland seems to have this sort of illustration in mind himself when he has characters appear without warning in the poem; e.g., Piers's first appearance: "Peter! quod a plouhman and potte forth his heued" (VII.182); for an account of the variations in medieval speaking gestures in religious art, see Barasch, *Giotto,* 15–39.

57. Cited in Camille, "Seeing and Reading," from John Damascene's account, *Patrologia Graeca* (*PG*) 94, co. 1231.

58. *Canterbury Tales* VIII.200–206, *The Riverside Chaucer,* 3d ed., ed. Larry Benson (Boston: Houghton Mifflin, 1987), and mentioned in a similar connection in Carruthers, *Book of Memory,* 341 n. 17.

59. See Barasch, *Giotto,* 23, fig. 4, for "announcing" hand and fig. 8 for "open" hand. Barasch makes no distinction between "the announcing hand" and the classical *declamatio* gesture (see his figs. 3 and 5 for the latter), but the distinction is useful in text-image relations work such as Camille's and in the present study.

60. For a reproduction of the plate and an excellent discussion of the portrait, see Derek Pearsall, *The Life of Geoffrey Chaucer* (Oxford: Blackwell, 1992); for the relevant stanzas see *Thomas Hoccleve: Selected Poems,* ed. Bernard O'Donaghue (Manchester, England: Carcanet Press, 1982): 97–98; Chaucer's hand points to line 4995. See also Michael Camille,

Notes to Chapter 4

"The Language of Images in England, 1200–1400," in *The Age of Chivalry: Art in Plantagenet England, 1200–1400* (London: Waterfield and Nicolson, 1987), 40.

61. Benskin, "Irish Adoptions," 56.

62. See, for instance, the "Kildare" poem that Wright called "A Song of the Times," *Political Songs*, 196.

63. Benskin, "Irish Adoptions," 47.

64. Scott, in *Facsimile*, lxxix. See also Lucy Freeman Sandler, *Gothic Manuscripts, 1285–1385: A Survey of Manuscripts Illuminated in the British Isles*, 2 vols. (London: Harvey Miller, 1985), illustration 328; and see chapter 1 in this volume on the figure of Pride in Add. 37049.

65. Compare Barasch, *Giotto*, fig. 4, in which the angel uses the same gesture.

66. Iconographically he recalls the male figure of adolescence in the *Omne bonum* (Royal 6.E.VI, pt. 1), fol. 51.

67. See chapter 2, n. 88.

68. Scott, in *Facsimile*, xl.

69. Wallis's distinction between narrating and representing figures who carry speech scrolls is inadequate for dealing with a complex literary narrative cycle like Douce; the distinction between signaling and identifying gives us a greater degree of delicacy.

70. Pearsall, "Manuscript Illustration." Maidie Hilmo has studied the way the figure of the beggar, discussed in this paragraph, and other related figures are turned or contorted in relation to the text. Also relevant here is her perception that the absence of frames "allows the pictures greater 'democratic' access to the script"; see Hilmo, "Transcending Boundaries."

71. In 1256 Laurence Somercote, a collector of the crusade taxes, gave an Englishman's view of the Irish: "What little they collect they spend inordinately. Because whatever part of their poor savings remains over they share generously or, as more often happens, they spend and throw away without caution"; Cotter, *Friars Minor in Ireland*, 129; trans. from W. W. Shirley, ed., *Royal Letters, 1216–1272*, Rolls Series (*Rerum Britannicarum Medii aevi Scriptores*), vol. 2 (London: HMSO, 1862), 117.

72. Justice, *Writing and Rebellion*.

73. See ibid., and Watson, "Censorship."

74. I would like to thank Malcolm Parkes for confirming my sense of this.

75. See, for instance, fol. 3, where he makes an effort at the features of secretary hand, such as one finds in fifteenth-century documents, in the extended Latin quotation ("Sum rex..."); note especially his use of secretary *d* and *g* in "deinceps" (Prol. 152a) and "grana" (156). The *anglicana formata*, as we have seen, is only used for the vernacular in the Dublin Red Book illustration; on the specialized development of an *anglicana formata* for vernacular writing, especially by Scribe D and Scribe Delta, see Doyle and Parkes, "Production of Copies."

76. Sandler, "Notes to the Illuminator"; J. J. G. Alexander, *Medieval Illuminators*, 52–71. Scribes also sometimes wrote notes to the illustrators, and even authors or patrons were known to do so on occasion, but most often it was a workshop supervisor or supervising scribe who performed this duty.

77. There are virtually no pictures of women in the cycle (only Mede and Mercy); the illustrator usually chose to portray a male in some instances in which the text explicitly calls for a female (as we have seen in the case of Pride), and even more commonly he ignores passages about women entirely (see, for instance, his handling of Wrath or his refusal to illustrate passages like IX.70–87). There is also the possibility that the manuscript was being produced *for* a male religious community, as we have seen, which would have influenced such pictorial choices as well. The dearth of saints and holy figures in the cycle also accounts for the lack of women to some extent. It is, of course, possible that a woman illustrator might not have taken an interest in illustrating members of her own sex; however, women illustrators, although known, were relatively scarce (see Alexander, *Medieval Illuminators*, 18–21).

78. Again, I would like to thank Linda Olson for allowing us to cite her unpublished paper, "A Fifteenth-Century Reading of *Piers Plowman*." Phillipa Hardman has suggested to us that the cropped descenders at the top of fol. 74r are in fact the remnants of notes to an illustrator. I think, however, that the two words were likely (before cropping) "lib~ ar~bit~um" (*liberum arbitrium*) (compare the descenders on these two words in the second to last line of fol. 73v), which is indeed the name of the character illustrated on fol. 74. And it is written in the rubricator's red—which would be very unusual for a *note* to the illustrator—and in any case tells the artist nothing about how to portray the figure (to say the least). Since this is one of the figures the rubricator "decorated," it seems more likely that he was highlighting and identifying the figure and the passage—in fact, the passage in question (XVI.181–200) was of great interest to medieval audiences; not only do annotators highlight it, but it was the one extracted from the poem by John Cok (see Kerby-Fulton and Justice, "Langlandian Reading Circles"). Moreover, we cannot find evidence that such red lettering (even partially cropped) occurs elsewhere in the manuscript, and we can only assume that since this is one of the most iconographically idiosyncratic and cryptic of the figures in the cycle, it was thought that identification was necessary (the identification may also have been written in red because the name is in Latin). We are grateful to Phillipa Hardman, however, for pointing this cropped inscription out to us.

79. On Griffiths' and Hilmo's forthcoming work, see preface, n. 11. Whether there might be more than one *painter* at work—that is, more than one person working up or finishing the underdrawings provided by the scribe-illustrator (which may have been exceedingly minimal in instances)—is difficult to say. The ideological unity and singularity of the cycle constitute the primary piece of evidence against such a division of labor. However, against this has to be weighed the fact that there is a noticeable difference in technical skill—*at least in the finished product*—between some illustrations: for instance, the king (figure 5) is much more skillfully executed than Reason (fol. 19), who immediately follows him. Moreover, Reason's face and hair have been poorly worked up and are crudely overlined in red rubricator's ink, whereas neither the faces of Conscience or the king (both of which are more skillfully finished) have been treated this way. There are also the outlines of more complex drapery visible in the *underdrawing* of Reason's garment, which the painter has made no attempt to replicate, suggesting that he was less skilled (or perhaps just more hurried?) than the person who originally drew the picture. Other instances in which the painter has been unable or unwilling to execute the complexities of the underdrawing include the architectural details on the castle (fol. 34) and the facial details of the schoolmaster (fol. 52). The fact that the knight (figure 11) remains unfinished gives us a good sense of the quality of the Douce underdrawings: the artist was definitely skilled in handling drapery, although this is sometimes obscured by the painting; as Mary Patricia Gibson has put it, it is difficult to see why the same person would draw so well and paint so poorly. More accomplished painting, or the attempt at more accomplished painting, seems to appear in pictures with the rarer colors, especially the blues: Conscience (figure 4), Wrath (fol. 26), and Sloth (figure 8) (note the attempt at white modeling in handling of the drapery, but the disastrous painting of the liripipe on the first). Instances such as this could be multiplied, but until further technical work is done, it is impossible to be certain what all the evidence adds up to.

80. See Hilmo, "Transcending Boundaries" and "Retributive Violence" (for a similar instance in the case of the saved thief on fol. 65).

81. See note 78 above.

82. See Hilmo, "Transcending Boundaries." For a helpful summary of the recent scholarship on the question of whether rubrication work was considered as scribal or artistic, see Adelaide Bennett, "Anthony Bek's Copy of the *Statuta*."

83. See note 79 above.

84. For the evidence that the annotator worked this way, see appendix 1.

85. We are grateful for Jeremy Griffiths' personal communication on this matter.

86. See Scott's discussion of each in *Facsimile*, nos. 18, 53. For the variants, see *Piers Plowman: The C Version*, ed. George Russell and George Kane (London: Athlone, 1997), VII.164.

87. See *Facsimile* (Pearsall, xix–xx; Scott, xxviii–xxix) for evidence and theories about how and when the illustrations were done in relation to the text. Jeremy Griffiths had planned, before his untimely death, to complete a spectrographic analysis. His results initially were inconclusive, but we hope that his literary executor will publish his later work on Douce.

88. We are grateful to Malcolm Parkes for suggesting this as an investigative methodology. For the one possible instance (a relation in subject matter across a single bifolium), see chapter 5.

89. See *The Ellesmere Chaucer: Essays in Interpretation*, ed. Martin Stevens and Daniel Woodward (San Marino, Calif.: Huntington Library, 1995).

90. See John B. Friedman, *Northern English Books, Owners, and Makers in the Late Middle Ages* (Syracuse, N.Y.: Syracuse University Press, 1995), 35 and n. 11.

91. Scott, in *Facsimile*, xxix.

5. Visualizing the Text

1. Michael Camille, "Art History in the Past and Future of Medieval Studies," in *The Past and Future of Medieval Studies*, ed. John Van Engen (Notre Dame, Ind.: University of Notre Dame Press, 1994), 365.

2. G. H. Russell, "Some Early Responses to the C-Version of Piers Plowman," *Viator* 15 (1984): 278–80.

3. See Camille, "Art History," 374. Recent studies by Christopher de Hamel and J. J. G. Alexander also point to the inevitable link between scribal interpretation and reception in a manuscript culture; for an example, see Sandra Hindman, *Sealed in Parchment: Rereadings of Knighthood in the Illuminated Manuscripts of Chrétien de Troyes* (Chicago: University of Chicago Press), 5. Hindman's introduction notes the dangers of ignoring the less costly manuscripts; their signs of wear and tear make the retrieval of a medieval reader possible: "Certain unexpected characteristics of the physical appearance of some of these manuscripts are singular. Even though many were evidently luxury productions...they are most often transcribed on crudely prepared, discolored parchment that has been torn, then mended. The corners of their pages are limp and dog-eared from extensive use, their luxurious miniatures now rubbed and worn. Food stains occasionally spot the pages. These factors have led art historians, typically attracted by deluxe, high-quality works produced in the emerging court environment of the Parisian capital, to turn away from Chrétien's manuscripts instead of taking them seriously as cultural artifacts and asking the relevant question: What can the now shabby condition of these manuscripts, coupled with other evidence provided by their texts and illustrations, tell us about their original use?"

4. Michael Camille, *Image on the Edge; The Margins of Medieval Art* (Cambridge, Mass.: Harvard University Press, 1992), 29.

5. For theoretical discussions of the New Art History, see Donald Preziosi, *Rethinking Art History: Meditations on a Coy Science* (New Haven, Conn.: Yale University Press, 1989), and David Freedberg, *The Power of Images: Studies in the History and Theory of Response* (Chicago: University of Chicago Press, 1989).

6. Elizabeth Salter, "*Piers Plowman* and the Visual Arts," in *English and International: Studies in the Literature, Art, and Patronage of Medieval England*, ed. Derek Pearsall and Nicolette Zeeman (Cambridge: Cambridge University Press, 1989), 256–66.

7. Ibid., 257.

8. Ibid., 258.

9. Mary Carruthers, *The Book of Memory* (Cambridge: Cambridge University Press, 1990), 201. Also see Susan K. Hagen, *Allegorical Remembrance: A Study of the* Pilgrimage of the Life of Man *as a Medieval Treatise on Seeing and Remembering* (Athens: Univer-

sity of Georgia Press, 1990), chaps. 1 and 2, "The Mirror and the Eye" and "Reasons, Tokens, Eyes, and Ears"; and Ivan Illich, "*Illuminatio* versus *Illustratio*," in *In the Vineyard of the Text: A Commentary to Hugh's* Didascalicon (Chicago: University of Chicago Press, 1993), 107–9.

10. On visual meditation and spiritual autobiography, see Denise Despres, *Ghostly Sights: Visual Meditation in Late Medieval Literature*, chap. 2, "Franciscan Meditation: Historical and Literary Contexts." On *compositio*, see Carruthers, *Book of Memory*, 197: "Composition is not an act of writing, it is rumination, cogitation, dictation, a listening and a dialogue, a 'gathering' (collectio) of voices from their several places of memory."

11. See Carruthers, *Book of Memory*, 191–93; Frances Yates, *The Art of Memory*, chap. 4, "Medieval Memory and the Formation of Imagery" (London: Routledge and Kegan Paul, 1966); and Despres, "Franciscan Meditation." A convincing discussion of medieval visual meditation, because it is couched in an argument in favor of recontextualizing images, is David Freedberg, "*Invisibilia per visibilia*: Meditation and the Uses of Theory," in *The Power of Images: Studies in the History and Theory of Response* (Chicago: University of Chicago Press, 1989), 161–191.

12. Carruthers, *Book of Memory*, 201.

13. Ibid., 143. See Yates, *Art of Memory*, 91: "These figures...stand out from their backgrounds, giving them an illusion of depth on a flat surface which was altogether new. I would suggest that both features may owe something to memory." There are numerous examples of such foregrounding for meditative and mnemonic drawings in English fourteenth- and fifteenth-century manuscripts. See Otto Pächt and J. J. G. Alexander, *Illuminated Manuscripts in the Bodleian Library, Oxford*, vol. 3, *British, Irish, and Icelandic Schools* (Oxford: Clarendon Press, 1973). See, for example, the marginal drawings illustrating Nicholas de Lyra's *Commentary on the Old Testament*, plate 99, fig. 1067a, Oxford, Bodleian Library, MS Laud Misc. 152, 154 (c. 1463); also the marginal illustrations from a fifteenth-century manuscript of *Dicts and Sayings of the Philosophers*, Oxford, Bodleian Library, MS Bodley 943 (27703), plate 102, figs. 1091b and c; a typical meditative image of the Crucifixion may be found in plate 91, fig. 969, Douce 240 (fifteenth century), a New Testament.

14. See Lesley Lawton, "The Illustration of Late Medieval Secular Texts, with Specific Reference to Lydgate's *Troy Book*," in *Manuscripts and Readers in Fifteenth-Century England*, ed. Derek Pearsall (Cambridge: Brewer, 1983), 41–69.

15. Wolfgang Kemp, "Visual Narratives, Memory, and the Medieval *Esprit du Systèm*," in *Images of Memory: On Remembering and Representation*, ed. Susanne Kuchler and Walter Melion (Washington, D.C.: Smithsonian Institution Press, 1991), 106.

16. Derek Pearsall and A. S. G. Edwards, "The Manuscripts of the Major English Poetic Texts," in *Book Production and Publishing in Britain, 1375–1557* (Cambridge: Cambridge University Press, 1989), 261.

17. Hagen, *Allegorical Remembrance*, 50.

18. See John B. Friedman, *Northern English Books, Owners, and Makers in the Late Middle Ages* (Syracuse, N.Y.: Syracuse University Press, 1995), esp. chap. 5, "'Hermits Painted at the Front': Images of Popular Piety in the North," 148–202.

19. Illich, *In the Vineyard*, 109. On the difference between *illuminatio*, in a context of monastic *lectio*, and *illustratio*, see 107–11.

20. Anne Hudson, *The Premature Reformation: Wycliffite Texts and Lollard History* (Oxford: Clarendon Press, 1988), 400: "The perception of the poem as a social document, and not the record of any theological or even mystical quest into which the readings of modern critics have transmuted it, is confirmed by the later works that certainly show its influence." Hudson's statement mistakenly identifies "mystical" with private spirituality and "theological" with clerical; mystical writers are not outside of the cultural and political conditions of book production, as Nicholas Watson's work on Julian Norwich and vernacular theology has demonstrated. Mystical and vernacular theological writers composed in the midst of censorship, reform, and book production impacted by social, economic,

Notes to Chapter 5

and political exigencies. See Nicholas Watson, "The Composition of Julian of Norwich's *Revelation of Love,*" *Speculum* 68, no. 3 (1993): 637–83. See also Watson's informative "Censorship and Cultural Change in Late Medieval England: Vernacular Theology, the Oxford Translation Debate, and Arundel's *Constitutions* of 1409," *Speculum* 70 (1995): 822–64.

21. Suzanne Lewis, *Reading Images: Narrative Discourse and Reception in the Thirteenth-Century Illuminated Apocalypse* (Cambridge: Cambridge University Press, 1995), 207. One might thus even view Douce 104 as reformist apocalyptic, based upon the methodology in Lewis's remarkable study. The Douce illustrator's reliance upon an earlier manuscript tradition and perhaps Matthew Paris's influence makes this an intriguing possibility; ibid., chap. 4, "The Ideology of the Book: Referencing Contemporary Crisis within Spectacular Structures of Power," 207.

22. Our thanks to Maidie Hilmo for providing us with a fifteenth-century description of the process of applying gold leaf as well as ground gold to parchment. Cennino D'Andrea Cennini directs the craftsman to use "ten or twenty leaves" to make "a tree look like one of the trees of Paradise"—no small sum, surely; see *The Craftman's Handbook: The Italian "Il Libro Dell' Arte"* (1437), trans. Daniel V. Thompson Jr. (New York: Dover, 1960), 102.

23. See Margaret Aston, *Lollards and Reformers: Images and Literacy in Late Medieval Religion* (London: Hambledon Press, 1984), esp. 147–64.

24. See Pächt and Alexander, *Illuminated Manuscripts,* plate 969 (and p. 84 on the manuscript provenance). The drawing provides further evidence of a fifteenth-century tradition of marginal illustration as well. The miniature depicts the Crucifixion and a scroll inscribed with "Thomas Pevere."

25. Aston, *Lollards and Reformers,* 164.

26. See ibid., 155.

27. Ibid., 159.

28. Anne Hudson, "Some Aspects of Lollard Book Production," in *Lollards and Their Books* (London: Hambledon Press, 1985), 184–86.

29. See figs. 25, 42–44 in Susan K. Hagen, *Allegorical Remembrance;* these are from Oxford, Bodleian Library, MS Laud Misc. 740, fol. 85v, and London, British Library, MS Cotton Tiberius A.7 fols. 58, 58v, 59v.

30. Scott, in *Facsimile,* xxxvii. This view contrasts with Carruthers's assessment that the manuscript is an "amateur" or "entirely personal production" (*Book of Memory,* 228–29), although Carruthers recognized immediately that the marginal figures serve various mnemonic purposes, as "*imagines rerum,*" "*imagines verborum,*" and as figures "associated with marginal *tituli*" (see 229).

31. Scott, in *Facsimile,* xxix.

32. Scott and Pearsall, in *Facsimile,* xxxvi–xxxvii.

33. Scott, in *Facsimile,* xxix n. 8.

34. MS Bodley 758 is particularly interesting as there are author and scribe portraits at the beginning and end of the *Meditations* (fols. 1 and 87v; see figures 43 and 44).

35. Charles Briggs's forthcoming study includes a discussion of London, Lambeth Palace Library, MS 150, which has a cycle of marginal illustrations like Douce 104 and is the source for Hoccleve. The cycle includes images remarkably like those in Douce 104, including a Senex figure, a flatterer, and a boaster, all clearly from the same tradition of moral and instructional literature.

36. Anne Middleton, "The Audience and Public of *Piers Plowman,*" in *Middle English Alliterative Poetry and Its Literary Background,* ed. David Lawton (Cambridge: Brewer, 1982), 104–5.

37. See Adelaide Bennett, "A Book Designed for a Noblewoman: An Illustrated Manuel des péchés of the Thirteenth Century," in *Medieval Book Production: Assessing the Evidence,* ed. Linda L. Brownrigg (Los Altos Hills, Calif.: Anderson Lovelace, 1990), 163–81.

38. Ibid., 166.

39. Ibid., 172.

Notes to Chapter 5

40. See ibid., 179 n. 11.

41. Scott, in *Facsimile*, xxx.

42. Ivan Illich discusses the marginal gloss in the context of a technological shift from monastic *lectio* (wherein the visible page is a record of speech) to scholastic *studium*: "But glosses were also written on the margin or between the lines. This way of glossing is a visual consequence of the mental process of monastic reading.... During the first quarter of the twelfth century a new kind of order appears on the manuscript page. Interlinear glossing becomes less frequent... the gloss is subordinated to the dominant main text. It is written in smaller letters.... The learned book has ceased to be a sequence of commentaries that are strung like beads on the thread of somebody else's narration. The author now takes it upon himself to provide the *ordinatio*. He himself chooses a subject and puts *his* order into the sequence in which he will deal with its parts" (97–99). Informed by Illich's description, we can see clearly how the Douce illustrator is not only providing marginal commentary, but in the process usurping the author's *auctoritas* to some degree by mapping out an *ordinatio*—a visual pattern of reading that highlights a theme or an argument; see Illich, "*Ordinatio*: Visible Patterns," 99–101; and Malcolm B. Parkes, "The Influence of the Concepts of *Ordinatio* and *Compilatio* on the Development of the Book," in *Medieval Learning and Literature: Essays Presented to Richard William Hunt*, ed. J. J. G. Alexander and M. T. Gibson (Oxford: Clarendon, 1976), 115–41. For two late medieval experiments with the marginal gloss and *ordinatio*, see Lucy Freeman Sandler, "*Omne Bonum: Compilatio* and *Ordinatio* in an English Illustrated Encyclopedia of the Fourteenth Century," in *Medieval Book Production*, ed. Brownrigg, 183–200; and Mary Ann Ignatius, "Christine de Pizan's 'Epistre Othea': An Experiment in Literary Form," *Medievalia et Humanistica*, n.s., 9 (1979): 132–33. For other interesting examples of marginal illustration from utility-grade manuscripts, see Dublin, Chester Beatty Library, MS 80, *Viridarium* (reproduced as figures 54 and 55), a manuscript featuring marginal images of the Seven Ages of Man; the author of the *Viridarium*, Jean Raynaud, was a teacher of law at Avignon (see Elizabeth Sears, "The Ages of Man in the Preacher's Repertory," in *The Seven Ages of Man: Medieval Interpretations of the Life Cycle* (Princeton, N.J.: Princeton University Press, 1986, 126). See also Pächt and Alexander, *Illuminated Manuscripts*, plate 1091, showing illustrations from Oxford, Bodleian Library, MS Bodley 954, late fourteenth century, *Dicts and Sayings of the Philosophers*, made by Stephen Scrope for Sir John Fastolf; and plate 811, miniatures, drawings, and diagrams in a fifteenth-century manuscript of tables, partly based on Nicholas de Lyra, composed by William Norton of Coventry in 1403 (Oxford, Bodleian Library, MS Laud Misc. 156), 72.

43. Michael Camille, "The Book of Signs: Writing and Visual Difference in Gothic Manuscript Illumination," *Word and Image* 1 (1985): 138.

44. See G. H. Russell, "Some Early Responses to the C-Version of Piers Plowman," *Viator* 15 (1984): 280.

45. See Scott, in *Facsimile*, appendix B, for a complete schema of illustrations passus by passus.

46. Catherine of Siena's *Dialogue* is an excellent example of the performative colloquy; Carruthers, *Book of Memory*, 186. Carruthers describes this meditative dialogue in relation to poetry: "What makes a poem...ethical is its construction...a recollecting subject, remembered 'dicta et facta'...and the remembering audience.... the ethical content is made by both the common and specific topics of death, love, and honour, recollected and spoken by somebody to somebody else in this poem, which thereby lodges as an experienced event in the memories of its audiences, memories that are made up equally of imagines (likenesses) and intentiones (responses)" (182). On meditation and the influence of silent reading, see Paul Saenger, "Silent Reading: Its Impact on Late Medieval Script and Society," *Viator* 13 (1982): 396–97.

47. Such is the case with the figure of Lechery on folio 25v, who is usually depicted as a woman. See Kathleen Scott's detailed notes on the Douce illustrator's rendering of the Seven Deadly Sins, specifically xlviii in *Facsimile*.

48. Scott, in *Facsimile*, lix.
49. Pearsall, *C-Text*, lines 285–86.
50. See Stephen B. Nichols, "Philology in a Manuscript Culture," *Speculum* 65 (1990): 7.
51. Ibid., 8.
52. Susan Hagen notes parallels in the rendering of the narrator of the *Pilgrimage of the Life of Man*: "Illustrations of the poem's opening sequences display the same emphasis upon the appearance of the Heavenly City within a mirror. In most illustrated manuscripts there are two initial miniatures, one showing the poet addressing his audience and the other depicting the dreamer sleeping." Hagen notes that the dreamer does not envision himself entering the city, but, rather, "an image of the Heavenly City generally appears above the head of the dreamer.... In this, the *Pilgrimage*'s illustrations are atypical of portrayals of literary dreamers. It is more customary—if some aspect of dream action is to be shown within the same frame—for the dreamer to be included as part of that action.... The distinction is subtle but suggestive: both the texts and illustrations of the *Pilgrimage* qualify that the dreamer does not dream of himself seeing the vision and then seeking the city; rather he sees the vision of the city in a mirror in a dream and then dreams of himself as a pilgrim to that same city. The mirror and its beautiful and compelling image exist elusively between the world of the poet-dreamer and that of the poet-dreamer's dream self"; see pp. 12–15 in *Allegorical Remembrance*. The iconography of the dreamer portraits in Douce 104 are discussed more fully in chapter 3.
53. Lewis, *Reading Images*, 21.
54. Ibid., 20.
55. Ibid., 21.
56. I am much indebted to Kathleen Scott's research on this figure; see Scott, in *Facsimile*, xxxviii–xxxix.
57. Ibid., liv–lv.
58. Ibid., lxvii–lxviii.
59. See passus XIV, lines 19–30.
60. See Scott, in *Facsimile*, lxvii n. 148. Also see *Sixty Bokes Olde and Newe*, ed. David Anderson (Norman, Okla.: The University of Oklahoma Printing Services, 1986), 106, MS Rosenbach 439/16, book 6, fol. 146v.
61. See Kathleen L. Scott, "The Illustrations of *Piers Plowman* in Bodleian Library Ms. Douce 104," *Yearbook of Langland Studies* 4 (1990): 59; and, in *Facsimile*, lxvii. For studies on the medieval faculty of the imagination, see Britton J. Harwood, "Imaginative in Piers Plowman," *Medium Aevum* 44 (1975): 252; A. J. Minnis, "Langland's Imaginatif and Late-Medieval Theories of Imagination," *Comparative Criticism* 3 (1981): 91; and Joseph Wittig, "Piers Plowman B, Passus IX–XII: Elements in the Design of the Inward Journey," *Traditio* 28 (1972): 272–73. There may have been a fifteenth-century tradition of marginal drawings of authors; Pächt and Alexander note the fifteenth-century addition of a marginal drawing of Thomas of Cantimpré to a fourteenth-century manuscript of *De lapidibus preciosis* (plate 962; Oxford, Bodleian Library, MS Rawl. C. 545, p. 84), as well as the fifteenth-century marginal sketch of Adalbertus Levita reading, added to a twelfth-century manuscript of the *Speculum* (plate 145; Oxford, Bodleian Library, MS Bodley 413, p. 17).
62. See Pearsall, *C-Text*, passus XIV, n. 1, p. 234.
63. On *affectus* as a moral disposition, see Minnis, "Langland's Imaginatif," 92. "The poem was directed primarily at the *affectus* or will and not the intellect" (91).
64. John Alford, "The Design of the Poem," in *A Companion to Piers Plowman*, ed. John A. Alford (Berkeley: University of California Press, 1988), 48.
65. A classic example is Bonaventure's penitential *Lignum vitae*; see Despres, *Ghostly Sights*, 28–35.
66. Carruthers, *Book of Memory*, 200–201.
67. See Despres, *Ghostly Sights*, 33–39. In his discussion of meditative texts, such as miracle tales, David Freedberg writes, "What we find in these tales are not generalized de-

scriptions of standard image types, but rather highly particularized descriptions of the tangible and distinctive characteristics of each image. Looks, features, garments, and colors are all described, even the physical condition of the object.... it is not the generalized Mother and Child who feature in these stories, but specific mothers and children...the more distinctive the better. We do not extend our empathy to humanity at large, not to the godhead which is intelligible only to the intellect. This is why, even when formulaic, the effort to differentiate is always plain" (Freedberg, *Power of Images*, 167).

68. The most common examples of visual glossing may be found in books of hours, especially where the text is in Latin so that the illustrations are the matter of meditation; see Christopher De Hamel, *A History of Illuminated Manuscripts* (London: Phaidon Press, 1994), esp. "Books for Everybody," 168–99.

69. Lillian Randall, *Images in the Margins of Gothic Manuscripts* (Berkeley: University of California Press, 1966).

70. This is, of course, the thrust of Camille's *Image on the Edge*; see also Madeline H. Caviness, "Patron or Matron? A Capetian Bride and a Vade Mecum for Her Marriage Bed," in *Speculum* 68 (1993): 333–62.

71. Camille, *Image on the Edge*, 42; emphasis added.

72. See Scott, in *Facsimile*, lxx, no. 54. Scott notes that this is "one of the few surviving English miniatures with a figure of Poverty."

73. Camille, "Book of Signs," 138.

74. Claire Donovan, *The de Brailes Hours: Shaping the Book of Hours in Thirteenth-Century Oxford* (Toronto: University of Toronto Press, 1991); see fig. 14, fol. 1 from the Matins of the Virgin, 43.

75. See Pearsall, *C-Text*, passus XI, n. 196, p. 203.

76. See Ruth Mellinkoff, *Outcasts: Signs of Otherness in Northern European Art of the Late Middle Ages* (Berkeley: University of California Press, 1993), 22: "A fool mocker wears a dagged cape, his identity as a fool confirmed by the powerless foolstick he insultingly offers to Christ. Although dagging is present in upper-class clothing during the fourteenth century, the dagged cape of this fool is identifying and stigmatizing." Mellinkoff also notes that, while the fool sometimes functions as a moral critic (the most famous example would be Lear's fool), he often symbolized "lack of responsibility, chaotic activities,...strange inner life" (30). Such is surely the case with Recklessness.

77. A classic example of this preaching strategy may be found in Alan of Lille, *The Art of Preaching*, trans. Gillian R. Evans (Kalamazoo, Mich.: Cistercian, 1981), chap. 3. Alan's sermon "On Despising Oneself" elaborates upon the theme of self-love through various uses of the mirror metaphor, concluding: "Look at yourself, then, in the mirror of reason...in the mirror of the senses...in the mirror of the flesh. Set yourself before three mirrors: first the mirror of providence...secondly, before the glass of circumspection...thirdly, in the glass of wariness. And so, through this threefold mirror, you will come to threefold vision of a clear conscience, divine contemplation and eternal life" (30).

78. See Barbara Raw, "Piers and the Image of God in Man," in *Piers Plowman: Critical Approaches*, ed. S. S. Hussey (London: Methuen, 1969), 143–79.

79. R. W. Hunt, "Manuscripts Containing the Indexing Symbols of Robert Grosseteste," *Bodleian Library Record* 4 (1953): 242.

80. Ibid., 247–48.

81. See ibid., 248, nn. 1, 2.

82. M. R. James called attention to this image; see R. W. Hunt, "Manuscripts," appendix n. 2, 251.

83. John Cok's theology manuscript annotations are another example of synthetic professional reading.

84. Suzanne Lewis, *The Art of Matthew Paris in the* Chronica Majora (Berkeley: University of California Press, 1988), 32.

85. Ibid., 31.

86. Scott, "The Illustrations of *Piers Plowman*," 4–5. I would disagree slightly with this assessment of the illustrator's principle of selection in subject matter; I am not convinced that he had a particular interest in allegory. To presume that he does suggests to me that the illustrator is being judged by his failure to adhere to illustrative trends in the manuscript culture of London, for example, where secular poetic works tend to offer art historians models of illustrative convention. See Scott's reassessment of this point in *Facsimile*, xxviii.

87. Lewis, *Art of Matthew Paris*, 35.
88. Ibid., 45.
89. Ibid., 58. Note, for example, the single figures on pp. 62, 63, and 132.
90. Ibid., 167.
91. Ibid., fig. 105.
92. Lewis, *Reading Images*, 251.
93. See Lewis, *Art of Matthew Paris*, 43.
94. Lewis, *Reading Images*, 251. Lewis cites a number of convincing examples from the Apocalypse—e.g. Malibu, J. Paul Getty Museum, MS Ludwig III.I.—but uses the initial on fol. 21v (fig. 195) to demonstrate this foreign punning aesthetic. The picture in the initial is the "familiar figure of a man warming himself before a fire from the Calendar representation for the month of February. As the figure pokes the fire and lifts one foot to be warmed, he creates a directional line of action that focuses on the word 'persecu-tus,' which breaks at that point, alerting the reader to the pun intended by his pointing gestures, because *perscrutus* can denote 'poking about.'" Needless to say, even Lewis's example of a "simple mnemonic" might escape a modern reader: "the text dealing with the Eternal Gospel (14:6–7) is introduced by a figure sowing grain (figure 194) from the Calendar iconography for October in contemporary Psalters. The sower's punning strategy draws the reader's eye to the word '*evangelium*' (gospel) in the third line of the adjacent text by pictorially miming the word *evagandus* (spreading or scattering)" (251).
95. Carruthers, *Book of Memory*, 229.
96. Sandler, "*Omne bonum*: *Compilatio* and *Ordinatio*," 183.
97. Ibid., 189.
98. See ibid. for James le Palmer's antifraternal polemic and fig. 6 for his marginal drawing of abandoned infants.
99. We would like to thank Maidie Hilmo of the University of Victoria for generously sharing her research with us on marginal illustration in Douce 104 and the Ellesmere manuscript. See her forthcoming "A Discourse on Vision and the Viewer in the Douce 104 Manuscript of William Langland's Piers Plowman," 2–3.
100. See Hilmo, "A Discourse," 6.

6. Visual Heuristics

1. See Tim William Machan, "Editing, Orality, and Late Middle English Texts," in *Vox Intexta: Orality and Textuality in the Middle Ages*, ed. A. N. Doane and Carol Braun Pasternak (Madison: University of Wisconsin Press, 1991), 229–45.
2. See ibid., 241, and 242–43 for a discussion of *Piers Plowman*.
3. See John Dagenais, "That Bothersome Residue: Toward a Theory of the Physical Text," in *Vox Intexta*, ed. Doane and Pasternak, 246–59.
4. The classic discussion of individualism as a medieval construct is in Caroline Walker Bynum, *Jesus as Mother* (Berkeley: University of California Press, 1982), chap. 3, "Did the Twelfth Century Discover the Individual?"
5. Derek Pearsall has reevaluated this assumption, and my discussion is largely indebted to his consideration of Chaucer's dreamer in *The Life of Geoffrey Chaucer* (Oxford: Blackwell, 1993), 86–87.
6. Ibid., 87.
7. Ibid.

Notes to Chapter 6

8. See, for example, Nicholas Watson, *Richard Rolle and the Invention of Authority* (Cambridge: Cambridge University Press, 1992), and "The Composition of Julian of Norwich's *Revelation of Love,*" *Speculum* 68 (1993): 637–83; Sarah Beckwith, "Problems of Authority in Late Medieval English Mysticism: Language, Agency, and Authority in the Book of Margery Kempe," *Exemplaria* 4 (1992): 171–200. On the epistemological and linguistic difficulties inherent in mystical utterance, see Steven T. Katz, "Mystical Speech and Mystical Meaning," in *Mysticism and Language*, ed. Steven T. Katz (Oxford: Oxford University Press, 1992), 3–41.

9. On the instability of the vernacular and conceptions of authorship, see Machan, "Late Middle English Texts," 230–36. Machan claims that "according to medieval literary theory a vernacular author was an impossibility, and whatever the notoriety of a Chaucer or a Gower, most surviving Middle English texts are, indeed, anonymous. Since Middle English lacked the stabilizing factors of prescriptive grammar and stylistics and often the identification of writer with text, the texts themselves presumably could not contain the *a priori* assumption of permanence. That is, as a work in the vernacular, any Middle English text necessarily lacked the lexical and thematic prestige associated with a text produced by an *auctor* in the language of *auctoritas*" (234).

10. Anne Clark Bartlett provides a fascinating discussion of this passage in her discussion of the "regendering" of medieval instructional texts, in *Male Authors, Female Readers: Representation and Subjectivity in Middle English Devotional Literature* (Ithaca, N.Y.: Cornell University Press, 1995), chap. 2, "Gendering and Regendering: The Case of *De institutione inclusarum.*"

11. Ibid., 50–51.

12. See Karma Lochrie, "The Disembodied Text," chap. 6 in her *Margery Kempe and Translations of the Flesh* (Philadelphia: University of Pennsylvania Press, 1991); see also Edmund Colledge and Romana Guarnieri, "The Glosses by 'M. N.' and Richard Methley to 'The Mirror of Simple Souls,'" *Archivio Italiano per la Storia della Pieta* 5 (1968): 357–82.

13. See Kathryn Kerby-Fulton, "Who Has Written This Book? Visionary Autobiography in Langland's C Text," in *The Medieval Mystical Tradition in England: Exeter Symposium V*, ed. Marion Glasscoe (Cambridge: Cambridge University Press, 1992), 101–16, for a review of this criticism and a reconsideration of autobiographical information in the context of religious visionary, rather than secular visionary, writing; see also Caroline M. Barron, "William Langland: A London Poet," in *Chaucer's England: Literature in Historical Context*, ed. Barbara A. Hanawalt (Minneapolis: University of Minnesota Press, 1992), 91–109; Anne Middleton, "William Langland's 'Kynde Name': Authorial Signature and Social Identity in Late Fourteenth-Century England," in *Literary Practice and Social Change in Britain, 1380–1530*, ed. Lee Patterson (Berkeley: University of California Press, 1990), 15–82; and Lawrence Clopper, "The Life of the Dreamer: The Dreams of the Wanderer in *Piers Plowman*," *Studies in Philology* 86, no. 3 (1989): 261–85.

14. See Laurence de Looze, "Signing Off in the Middle Ages: Medieval Textuality and Strategies of Authorial Self-Naming," in *Vox Intexta*, ed. Doane and Pasternak, 162–78; and Sylvia Huot, "Authors, Scribes, *Remanieurs*: A Note on the Textual History of the *Romance of the Rose*," in *Rethinking the Romance of the Rose*, ed. Kevin Brownlee and Sylvia Huot (Philadelphia: University of Pennsylvania Press, 1992), 203–33.

15. See de Looze, "Signing Off," 165.

16. I am here referring to Middleton's assertion that "the anagrammatic signature ... is the literary equivalent of the rebus or visual pun, and like it, doubles and foregrounds the number and complexity of the acts required for its decoding.... the wit of the anagrammatic signature thus derives from the perpetual double life of the text, its claims to represent the spoken and audible voice ... as well as visible signs representing the meaning of things.... it tends to problematize rather than celebrate the written as a means of stabilizing communicative authority"; Middleton, "William Langland's 'Kynde Name,'" 35.

17. See John Dagenais, "The Bothersome Residue: Toward a Theory of the Physical Text," in *Vox Intexta*, ed. Doane and Pasternak, 252–53.

18. Peter Brieger, "Pictorial Commentaries to the Commedia," in P. Brieger, M. Meiss, and C. S. Singleton, *Illuminated Manuscripts of the Divine Comedy*, vol. 1 (Princeton, N.J.: Princeton University Press, 1969), 88–89; see also Kerby-Fulton, "Visionary Autobiography," 108–10.

19. Brieger, "Pictorial Commentaries," 90.

20. See Kerby-Fulton, "Visionary Autobiography," 107–8; and Lawrence Clopper, "Need Men and Women Labor? Langland's Wanderer and the Labor Ordinances," in *Chaucer's England*, ed. Barbara Hanawalt (Minneapolis: University of Minnesota Press, 1992), 112–13.

21. See John Burrow's seminal article, "Langland Nel Mezzo Del Cammin," in *Medieval Studies for J. A. W. Bennett*, ed. P. L Heyworth (Oxford: Oxford University Press, 1981), 35–39. Burrow was discussing the B text when he raised this unpopular issue.

22. Daniel Poirion, "From Rhyme to Reason: Remarks on the Text of the *Romance of the Rose*," in *Rethinking the* Romance of the Rose, ed. Brownlee and Huot, 65.

23. Susan K. Hagen, *Allegorical Remembrance: A Study of* The Pilgrimage of the Life of Man *as a Medieval Treatise on Seeing and Remembering* (Athens: University of Georgia Press, 1990), 15; see figs. 1–9 for various illuminators' interpretations of this subtle narrative strategy.

24. *The Book of Margery Kempe*, ed. Sanford Brown Meech, EETS 1940, o.s. 212 (Oxford: Oxford University Press, 1940), p. 186, line 15. For a general discussion of this metaphor, see RitaMary Bradley, "The Speculum Image in Medieval Mystical Writers," in *The Medieval Mystical Tradition in England: Papers Read at Dartington Hall, July 1984* (Cambridge: Brewer, 1984), 9–26.

25. See Steven F. Kruger, "Mirrors and the Trajectory of Vision in Piers Plowman," *Speculum* 66 (1991): 74–91.

26. Anne Middleton, "The Audience and Public of *Piers Plowman*," in *Middle English Alliterative Poetry and Its Literary Background: Seven Essays*, ed. David Lawton (Cambridge: Cambridge University Press, 1982), 117.

27. See Lawrence M. Clopper, "The Life of the Dreamer: The Dreams of the Wanderer in *Piers Plowman*," *Studies in Philology* 86, no. 3 (1989): 263.

28. See David Hult, *Self-Fulfilling Prophecies: Readership and Authority in the First Roman de la Rose* (Cambridge: Cambridge University Press, 1986), 74–93.

29. See Scott, "Illustrations of *Piers Plowman*," 17, and the extensive list of dreamer portraits Scott provides. It is also possible that this is an author portrait, signifying not the historical author but the authorial imaginative faculty, and that the agricultural instrument is a scribe's knife; see Scott's discussion on p. 11.

30. See Susan K. Hagen, "The Mirror and the Eye," in *Allegorical Remembrance*, 7–29 (see introduction, n. 30). Hagen provides a number of plates of the sleeping dreamer in figs. 1–8; of special interest are plates 5, 6, and 8. In plate 5, Paris Bibliothèque Nationale, MS fr. 823, fol. 1 (1393), the first image we see is that of the poet writing, and thus the image of a retrospective narrator; the next quadrant illustrates the dreamer and the mirror. In British Library MS Harley 4399, fol. 1, an early-fifteenth-century manuscript, the first image we see is that of the poet preaching (with his pointed finger emphasizing speech) from a pulpit to a rapt audience. Clearly this image underscores the oral and performative nature of the text, as does another fifteenth-century manuscript, Paris Bibliothèque Nationale, MS fr. 376, fol. 1.

31. See Kerby-Fulton's discussion in "Visionary Autobiography," 101–4; see also Robert E. Lerner, "Ecstatic Dissent," *Speculum* 67, no. 1 (1992): 33–57.

32. See Peter Dinzelbacher, *Vision und Vision-literature im Mittelalter* (Stuttgart: Hiersemann 1981), 65–77.

33. See Malcolm Richardson, "Hoccleve in His Social Context," *Chaucer Review* 20, no. 4 (1986): 313; and more recently, Derek Pearsall, "Hoccleve's *Regement of Princes*: The Poetics of Royal Self-Representation," *Speculum* 69, no. 2 (1994): 386–410.

34. See Sears, "The Ages of Man," 121–33; Sears convincingly argues for the pervasive influence of "Ages of Man" iconography through the manuscript traditions of compendia

Notes to Chapter 6

like the Franciscan Bartholomaeus Anglicus's *De proprietatibus rerum*, composed circa 1230. Sears notes that "the wealth of extant manuscript copies and the large number of printed editions, not only in Latin but also in French, English, Italian, Provençal, Spanish, and Dutch indicate a long and continuous popularity" (127–28). An example of an early-fifteenth-century compendium with an Irish provenance containing marginal Seven Ages illustrations is Chester Beatty Library, MS 80, fols. 6v and 7. The writer, Jean Raynaud, was a teacher of law at Avignon; he included the text of Thomas of Cantimpre's *Liber de natura rerum* in his manuscript but made significant additions and titled the treatise the *Viridarium* (figures 54–55). Also see Françoise Henry and Genevieve Marsh-Micheli, "Manuscripts and Illuminations, 1169–1603," in *A New History of Ireland*, vol. 2, *Medieval Ireland, 1169–1534*, ed. Art Cosgrove (Oxford, 1987), 801. The evidence suggests that many fourteenth- and fifteenth-century Irish compendia with such homiletic materials "derived from school texts copied probably by Irish students in some of the continental universities renowned for their medical courses, such as Montpellier, Padua, and Salerno. They were probably as divorced from practical Irish medicine as some of the legal texts were from the actual law practice. But copying them was a normal occupation for an *ollamn* of medicine and their possession enhanced his status." The result is compilations of the lives of Irish saints and Irish homilies beside Continental texts like the "Meditations of the Pseudo-Bonaventure" or a manuscript containing lives of saints, homilies, and prayers, with an "excursion into mythology" such as the "Life of Hercules" (804–5). Such Irish scribal practice, and the fact that Irish scribes appeared to belong to wandering families in the fourteenth and fifteenth centuries, add to their eclectic nature and support our discussion of the influence of utility-grade manuscript drawing on the iconography of Douce 104.

35. Burrow, "Langland Nel Mezzo Del Cammin," 24.
36. Scott, in *Facsimile*, lxvii.
37. Scott notes that the head in hand is connected to the human imaginative powers and that there are miniatures in manuscripts of Lydgate's *Fall of Princes* as well as in Boccaccio manuscripts in which figures composing or recollecting dreams or visions are drawn in this position. It is important that in the Rosenbach miniatures that Scott describes, these figures are connected specifically to authorship (*Facsimile*, lxvii).
38. Clopper, "Life of the Dreamer," 264.
39. Scott, in *Facsimile*, lxviii; see, however, Chenu, "Auctor, actor, autor.".
40. See Carruthers, *Book of Memory*, 198–99.
41. Ibid., 199.
42. Pächt and Alexander, *Illuminated Manuscripts*, no. 794, p. 70 and plates.
43. See Hult, *Self-Fulfilling Prophecies*, 75–101.
44. Ibid., 81.
45. Ibid., 95.
46. Robert O. Payne warns us that critics must use caution when exploring late medieval self-images of the poet: "Because we are dealing with self-images, we may (as too many historical critics have warned us) press them too hard for direct personal revelations, and when those are not forthcoming, dismiss the images as 'merely conventional.' On the other hand, seeing such imagery as conventional, we may fail to pursue adequately its integration into the strategies and purposes of various poems and so miss much of what the poems do after all reveal about their authors' attitudes toward their craft and themselves as practitioners of it"; Payne, "Late Medieval Images and Self-Images of the Poet: Chaucer, Gower, Lydgate, Henryson, Dunbar," in *Vernacular Poetics in the Middle Ages*, ed. L. Ebin, Studies in Medieval Culture 16 (Kalamazoo, Mich.: Medieval Institute, 1984), 260.
47. J. A. Burrow, *The Ages of Man* (Oxford: Oxford University Press, 1988), 71.
48. See *Fasciculus Morum: A Fourteenth-Century Preacher's Handbook*, trans. and ed. Sigfried Wenzel (University Park, Pa.: Pennsylvania State University Press, 1989), 431.
49. For discussions of these various schema, see Samuel C. Chew, *The Pilgrimage of Life* (New Haven, Conn.: Yale University Press, 1962); Burrow, *Ages of Man*; and Sears,

Notes to Chapter 6

Ages of Man. See plate 4, "Wheel of the Ten Ages of Man," in *The Psalter of Robert de Lisle,* ed. Lucy Freeman Sandler (Oxford: Oxford University Press, 1983).

50. See Sears, *Ages of Man,* 139–40.

51. See Burrow, *Ages of Man,* 70.

52. See fig. 84, autobiographical schema, *Opicinus de Canistris, Biblioteca Apostolica Vaticana, MS. Pal. lat. 1993,* fol. 11r, in M. W. Evans, *Medieval Drawings* (London: Hamlyn, 1969). See also Richard Solomon, *Opicinus de Canistris* (London: Warburg Institute, 1936), 205–15.

53. Ibid., description of plate 84.

54. See Camille, *Image on the Edge,* 14.

55. See Elizabeth Kirk, *The Dream Thought of Piers Plowman* (New Haven, Conn.: Yale University Press, 1972), 49; and Despres, *Ghostly Sights,* 130–32.

56. Scott, in *Facsimile,* xlv–xlvi.

57. The topoi of physical indulgence, be it material or sexual, is associated with youth in nearly every medieval work of conversion I can think of, including Augustine's *Confessions,* Abelard's *Historia,* Bonaventure's *Life of Francis,* and *The Book of Margery Kempe.*

58. See the figure of "Adolescens" on folio 58 of the *Omne Bonum,* reproduced as fig. 328 in Sandler, *Gothic Manuscripts.*

59. See fig. 81 and pp. 138–40 in Sears, *Ages of Man.*

60. See ibid., plate 79 of Pierpont Morgan Library, MS G. 50, fol. 29, and her discussion on pp. 138–39.

61. See ibid., 147–48.

62. See V. A. Kolve, *Chaucer and the Imagery of Narrative* (Stanford, Calif.: Stanford University Press, 1984); esp. chap. 2, "Chaucerian Aesthetic: The Image in the Poem," 59–84. Kolve identifies these clusters as "symbolic images known from other medieval contexts, both literary and visual, where their meanings are stipulative and exact, unmediated by the ambiguities and particularities of fiction" (61).

63. Ibid., 168.

64. Quoted in ibid., 168–69. Kolve points to the Black Knight's confession as an example of this typology: "For hyt was in my firste youthe, / And thoo ful lytel good y couthe, / For al my werkes were flyttynge / That tyme, and al my thoght varinge. / Al were to me ylyche good / That I knew thool but thus hit stood."

65. E. Talbot Donaldson, *"Piers Plowman": The C-Text and Its Poet,* Yale Studies in English 113 (New Haven, Conn.: Yale University Press, 1949), 202–19.

66. See Clopper, "Life of the Dreamer," 266.

67. See R. W. Frank, *Piers Plowman and the Scheme of Salvation* (New Haven, Conn.: Yale University Press, 1957), 48–49; Despres, *Ghostly Sights,* 133.

68. Scott, in *Facsimile,* lxii.

69. See the discussion of the Giraldian illustrative tradition in chapter 2.

70. Middleton, "William Langland's 'Kynde Name,'" 47.

71. Ibid., 42. I would like to thank Lawrence Clopper for providing me with his unpublished essay "A Search for Wille Longelonde," which discusses the C text as an autobiographical poem.

72. See Middleton, "William Langland's 'Kynde Name,'" 42: "What the disposition of the authorial name in his poem discloses, however, is Langland's progressively deeper understanding and more fully conscious acceptance—comparable to that of Augustine—of both the literary and social consequences of developing a philosophic and spiritual quest in the narrative form of an apparently historically specific life-story."

73. I would like to thank Maidie Hilmo for providing me with an outline of her lecture "The Illustrations of Recklessness and Fortune in Bodleian Library MS Douce 104." She noticed the flakes of gold inside the ascending part of Fortune's Wheel when she examined the manuscript under ultraviolet light.

74. See Pearsall, *C-Text,* n. 196.

75. This reading is specific to Douce 104; in Pearsall's edition of the C text it appears as "That wit shal turne to wrechednesse for Wil hath al his wille!" (XII.2).
76. See Scott, in *Facsimile,* lxiv.
77. Mary Dove, *The Perfect Age of Man's Life* (Cambridge: Cambridge University Press, 1986), 107.
78. Ibid., 105.
79. The Douce illustrator understood the importance of this argument and chose to represent the thief on fol. 65r (XIV.145–59) despite the fact that "no representative types of a thief, as a single figure, are known outside of this manuscript" (Scott, in *Facsimile,* lxviii). This seems typical of the Douce illustrator, who often works against or outside of iconographic conventions.
80. See Sylvia Huot, *The Romance of the Rose and Its Medieval Readers* (Cambridge: Cambridge University Press, 1993), 285–322.
81. See Sears, *Ages of Man,* figs. 61, 62, 81 — all of which have the same kind of marginal illustrations as Douce 104, despite the fact that they are legal, scientific, and theological manuscripts.
82. See Lucy Freeman Sandler, *The Psalter of Robert De Lisle* (Oxford: Oxford University Press, 1983), figs. 52–55.
83. Reproduced in Dove, *Perfect Age,* 80.
84. See for example Pächt and Alexander, *Illuminated Manuscripts,* fig. 1018a, Oxford, Bodleian Library, MS Bodley Rolls I (2974), a fifteenth-century manuscript of George Ripley's *Alchemical Roll.*
85. BL, Egerton MS 2572, fol. 51, reproduced in Michelle P. Brown, *Understanding Illuminated Manuscripts: A Guide to Technical Terms* (Malibu, Calif.: J. Paul Getty Museum, 1994), 85.
86. Scott points out that, while there are many illustrations in English manuscripts of physicians holding up jordans, in only two scenes is the doctor a religious, and only one of these is a friar; see London, British Library, MS Royal 17 C.XV, medical miscellany, fol. 104; Scott, in *Facsimile,* n. 187.
87. Scott, "Illustrations of *Piers Plowman,*" 76.
88. See Stephen A. Barney, "Generic Influences on *Piers Plowman,*" in *A Companion to Piers Plowman,* ed. Alford, 117–33.
89. Elizabeth Petroff, *Medieval Visionary Women* (Oxford: Oxford University Press, 1986), 22.
90. See Nicholas Watson, *Richard Rolle and the Invention of Authority* (Cambridge: Cambridge University Press, 1990); and Ralph Hanna III, "Will's Work," in *Written Work: Langland, Labor, and Authorship,* ed. Steven Justice and Kathryn Kerby-Fulton (Philadelphia: University of Pennsylvania Press, 1997).
91. See Kerby-Fulton, "Piers Plowman and the Medieval Visionary Tradition," in *Reformist Apocalypticism and* Piers Plowman (Cambridge: Cambridge University Press, 1990), 76–132.
92. Ibid., 116. See also Kathryn Kerby-Fulton, "Langland and the Bibliographic Ego," in *Written Work,* ed. Justice and Kerby-Fulton, 67–143.
93. See Roger Ellis, "'Flores Ad Fabricandum...Coronam': An Investigation into the Uses of the Revelations of St. Bridget of Sweden in Fifteenth-Century England," *Medium Aevum* 52 (1983): 163–86.
94. Ibid., 172.
95. Ibid., 173.

Conclusion

1. Caroline M. Barron, "William Langland: A London Poet," in *Chaucer's England: Literature in Historical Context,* ed. Barbara Hanawalt (Minneapolis: University of Minnesota

Press, 1992), 93. See also Derek Pearsall, "Langland and London," in *Written Work*, ed. Justice and Kerby-Fulton, 185–207.

2. See S. Ogilvie-Thomson, "An Edition of the English Works of Longleat 29," (D. Phil. thesis, Oxford University, 1980), 205.

3. See index of manuscripts cited under (for Rolle) Longleat 29, Bodley e Mus. 232; (for the Northern Homily Cycle) Huntington Library, HM 129; (for the *Secreta*), chapter 4 and Kerby-Fulton and Justice, "Langlandian Reading Circles."

4. See Helen Barr, *The Piers Plowman Tradition* (London: Dent's, 1993).

5. Steven Justice, *Writing and Rebellion*, 104–6.

6. Wendy Scase, "Two Piers Plowman C-Text Interpolations: Evidence for a Second Textual Tradition," *Notes and Queries*, December 1987, 456–63.

7. See Kathryn Kerby-Fulton, "Langland in His Working Clothes? Scribe D and the Ilchester Manuscript," in *Essays in Honor of Derek Pearsall*, ed. A. Minnis (forthcoming).

8. Clanchy, *From Memory to Written Record*, 248. See also Sandra Hindman's discussion of the seal as a preliterate oral transaction and the source of Manessier's pun in *Le Conte del Graal* where he concludes: "Que li rois Artus seella. / Encor le puet on veoir la, / Tot seelle en parchemin, / Cil qui errent par le chemin" (All those who travel the road will still see the story there sealed in parchment) (198). Hindman explains that the term "sealed" here "employs the language of orality in which a seal witnesses an oral transaction. Then in a much richer, more subtle metaphor...he equates the traveling knight with the reader" (199). The same kind of tension (historically situated by Hindman in the various regions that produced Chrétien manuscripts) between the authority of the written word and the spoken narrative, signaled visually in the manuscript, occurs in Douce 104.

9. Derek Pearsall, "Poverty and Poor People in *Piers Plowman*", in *Medieval English Studies Presented to George Kane*, ed. E. Kennedy et al. (Woodbridge, England: Brewer, 1988), 167–85.

10. Lester K. Little, *Religious Poverty and the Profit Economy in Medieval Europe* (Ithaca, N.Y.: Cornell University Press, 1978; reprint, 1992), 28. On this tendency to view the poor as sinful and parasitic, see Michael Mollat, *The Poor in the Middle Ages: An Essay in Social History*, trans. Arthur Goldhammer (New Haven, Conn.: Yale University Press, 1986); and David Aers, "Piers Plowman and Problems in the Perception of Poverty: A Culture in Transition," *Leeds Studies in English* 14 (1983): 5–25. For an Irish context, see T. K. Moylan, "Vagabonds and Sturdy Beggars: Poverty, Pigs, and Pestilence in Medieval Dublin," in *Medieval Dublin: The Living City* (Dublin: Irish Academic Press, 1990).

11. John A. Burrow, "Words, Works, and Will: Theme and Structure in Piers Plowman," in *Piers Plowman: Critical Approaches*, ed. S. S. Hussey (London: Methuen, 1969), 118.

12. On the dreamer's "inward journey" more generally, see Joseph Wittig, "Piers Plowman B. Passus IX-XII: Elements in the Design of the Inward Journey," *Traditio* 28 (1972): 211–80.

13. See Pearsall, *C-Text*, passus X, p. 178 n. 2. Also see Penn Szittya, *The Antifraternal Tradition in Medieval Literature* (Princeton, N.J.: Princeton University Press, 1986); E. Talbot Donaldson, *Piers Plowman: The C-Text and Its Poet*, Yale Studies in English Literature 113 (New Haven, Conn.: Yale University Press, 1949); and Robert Worth Frank Jr., *Piers Plowman and the Scheme of Salvation*, Yale Studies in English 136 (New Haven, Conn.: Yale University Press, 1957), 48–49. On the possibility that these are the robe of a hermit, see Ralph Hanna III, "Will's Work," in *Written Work*, ed. Justice and Kerby-Fulton, and his discussion in *William Langland*, Authors of the Middle Ages, no. 3 (Newcastle upon Tyne: Athenaeum Press, 1993), 23.

14. Carruthers, *Book of Memory*, 186.

15. Michael Camille, "Seeing and Reading: Some Visual Implications of Medieval Literacy," *Art History* 8 (1985): 28.

16. Scott (*Facsimile*, lx) had thought that this figure was Cain, but this isn't iconographically possible. This figure is not a man, but a youth, according to the iconography of the *Ages of Man*. He has a round, undeveloped face and curly blond hair. It is true that

Wit's discourse on "unholy" progeny cites Cain as the product of a sinful union of Adam and Eve during a period of penance, but the Douce figure has none of the standard attributes of Cain in medieval iconography, nor does the illustrator, with his tendency toward literalism and iconomachia, reproduce biblical figures unless necessary (see Pearsall, *C-Text,* 189 nn. 212, 219).

17. Barbara A. Hanawalt's research provides considerable evidence of the casual acceptance of bastards in fourteenth- and fifteenth-century English communities, despite the complications they posed for the proper succession of land: "Common law and church law differed from customary law but were also generous in recognizing the legitimacy of children"; see 72–73, 194–197 in Hanawalt, *The Ties That Bound: Peasant Families in Medieval England* (Oxford: Oxford University Press, 1986).

18. Justice, *Writing and Rebellion,* 106.

19. Ibid.

20. It was quite likely the patron who had suppressed, or discouraged the completion of, as we have seen, the images of the devil (and Castle of Care), Abraham, the angel, and perhaps the knight—possibly for polemical reasons.

Appendix 1

1. I am grateful to Malcolm Parkes for confirming that the hand of the main text is rather old-fashioned. For an instance of the two forms of *anglicana formata* appearing in the same document, see the plate of Oxford, Bodleian Library, MS Douce 257 in Parkes, *English Cursive Hands, 1250–1500* (London: Scolar Press, 1979), plate 2(i), where a single scribe has copied Alexander de Villa Dei's "Massa Compoti" in the formal script and the commentary in the cursive script. This manuscript, however, dates from over forty years before Douce 104, and the comparison serves to confirm the assumption that Douce 104 was created in a provincial setting. See Pearsall and Scott for further discussion of the manuscript's apparent provincialism.

2. In addition to Parkes, see Lucas, "Capgrave," for an illuminating paleographical demonstration of the same scribe handling two scripts.

3. Malcolm Parkes, "Punctuation, or Pause and Effect," in *Medieval Eloquence,* ed. James J. Murphy (Berkeley: University of California Press, 1978), 127–42. See also George Kane, "The Text," in *A Companion to Piers Plowman,* ed. John Alford (Berkeley: University of California Press, 1988), 175–200, for a far less positive view of the role of correctors.

4. Pearsall and Scott mention his consistent substitutions of "trewþ" and "trewe" for "leaute" and "lele," which we take to be dialectically motivated as well.

5. Compare the annotation and the main text on fol. 61r (see appendix 2) with Pearsall XIII.130.

6. For a transcription of many sets of *Piers* annotations, see Marie-Claire Uhart, "The Early Reception of Piers Plowman" (Ph.D. dissertation, University of Leicester, 1986); see also chapter 3, note 1, for a list of other transcriptions of *Piers* annotations.

7. This observation explains some of the odd readings like "kissed" for the West Midlands "cused" at Prol. 95, fol. 2.

8. The scribe could, of course, be translating from an exemplar annotated in West Midlands dialect, but there is no apparent evidence for this. The hand of the annotator is very close to the hand of Longleat 29 and Bodley e Mus. 232, which suggests the possibility of scribes of shared training in the Pale district; see chapter 3, note 24.

Appendix 2

1. It should, however, be noted that flourishes at the ends of words that could be either abbreviations or otiose strokes are not indicated in the text by apostrophes because the scribe of the Douce annotations has a tendency to use hairlines to trace otiose strokes, and thus they are usually distinguishable from his deliberate abbreviation marks; see Mal-

colm Parkes, *English Cursive Hands, 1250–1500* (London: Scolar Press, 1979), xxix-xxx. In any case, according to Angus McIntosh and M. L. Samuels, final *e* has no morphological significance in Anglo-Irish dialect; see their "Prolegomena to a Study of Mediaeval Anglo-Irish," *Medium Aevum* 37 (1968): 5.

2. E.g., -*it* or -*yt* for ME -*ith*, -*yth*; see McIntosh and Samuels, "Prolegomena," 5. The abbreviation ~ has been expanded not as ME *ur*, but rather as Anglo-Irish *wr*, in accordance with typical spellings elsewhere in the manuscript (e.g., "fayto*wrs*" [VIII.124]; cf. "faytowrs" [XI.54]). The abbreviation that indicates a plural or genitive that has been expanded as *is*, *es*, or *ys* (and italicized), with reference, where possible, to the same word fully spelled elsewhere in the annotations; in instances in which the word does not occur elsewhere it has been expanded (and italicized) as *is*, which is this scribe's spelling of choice, judging by the frequency of its occurrence in unabbreviated words (*ys* occurs only slightly less often, and *es* least of all). However, it must be noted that the scribe often spells the same word a variety of ways, for example, "prestys" (I.184), "prestis" (III.463), "prestes" (XIV.251), which makes any such attempt at standardization seem slightly anachronistic. The Douce annotator's preference for *is* (or *ys*) is interesting in the light of John Fisher's study of B-text manuscripts in which he found that only three regularly use the *is/ys* spellings, the others conforming to the Chancery standard *es*; see his "*Piers Plowman* and the Chancery Tradition," in *Medieval English Studies Presented to George Kane*, ed. Edward Donald Kennedy, Ronald Waldron, and Joseph S. Wittig (Woodbridge, England: Brewer, 1988), 274.

3. Parkes, *English Cursive Hands*, xxviii–xxix.

4. The later owner, antiquarian Francis Douce (1757–1834), made several annotations in the manuscript, which are, of course, easily distinguishable from those of the medieval annotator. There are also a few corrections or textual additions in the margins (e.g., fol. 4v) and some miscellaneous pen trials (e.g., fol. 45), plus a curious, barely legible vertical note on fol. 12v in a later hand.

5. The first two notes on 23v at passus V.169 and 178 are in a different hand. The note on 90v at passus XIX.252 may also be in another hand. For a description of the hand of the annotating scribe, see appendix 1.

Index

❖

Note: There are three idiosyncrasies in the following index. (1) In the absence of a bibliography, modern scholars are comprehensively indexed. (2) Langland's personifications are listed under their own names; concepts with the same names can be distinguished by the use of lowercase (e.g., "Simony" and "simony"). (3) *Piers Plowman* characters discussed textually appear in this index, while discussion of the characters as illustrations in Douce 104 appear in the index of illustrations in Douce 104.

Abell, William, 30, 66, 75
Abraham, 164. *See also* index of illustrations in Douce 104: Abraham, unfinished
Activa Vita, 31. *See also* index of illustrations in Douce 104: Activa Vita
Adam, 132; as symbol of sinning, 51
Aelred of Rievaulx, 148; *De institutione inclusarum*, 148
Aers, David, 250 n. 10
Africa, Dorothy, xv, 220 n. 29
Ages of Man, 5, 156–62, 164, 165
Alan of Lille, 243 n. 77
Alexander of Hales, 76–77. *See also* biblical *modi*
Alexander, Jonathan J. G., 25, 43–44, 205 n. 6, 206 nn. 5, 7, 209 n. 52, 211 n. 22, 213 n. 40, 48, 214 n. 57, 219 n. 11, 229 n. 27, 234 n. 40, 236 nn. 76–77, 238 n. 3, 239 n. 13, 240 n. 24, 241 n. 42, 242 n. 61, 247 n. 42, 249 n. 84
Alford, John, 132, 209 n. 51, 212 n. 28, 219 n. 13, 242 n. 64
Allen, J.B., 10, 80, 208 n. 47, 230 n. 43, 231 n. 57
alliteration, 57
Ambrose, Saint, 30
Anderson, David, 242 n. 60
angel. *See* index of illustrations in Douce 104: Angel, unpainted
Anglo-Ireland, xii, xiii, xiv, 7, 11, 17–18, 22, 27–28, 33–34, 37–39, 41, 46, 50–51, 56, 58–60, 76, 78, 93–94, 97–102, 169, 176; civil service, 92–93; iconographical tradition, xii; literature, 7, 208 n. 33; musical culture, 34; poetry, 39, 56, 60, 85, 105; readers, 7. *See also* readers, Anglo-Irish; satire, Anglo-Irish
animals, 4, 22, 28, 32, 139, 141, 143, 172–73, 175. *See also* index of illustrations in Douce 104: Piers's oxen; Sleeping bishop and wolf with sheep; Two beasts
annotations, types of: ethical pointers, 73, 76, 86; linguistic glosses, 73; literary responses, 76, 79; narrative reading aids, 76; narrative summary notes, 73, 86; polemical comments, 71, 73, 76, 77, 78; source glosses, 73
annotator of HM 143 (*H*), 68, 74, 77–78, 79–90, 177, 178
Anselm, Saint, 141
Anthony, Saint, 30
Antichrist, 18, 20, 128. *See also* index of illustrations in Douce 104: Antichrist
anticlericalism, 19, 21, 27, 29, 56, 59, 77–78, 232 n. 10; *See also* satire, anticlerical
anti-intellectualism, 84–85, 101
antimendicantism, 7, 11, 18, 22–24, 26, 28, 33, 35–37, 39, 81, 83–84, 89, 91, 173, 230 n. 48. *See also* FitzRalphian tradition; satire, antimendicant
apocalypticism, 21, 22

253

Index

apologia (C.V), 24, 81, 86–88, 130–31, 149, 151–52, 158, 160, 166, 218 n. 119
apostolic life, 124, 137, 138. *See also* poverty, apostolic
Aquinas, Saint Thomas, 77
Arundel, Thomas (archbishop), 8, 20. *Constitutions*, 8, 211 n. 17
Aston, Margaret, 124, 213 nn. 43, 45, 214 n. 56, 215 n. 70, 240 nn. 23, 25–27
Augustine, Saint, 30, 64, 83, 120, 141, 148, 151, 154, 160, 161; *City of God*, 62; *Confessions*, 120, 148, 248 n. 57
Augustinians, 70, 72
Austin, J. L., 207 n. 23
authority, 5, 6, 7, 17, 22, 39, 81, 108, 139, 166, 168, 170; church, 20, 23, 25, 31, 93–94; clerical, 18, 23, 170; ecclesiastical, 17, 24, 25, 30, 170; Latin and vernacular, 130; lay, 30, 63; legal, 66, 170; moral, 136; papal, 18, 212 n. 26; political, 17, 123; royal, 18, 55; spiritual, 30, 62, 121, 143; textual, 129, 149; written, 129
authorship, 132, 147, 148, 153, 154, 155; authorial intention, 1, 145; authorial signing, 149; self-presentation, 149
autobiography, 149, 150, 159; spiritual, 120, 132, 152, 154, 156, 158, 162–63, 166

Baker, J. H., 218 n. 7, 219 n. 10
Bakhtin, Mikhail, 227 n. 13
Baldwin, Anna, 219 n. 13
Ball, John, 7, 35, 65, 170, 175, 218 n. 19, 225 n. 99; Ball letters, 9
Barasch, Moshe, 105, 205 n. 9, 225 n. 91, 235 nn. 56, 59, 236 n. 65
Barney, Stephen A., 249 n. 88
Barn of Unity, 4
Barr, Helen, 208 n. 35, 250 n. 4
Barron, Caroline, 169, 245 n. 13, 249 n. 1
Bartlett, Anne Clark, 245 nn. 10–11
Bartlett, Robert, 52, 222 nn. 51–52
bas de page, 12, 126, 139, 209 n. 55
bastardy, 7, 26, 35, 53, 87, 89, 135, 170, 251 n. 17. *See also* index of illustrations in Douce 104: Young bastard
Baxter, Margery, 38
beauty, censoring of female, 61, 108, 224 n. 88
Beckwith, Sarah, 245 n. 8
Bede, Saint, 141
beggars, 51, 53, 64–66, 79, 138. *See also* index of illustrations in Douce 104: Beggar
begging, 7, 34, 110, 170
Belling of the Cat, 32, 57

Benedictines, 51, 57, 223 n. 73
Bennett, Adelaide, xvi, 47, 218 n. 7, 219 n. 10, 220 nn. 21, 24–27, 39, 237 n. 82, 240 nn. 37–39
Benskin, Michael, 106, 216 n. 96, 219 n. 111, 218 n. 1, 223 n. 67, 226 n. 3, 232 n. 5, 233 nn. 20, 26, 235 n. 45, 236 nn. 61, 63
Benson, C. David, 226 n. 1, 229 n. 28
Benson, Larry, 235 n. 58
Bernard, Pat, xvi
Bernard, Saint, 27
Berry, Henry F., 97, 215 nn. 74, 77–79, 218 n. 6, 231 n. 2, 233 nn. 22, 24–25, 234 n. 30
biblical commentaries, 58, 121
biblical *modi*, 76–77
Blackfriar's Council (1382), 7, 216 n. 99
Blazejewski, John, xvi
Bliss, Alan, 56, 59, 210 nn. 3, 5, 217 n. 105, 223 nn. 67–68, 224 n. 82, 233 n. 12
Blumenthal, Uta-Renate, 213 n. 45
boats, 13, 30, 50–51, 140, 143. *See also* index of illustrations in Douce 104: Boat as flood symbol
Boffey, Julia, 227 n. 14, 228 nn. 16–19
Book of Margery Kempe, The. *See* Kempe, Margery
books of hours, 12, 13, 26, 29, 31, 55, 65, 110, 159, 243 n. 68
Boyle, Leonard E., 20, 211 nn. 12, 14–15
Bradley, RitaMary, 246 n. 24
bread, 49, 64–65
Bretoner, 106, 136. *See also* index of illustrations in Douce 104: Wastor
Brewer, Charlotte, 216 n. 93
brewer, 79
bribery, 87, 109
Bridget of Sweden, 166, 167; *Revelations*, 166, 167
Brieger, Peter, 150, 206 n. 6, 246 nn. 18–19
Briggs, Charles, 240 n. 35
Brooks, John, 58, 223 n. 75, 224 nn. 76–77
Brown, A. L., 232 n. 4
Brown, Michelle P., 249 n. 85
Brownlee, Kevin, 206 nn. 4, 6
Brownrigg, L. L., 206 nn. 4, 6
Bruce, Edward, 60
Bruges, Walter de, 58
Brusendorff, Aage, 72, 227 n. 14, 228 nn. 17–18, 20, 229 n. 28
Bryer, Ronald, 223 nn. 70, 72
Burrow, John A., 151, 153, 173, 246 n. 21, 247 nn. 35, 47, 49, 248 n. 51, 250 n. 11
busts: in margins, 13, 22, 99, 100, 101, 137, 140–43

Index

Butler, James, 59, 93, 210 n. 5
Bynum, Caroline Walker, 244 n. 4

Caiaphas, 29. *See also* index of illustrations in Douce 104: Caiaphas
Cain, 51, 175, 222 n. 46, 250 n. 16
Calkins, Robert, 219 n. 17
Cambrensis, Giraldus, 11, 34, 49, 51, 59, 208 n. 48; *Conquest of Ireland,* 59; *Expugnatio hibernica,* 51, 52, 59, 60; *Topographia hibernica,* 34, 51, 52, 53, 208 n. 48, 234 n. 42. *See also* Giraldian tradition
Camille, Michael, xvii, 5, 45, 103, 134, 174, 205 n. 9, 207 n. 24, 218 n. 7, 219 n. 12, 16, 18–19, 220 n. 20, 223 n. 62, 235 nn. 50–52, 54–55, 57, 59, 236 n. 60, 238 nn. 1, 3–4, 241 n. 43, 243 nn. 70–71, 73, 248 n. 54, 250 n. 15
Canterbury Tales, The. See Chaucer, Geoffrey
Capgrave, John, 69–72, 74–75, 88–90, 92, 178, 209 n. 54, 227 n. 10, 229 n. 27; *Commentarius in Genesim,* 70; *nota mark of,* 70–71, 73, 75
Carmelites, 36, 216 n. 93
Carruthers, Mary, 4, 103, 121, 144, 207 n. 19, 208 n. 45, 234 n. 40, 235 nn. 48, 58, 238 n. 9, 239 nn. 10–13, 240 n. 30, 241 n. 46, 242 n. 66, 244 n. 95, 247 nn. 40–41, 250 n. 14
Cart of Christendom, 4
Carter, Ronald, 207 n. 21
Carthusians, 63
Catherine of Siena, 166; *Dialogues (The Orchard of Syon),* 166, 241 n. 46
Caviness, Madeline H., 243 n. 70
Chambers, R. W., 226 n. 6
Charity, 140
Chart, David, 215 n. 72
Chaucer, Geoffrey, 72, 85, 105, 119, 147–49, 153, 159, 167; *Canterbury Tales,* 5, 73, 89, 159; *Second Nun's Tale,* 104; Wife of Bath, 73
Chenu, M.-D., 230 n. 44
Chess of Love, The, 160
Chew, Samuel C., 247 n. 49
Christ, 26, 29, 30, 71, 85, 100, 124, 135, 140, 163, 164; body of, 29; life of, 28
Christianson, Paul, 213 n. 47
Chronica majora. See Paris, Matthew
chronicles, 13, 44, 50, 54, 56, 90, 92, 121, 125, 140, 142, 144, 166, 171
Church, 140
City of God. See Augustine, Saint

civil service, xiii, 12, 17, 23–24, 43, 47, 49, 50, 57, 72, 78, 92, 96, 99, 102. *See also* Exchequer, Court of
Clanchy, M. T., 102, 103, 171, 207 n. 22, 220 nn. 20, 22, 25, 28, 235 nn. 46, 50, 52, 250 n. 8
Clark, J. P. H., 216 n. 91
Clarke, Howard, 223 n. 68
Clergy, 128, 154, 160
clergy, 20, 25; secular, 7, 20–21, 23, 26, 57, 61, 74, 78, 86, 88, 90. *See also* anticlericalism
clerical concubinage, 19, 215 n. 82
Clopper, Lawrence M., xvii, 213 n. 46, 216 n. 95, 245 n. 13, 246 nn. 20, 27, 247 n. 38, 248 nn. 66, 71
clothing, 5, 18–19, 23–24, 32, 36, 40, 61–63, 96, 98, 106–8, 112–13, 125, 136–38, 145, 154–55, 163
Coburn, Jeanne, 215 n. 68
coins. *See* money
Cok, John, 30, 70–71, 74–75, 90, 214 n. 57, 229 nn. 26–27, 237 n. 78, 243 n. 83
collatio, 120, 132, 154, 155
Colledge, Edmund, 224 n. 79, 245 n. 12
colophon, 42, 48, 78, 94, 213 n. 47, 218 n. 6
color, use of, 41, 44, 82, 100, 115, 123–24, 180; black, 113, 154; blue, 5, 113, 123, 136, 159; brown, 45, 113; gray, 131, 144, 152; gray-blue, 154; green, 45, 96, 136, 145; orange, 136, 159; orange-red, 96; pastels, 111; pink, 113, 123, 136; red, 5, 45, 96, 113, 138, 154; reddish-brown, 63; russet, 163; tan, 131, 152; white, 113, 154, 159; yellow, 45, 96, 113
Colton, John (archbishop), 34
Concupiscencia Carnis, 82, 162
confession, of seven sins, 129
Conquest of Ireland. See Cambrensis, Giraldus
Conscience, 29–30, 35, 54–55, 66, 86, 88, 136, 158. *See also* index of illustrations in Douce 104: Conscience
conscience, 129
Constitutions. See Arundel, Thomas
Contemplatif, 64. *See also* index of illustrations in Douce 104: Contemplatif
Copeland, Rita, xv, 217 n. 106
Corrigan, Kathleen, 234 n. 40
Cosgrove, Art, 92, 101, 205 n. 5, 209 n. 50, 215 n. 76, 231 nn. 1–2, 232 n. 8
Cotter, Francis J., 230 nn. 38, 47, 236 n. 71
courtly love tradition, 120

255

Index

Covetousness. *See* index of illustrations in Douce 104: Covetousness
crosses, 30, 124
crowns, 50, 86, 89, 109, 143
crucifixes, 30, 53, 63, 124
Crucifixion, 3, 29, 137
Crumpe, Henry, 37, 38, 41, 210 n. 2, 216 n. 99
Cursor Mundi, 126
Curtis, Edmund, 224 n. 79
cutpurse, 79

Dagenais, John, 150, 244 n. 3, 245 n. 17
Dante, 76–77, 150; *Divine Comedy*, 150
David, King, 29
Dean, James, 214 n. 64, 217 n. 113
De Brailes Hours, The. See index of manuscripts: London, British Library, MS Additional 49999
De Brailes Psalter. See index of manuscripts: Cambridge, Fitzwilliam Museum, MS 330, no. 4
de Canistris, Opicinus, 157
declamatio. See speaking gestures
deconstructionism, 147
Decretals. See index of manuscripts: London, British Library, MS Royal 10.E.IV. *See also* Gregory, Saint
Deguilleville, Guillaume de, 103, 235 n. 53; *Pèlerinage de la vie humaine*, 126, 150, 151, 152, 153, 166
de Hamel, Christopher, 209 n. 56, 238 n. 3, 243 n. 68
De hebraicis quaestionibus. See index of manuscripts: London, British Library, MS Royal 5.D.X
De Lisle Hours. *See* index of manuscripts: New York, Pierpont Morgan Library, MS G.50
De Lisle Psalter. See index of manuscripts: London, British Library, MS Arundel 18
De mansionibus filiorum Israel. *See* index of manuscripts: London, British Library, MS Royal 5.D.X.
Dennison, Lynda, 219 n. 8
Despensers, 18, 57, 58, 224 n. 79
Despres, Denise L., 12, 209 n. 54, 239 nn. 10–11, 242 nn. 65, 67, 248 nn. 55, 67
devotion, 35, 38, 75, 90, 122, 124
devotional works, 30, 75, 121, 125, 126, 148, 156
diagrams, 157; tree, 32
dialect: Anglo-Irish, 181; Hiberno-English, 59, 208 n. 33; Middle Hiberno-English

(MHE) of Douce 104, xii, xiii, 1, 2, 7, 18, 42, 68, 115–16, 180; South West Midlands (SWM), 56; West Midlands, 56, 179, 180
Digger. *See* index of illustrations in Douce 104: Digger
Dimock, James, 234 n. 42
Dinzelbacher, Peter, 246 n. 32
Dobest, 28, 132, 173
Dobet, 132, 173, 174. *See also* index of illustrations in Douce 104: Dobet
documents: legal, 11, 207 n. 21 ; sealed, 13, 22, 45, 49, 171
Dominic, Saint, 30
Dominicans, 36, 66, 141, 216 n. 87, 93
Donaldson, E. Talbot, 160, 210 n. 66, 248 n. 65, 250 n. 13
Douce, Francis, 252 n. 4
Douce 104: annotator of (D), 6–9, 42, 67, 68, 70, 73–74, 76, 77–90, 94, 97, 100, 122, 128, 130–31, 133, 135, 137, 141, 144, 149, 150–51, 166, 169, 170–75, 177–80; corrector of, 42, 68–69, 81, 94, 114, 175, 177–79, 180, 206 nn. 9–10; low-budget production of, 1, 3, 9–10, 22, 31, 101, 108, 111, 113, 114, 115, 116, 123, 126, 208 n. 46; patron of, 1, 2, 8, 17, 27–28, 29, 33, 42, 61, 63, 66, 67, 73, 89, 92, 115, 134, 172, 175–176, 206 n. 8; rubrication of, xiv, xv, 5, 8, 96, 105, 112–13, 119, 136, 171, 172–73; scribe-illustrator of, xiii, xiv, xv, 1, 3, 4–10, 11, 13–14, 17, 18–19, 21–23, 25–36, 39–41, 42, 44, 45, 47–48, 49–56, 60–61, 62, 63–67, 68, 78, 82, 85, 87, 88, 89, 92, 93–103, 105, 106–10, 111–12, 114–16, 119–40, 141–43, 144, 145, 147, 149, 150, 151–54, 155, 156, 158, 159, 161–66, 167–68, 169, 170–74, 177–79
Douce 104 illustrations: avoidance of orthodox religious iconography in, 4, 26, 122; meditative function of, 61, 116, 120–21; mnemonic function of, 116, 121, 139, 173; neglect of setting in, 3–4
Douie, D. L., 220 n. 23
Dove, Mary, 163, 249 nn. 77–78, 83
Dowel, 113, 129, 160, 161, 170, 173, 174
Doyle, A. Ian, 8, 74, 75, 208 n. 40, 228 nn. 22, 25, 236 n. 75
dreamer, 5, 30, 54, 84, 87, 111, 123, 129–33, 149–54, 158, 160–63, 166. *See also* index of illustrations in Douce 104: Will
dream vision, 9, 120–23, 126, 128–32, 147, 149, 153, 155, 166–67

Index

Dronke, Peter, 206 n. 6, 230 n. 42
Dublin, 102, 110, 169
Dublin-Pale region, 8, 17, 57, 94, 169
Dublin Public Record Office, destruction of, 23
Dutschke, C. W., 219 nn. 9–10, 14, 221 nn. 33, 37, 223 n. 62, 234 nn. 38–39

Economou, George, 193
Edward IV, 70, 71
Edward III, 145
Edwards, A. S. G., 227 n. 14, 228 nn. 16, 18–19, 239 n. 16
Edwards, R. Dudley, 212 n. 34, 232 n. 12
Elde, 79. *See also* index of illstrations in Douce 104: Elde
Elliott, Margaret, 219 n. 12
Ellis, Roger, 167, 249 nn. 93–95
Emmerson, Richard, 210 n. 65, 212 n. 24
emotion, 44, 75, 90, 109, 122, 128, 133, 147
Envy. *See* index of illustrations in Douce 104: Envy
Evans, Gillian R., 243 n. 77
Evans, M. W., 225 n. 92
Exchequer, Court of, 11, 23–24, 44–46, 49, 89, 95, 96, 169, 173; Dublin, xiii, xv, 47, 58, 97; Westminster, xiii. *See also* civil service; Red Book of the Exchequer; *signa*, Exchequer
Expugnatio hibernica. *See* Cambrensis, Giraldus
eye, inner, 120

facial features, 23, 31, 44, 61, 64, 108
Fall of Princes. See Lydgate, John
Fals, 108
family, 25, 172
Fasciculus Morum, 156
Fauntelete, 164
Feast of of Patience, 79
Ferster, Judith, 224 n. 81, 231 n. 3
Fincke-Keeler, Margaret, xvi
Finter, Kathryn, 205 n. 4
first person, use of, 79, 87
Fisher, John, 252 n. 2
FitzRalph, Richard (archbishop of Armagh), 7, 18, 33–39, 53, 98, 173; *De pauperie salvatoris*, 39; FitzRalphian tradition, 27, 37–39, 61, 208 n. 33
Fletcher, Alan, xvii, 34, 210 n. 3, 211 n. 17, 215 n. 74, 223 n. 68
Flett, Allison, 235 n. 49
Flower, Robin, 223 n. 66
fool, 137, 138

Fortune, 82, 153, 154. *See also* index of illustrations in Douce 104: Fortune's wheel
Four Ages of Man, 157
Fox, Peter, 234 n. 27
Francis, Saint, 30, 38
Franciscans, 7, 27, 31, 36, 37, 38–39, 61, 66, 141, 173, 216 n. 96, 217 n. 62
Frank, Robert Worth, Jr., 248 n. 67, 250 n. 13
Freedberg, David, 238 n. 5, 239 n. 11, 242 n. 67
friars, 7, 18, 22, 35–36, 37, 79, 138. *See also* Dominicans; Franciscans
Friedman, John B., 225 n. 105, 238 n. 90, 239 n. 18
Froissart, Jean, 147
Fulton, Gordon, xviii, 207 n. 21

gaze, 19, 61, 108, 110–11, 135–39, 155, 163, 164, 174
Germanus of Constantinople, 55
gestures: of despair, 145, 163; of devotion, 36; of grief, 35, 53; of guilty surprise, 40; of humility, 174; of interiority, 60; of vernacular reading, 111. *See also* speaking gestures
Gibson, Gail McMurray, xvi
Gibson, Mary Patricia, xvii
Gilbert, John T., 208 n. 25, 212 n. 33, 224 n. 79, 232 n. 12, 233 n. 15, 234 n. 36
Gilliland, Corinna, xvii
Giraldian tradition, 10, 11, 13, 46, 48–56, 110, 141, 209, 209 n. 48. *See also* Cambrensis, Giraldus
Glutton, 32. *See also* index of illustrations in Douce 104: Glutton
gold, xiv, 5, 120, 125, 205 n. 3, 240 n. 22, 248 n. 73; dust, 31, 62, 66, 123, 124, 138, 161, 170, 172; leaf, 27, 123, 218 n. 120; spray, 119, 123
goliardic verse, 38, 56
Gould, Karen, 217 n. 104
Gower, 73, 74, 96, 227 n. 10
Grace, xiv, 66
Grady, Frank, 231 n. 50
Gransden, Antonia, 221 n. 37, 222 n. 53, 223 n. 54
Great Malvern Priory, 57
Green, Richard Firth, 227 n. 14
Gregorian Reform, 27, 213 n. 45
Gregory, Saint, 30, 85, 103, 104; *Decretals*, 43
Griffiths, Jeremy, 112, 114, 205 n. 11, 237 nn. 79, 85, 238 n. 87

Index

Grimbald, 104
Grindley, Carl, xvii, 68, 226, 226 nn. 1–2, 5, 228 n. 23, 229 nn. 28, 31, 230 nn. 32, 40, 45, 231 n. 55
Grosseteste, Robert, 6, 69, 140
grotesques, 32, 33, 40, 122
Guarnieri, Romana, 245 n. 12
Guild Book of the Barber Surgeons of York. See index of manuscripts: London, British Library, MS Egerton 2572
guilds, 35
Guth, De Lloyd, xvi, 205 n. 8, 232 n. 12

Hagen, Susan K., 208 n. 30, 235 n. 53, 238 n. 9, 239 n. 17, 240 n. 29, 242 n. 52, 246 nn. 23, 30
hagiography, 166
hair, 22, 97, 98, 108, 112, 113. See also tonsure
Hall, Hubert, 212 nn. 30–31, 220 nn. 21, 38, 231 n. 64
Halligan, Theresa, 231 n. 50
Hammond, Eleanor P., 72, 227 n. 14
Hanawalt, Barbara A., xv, 251 n. 17
hands. See index of illustrations in Douce 104: Hand holding ball; Hand holding coins; Pointing hand (fol. 75v); Pointing hand (fol. 79v)
Hanley, W. de, 45
Hanna III, Ralph, 211 n. 18, 222 n. 50, 223 n. 73, 249 n. 90, 250 n. 13
Hardman, Phillipa, 237 n. 78
Harris, Kate, 228 n. 24
Harrowing of Hell, 3
Harwood, Britton J., 242 n. 61
hats, 125, 141. See also headdress; headgear
Hazelden, R. B., 226 n. 6
headdress, 100, 107, 109, 161. See also hats
headgear, 100, 145. See also hats
Heinlen, Michael, 69, 178, 226 n. 7
Henry, Françoise, 99, 232 n. 11, 233 nn. 12, 27, 234 nn. 28, 33, 35, 235 n. 43, 247 n. 34
Heuser, W., 216 n. 96, 217 nn. 109, 112
Hilmo, Maidie, xvi, xvii, 40, 60, 65, 96, 112, 114, 205 n. 11, 214 n. 65, 216 n. 90, 218 nn. 118, 120, 221 n. 40, 222 n. 47, 224 nn. 88, 91, 102, 231 n. 49, 236 n. 70, 237 nn. 79–80, 82, 240 n. 22, 244 nn. 99–100, 248 n. 73
Hilton, Walter, 166
Hindman, Sandra, 206 nn. 4, 6–7, 238 n. 3, 250 n. 8

Historia Anglorum. See index of manuscripts: London, British Library, MS Royal 14.C.
historiated initials, 40, 44, 47, 48, 119, 127, 130, 152, 159, 206 n. 3
Hoccleve, Thomas, 17, 23, 96, 105, 153, 157, 240 n. 35; *De Regimine Principium*, 127
Hogg, James, 212 n. 24
Holkam Bible Picture Book. See index of manuscripts: London, British Library, MS Additional 47682
Holub, Robert C., 227 n. 13
Holy Church, 20, 31. See also Unity
Holynesse, 162
homophony, 143–44
Honorius of Autun, 27, 30
Hosse, Nicholas, 233 n. 13
Hours of Catherine of Cleves, The, 65–66
hours. See books of hours
Hudson, Anne, 27, 125, 208 nn. 37, 39, 41, 216 nn. 99–100, 217 n. 102, 239 n. 20, 240 n. 28
Hult, David, 155, 162, 246 n. 28, 247 nn. 43–45
Humphrey, Duke, 70, 71
Hunger, 65, 128; See also index of illstrations in Douce 104: Hunger
Hunt, R. W., 141, 209 n. 62, 243 nn. 79–82
Huot, Sylvia, 115, 149, 163, 206 nn. 4–6, 245 n. 14, 249 n. 80

iconomachia, 26, 30, 31, 41, 119, 122–23, 124–25
Ignatius, Mary Ann, 241 n. 42
Illich, Ivan, 122, 239 nn. 9, 19, 241 n. 42
illustration: document, 29, 130; historical book, 56; legal book, 11, 13, 26, 43–44, 45, 46, 47, 48, 50, 56, 66, 102, 108, 214 n. 53; Lollard book, 33, 39, 41; unframed marginal, 1, 3, 9, 10, 13, 23, 28, 31, 33, 45–46, 48, 51, 52, 54, 60, 61, 100, 155. See also Douce 104 illustrations; index of illustrations in Douce 104
Imaginatif, 14, 80, 132–33, 153–54, 155, 156. See also index of illustrations in Douce 104: Imaginatif
imagination, 120–21, 128
Imray, Jean, 226 n. 106
interiority, 147, 151–52
Isaiah, 82
Iser, Wolfgang, 72, 88, 227 n. 13

James, M. R., 221 n. 39, 231 n. 54, 243 n. 82
Jauss, Hans Robert, 72, 88, 227 n. 13

Index

Jerome, Saint, 30, 141
Job, 77, 90
John, Saint, 131
John Chrysostom, Saint, 104
John of Worcester, 104
John the Baptist, 82
Jones, Holly, xvi
Jouris, Pamela, xvii, 234 n. 40
Julian of Norwich, 151, 152, 167
Justice, Steven, xiv, xvii, 7, 35, 110, 175, 208 nn. 36, 38, 210 nn. 1, 5, 211 n. 21, 212 n. 28, 215 n. 83, 217 nn. 106–107, 218 n. 119, 220 nn. 22–23, 221 n. 43, 223 n. 58, 224 n. 81, 225 n. 99, 226 n. 6, 228 n. 22, 229 nn. 26, 28, 231 n. 54, 232 nn. 4, 6, 233 n. 19, 234 nn. 31, 41, 236 nn. 72–73, 237 n. 78, 250 nn. 3, 5, 251 nn. 18–19

Kane, George, 179, 210 nn. 66, 4, 238 n. 86, 251 n. 3
Kashe, R. E., 214 n. 66, 223 n. 74
Katz, Steven T., 245 n. 8
Kemp, Wolfgang, 239 n. 15
Kempe, Margery, 120, 148, 151–52, 158–59, 166–67; *Book of Margery Kempe*, 120, 151, 166–67, 248 n. 57
Kennedy, Kevin, xvii, 233 n. 16
Ker, N. R., 224 n. 80
Kerby-Fulton, Kathryn, 208 n. 38, 210 nn. 1, 5, 211 nn. 13, 21, 212 nn. 24, 28, 35, 213 n. 41, 214 n. 50, 216 n. 95, 220 nn. 22, 23, 221 n. 43, 222 n. 50, 223 n. 56, 224 n. 81, 225 n. 99, 226 n. 6, 228 n. 22, 229 nn. 26, 28, 231 nn. 54, 59, 63, 66, 232 nn. 4, 6, 233 n. 19, 234 nn. 31, 41, 237 n. 78, 245 n. 13, 246 nn. 18, 20, 31, 249 nn. 91–92, 250 nn. 3, 7
Kildare Gospels. *See* index of manuscripts: London, British Library, MS Harley 913
king, 55. *See also* index of illustrations in Douce 104: King
Kirk, Elizabeth, 248 n. 55
Kitzinger, Ernst, 213 n. 45
knight, 136. *See also* index of illustrations in Douce 104: Knight, unpainted
Kolve, V. A., 159, 248 nn. 62–64
Kruger, Steven F., 246 n. 25

laity, 20, 26, 29, 33–34, 35, 40, 60, 62–64, 70, 78, 92, 124, 127, 138, 156. *See also* authority, lay; literacy, lay; patronage, lay; readers, lay
Langland, William, xiii, 1, 7, 9, 11–12, 19–22, 28, 44, 57–58, 66–67, 76–77, 87, 90–91, 137, 148, 149, 152, 166–68, 174; *Piers Plowman*, 1, 4, 6, 7, 8, 9, 25, 38–39, 56, 59, 69, 93, 94, 119–20, 125, 142, 149, 165; *Piers Plowman*, narrative structure of, 3, 8, 130; *Piers Plowman*, reception of, 13–14, 17–18, 57–58. *See also* readers, of *Piers Plowman*
Lawton, Leslie, 207 n. 15, 209 n. 53, 239 n. 14
Lawyer. *See* index of illustrations in Douce 104: Lawyer
Lazarevich, Gordana, xvi
Leclerq, Jean, 214 n. 61
Leff, Gordon, 210 n. 2
Lerner, Robert E., 246 n. 31
Lewis, Suzanne, 51, 52, 131, 141, 142, 144, 209 nn. 55, 57, 61–62, 214 n. 63, 221 nn. 36, 39, 43, 46, 222 nn. 47–48, 51, 223 nn. 59, 64, 225 n. 90, 235 n. 53, 240 n. 21, 242 nn. 53–55, 243 nn. 84–85, 244 nn. 87–94
Liar, 207 n. 21; *See also* index of illustrations in Douce 104: Liar with charter
Liberum Arbitrium, 79, 140. *See also* index of illustrations in Douce 104: Liberum Arbitrium
Life of St. Alban. See Paris, Matthew
literacy, 12, 13, 21, 66, 84, 125, 127; Latin, 25, 33, 88; lay, 14; visual, 2, 17, 21, 28, 41, 127
Little, Lester K., 250 n. 10
Little Malvern Priory, 57
Lochrie, Karma, 245 n. 12
Lollardy, 7, 27, 32, 33, 37, 41, 90, 124, 125, 208 n. 33
Long, Joseph, 210 nn. 3, 5, 217 n. 105, 233 n. 12
Looze, Laurence de, 149, 245 nn. 14–15
Lovelich, Henry, 75; *Graal*, 75; *Merlin*, 75
Lucas, Angela, 217 nn. 110–11, 218 n. 1, 233 n. 26
Lucas, Peter, 70, 71, 227 nn. 10, 12
Lunatic lollar. *See* index of illustrations in Douce 104: Lunatic lollar
Luttrell Psalter, the, 62, 133
Lydgate, John, 3, 72, 73, 74, 119; *Fall of Princes*, 73; *Troy Book*, 3, 127
Lyf, 165

Machan, Tim William, 244 nn. 1–2, 245 n. 9
Machaut, Guillaume de 147
manicules, 100, 101, 102, 128, 140, 145, 155
manuscript: pouncing, 114; pricking, 114; ruling, 115

Index

manuscripts: devotional, 155, 159; legal, 43, 45, 47, 92, 105, 121, 140, 142, 144, 153, 171, 205 n. 10, 218 n. 7, 219 n. 10, 221 n. 39; luxury, 119, 123, 126, 145; scribe-illustrated, 1–2, 9, 10–14, 64, 94; utility-grade, 10, 12, 119, 125, 153, 155, 174, 241 n. 42, 247 n. 34; Wycliffite, 125. *See also* index of manuscripts

marriage, 25, 35, 89–90, 97

Marsh-Micheli, Genevieve, 99, 232 nn. 11–12, 233 n. 27, 234 nn. 28, 33, 35, 235 n. 43, 247 n. 34

Mary Magdalene, 39, 169

Massa, Michael de, 126, 155; *Writings on the Passion. See* index of manuscripts: Oxford, Bodleian Library, MS Bodley 758

Mathews, Josephine, xvi, 220 n. 23

McClintock, H. F., 46, 212 n. 30, 220 nn. 22–23

McGann, Jerome, 206 n. 11

McIntosh, Angus, 208 n. 33, 210 n. 7, 218 n. 1, 223 n. 68, 226 n. 3, 233 n. 20, 252 nn. 1–2

Mead, Stephen, xviii

Mechtild of Hackeborn, 85, 231 n. 50

Mede, 47, 55, 66. *See also* index of illustrations in Douce 104: Mede at Westminster; Mede confessing to friar; Mede riding on sheriff; Mede with chalices

medieval literary theory, 6, 80

meditation, 11, 120–21, 124, 125, 128, 131, 132–33, 147, 156, 157, 159; and images, 121

Medveder, P. N., 227 n. 13

Medylton, Ralph, 155

Meech, Sanford Brown, 246 n. 24

Mellinkoff, Ruth, 100, 219 n. 19, 230 n. 49, 234 n. 37, 243 n. 76

memory, 120–21, 128, 132, 145, 147, 151, 153, 154, 155; and reading, 128; treatises, 121

mendicancy, 18. *See also* antimendicantism

merchants, 44, 47, 48, 107, 123, 215 n. 84

Mercy. *See* index of illustrations in Douce 104: Mercy

Michael, M. A., 219 n. 10, 220 nn. 28–30, 32, 221 n. 34

Middle Hiberno-English (MHE). *See* dialect

Middleton, Anne, 88, 151, 161, 221 n. 42, 222 n. 50, 229 n. 28, 231 n. 62, 240 n. 36, 245 nn. 12, 16, 246 n. 26, 248 nn. 70–72

Minnis, A. J., 229 n. 28, 230 nn. 33–35, 242 nn. 61, 63

minstrels, 31, 34, 93, 97, 98, 111

mirror, 151, 153, 159, 161, 242 n. 52, 243 n. 77

Mirrors of Middle Earth, 151

miscellanies, religious, 127

misericords, 32, 57, 214 n. 67

mnemonics, 6, 11, 25, 29, 32–33, 39, 43, 47–48, 65, 69, 84, 99, 101, 107, 124, 126, 140–41: oral, 129; visual, 13, 44, 50, 129, 174

model books, 3, 30, 54, 56, 60, 114, 134. *See also* pattern books

Modus tenendi parliamentorum, 93, 232 nn. 4, 6–7

Mollat, Michael, 250 n. 10

money, 13, 47, 48, 123, 220 n. 30. *See also* index of illustrations in Douce 104: Hand holding coins; Merchant counting money

Moore, Deborah, xvi

Mortimer, Roger de, 58

Mortimers, 57, 58, 59, 224 n. 80

Moylan, T. K., 225 n. 100, 250 n. 10

Mulchahey, Michèle, 216 n. 93

Mum and the Sothsegger, 9, 170

murder, 38, 98

Murphy, Margaret, 232 n. 10

mystical works, 120, 128, 147, 148, 150, 152

Need, 21

Nelson, Paul, 234 n. 29

Netter, Thomas, 216 n. 88

New Art History, 120, 238 n. 5

New Criticism, 6, 14, 147, 150

New Historicism, 120

New Troy, 55, fig. 46

Nichols, Stephen B., 8, 130, 208 n. 42, 242 n. 50

Oculus sacerdotis. See index of manuscripts: Hatfield House, Hertfordshire, Cecil Papers MS 290 (the Hatfield Manuscript)

O'Donaghue, Bernard, 235 n. 60

Ogilvie-Thompson, S. J., 250 n. 2

Oireachtaigh, David Mág, 34

Olson, Linda, xvii, 237 n. 78

Omne bonum. See index of manuscripts: London, British Library, MS Royal 6.E.VI–VII; *see also* Palmer, James le

ordinatio, 5, 12–13, 75, 113, 143, 207 n. 25, 241 n. 42; *See also* visionary *ordinatio*

Pacht, Otto, 234 n. 40, 239 n. 13, 240 n. 24, 241 n. 42, 242 n. 61, 247 n. 42, 249 n. 84

Palgrave, F., 221 n. 41
Palmer, James le, 11, 13, 22–25, 44, 144–45, 208 n. 48, 209 n. 48. *See also* Omne bonum
Palmere, William, 65
pardon of Truth, 128, 129
Paris, Matthew, xii, 11, 13, 24, 28, 48–52, 55, 61, 62, 65, 86, 115, 140–45, 208 n. 48; *Chronica majora*, 13, 49, 140, 142–43; *Life of St. Alban*, 100
Parkes, Malcolm B., xiii, xvi, 13, 74, 179, 181, 205 n. 1 (preface), 207 n. 25, 213 n. 44, 228 n. 22, 229 nn. 28, 32, 236 nn. 74, 75, 238 n. 88, 241 n. 42, 251 nn. 1 (app. 1)– 3, 252 nn. 13
Parliament of the Three Ages, the, 156
Partridge, Stephen, 229 n. 31
pastoral care, 20, 35, 58, 61, 64, 89
pastoral manuals, 20, 21, 25, 30, 58, 62, 64, 211 n. 18
Patience, 32, 65, 79. *See also* index of illustrations in Douce 104: Patience
patronage, 75, 115, 123; female, 127; lay, 127, 155. *See also* Douce 104, patron of
pattern books, 13, 61, 123, 141, 142, 168. *See also* model books
Patterson, Annabel, 1, 71, 205 n. 1 (intro.), 227 n. 11
Paul, Saint, 61, 104, 138
Paul the Hermit, 30
Payne, Robert O., 247 n. 46
Peace, 66–67, 79
Pearce, E. H., 223 n. 71
Pearl Poet, 167; *Pearl*, 3
Pearsall, Derek, xiii, xvii, 9, 65, 109, 110, 113, 148, 171, 193, 205 nn. 2 (preface), 3, 11–12, 2 (intro.), 207 nn. 25, 27, 208 nn. 31–32, 46, 209 n. 53, 211 n. 23, 214 nn. 58, 62, 215 n. 69, 216 n. 89, 218 nn. 2–5, 221 n. 45, 223 nn. 63, 69, 224 n. 78, 225 nn. 92, 94, 100–101, 227 n. 10, 228 nn. 18–19, 229 n. 28, 230 nn. 37, 41, 231 nn. 52, 60, 235 n. 60, 236 n. 70, 238 n. 87, 239 n. 16, 240 n. 32, 242 nn. 49, 62, 243 n. 75, 244 nn. 5–7, 246 n. 33, 248 n. 74, 249 n. 75, 250 nn. 1, 9, 13, 251 nn. 1 (app. 1), 4, 6
Pecham, John (archbishop), 46, 48
penitential narrative, 152
Perkyn, 129
Perrers, Alice, 46, 213 n. 42
Peter, Saint, 61
Peter of Icham, 54
Petroff, Elizabeth, 249 n. 89

phallic symbols, 40; noses as, 40; swords as, 19, 24, 95, 106, 107, 158
Piehler, Paul, 9, 208 n. 44, 231 n. 58
Piers Plowman. See Langland, William
Pierce the Ploughman's Crede, 8, 9, 39, 170, 172
piety. *See* devotion
Pilgrim. *See* index of illustrations in Douce 104: Pilgrim
pilgrimage, 122, 124, 125, 172; of life, 5, 156
Pilgrimage of the Life of Man, The. See Deguilleville, Guillaume de, *Pèlerinage de la vie humaine*
pillory, 49–50
Plummer, Charles, 76, 229 n. 29
Plummer, John, 216 n. 93, 225 n. 103
Poiron, Daniel, 151, 246 n. 22
poor, 13, 31, 53, 59, 61, 64–66, 85, 87, 110–11, 123–25, 134–35, 138, 166, 170–71, 175, 250 n. 10. *See also* index of illustrations in Douce 104: Crouched poor man
Porete, Marguerite, 148, 168
portraits: of Antichrist, 21, 211–12 n. 24; author, 39, 40, 54, 152, 155, 167; dreamer, 130, 160, 163, 165; scribal, 54, 127
posture, 53, 126, 132, 134; of despair, 134; head in hand, 132, 133
poverty, 7, 18, 27, 37, 56, 60, 83, 85, 110, 142, 171, 208 n. 34; apostolic (patient), 125, 137, 162, 172, 173; of Christ's, 125; holy, 62; reckless, 172; spiritual, 123; voluntary, 87
prayer, 121
precious metals. *See* gold; silver
Prestwich, Michael, 220 n. 21
Preziosi, Donald, 238 n. 5
Pride. *See* index of illustrations in Douce 104: Pride
Priest with Pardon. *See* index of illustrations in Douce 104: Priest with pardon
Pronay, Nicholas, 232 nn. 4, 7
prophecy, 140
Proud priest, 19. *See also* index of illustrations in Douce 104: Proud Priest
psychomachia, 136, 156
punishment, images of, 49–50
puns, 10, 53, 83, 87, 115, 143–44, 222 n. 48, 244 n. 94
Purnele, 32, 158

Queen Mary Psalter. See index of manuscripts: London, British Library, MS Roy.2.B.VI

Index

Quick, Anne Wenley, 211 nn. 18–19, 219 n. 13

Randall, Lillian, 133, 214 n. 60, 216 nn. 93–94, 243 n. 69
Raw, Barbara, 243 n. 78
readers: Anglo-Irish, xii, 18–19, 20; clerical, xii, 12, 14, 23–24, 45; cloistered, 31; of Douce 104, 27–28, 122–24, 129, 133, 138–39, 141–42, 145–49, 154, 156, 160, 166, 170, 171, 178; expectations of, 1, 6, 17, 26, 72; female, 127, 148; lay, 12, 45, 78, 88, 127; of *Piers Plowman*, xii, 6, 8, 9, 22, 25, 30, 47, 58, 65, 77–78, 88, 130; professional, xii, 2–3, 6, 23, 42, 69, 70, 72, 75, 78, 79, 81, 92, 119, 130, 141, 148, 149, 169, 173, 176
reading: "clericist," 17; contemplative, 127; devotional, 126; ethical, 145, 152; medieval, 8, 14, 73, 76, 79, 126, 127, 144, 155, 158, 173; meditative, 120, 165; monastic, 74, 81, 86, 90, 122; orality of medieval, 5, 103, 163; participatory, 122, 147; performative, 9, 12, 45, 129; private, 81, 125, 126; public, 125; self-reflexive, 8, 9, 54, 122, 127; silent, 5, 8–9, 45, 103, 104, 105, 129; vernacular, 25, 69–70, 208 n. 39
Reason, 29, 30, 86, 88, 154, 158. *See also* index of illustrations in Douce 104: Reason
rebel letters (of 1381), 170. *See also* Ball, John
Rebel Rising of 1381, 7, 8, 9, 87. *See also* Ball, John
reception theory, 72
Recklessness, 81–84, 128, 137, 164. *See also* index of illustrations in Douce 104: Recklessness
Red Book of the Exchequer, 49, 102, 114; Dublin, 23–24, 25, 26, 47, 49, 94, 95, 97, 109; Westminster, 11, 24. *See also* Exchequer, Court of
Remnant, G. L., 214 n. 67
Revard, Carter, xvi, 224 n. 80
Rhys, Ernest, 207 n. 16
Richardson, H. G., 233 n. 13
Richardson, Malcolm, 246 n. 33
Richard the Redeless, 7, 170
Rickert, Margaret, 216 nn. 88, 91, 223 n. 62
Rigg, A. G., 216 n. 93
Robbins, Rossell Hope, 217 n. 102
Rolle, Richard, 63, 74, 126, 166–67, 169; *Northern Homily Cycle*, 169

Romance of the Rose, The, 145, 147, 151, 152, 155, 163, 165
roundels, 40
Rouse, Mary, 227 n. 9
Rouse, Richard, 227 n. 9
Ruiz, Juan (archpriest of Hita), 150; *Libro de buen amor*, 150
Russell, George H., 75, 119, 128, 207 n. 26, 226 n. 1, 228 n. 25, 229 n. 28, 238 n. 86, 241 n. 44

Saenger, Paul, 8, 69, 178, 207 n. 22, 208 n. 43, 226 n. 7, 235 n. 52, 241 n. 46
Saint Bartholomew's Hospital, 75
Salter, Elizabeth, 4, 38, 120, 121, 207 n. 20, 215 n. 69, 238 nn. 6–8
salvation, 82, 83, 85, 87
Salvation History, 50
Samaritan, 140
Samuels, M. L., 218 n. 1, 223 n. 68, 226 n. 3, 252 nn. 1–2
Sandler, Lucy Freeman, 36, 145, 206 n. 7, 209 nn. 48, 55, 57, 61, 211 n. 11, 212 nn. 27, 36, 213 n. 38, 216 n. 92, 219 nn. 14–15, 234 n. 40, 236 nn. 64, 76, 241 n. 42, 244 nn. 96–98, 248 n. 58, 249 n. 82
satire, 17, 24, 33, 37, 39, 41, 45, 58, 78, 79, 99, 107, 166, 219 n. 19; Anglo-Irish, 56, 57, 208 n. 33; anticlerical, 27, 59; antimendicant, 7; clerical, 51, 101; ecclesiastical, 7, 60, 139; political, 60
Sayles, G. O., 93, 232 n. 4, 233 n. 13
Scase, Wendy, 77, 78, 170, 216 n. 99, 230 n. 36, 231 n. 56, 250 n. 6
Schaap, Tanya, xvii, 226 n. 1
Schibanoff, Susan, 229 n. 28
Schmidt, A. V. C., 91
Schulz, H. C., 226 n. 6
Scott, Kathleen, xiii, xvi, 3, 5, 9, 29, 65, 96, 106, 112, 116, 126, 127, 129, 132, 154, 158, 160, 164, 165, 205 nn. 2 (preface), 11, 2 (intro.), 206 nn. 3, 13, 207 nn. 17, 25, 207 27–28, 208 nn. 32, 46, 210 n. 5, 211 n. 23, 213 nn. 44, 49, 214 nn. 54–55, 58, 216 n. 88, 217 n. 114, 218 n. 116, 219 nn. 3, 8, 17, 223 nn. 60, 69, 224 n. 81, 225 nn. 92, 94, 233 nn. 14, 18, 236 nn. 64, 68, 238 nn. 86–87, 91, 240 nn. 30–33, 241 nn. 41, 45, 47–48, 242 nn. 56–58, 60–61, 243 n. 72, 244 n. 86, 246 n. 29, 247 nn. 36–37, 39, 248 nn. 56, 68, 249 nn. 76, 79, 86–87, 250 n. 16, 251 nn. 1 (app. 1), 4

Index

scribe-illustrators, xii, xiii, xv, 17, 46, 53, 64, 78, 95–96, 115, 143; general characteristics of, 10–13. *See also* Cambrensis, Giraldus; Douce 104, scribe-illustrator; Palmer, James le; Paris, Matthew
script: *anglicana formata* in Douce 104, 95, 112, 177
Scripture, 53, 54, 84, 136, 160–61, 166
Sears, Elizabeth, 241 n. 42, 246 n. 34, 247 n. 34, 248 nn. 49–50, 59–61, 249 n. 81
Secreta secretorum. See Yonge, James
self-reflexivity, 53, 123, 130, 155
Seven Ages of Man, 127, 157
Seven Deadly Sins, 127, 157–58, 165, 241 n. 47
Seven Vices of Corrupt Nature, 127
sexuality, 25, 35, 64, 89, 148, 151, 158
Sheehan, M. W., 216 n. 90
Shirley, John, 70, 71, 72, 73, 74, 227 n. 14
signa, Exchequer, 23, 24, 28, 32, 46, 49, 50, 86, 95. *See also* civil service; Exchequer, Court of
silence, female, 108–9
silent witnesses, 9, 61, 105, 106, 108, 109, 110, 111
silver, 36, 62, 65, 111, 216 n. 90
Simon (abbot of Ramsay), 141
Simony, 207 n. 21
simony, 24, 26, 87, 144
Simpson, James, 211 n. 17, 219 n. 13
Simpson, Paul, 207 n. 21
skeletons, 164. *See also* index of illustrations in Douce 104: Skeleton
Skemer, Don C., 46, 220 n. 25
Sloth, 159. *See also* index of illustrations in Douce 104: Sloth
Smetana, Cyril, 227 n. 10, 229 n. 27
Smith, Jeremy, xvi, 180, 208 n. 33, 223 n. 68, 226 n. 3
social realism, 13, 25, 26, 41, 45, 48, 52, 54, 64, 66, 97, 110, 122, 233 n. 12
Solomon, 82
Solomon, Richard, 248 nn. 52–53
Somercote, Laurence, 236 n. 71
speaking gestures, 61, 85, 103, 171, 207 n. 21; announcing, xv, 22, 54–55, 62, 107; *declamatio*, xv, 19, 44, 46, 60, 104, 105, 106, 107, 144, 174, 212 n. 26; open hand, xv, 105. *See also* teaching gesture
speaking voices, 102, 103
speech scrolls, 55, 95, 102, 103, 105, 108, 155, 156
Spencer, H. Leith, 211 n. 17

spice box, 39
Stapelton, Sir Miles de, 155
Statuta angliae, 46
Statutes of Kilkenny, 34, 59, 93, 97, 98, 105, 215 nn. 77–78, 80, 232 n. 8
Statutes of Labourers, 97
Statutes of Provisors, 97
Steele, Robert, 232 n. 9, 234 n. 41
Stones, E. L. G., 220 n. 22
Strayler, Alan, 219 n. 20
Strohm, Paul, 227 n. 13, 234 n. 32
Stubbs, William, 221 n. 35
Swayne, John (archbishop of Armagh), 33; *Register*, 215 nn. 72–74, 77, 82, 232 n. 8
Synagoga, 143
Szittya, Penn, 212 n. 25, 217 nn. 102–3, 250 n. 13

Tateshal, Joan, 127
Taylor, John, 221 n. 38, 232 nn. 4, 7
Taymouth Hours, The. See index of manuscripts: London, British Library, MS Yates Thompson 13
teaching gesture, 36, 62, 63–64
Templars, 89, 90
Ten Commandments, 127
Thomas à Becket, Saint, 46, 212 n. 30
Thompson, John, 227 n. 14, 228 nn. 16–17, 19
Thomson, R. M., 212 n. 24, 225 n. 97
Thomson, S. Harrison, 227 n. 8
Thorp, Nigel, 219 n. 10
Three Estates, 55, fig. 60
Three Living and the Three Dead, The, 156, 164
Tom Stowe, 29, 130. *See also* index of illustrations in Douce 104: Tom Stowe
Tom Two-Tongue. *See* index of illustrations in Douce 104: Tom Two-Tongue
tongues, as mnemonics or emphasizing speech, 32, 100–101, 102, 129
tonsure, 19, 24, 31, 54, 62, 106, 127, 129, 171, 174. *See also* hair
Topographia hibernica. See Cambrensis, Giraldus
Tournament, 3
Trajan, 83–84, 104. *See also* index of illustrations in Douce 104: Trajan
Tree of Charity, 4, 32, 89, 90
Trinity, 90
Troy Book. See Lydgate, John
Truth, 108
Tucker, Marcia, xvi
Turville-Petre, Thorlac, 217 n. 105, 223 n. 67

263

Index

Uhart, Marie Claire, 77, 226 n. 1, 228 n. 17, 229 n. 31, 251 n. 6
Unity (Holy Church), 18–20, 128
Usk, Thomas, 96, 234 n. 32

Vaughan, Richard, 51, 209 n. 49, 212 n. 32, 221 nn. 39, 46
vernacular books, 21, 59, 122, 126, 127
Vernon manuscript. *See* index of manuscripts: Oxford, Bodleian Library, MS English Poetry a.1
Vicar. *See* index of illustrations in Douce 104: Unlearned vicar
Virtues and Vices, 127
visionaries, female, 166
visionary experience, 151, 153, 166
visionary *ordinatio*, xii, 13, 121, 122, 129, 139, 141, 147, 149, 173
visionary works, 4, 53, 103, 148, 151, 166–67
visualization, 155
voicing figures, 104–5
Voloshinov, V. N., 227 n. 13

Wales, Katie, 207 n. 23
Wallis, M. 104, 105, 235 n. 49, 236 n. 69
Walsh, Kathleen, 34, 35, 210 nn. 2, 6, 8–9, 215 nn. 72, 74, 82, 216 nn. 85–86, 97–98, 218 n. 115
Walsingham, Thomas, 219 n. 20
Wanley, Humphrey, 39
Wastor. *See* index of illustrations in Douce 104: Wastor
Waterford Charter Roll. *See* index of manuscripts: Waterford, Ireland, Archives of the Munical Corporation of Waterford, Waterford Charter Roll
Watson, Nicholas, 208 n. 39, 211 n. 17, 225 nn. 95, 98, 228 n. 24, 236 n. 73, 239 n. 20, 240 n. 20, 245 n. 8, 249 n. 90
Watt, J. A., 205 n. 5, 233 nn. 21, 25
Watt, John, 224 nn. 83–86
Wenzel, Siegfried, 207 n. 29, 208 n. 30
Westminster, 93, 96, 97
Wethamstede, John (abbot of Saint Albans), 8, 219 n. 20
Wheel of Fortune, 127, 137, 159. *See also* index of illustrations in Douce 104: Fortune's Wheel
Whittington, "Dick," 66
Wilkins, David, 211 n. 17
Will, 5, 21, 30, 53–54, 79–81, 84, 87, 132, 151, 153, 160, 164, 173. *See also* dreamer; index of illustrations In Douce 104: Will; Will writing

William of Pagula, 20, 27
Windeatt, B. A., 229 n. 28, 230 n. 39
Wit, 170, 175
Wittig, Joseph, 242 n. 61, 250 n. 12
Wood, R. A., 225 n. 99
Woolf, Rosemary, 3, 4, 206 n. 12, 207 n. 14
workshop tensions, xi, 8, 67, 102, 128, 172, 173, 206 n. 8
Wormyngton, John, 58
Wrath. *See* index of illustrations in Douce 104: Wrath
Wright, Thomas, 217 n. 102, 226 n. 107, 236 n. 62
Wrong, 55, 67
Wyclif, John, 27, 33, 37, 53, 61
Wycliffitism, 30, 36, 38, 39, 40

Yates, Frances, 239 nn. 11, 13
Yonge, James, 59, 93–94, 101, 234 nn. 28, 41; *Secreta secretorum*, 59, 93, 94, 169, 215 n. 80, 231 n. 3
Youth, 82, 154

Index of Illustrations in Douce 104

Note: For the folio number location of these illustrations in the manuscript, see appendix 2. The entries in this index have been named according to those given to the illustrations listed in appendix 2.

Abraham, unfinished, 29, 62, 189, 206 n. 13, 251 n. 20
Activa Vita, 64, 111, 128, 188, fig. 29
Angel, unpainted, 33, 189, 251 n. 20
Antichrist, 21–22, 191, fig. 35
Beggar, 96, 110, 134, 186, 223 n. 55, fig. 23
Blind man, 125, 129, 138, 170, 171–72, 185, 223 n. 55, fig. 17
Boat as flood symbol, 50–51, 140, 143, 185, fig. 14
Caiaphas, 99, 141, 190
Castle of Care and devil, 28, 182, 213 n. 49, 223 n. 65, 225 n. 88, 251 n. 20
Clerk, 186
Conscience, 40, 60, 99, 113, 114, 172, 183, 209 n. 58, 214 n. 55, 237 n. 79, fig. 4
Contemplatif, xiv, 63–64, 129, 135, 141, 185, fig. 10
Corrupt friar, 36, 139, 188

Index

Covetousness, 48, 107, 108, 184, 215 n. 84, 220 n. 31
Crouched poor man, 65, 188
Devil, 28, 40, 190, 224–25 n. 88
Digger, 40, 50–51, 65, 131, 185, fig. 13
Dobet, 4, 61, 62, 138–39, 170, 174, 186, 216 n. 87, fig. 21
Elde, 114, 124, 125, 132, 135, 162–63, 172, 187, 223 n. 55, fig. 26
Envy, 10, 96, 113, 137, 184, 215 n. 84
False friar, 23, 36, 40, 138, 139, 170, 172, 185, fig. 18
Fortune's wheel, 137, 159, 161–62, 186, 209 n. 57, 248 n. 73, fig. 25
Franciscan friar, 4, 10, 36, 61, 128, 160, 170, 173, 186, fig. 20
Friar physician, 36, 40, 66, 165, 191, fig. 38
Glutton, 114, 159, 184
Hand holding ball, 32, 189
Hand holding coins, 187
Hunger, 8, 106, 114–15, 136, 185, 214 n. 51, 225 n. 104
Imaginatif, 14, 61, 132, 133, 154, 155, 156, 160, 163, 187, 221 n. 34, fig. 28
King, 44, 54–55, 60, 61, 99, 114, 135, 136, 183, 214 n. 55, 219 n. 14, 220 n. 32, 237 n. 79, fig. 5
Knight, unpainted, xv, 55, 61, 62, 63–64, 95, 114, 185, 237 n. 79, 251 n. 20, fig. 11
Lawyer, xv, 4, 33, 40, 48, 61, 66, 95, 96, 99, 114, 144, 170, 185, fig. 15
Learned friar, 36, 139, 188
Lechery, 107, 113, 156, 158–59, 184, 241 n. 47, fig. 7
Liar with charter, 4, 45, 66, 128, 129, 130, 171, 182, 207 n. 21, 210 n. 62, 219 n. 20
Liberum Arbitrium, 188
Lunatic lollar, 31–32, 40, 61, 99, 124, 137–38, 139, 170, 174, 178, 185, 223 n. 55, 234 n. 36, fig. 16
Man on gallows, 29, 48, 49, 99, 112, 188, 222 n. 47, fig. 32
Manor of Truth, 55–56, 184
Mede at Westminster, 99, 108, 113, 115, 183, fig. 3
Mede confessing to friar, 4, 33, 36, 37, 66, 139, 183
Mede riding on sheriff, 66, 99, 109, 115, 139, 182, fig. 2
Mede with chalices, 109, 182
Merchant counting money, xiv, 99, 123, 190, 220 n. 31, fig. 34
Mercy, 60–61, 108, 109, 114, 115, 189, 224–24 n. 58, fig. 33
Patience, 124, 125, 129, 138, 164, 172, 188, 225 n. 96, fig. 30
Physician, 191
Piers, 44, 62, 132, 185, fig. 10
Piers's oxen, 190, 207 n. 18
Pilgrim, 114, 125, 184, 215 n. 68, fig. 9
Pointing hand (fol. 75v), 188
Pointing hand (fol. 79v), 188
Pride, 32, 35, 123, 135, 158–59, 162, 184, 215 n. 68
Priest, 187
Priest with pardon, 22–23, 24, 28, 45, 61, 62, 99, 129, 130, 171, 186, 210 n. 62, 219 n. 20, fig. 19
Proud priest, 19, 24, 40, 60, 66, 106, 108, 191, fig. 37
Reason, 40, 60, 99, 113, 136, 183, 209 n. 58, 237 n. 79
Recklessness, 4, 40, 66, 137–138, 156, 159, 161, 162, 172, 186, 209 n. 57, 243 n. 76, fig. 25
Schoolmaster beating child, 61, 96, 186, 237 n. 79
Skeleton, 114, 135, 188, fig. 31
Sleeping bishop and wolf with sheep, 22–23, 28, 49, 55, 66, 113, 139, 143, 170, 172–73, 186, 207 n. 18, 209 n. 55, fig. 18
Sle3th, 98, 191, fig. 36
Sloth, 113, 131, 156, 159, 160, 162, 172, 184, 237 n. 79, fig. 8
Thief, 187, 249 n. 79
Tom Stowe, 29, 48, 50, 66, 88, 99, 130, 184, 209 n. 60, 235 n. 47, fig. 6
Tom Two-Tongue, 32, 191
Trajan, 4, 40, 66, 85, 99–101, 141, 187, 235 n. 47, fig. 27
Two beasts, 186
Unlearned vicar, 61–62, 141, 190
Wastor, 8, 40, 44, 50, 66, 105–6, 108, 115, 136, 185, 214 n. 51, 225 n. 104, fig. 12
Will, 14, 131, 135, 152, 154, 160, 163, 182, fig. 1
Will writing, 4, 53, 87, 135, 155, 156, 160–61, 186, 209 n. 57, fig. 24
Wrath, 113, 159, 184, 237 n. 79
Young bastard, 26, 35, 44, 48, 53, 99, 135, 145, 174, 175, 186, 219 n. 14, fig. 22

Index of Manuscripts

Belfast
    Public Record Office of Northern Ireland
        D 10 4/2/3: 215 n. 75

Index

Cambridge
  Corpus Christi College Library
    MS 16 (Chronica majora): 11, 49, 143, 221 nn. 39–40, 221 nn. 43–44, 222 n. 47, 223 n. 64, 231 n. 54, fig. 48
    MS 26 (Chronica majora): 11, 49, 222 nn. 47–48, 231 n. 54
    MS 80: 75
    MS 171: 221 n. 37
    MS 180: 39–40
  Fitzwilliam Museum
    MS 330 (De Brailes Psalter): 159
  Gonville and Cauis College Library
    MS 669*/646: 74
  Saint John's College Library
    MS 17: 141
  Trinity College Library
    MS R.3.14: 206 n. 3
    MS R.3.20: 228 nn. 20–21
  University Library
    MS Dd. 1.17: 222 n. 50
    MS Ff. 1.27: 11, 214 n. 52, 215 n. 81, 222 n. 51, 223 n. 58, fig. 50
    MS Gg. 1.1: 224 n. 80
    MS Gg. 4.12: 71

Cambridge, Massachusetts
  Harvard Law School Library
    MS 12: 47, 48, 49, 60, 107, 219 n. 10, 220 nn. 30–32, 221n. 34, figs. 51–53

Dublin
  Chester Beatty Library
    MS 80: 164, 241 n. 42, 247 n. 34, figs. 54–55
  King's Inn
    MS 17: 232 n. 11
  National Library
    MS 700: 52, 215 n. 81, 224 n. 80
  Public Record Office of Ireland
    Parliament Roll of 1429: 210 n. 7
  Royal Irish Academy
    MS 23: 232 n. 11, 235 n. 43
  Trinity College Library
    MS 177: 100
    MS 212: 57, 58, 222 n. 50, 228 n. 17
    MS 213: 222 n. 50
    MS 1440: 233 n. 27

Durham
  Durham Cathedral Library
    MS C.I.4: 50

Edinburgh
  National Library of Scotland
    MS Advocates 72.1.2: 232 n. 11, 233 n. 18

Glasgow
  Glasgow University Library
    MS General 335: 219 n. 10

Hatfield House, Hertfordshire
  Marquess of Salisbury
    MS Cecil Papers 290 (Hatfield manuscript): 19–20, 21, 24, 27, 30, 211 n. 11, fig. 56

Lincoln, United Kingdom
  Lincoln Cathedral Library
    MS 218: 11, 21, 22, 25, 27, 30, 60, 61, 64, 105, 211 n. 20, 211–12 n. 24, 225 n. 97, figs. 57–58

London
  British Library
    MS Additional 10392: 75
    MS Additional 16165: 72, 73
    MS Additional 22720: 126
    MS Additional 29729: 228 nn. 15–16
    MS Additional 35157: 226 n. 1
    MS Additional 35287: 228 n. 17, 229 n. 31
    MS Additional 37049: 11, 12, 21, 22, 25, 32, 54, 55, 62, 63, 64, 105, 127, 156, 157, 159, 207 n. 20, 211–12 n. 24, 214 n. 52, 236 n. 64, figs. 59–61
    MS Additional 47680 (Secreta secretorum): 59, 93, 94, 169, 215 n. 80, 231 n. 3
    MS Additional 47682 (Holkam Bible Picture Book): 4
    MS Additional 49999 (de Brailes Hours): 135
    MS Arundel 18 (Psalter of Robert de Lisle): 127, 156, 159, 164, 225 n. 104, fig. 62
    MS Cotton Cleopatra B.II: 37, 217 n. 105
    MS Cotton Nero D.I: 214 n. 63
    MS Cotton Nero D.VII: 219 n. 20
    MS Cotton Tiberius A.7: 240 n. 29
    MS Egerton 2572 (Guild Book of the Barber Surgeons of York): 165, 249 n. 85
    MS Harley 225: 73

Index

MS Harley 913 (Kildare manuscript): 39, 53, 56, 59, 225 n. 104, 226 n. 107, 235 n. 45
MS Harley 2251: 228 n. 18
MS Harley 2253: 58, 224 n. 80
MS Harley 3724: 56, 99, 101, 222 n. 51, 223 n. 66, 232 n. 11, fig. 63
MS Harley 4399: 246 n. 30
MS Harley 4605: 44, 219 n. 12
MS Harley 6041: 222 n. 50
MS Harley 6563: 224 n. 88
MS Harley 7333: 73
MS Royal 2.B.VII (Queen Mary Psalter): 55
MS Royal 5.D.X: 141
MS Royal 6.E.VI-VII *(Omne bonum)*: 11, 21, 22, 23, 24, 25, 31, 36, 43, 47, 60, 62, 106, 144, 208 n. 48, 209 n. 55, 212 nn. 24, 27, 38, 219 n. 14, 236 n. 66, figs. 64–67
MS Royal 10.E.IV *(Decretals)*: 44, 219 n. 12
MS Royal 13.A.XIV: 222 n. 51
MS Royal 13.B.VIII: 52, 215 n. 81, 223 n. 54
MS Royal 14.C: 143
MS Royal 17.C.XV: 249 n. 86
MS Stowe 17: 37, 216 n. 93
MS Yates Thompson 13 (Taymouth Hours): 164
Burlington House, Society of Antiquaries
MS 687: 211 n. 18
Lambeth Palace Library
MS 1106: 221 n. 37
MS 150: 240 n. 35
Public Record Office
E 36/268: 220 n. 22, fig. 69
E 36/273: fig. 69
E 36/274 (Liber A): 23, 46, 220 nn. 22–23, fig. 69
Saint Bartholomew's Hospital Cartulary: 30, fig. 68

Longleat House, Wiltshire
Marquess of Bath
MS 29: 228 n. 24, 234 n. 34, 250 n. 2, 250 n. 3, 251 n. 8

Malibu, California
J. Paul Getty Museum
MS Ludwig III.1: 235 n. 53, 244 n. 94

New York
Pierpont Morgan Library
MS G. 50 (De Lisle Hours): 55, 159, 248 n. 60
MS M. 812: 45, 50, 219 n. 19, 220 n. 20, fig. 70

Oxford
Bodleian Library
MS Bodley 277: 40, 217 n. 114, 218 n. 15
MS Bodley 413: 242 n. 61
MS Bodley 758: 126, 240 n. 34, figs. 43–44
MS Bodley 851: 216 n. 93, 222 n. 50, 226 n. 1
MS Bodley 943: 239 n. 13
MS Bodley 954: 241 n. 42
MS Bodley 978: 30, 33, 139, 217 n. 114, figs. 40–42
MS Bodley e Mus. 232: 228 n. 24, 250 n. 3, 251 n. 8
MS Bodley Rolls I (2974): 249 n. 84
MS Digby 98: 217 n. 102
MS Digby 102: 226 n. 1
MS Douce 104: passim, figs. 1–39. See also index of illustrations in Douce 104; general index
MS Douce 240: 124, 239 n. 13
MS Douce 257: 251 n. 1 (app. 1)
MS Douce 323: 226 n. 1
MS English Poetry a.1 (Vernon manuscript): 126, 148
MS Laud Misc. 152: 239 n. 13
MS Laud Misc. 154: 239 n. 13
MS Laud Misc. 156: 241 n. 42
MS Laud Misc. 720: 10–11, 51–52, 222 n. 51, fig. 45
MS Laud Misc. 730: 54, 55, fig. 46
MS Laud Misc. 740: 240 n. 29
MS Rawlinson B. 488 (Yellow Book of Lecan): 233 n. 15
MS Rawlinson B. 505: 235 n. 43
MS Rawlinson C. 32: 235 n. 42
MS Rawlinson C. 545: 242 n. 61
MS Rawlinson G. 185: 99, 101, 234 n. 36
MS Rawlinson Poet. 137: 226 n. 1
Corpus Christi College Library
MS 201: 206 n. 3
MS 157: 235 n. 54
Merton College Library
MS 319: 40, 43, 216 n. 88, fig. 47
Oriel College Library
MS 32: 70

Index

Paris
  Bibliothèque Nationale
    MS fr. 376: 246 n. 30
    MS fr. 823: 246 n. 30
    MS fr. 25526: 163

Prague
  Prague University Library
    MS VIII.C.3 (1472): 217 n. 114

Princeton, New Jersey
  Princeton University Library
    MS Scheide 30: 47, 60, 219 nn. 10–19, 220 n. 21, 221 n. 39
    MS Taylor Medieval I: 127

Rome
  Biblioteca Apostolica Vaticana
    MS Pal. lat. 1993: 157, 248 n. 52

San Marino, California
  Huntington Library
    MS Ellesmere 7 H 8: 44
    MS Ellesmere 26 C 9 (Ellesmere Chaucer): 5, 119, 207 n. 24
    MS Ellesmere 34 B 23: 221 n. 33
    MS HM 128: 211n. 18, 222 n. 50
    MS HM 129: 99, 232 n. 11, 234 n. 39, 250 n. 3, fig. 49
    MS HM 137: 231 n. 65
    MS HM 143: 50, 68, 73, 74, 77–78, 79–90, 177, 178, 222 n. 50, 226 nn. 1–2, 6, 228 n. 17, 229 nn. 28, 30–31, 229–30 n. 32
    MS HM 923: 221 n. 33
    MS HM 932: 219 n. 9
    MS HM 19920: 219 n. 10, 223 n. 62
    MS HM 19999: 43
    MS HM 30319: 221 n. 37

Vienna
  Österreichische Nationalbibliothek
    MS 3923: 217 n. 102

Waterford, Ireland
  Archives of the Munical Corporation of Waterford
    Waterford Charter Roll: 11, 220 n. 25, 233 nn. 12, 27

MEDIEVAL CULTURES

VOLUME 7
Edited by Clare A. Lees
Medieval Masculinities: Regarding Men in the Middle Ages

VOLUME 6
Edited by Barbara A. Hanawalt and Kathryn L. Reyerson
City and Spectacle in Medieval Europe

VOLUME 5
Edited by Calvin B. Kendall and Peter S. Wells
Voyage to the Other World: The Legacy of Sutton Hoo

VOLUME 4
Edited by Barbara A. Hanawalt
Chaucer's England: Literature in Historical Context

VOLUME 3
Edited by Marilyn J. Chiat and Kathryn L. Reyerson
The Medieval Mediterranean: Cross-Cultural Contacts

VOLUME 2
Edited by Andrew MacLeish
The Medieval Monastery

VOLUME 1
Edited by Kathryn Reyerson and Faye Powe
The Medieval Castle

Kathryn Kerby-Fulton is professor of English at the University of Victoria, Victoria, British Columbia, and a member of the Institute for Advanced Study at the School of Historical Studies, Princeton University.

Denise L. Despres is professor of English and Humanities at the University of Puget Sound, Tacoma, Washington.